Political Deliverance

Political Deliverance

The Mormon Quest for Utah Statehood

EDWARD LEO LYMAN

With a Foreword by
Leonard J. Arrington

UNIVERSITY OF ILLINOIS PRESS
Urbana and Chicago

© 1986 by the Board of Trustees of the University of Illinois
Manufactured in the United States of America
C 5 4 3 2 1

This book is printed on acid-free paper.

Library of Congress Cataloging in Publication Data

Lyman, Edward Leo, 1942–
   Political deliverance.

   Bibliography: p.
   Includes index.
   1. Utah—Politics and government.   2. Mormons—
Utah—Political activity—History—19th century.
3. Statehood (American politics)   I.   Title.
F826.L95   1986   979.2'02   85–1204
ISBN 0–252–01239–9 (alk. paper)

To my wife and my mother

Contents

Foreword

Rarely, all too rarely, a work of history appearing from an unexpected quarter is so fresh and fine that it causes old timers and experts to sit up and take notice. So it was when the article on "Isaac Trumbo and the Politics of Utah Statehood" appeared in the *Utah Historical Quarterly* in 1973. Written by Edward Leo Lyman, a high school history teacher and wrestling coach in southern California, the article presented new information that compelled reevaluation of what was then known about what happened in Washington, D.C., and in Utah in the final years of the nineteenth century. Several of his articles of equal worth in the understanding of western American history soon appeared in other historical journals—*Idaho Yesterdays*, *Southern California Quarterly*, *Arizona and the West*, and *Dialogue: A Journal of Mormon Thought*.

Now Coach Lyman is Doctor Lyman, and in *Political Deliverance* he brings so much more information to light regarding the coming of Utah statehood that it causes us to revise our understanding of this crucial event in the history not only of Mormonism, but of the entire American West. Thus Lyman's work is revisionist in the very best sense; the author provides so much new data from so many previously unmined sources that the popular understanding of how plural marriage began to be abandoned and how statehood came to Zion will have to be reassessed.

Without taking anything away from his industry and perseverance, it has to be pointed out that to some extent *Political Deliverance* is an important book because its author appeared at the right place at the right time with the right set of historical questions. During the decade in which he researched this work, Dr. Lyman was able to use the vast store of documents that had previously been unavailable. These he used not only with

sensitivity and respect, but also with the intuition of a detective, following leads and clues that sent him into libraries and archives across the
nation.

This work, which reports the outcome of his tenacious investigations,
provides new information and draws significant conclusions in nearly
every chapter. As a result, what is written here will be of great interest to
students of Mormonism and of the American political process. An earlier
draft of *Political Deliverance*, which was Lyman's doctoral dissertation,
won the first William Grover and Winifred Foster Reese Award for best
dissertation on a topic in Mormon history. In this book Lyman has shown
remarkable objectivity and thoroughness in writing about a pivotal period in Mormon history. *Political Deliverance* is an indispensable and welcome addition to the significant University of Illinois Press series of books
on western American history.

Leonard J. Arrington

Introduction

This present study traces the course of Mormon officials and their agents as they overcame the seemingly insurmountable barriers blocking admission of Utah as a state. The most crucial issues to be resolved, as recognized by contemporaries and historians ever since, were the practice of plural marriage (usually called polygamy, although polygyny is more technically correct) and the long-standing practice of high church officials virtually dictating the political course they expected their followers to pursue. The "Mormon question," which was a series of variations on the themes of polygamy and church interference in politics, had loomed large in the nation's consciousness during much of the last half of the nineteenth century.

There is no doubt that the First Presidency of the Church of Jesus Christ of Latter-day Saints[1] was involved in every phase of the statehood efforts. Whatever the role of the so-called Council of Fifty in earlier Mormon history, this body was not in evidence during the 1880s and 1890s when the presidency, acting as a committee on statehood, was rather fully preoccupied with political and economic affairs related to Utah and the Latter-day Saints.[2] Despite the consistent outcry against church leaders' interference in matters most Americans deemed beyond the proper realm of ecclesiastical activity, the tradition inherited from founding prophet Joseph Smith and his successor Brigham Young fully encompassed this intervention as within the legitimate area of concern of the presidency. The unique Mormon philosophy regarding church, state, and citizenship allowed the church hierarchy and its followers, who paid higher allegiance to church than state, to proclaim to be loyal citizens, while sometimes ignoring, defying, or at least practicing passive disobedience toward federal laws and decrees and at other times making statements that appeared to be less than candid.[3] Thus the critics had fully justifiable grounds for their allegations of church interference, although the Saints were equally convinced they were right.

Research for this work has convinced me that the practice of plural marriage among the Latter-day Saints was the foremost obstacle to admission of Utah as a state. I am certainly aware of the number of statements by contemporary opponents of the Mormons that polygamy was simply a pretext useful in arousing public indignation and stimulating political support for their own aims of limiting the political power of the church leaders. These statements, particularly one made in his later years by former Idaho Senator Fred T. Dubois, have led two of the foremost students of Mormon politics, Klaus J. Hansen and Gustive O. Larson, to contend similarly that raising the polygamy issue was simply a means of attacking the more serious problem of church involvement in political affairs. While there is no reason to deny that such was the case for Dubois, for Senator George F. Edmunds, and *Salt Lake Tribune* editor C. C. Goodwin, polygamy was still the real objection of most in Congress, the body ultimately responsible for Utah's admission.[4]

One of the first attempts to achieve Utah statehood, at what might otherwise have been a most opportune time during the Civil War, shattered against the Mormon refusal to abandon polygamy. Soon after, two ranking leaders of the House of Representatives journeyed to Utah and specifically informed church leaders that such abandonment was an absolute prerequisite for statehood. This was more than a decade before the arguments about church interference in politics were effectively formulated.

In the late 1880s, when many Democrats were fully sympathetic with the sixth attempt at Utah statehood, congressional party leaders gave church officials numerous opportunities for concessions on the matter, and since each was firmly rejected, this most concerted effort at admission also failed. In 1890 there was no question that the Republican party not only demanded retrocession but also was prepared to act with unprecedented severity if such demands were not met. After the resultant Woodruff Manifesto, other obstacles to statehood were removed with considerable dispatch.

It is clear that politicians were more angered by the interference of Mormon leaders when the results were detrimental to the interests of their party than when potentially favorable to them. In 1887 members of the Democratic Cleveland administration not only witnessed but also actively participated in some of the most flagrant instances of church interference in Utah politics ever documented. And yet they were fully supportive of the

Mormon statehood attempt then in progress. On the other hand, after a rather amazing political about-face among the highest church leaders and a majority of the Utah Saints, in the 1895 campaign for election of the first state officers, the Democrats protested loudly, but legitimately, against an equally outrageous instance of church interference to the detriment of their party. And yet, despite the fact that the timing of this episode could have caused President Grover Cleveland and other powerful party members to block or at least delay impending statehood, even such an extreme example of Mormon political involvement was not sufficient to prevent the wronged party from continuing to cooperate with those seeking Utah's admission.

The consistent torrent of Republican criticism of Mormon political activity subsided markedly when cordiality between the former combatants, the leaders of the Republican party and Mormon general authorities, began to be established. At that point Republican officials urged First Presidency counselor George Q. Cannon and his associates to do whatever was necessary to create a closer balance between the parties in Mormondom. This undoubtedly necessitated some direct political action, but since it was clearly advantageous to the Republicans, it was not criticized by party leaders. And when the Utah Enabling Act finally passed, repayment for services rendered by unnamed party members included obligations, which it was assumed church leaders would accept, of guaranteeing continued Republican electoral victories indefinitely in Utah. This would have demanded the ultimate in political interference by ecclesiastical officials.

Church agents had little apprehension about mentioning the voting strength at their command as they conferred with high officials of both parties. They were playing on the vital interest each party held in enhancing the number of congressional votes they possessed in an era when the two parties had often been most closely balanced. In the 1880s it was the Democrats who were promised political dominance in the several western states and territories where Mormon voters supposedly held the balance of power. By the early 1890s some Republican leaders were arguing that possibly the Mormon vote held decisive sway in as many as eight or ten states and might even be the determining factor in which party received the majority of electoral votes in the next presidential contest. These were truly extravagant claims, but were utilized during the Mormon struggle for Utah statehood.

If cessation of political activity by the Mormon hierarchy was not mandated, regularization of political affairs in Utah certainly was. Leaders of both parties encouraged the break-up of the Mormon People's party and the Gentile Liberal party. This work traces these developments in considerable detail for the first time. Division was largely accomplished in 1891, and thereafter the party struggles sometimes proved difficult for Mormon partisans, including general church authorities, who now faced each other for the first time as Democrats and Republicans. Yet the progress made through these new political organizations, each including Mormons and Gentiles in common cause, significantly enhanced normalization of social relationships between formerly rival factions of Utah citizens and were thus an important step toward statehood.

Division of the Utah parties along national political lines clearly worked to the advantage of the Republicans. This was partly the result of the foresight of James G. Blaine and others who were seeking means for a permanent congressional majority after two decades of frustrating shifts in the balance of power. Blaine was also the leading proponent of Republicans adopting the high protective tariff issue as their primary campaign focus just at the time when Mormon leaders were becoming disenchanted with the Democrats not only for their low tariff stance, but also because of a seeming lack of commitment to protect the Saints' interests when they had the opportunity. The same Blaine-James S. Clarkson wing of the Republican party urged that the party adopt a more tolerant position related to the cultural diversity that Republican crusaders had previously sought to repress. Their former adversaries, the Mormons, were among the beneficiaries of this policy.

It has sometimes been argued that since plural marriage was dying naturally in Mormondom, there was little actual justification for the so-called anti-polygamy raid imposed by the federal government in the late 1880s. I have seen no evidence to bolster this thesis and much to indicate that the Saints' peculiar institution would have continued to flourish, at least among the Mormon elite who would lead the church, for at least another generation. Although some Utah Gentiles undoubtedly advocated stringent measures as a means of maintaining political dominance in the territory, while comprising a small minority of the citizenry, many federal appointees involved in the raid were sincere and capable men fully committed to the best interests of the nation.

Many have assumed that the Wilford Woodruff Manifesto of 1890 was an abrupt announcement decisively ending polygamy among the Mormons. In fact, it was probably not intended that when the church leaders announced cessation of plural marriages within the United States that such would be a permanent situation. It was likely no more than a strategic retreat necessary at the time not only to prevent enactment of the Cullom-Struble bill and to further enhance cordiality with the Republican party but also to appreciably increase the possibilities for statehood. There were several subtle changes concerning the theory and public prac-

tice of polygamy that place the manifesto within a sequence of developments through which some within the Mormon hierarchy sought to separate the church from responsibility for the continued practice of plural
marriage. If individuals thereafter failed to comply with the official declaration of the church president, duly ratified by the L.D.S. membership at
a general conference, government officials could no longer legitimately
blame the Mormon church as a body for the private noncompliance of
those who might now be publicly regarded as dissidents. Thus the opposition to statehood, which centered on the continued church sponsorship of polygamy, would be diminished.

It is doubtful if most Americans would have given much thought to the
marital or political activities of a group so geographically removed from
the mainstream had it not been for artificial stimulation, for whatever
motives, by a segment of the nation's clergy and press, often in collaboration with their counterparts in Utah. Since neither total abandonment of
plural marriage nor total abstinence from political affairs was actually intended by the church hierarchy, perhaps the greatest challenge in the
Mormon quest for Utah statehood was to remove these issues from the
forefront of public consciousness and discussion.

A public relations machine allied with the L.D.S. leaders played a crucial role in neutralizing the overwhelmingly adverse public image of the
Mormons during the last decade prior to achievement of statehood in
1896. These efforts focused on pursuading a dominant element of the
printed media to treat the Saints more favorably than heretofore. While
some documentation of their success is possible, the ultimate measure of
the accomplishment was the near absence of opposing debate when the
enabling act finally passed each house of Congress. This could only be
possible if members of Congress were assured that their constituents had
been pacified and would not be alarmed by their support of something
that had formerly been so controversial as Utah's admission as a state.

Certainly the details surrounding passage of the Utah Enabling Act
must necessarily be traced herein. And discussion of the complex role of
lobbyists, including the debts they incurred in the cause of statehood,
along with the Mormon efforts to extricate themselves therefrom is a revealing aspect of the book. The political developments in Utah on the eve
of statehood have also been treated at considerable length.

A dozen years of work on this book have incurred debts too numerous
to fully mention. I am appreciative of the many kindnesses extended at
the far-flung libraries and archives utilized in this study. Particularly helpful were Virginia Lowell Mauck, assistant curator of manuscripts at the
Lilly Library, Indiana University; Ron Watt of the staff of the Archives of
the Church of Jesus Christ of Latter-day Saints; and Velia Brown of the

University of California, Riverside, interlibrary loan department. Among the many who have offered valuable suggestions and criticisms at various stages of development of the manuscript were Thomas G. Alexander, A. R. Mortensen, Hal Bridges, Scott Kenney, Jan Shipps, Ronald W. Walker, and R. Hal Williams. Van L. Perkins and Robert V. Hine deserve special thanks for giving far more than the usual encouragement and attention during the formative stages of the study and the historian and for continuing helpful advice and interest during the subsequent stages of both. Similarly, to Leonard J. Arrington, I owe a great debt of gratitude for offering me the initial opportunity to probe the holdings of the church archives and for the constant nurturing of a whole generation of budding historians of Mormonism and other subjects, among whom I am honored to be numbered. I have also appreciated my association with the University of Illinois Press staff, particularly Susan L. Patterson who has greatly improved the readability of the book through her deft changes in the sentence structure. And to my wife, Pam, who besides the usual sacrifices of time, vacations, and resources, typed the entire manuscript through four different revisions, I owe a debt I have already commenced to repay.

NOTES

1. The president of the church holds the highest office and is revered as a prophet. He is assisted by counselors, usually two, who with him comprise the First Presidency, the highest council of the church. The Quorum of Twelve Apostles comprises the second council, which temporarily supersedes the presidency upon the death of the president. The Seven Presidents of Seventy is the third council. These officers, together with the three-man Presiding Bishopric and one Patriarch are the general authorities of the church. The stake is the local church organization similar to a Roman Catholic diocese and is comprised of from five to fifteen wards or local congregations. There is a three-man stake presidency in charge of each stake and a similar bishopric over each ward. Each level is carefully obedient to its ecclesiastical superiors. See also G. Homer Durham, "Administrative Organization of the Mormon Church," *Political Science Quarterly* 57 (Mar. 1942), 51–71.

2. See pp. 52, 65n23 below, and also Bibliographical Essay, pp. 303–4.

3. Therald N. Jensen, "Mormon Theory of Church and State" (Ph.D. diss., University of Chicago, 1938); Gaylon L. Caldwell, "Mormon Conceptions of Individual Rights and Political Obligation" (Ph.D. diss., Stanford University, 1952).

4. See pp. 23, 38–39n42 below, and also Klaus J. Hansen, *Quest for Empire: The Political Kingdom of God and the Council of Fifty in Mormon History* (East Lansing, 1967), 170; Gustive O. Larson, *The "Americanization" of Utah for Statehood* (San Marino, Calif., 1970), 281.

1

Utah Statehood and the Mormon Question, 1849–86

From their first arrival in the Great Basin, the Mormon leaders were aware that the more self-government they could maintain the better. Admission as a full-fledged state, with its inherent privileges of local autonomy, was the ideal. The Latter-day Saints had been warned about the low-type politicians likely to seek appointive office if the region were transformed into a territory under the direct control of Congress. In 1849, aided by prominent Democratic Senator Stephen A. Douglas, Mormon emissaries from the just-established provisional state of Deseret sought special permission for local citizens to elect their own territorial officials. Memorials seeking outright statehood for Deseret were sent at about the same time from Salt Lake City. However, there was no positive action on either request. Late in March, 1850, John M. Bernhiesel, the Mormon delegate to Congress, informed church leaders that Senator Douglas had concluded Congress would not legitimize Deseret with statehood. Part of the problem was that the Mormon settlements did not yet have the 60,000 eligible voters usually required for admission as a state. And there was clearly no disposition to allow the Mormons to control the truly enormous domain encompassed by the proposed state of Deseret.[1]

In the ensuing months, Deseret's fortunes were entwined in the bitter pre–Civil War controversy over slavery. Douglas, as chairman of the Senate Committee on Territories, soon felt compelled to report bills to establish the territories of Deseret and New Mexico. And thereafter not only was the name changed to Utah but also the size of the territory was drastically reduced. Utah became a territory as part of the famous Compromise of 1850. But with the other weighty matters contained therein, there was almost no consideration of Utah's needs. Fortunately for the Mormons, Bernhiesel's friend, Millard Fillmore, had just assumed the presidency upon the death of Zachary Taylor. Bernhiesel convinced the new president of the good character of Brigham Young, who was thereupon appointed governor of Utah.[2]

Unfortunately, some of the other territorial officials Fillmore selected quickly became disenchanted with Young and the general conditions in Utah. Several of them returned to Washington, D.C., with damaging reports of Mormon disregard for consitituted authority and the actual danger in which non-Mormon Gentiles found themselves within the territory. From then on the Mormon question would generate increasing hostility in the East.

The most important of the allegations was that some Mormons were engaging in the practice of plural marriage. Such reports had not been uncommon for most of a decade. Not long after the storm of the "runaway officials" blew over, church leaders apparently recognized that there was no purpose in denying the existence of polygamy. At a conference held in the late summer of 1852, church authorities acknowledged that the doctrine of plural marriage had been accepted as a divinely instituted obligation among some of the most faithful adherents of the Latter-day Saint religion. At that time there was no actual law against polygamy, but certainly many citizens throughout the nation were shocked by this admission. Church authorities were cognizant of the need to counteract the adverse press comments generated by the acknowledgment of polygamy. Establishing a pattern followed in later years, Young sent one of his most trusted lieutenants, Jedediah M. Grant, east to assist Bernheisel in that task, which aimed especially at neutralizing negative newspaper articles published there.[3]

Amid the rising current of antagonism toward their peculiar institution, Mormon leaders unwisely embarked on their second attempt at statehood in 1856. Democratic President Franklin Pierce's willingness to allow Young to continue as governor beyond his regular term may have been interpreted as sufficient favor to encourage another constitutional convention. But when Apostles John Taylor and George A. Smith brought the completed document to the nation's capital and conversed with Bernhiesel, they realized that the statehood attempt could not only be totally futile, but also might generate formidable obstacles to future attempts. Senator Douglas advised the Mormons to wait quietly until his popular sovereignty principles were more fully implemented. But it was too late. The presence of the Mormon petitioners generated considerable press comment. Although newspapers like the *New York Herald* favorably contrasted orderly Utah with "Bleeding Kansas" and expressed willingness to admit the Mormon state, polygamy and all, Republican papers took the opposite view.

One Ohio editor anticipated the statement in the platform of the infant Republican party when he exclaimed, "What a tricolor for freemen, for Americans, for religion, for progress to contemplate—Democracy—Slavery—Polygamy—."[4] It was clearly the intent of the 1856 Republican National Platform Committee, which included such notable antislavery advocates as Ebeneezer R. Hoar, David Wilmot, and Joshua R. Giddings, to use the practice of polygamy to strengthen the case in the public mind against slavery by coupling both offenses in the same phrase. Thus was born the famous election year platform plank that resolved that since the federal government possessed broad-ranging powers over territories, it was "both the right and the imperative duty of Congress to prohibit in the territories those twin relics of barbarism—polygamy and slavery."[5] Yet despite this statement, Mormonism and polygamy apparently played a minor role in the ensuing campaign. There was, however, plenty of reference to plural marriage during congressional debates. And some gave credence to a fraudulent handbill that advised almost nonexistent Pennsylvania Mormons to support the Democratic presidential candidate, James Buchanan.[6]

Buchanan's subsequent election would prove a cause of regret for the Utah Saints. Although the president-elect had been involved in national politics much too long to be unaware of the Mormon question, that the subject was unmentioned in his inaugural address indicates that Utah matters were of little concern to him as he began his presidency. But in an administration that sorely needed to devote attention and decisiveness to preserving the union, the Mormons eventually received an inordinate amount of Buchanan's attention. The events of the so-called Mormon War need not be recounted. It is sufficient to say that the Buchanan administration, acting without good information or judgment, sent a large contingent of U.S. Army troops under Albert Sidney Johnston to show the Mormons who possessed the ultimate power in the United States. The best historical account of this Mormon conflict has concluded that the government's decision was easier because it was assumed that rather than being faced with widespread resistance, many Mormons would welcome the soldiers as liberators from theocratic tyranny. The level of this miscalculation justifies labeling the entire fiasco "Buchanan's blunder."[7]

In December, 1860, as the states of the lower South were seceding from the union, new Utah delegate William H. Hooper expressed confidence that most of the Republicans then gaining control of the House of Representatives would vote for admission of Utah as a state. This suggestion quickly generated a third attempt at statehood. Although the newly seated Governor John W. Dawson vetoed a legislative attempt to call a constitutional convention into session, the citizens acted independently of governmental authority by organizing mass meetings throughout the settlements as a means of selecting delegates. The convention met on January 20, 1861, drafting a constitution and memorial for a state government still named Deseret. The document was duly ratified and state officers were even elected. Since the entire movement was accomplished without dissenting votes, it was undoubtedly orchestrated once again by the church hierarchy.

The new constitution provided that the governor-elect, predictably Brigham Young, could call the state legislature into its first session, which he did in mid-April. In the message delivered at that time, "Governor" Young quoted a statement that President Abraham Lincoln's recently installed secretary of state, William H. Seward, had made in reference to Kansas—"the Constitution of the United States prescribed only two qualifications from new states, namely, a substantial civil community and a republican government." The statement was cited, as it had been used originally, as argument against any specific minimum population being necessary before statehood could be granted.[8]

The legislature remained in session only four days, but among its actions was the election of Hooper and George Q. Cannon as the U.S. senators from Deseret. Although they and Delegate Bernhiesel expended considerable effort in Washington, D.C., they did not even come close to achieving statehood. At the end of 1862, James M. Ashley, chairman of the House Committee on Territories, reported enabling acts for the admission of Nebraska, Colorado, Utah, and Nevada. But by that time an anti-polygamy bill had been passed, which guaranteed that the Utah measure would die on the House calendar.

Historians have long understood that it was the stubborn stand by Latter-day Saints on the issue of polygamy that prevented achievement of statehood. Orson F. Whitney, a contemporary who wrote the most extensive historical treatment of the era and who had access to inside information from the church hierarchy, concluded that "had the Mormons been willing to abandon polygamy in 1862, thus meeting the Republican party half way, it was not improbable that Utah, in view of her loyal attitude, might have been admitted into the Union." But since there was no real consideration of abandoning the doctrine or practice, it appears that again the attempt at statehood was ill-advised.[9]

On the other hand, Mormon agents had reason to believe that persistent anti-polygamy clamor would continue to be ignored in the most important circles of Congress. Although Justin Morrill had introduced a bill prohibiting polygamy at each new term of Congress since 1856, none had gotten very far. The subject had, on occasion, been hotly debated, but discussion had been considerably colored by the slavery question. Typical of the objections expressed by southern congressmen was that of Lawrence Branch, who warned his colleagues that "if we can render polygamy criminal, it may be deemed that we can also render criminal that other twin relic of barbarism, slavery." So long as such fears persisted, there was no danger of the powerful southern bloc allowing such a precedent to be set. Besides this, the Republican party virtually ignored the Mormon and polygamy issues during their 1860 national election campaign.[10]

It was just after the Republicans succeeded in electing Lincoln that Hooper wrote the letter which initiated the third statehood movement. From the preceding events he had surmised that in light of the secession crisis then becoming ominous—which included the suggested possibility of a similar move by the Mormon commonwealth—leading northern politicians had revised their views considerably on polygamy and the Mormons. However, Hooper had misjudged the situation. By the opening of the Thirty-seventh Congress late in 1861, with southern Democrats having departed when their states chose the Confederacy, the Republican party was in control. Thus, when Morrill again introduced the bill to make polygamy a crime, he had reason to hope his party would finally fulfill its commitment to abolish this other twin relic. The Vermont congressman was correct. Bernhiesel made no open effort to check the measure's progress in the House. Nor was there any better success in blocking the bill in the Senate. In fact, such quick passage of the Morrill Act can be justified only when viewed in the context of the Civil War crisis and the flood of legislation the frustrated Republican members had so long wished to pass. Lincoln signed the bill into law July 1, 1862, thus placing on the statute books the first congressional legislation aimed at the Church of Jesus Christ of Latter-day Saints, and the first action of what proved to be an extended anti-polygamy crusade.[11]

Although Young's often-bombastic rhetoric could be, and on occasion was, construed to indicate the Mormons were less than loyal to the war-torn union, they remained supportive of the U. S. government. President Lincoln recognized this and indicated his own trust in the Saints by accepting their offer for manpower necessary to protect the recently completed transcontinental telegraph line and certain important wagon roads of the West.[12] But the president also accepted the services of a detachment of California volunteers under the command of Patrick Edward Connor, ordered to establish Camp Douglas on the benchland overlooking Salt Lake City. These soldiers were decidedly unfriendly to their religious neighbors, and the army post quickly became the center of anti-Mormon activity in the territory. Connor conscientiously sought to stimulate a large influx of Gentiles by granting generous furloughs to any of his men willing to prospect for mineral wealth in Utah's mountain ranges. He recognized that a mining rush was the most logical means of increasing the non-Mormon population sufficiently to overcome the domination of the Latter-day Saints.[13]

As the Civil War drew toward its end, the president showed a clear disinclination to perpetuate strife in Utah. When he was approached concerning what he intended to do about the Mormons, whom he had known in his earlier Illinois years, he characteristically replied with a story about a tree stump back on his farm that "was too heavy to move, too hard to chop, and too green to burn. So we just plowed around it," implying that he intended to leave the Saints alone.[14] In his uniquely diplomatic way, Lincoln removed Governor Stephen Harding, who was particularly objectionable to the Mormons, while attempting to assuage Gentiles by replacing Chief Justice John F. Kinney, whom they considered overly submissive to the Saints.

Soon after, the church hierarchy and its obedient followers rewarded Kinney by electing him Utah's first non-Mormon delegate to Congress. In that capacity he not only had occasion to defend his constitutents in the practice of their religious principles, but also to introduce yet another bill aimed at admission of Utah into the union. In a two-hour address before the House on March 7, 1864, Kinney favorably contrasted Utah's population to that of neighboring territories then seeking entrance, calling them "infants in age and population when compared to Utah." But his efforts proved no more successful than that of his predecessors, and no perceptible progress was made toward the goal.[15]

The stumbling block continued to be polygamy, as visits to Utah by several prominent congressmen the following summer made clear. House Speaker Schuyler Colfax, after a week in Salt Lake City, which included interviews with prominent church leaders, warned pointedly that statehood would not be attained until the offensive marriage practices had ceased. The speaker even suggested that the Mormon authorities should supply their people with a counterrevelation on the subject of plural marriage. Young's only response was to defend the practice on scriptural grounds, declaring that God had, in the latter days especially, commanded it. Two weeks later, Ashley arrived in the Mormon capital. He was perceptibly more friendly to the Saints than Colfax and apparently more interested in determining exactly where the church leaders stood on polygamy. But after freely discussing L.D.S. relations with the government, Ashley too expressed doubt that anything positive could be done without some marked Mormon concessions. He explained that outside religious groups were generating tremendous political pressures on his associates and that under such conditions there was little reason to hope for Utah statehood in the near future.[16]

Despite the clearly pessimistic views by two of the men best able to assess Utah's chances for admission into the union, the Mormon leaders soon launched another effort in that direction. At the beginning of the next territorial legislative session in January 1867, the lawmakers adjusted Utah's delegate elections to better conform with similar ones throughout the nation. At the same time the Constitution of the State of Deseret, amended to accept boundary limitations previously imposed by Congress, was readopted by the Mormon electorate. Delegate Hooper was once again directed to introduce the constitution and an accompanying memorial in the lower house. But again there was no favorable action on the measure.

Even more quixotic was a second memorial drafted by the same Utah legislature requesting Congress to repeal the 1862 anti-polygamy act on the grounds that to Latter-day Saints the plurality of wives was a divinely instituted doctrine proclaimed by the church at least ten years prior to passage of any law against it. Besides being a violation of the first amendment guarantee of freedom of religion, the Mormon legislators argued that the Morrill Act was an ex post facto law as far as they were concerned. But given the climate of hostility existing in Congress and most of the members' constituencies, such a petition indicates Mormon leaders were seriously out of touch with political reality on the national scene.[17]

In fact, much of Utah politics at this juncture was so clearly disharmonious with accepted American values as to detract from Young's reputation for shrewdness. Mormon leaders denounced political parties as divisive and argued that running more than one candidate for office was disruptive to the political order. Citizens of the Kingdom of God, they preached, exercised their freedom through sustaining the decisions of their ecclesiastical leaders and voting unanimously for the candidates selected by them. Not only did the Mormon voters obediently follow this course, but also territorial legislators selected by them were encouraged to "follow council" so that the votes on issues before them were frequently unanimous.

On the other hand, Young had reason to remain aloof from the supposedly less enlightened outside world and its standards. His preoccupation was with preparing his people to usher in the Kingdom of God on Earth, and many of his political actions may have been mainly for effect at home. Although by the mid-1860s the secret Council of Fifty was clearly subordinated by the official L.D.S. hierarchy, it too served as a mechanism through which Young and his associates maintained a political identity even after the appointive territorial offices passed largely into Gentile hands.[18]

As the decade of the 1860s drew to a close, a substantial body of non-Mormons emerged in Utah, conscious of their inferior status within the territory. When the congressional elections of 1867 approached, a small informal group of Gentile businessmen concluded that if they intended to remain in Utah, they needed to organize and "oppose the political control of the priesthood" of the dominant church. They therefore nominated William McGroarty to run against incumbent Hooper in the contest for delegate. Although the non-Mormon candidate received only 105 votes, McGroarty challenged the Mormons' seat in a partially successful attempt to focus the attention of Congress and the nation on political conditions then prevalent in Utah.[19]

Subsequently, with the full support of the appointed officials, Utah Gentiles began initiating a series of legislative remedies for which they found willing champions in Congress. Among those who introduced such bills in the late 1860s were Ashley, Benjamin Wade, Aaron H. Cragin, and Shelby M. Cullom. The several measures aimed generally at taking appointive powers, especially of law enforcement officials and juries, away from the popularly elected legislature and placing those prerogatives in the hands of the federally appointed executive branch of territorial government. Yet despite considerable effort and expense in behalf of these bills, the decade of the 1870s arrived with none of the legislation having been enacted into law.[20]

The completion of the transcontinental railroad in 1869 ended Utah's isolation and ushered in an era of increased Mormon-Gentile hostility. In fact, two distinct societies emerged to coexist, none too peaceably within the territory. The rival factions developed rival religious, social, educational, and economic organizations. Few members of either group ventured from their own domain into the other. At the time there was not even any fraternal or commercial organization that bridged the chasm.[21]

In 1870 the non-Mormons organized the Liberal party, which most markedly divided Utah citizens for more than twenty years. By that time the mining activity and other enterprises stimulated by the railroad had attracted a sizable Gentile population, with good prospects for continued growth. This was enhanced by the not unrelated schismatic movement through which a number of prominent Mormons broke away from the main body of Saints in disagreement over the arbitrary political and economic policies of Young. These "Godbeites" joined with the Gentiles for political purposes, with members of both groups calling for all who opposed "despotism and tyranny in Utah" and who favored separation of church and state there to unite in a convention to be held July 16 at the new Gentile stronghold of Corrine. The old soldier Patrick Edward Connor was elected chairman of the proceedings and those present nominated U. S. Registrar of Public Lands George R. Maxwell as a congressional candidate from the party then officially named the "Liberal Political Party of Utah." In the ensuing election the Liberal candidate garnered but 1,500 votes, some of which were allegedly fraudulent, but it was nevertheless a significant improvement over the previous contest of McGroarty.[22]

As Robert N. Baskin, one of the leading figures in both congressional campaigns pointed out, the Liberal party movement throughout its history was motivated by the aim "to correct the abuses prevalent in Utah and to establish republican American rule in place of usurped rule of the priesthood of the Mormon church." Liberals subsequently organized the semisecret Gentile League, later called the Loyal League, which often maintained Baskin and other lobbyists at Washington, D.C., for the purpose of sponsoring and pressuring for anti-polygamy legislation. This, as some of their number admitted on several occasions, was simply the most effective way to generate the support necessary to take political power away from the church hierarchy. The Liberals were also the leading opponents of the Mormon efforts for statehood, which according to them would permanently enthrone the priesthood in power.

The non-Mormon minority certainly had much to gain by maintaining territorial status in Utah. As long as the federal government exercised power through appointment of executive and judicial officers and held extensive veto powers over "inappropriate" legislative enactments, the Gentiles enjoyed governmental power superior to that held by the Mormon majority. This was most immediately beneficial not only in the favorable treatment of federal officials directly, but the mining interests, almost entirely in the hands of closely associated non-Mormons, largely escaped taxation of their property through gubernatorial vetoes of legislation aimed at that purpose. It was thus not uncommon for non-Mormons to argue that to place government entirely in the hands of the majority would severely harm their business affairs in Utah.[23]

Although the Liberals were thwarted in their initial legislative attempts to strengthen their hand against the Utah polygamists, they were more successful in securing appointment of key territorial officials who sympathized with their aims. President Ulysses S. Grant appointed J. Wilson Shaffer as governor and James B. McKean as chief justice of the Territorial Supreme Court. They took office in mid-1870 and assisted by enthusiastic Utah Gentiles, the two embarked on a so-called anti-Mormon crusade. McKean stripped the church-dominated probate courts of jurisdiction in criminal matters and severely restricted Mormon participation on juries. He also refused to allow the territorial marshal and attorney to function in the federal courts in cases affecting the territory. Thus the number of indictments and convictions of Mormon polygamists mounted to unprecedented heights.

The Utah prosecutions by administration appointees received the full endorsement of President Grant, and when these efforts were thwarted through the Englebrect decision of the U.S. Supreme Court, he lent his voice to securing passage of the legislation necessary to legalize the special tactics deemed necessary to curb the "Mormon menace."[24] In his annual message to Congress of December 1872, Grant urged "the ultimate extinguishment of polygamy." This was further stressed the following February in a special message in which the president outlined the kind of legislation necessary to solve the problem. A bill to that effect was introduced by Senator F. T. Freylinghuysen, and aided by Grant's urging, it passed the Senate. The president continued to exert special efforts in its behalf in the House—purportedly even threatening to use troops to solve the Utah problem if it were not soon solved more peaceably by Congress. But personal support by the president notwithstanding, the Freylinghuysen bill did not become law.[25]

There had been petitions opposing as well as supporting the bill's passage, but indications are that Mormon agents benefited even more fully from the influence of a "few key friends" in the House of Representatives, including Speaker James G. Blaine. Although Blaine was a Republican, he would soon be the leader of the "Halfbreed" faction that, on occasion rather bitterly opposed the "Stalwart" wing of the party to which Grant and his closest supporters belonged. Upon failure of the Freylinghuysen bill, it was disclosed that the anti-Mormon Republicans were "swearing mad" and openly accused Speaker Blaine, the chairman of the House Committee on Territories, and members of the judiciary committee of having been lavishly bribed by the Mormons.

However accomplished, the Mormon success in blocking the Freylinghuysen bill proved to be short-lived. In his annual message at the end of 1873, President Grant again called for legislation necessary to solve the Mormon problem. Early in the following session of Congress, Luke P. Poland introduced a bill similar to the one that had failed the year before. The Poland Act became law on June 23, 1874, and was to be the basis for the repeated attempts at prosecution of Mormon polygamists throughout the ensuing decade.[26] Yet the Poland Act was considerably less than Gentile advocates of stringent measures had hoped for. In the last stages of progress through the Senate, Aaron A. Sargent, known to be a loyal representative of Southern Pacific Railroad interests, threatened filibuster-type delays if the law were not moderated at least in some jury selection provisions. The proponents grudgingly acquiesced and enacted a law in which the probate judge still retained some power in selecting jurists, even where polygamy cases were concerned. Utah Gentiles continued to lament these developments for years to come.[27]

Those who aimed at a harsher law were unsuccessful largely because of the contrary efforts of the new Utah delegate to Congress, George Q. Cannon. A boyhood emigrant from England, Cannon had served effectively as a missionary and newspaper spokesman for the church, eventually becoming one of Young's closest confidants. Upon Young's death in 1877, Cannon emerged as a dominant member of the Mormon hierarchy, and from then until after Utah statehood had been achieved in 1896, he was the central figure in the political affairs of the church. On occasion, Cannon's rivals referred to him as the premier of the Mormon kingdom or the power behind the throne. Indeed, he was younger and more energetic than either John Taylor or Wilford Woodruff, whom he served as first counselor in the First Presidency, when they each in turn succeeded to the position of president of the Church of Jesus Christ of Latter-day Saints. His experience in worldly affairs, especially national politics, gave him insights beyond those of either of the men sustained by their followers as prophets. Despite their considerable dependence upon his advice, Counselor Cannon regarded himself as the loyal subordinate of the men he recognized as possessing superior ecclesiastical authority. Nevertheless, there is no question that most of the strategy and activity aimed at statehood emanated from him.[28]

Cannon's initial election as delegate to Congress was in connection with the fourth distinct effort to gain statehood. This time, to a greater extent than previously, the effectiveness of the anti-Mormon prosecutions and the bitterness of the federally appointed executive officers made the bid for admission one to alleviate real rather than simply anticipated misrule. Early in January, 1872, the Utah legislature convened in regular session and again enacted a bill providing for a constitutional convention. The proposal was promptly vetoed by Shaffer's successor, the like-minded Governor George L. Woods, but the legislature accomplished the same purpose through a joint resolution. The resultant convention, which met February 19, differed from such previous gatherings in that non-Mormons, selected at mass meetings clearly independent of Mormon control, also participated. Of the nineteen delegates representing Salt Lake County, eight were Gentiles, including Hadley D. Johnson, a former congressman and General Eli M. Barnum, who was chosen president of the convention.

When the convention settled down to the regular business of accomplishing statehood, another non-Mormon, Thomas Fitch, expressed complete sympathy with the need for Utah's admission into the union, but observed realistically that this could not be accomplished without certain concessions. He claimed no personal aversion toward the institution of polygamy but pointed out that the nation would no longer tolerate it. He further warned that if the Mormons present did not make the adjustments necessary to gain a state government themselves, the time was close at hand when their foes would organize one upon such terms as would ostracize the most honored Mormon citizens from public life and might even disfranchise the entire body of L.D.S. citizens. Although the legislators were not disposed to go so far as Fitch suggested, as a partial concession to him one section of the new constitution inquired of Congress as to the conditions that must be met in order to satisfy the nation on the subject of plural marriage. They further added a pledge to abide by whatever the terms might be, providing the majority of Utah's legal voters accepted that pledge at the polls. Upon adoption and ratification of the document, Fitch and Cannon were selected to convey the constitution to Washington, and assisted by outgoing Delegate Hooper, it was presented to Congress.[29]

The possibility that this concerted attempt at statehood might succeed aroused the anti-Mormons to greater activity than ever before. Meetings were held to denounce both convention participants and the document they produced. Great effort was expended in most Gentile communities throughout the territory to gather signatures on petitions which eventually occupied fifty three pages in the same printed volumes of congressional documents containing the proposed Utah constitution. The Liberal party also dispatched Baskin and several other lobbyists to Washington to warn the administration of the disastrous effects that local self-government would bring to the non-Mormon minority. These efforts certainly bolstered the majority in Congress in their predispositions to do nothing on the Utah question. There was not even an answer to the convention inquiry concerning what conditions might need to be met to draw Utah closer to admission as a state.[30]

Almost simultaneous with the unsuccessful statehood attempt was the first real effort to align Utah voters with the Democratic and Republican parties of the United States. In mid-March, 1872, a group comprised of Mormons and Gentiles issued a call for all inclined to be Republicans to send representatives to a convention to be held in Salt Lake City during the first week in April. Soon after, a group of Utah Democrats published a like notice informing those preferring their party of a similar kind of gathering. Both conventions were held and the participants were reported to be enthusiastic. The Republican meeting selected two delegates to represent the territory at the approaching national party convention. But when those so honored arrived there, their application for Utah's seats was rejected in favor of rival claimants sent by the Republican arm of the Utah Liberal party.

The Democrats did not send any delegates to the 1872 national convention, but later that summer over 4,000 Mormons and friendly Gentiles staged several days of demonstrations in favor of Horace Greeley, who had been put forward by anti-Grant Republicans and subsequently nominated as the Democratic party presidential candidate. The Utah support for Greeley was meaningless as far as actual votes were concerned, but it did indicate prevailing party preferences.[31]

In the succeeding presidential election contest of 1876, the Utah Democrats again attempted to be involved during the national campaign. By this time there was a territorial Democratic central committee separate and distinct from the Liberal party, which called for a convention to select delegates to the national convention to be held at St. Louis. Mormons participated freely in all aspects of these proceedings. Apparently for this reason, Liberal Democrats also convened in a rival gathering, which declared itself the legitimate representative of the party in the territory. This effort to thwart recognition of the party organization that had harmoniously integrated Mormon and Gentile Democrats was sufficiently successful to drive most Latter-day Saints back into the church-controlled political organization, by then called the People's party, where they would remain until a more successful attempt to divide along national party lines in 1891. As historian Gustive O. Larson has observed, by thus blocking the effort to divide Utah citizens along normal political lines, the Liberals appreciably enhanced their primary aim of delaying statehood for two decades.[32]

Once Cannon established himself in Congress and learned from the difficult experience with the Poland Act struggles of 1874, he became an effective defender of the Mormons. From that time until late 1881, he was able to stifle literally all of a substantial amount of legislative proposals deemed to be inimical to church interests. It must be conceded that the delegate enjoyed an advantage not available to his predecessors since 1859—the Democrats controlled the House of Representatives from March, 1875, to March, 1881. Besides the understandable predilection of southern party members to oppose anything reminiscent of carpetbag reconstruction, the Democrats were generally more inclined to favor the local self-government that the Mormon hierarchy aspired to for their empire. And with the long-standing record of Republican hostility manifested through the majority of territorial officials, as well as the congressional legislation and Republican party platforms, it was accurately assumed that most Mormons were strongly sympathetic with the Democrats.

Democratic leaders were not unmindful of the advantage Utah's admission would be for them, nor were their Mormon counterparts. On occasion Cannon encouraged this thinking. During the 1876 dispute over whether Rutherford B. Hayes or Samuel J. Tilden had been elected president, the Utah delegate confidentially assured the Democratic contender, Tilden, of the widespread support he possessed among the Latter-day Saints. Cannon further confided that if the Democrats were to grant statehood to Utah, "they would reap the gratitude of the people," presumably in the form of voter support for that party. Unfortunately for any pursuit of such a proposal, the Republican candidate was ultimately designated as the duly elected president.

In 1879, during one of the few congressional sessions in which the Democrats controlled the Senate as well as the House, Fernando Wood, one of the senior Democratic political leaders, quietly approached Cannon. The New York congressman, whose earlier demonstrations of hostility toward Mormonism made clear he was acting entirely out of partisan interest, proposed that "if Utah would become a solely Democratic state," he would work to secure admission. However, Wood was unable to generate sufficient support for his scheme because, it developed, too many congressional Democrats were "tender footed" concerning the proposition to aid the Mormons. Throughout Cannon's congressional career, he noted with disgust the "cowardice" and lack of unity among Democrats on the Mormon question.[33] In fact patience with that party, worn thin during his decade in Washington, was probably an important factor in Cannon's ultimate decision in 1890 to switch his considerable influence and personal sympathies to the Republicans. But until then he continued to work with the Democrats and usually sat on their side of the aisle.

Although the Liberals continued to enjoy considerable success in generating negative comments on the Mormon question, particularly from the nation's newspapers and clergymen, they were far from impressive in the more substantive political results they had been anxious to achieve. By the late 1870s, the Liberal cause actually appeared to be languishing in a near-hopeless condition as far as any chance at further legislation against the Mormons was concerned. At times Liberals had not even bothered to run candidates in opposition to the People's party in some important Utah elections.[34]

However, the anti-Mormon cause received new impetus in 1879 with a U.S. Supreme Court decision in the Reynolds case. Throughout the years since passage of the Morrill Anti-polygamy Act, the Latter-day Saints maintained that the law was an unconstitutional infringement upon their freedom of religion and was thus virtually ignored by them. They expected it to be eventually overturned by a fair-minded tribunal, and finally in 1874 church authorities apparently made an agreement with U.S. attorney William Carey that they would provide the defendant and evidence necessary for a test case. George Reynolds, a young secretary to the First Presidency, who had taken a second wife only a few months previously, was thus indicted and tried under the 1862 statute in the territorial courts. His second bride and other witnesses voluntarily provided the testimony that eventually convicted him. The case was ultimately appealed to the Supreme Court, where it was heard on November 14 and 15, 1878. Two months later Chief Justice Morrison Waite issued the unanimous decision, which upheld the law making the practice of plural marriage a criminal offense.[35]

The high court decision was widely hailed as striking the death blow at Mormon polygamy. It marked such a change in the federal government actions toward Utah and her recalcitrant religionists as to be a turning point in the history of the territory. Yet, although Cannon noted a flood of bills introduced to codify the nation's prevailing anti-Mormon mood, he was also the recipient of numerous offers of leniency toward the Saints, if they would but avail themselves of the opportunity and promise in the future to accept the decision as binding upon them. These came from President Hayes, Vice-President William A. Wheeler, Supreme Court Justice Stephen J. Field, and leaders of both houses of Congress. Such overtures were apparently not seriously considered because within a few days, church president John Taylor clearly indicated the intention to continue resistance to the Morrill law. In an interview with a territorial official with close connections to high authorities in Washington, D.C., Taylor was asked the question of what effect Waite's decision would have on the Saints. He replied that he did not think that it would have any effect other than to unite his people and strengthen their faith and resolve toward continued resistance.[36]

The first notable change in Utah following the Reynolds decision was appointment of Eli H. Murray as governor. This Kentucky Republican united with the clique of Liberals most hostile to the Latter-day Saints and soon became the "executive agent" of the "anti-Mormon ring." Murray's term was most notable for the extreme measures he advocated and enforced and for the frequent use of his veto power in frustrating legislative enactments of the Mormon lawmakers. Governor Murray also headed the solely Gentile committee formed to arrange for the visit of President Hayes and party to Utah in September, 1880. Although a stop at the Temple block in Salt Lake City was on the itinerary, there was a suspected attempt to isolate the president from much of the positive contact the Latter-day Saints wished to have with him.[37]

Clearly there was no change in Hayes's views of the Saints. Within three months his final message to Congress contained statements on the Mormon question more damaging to the church cause than those of his speech the year before. Hayes proposed that in order to curb the expanding "political power" of the Mormons, which threatened the principle of separation of church and state, an appointive commission should be formed to replace the elected Utah legislative assembly. He also recommended that the right to vote, hold office, and sit on juries be denied not only to practicing polygamists but also to all those who upheld and believed in that principle. These instructions were not immediately acted upon, but they were reemphasized and further enhanced the following March in the inaugural address of James A. Garfield. And since the tragic assassination of Garfield made Chester A. Arthur president by the end of the summer of 1881, the country experienced the unique phenomenon of three different Republican presidents in one year calling for Congress to act with decisiveness and, if necessary, harshness to solve the Mormon question. By year's end matters were clearly moving in the direction recommended by the presidents.[38]

On December 13, 1881, Senator George F. Edmunds introduced a comprehensive bill like the one President Hayes and others had called for. It alleviated the flaw in the previous law, which had demanded proof of actual polygamous marriage or marital relations in order to attain convictions for polygamy, by providing for the much more easily substantiated "unlawful cohabitation." Unlawful cohabitation was made a misdemeanor punishable by six months' imprisonment and a fine of up to $600 to be imposed upon anyone convicted of living with a woman alleged to be a plural wife. Also under the Edmunds bill, polygamists and cohabitants were to be disqualified from voting, holding public office, and from serving on juries. And the law declared that all election and voter registration offices be vacated and filled by a five-member Utah commission charged with the oversight of all future election matters in the territory.[39]

Less than a month after the Edmunds bill was introduced, it was reported favorably from the Senate Judiciary Committee, of which its sponsor was chairman. In heated floor debate Democrats, notably from the southern states, argued that although they too wished polygamy to be eradicated, the proposed law was far too dangerous in the penalties and restrictions imposed upon citizens. Senator J. T. Morgan voiced common concern when he stated that he was "not willing to persecute a Mormon at the expense of the Constitution of the United States." On the other side of the question, Edmunds allegedly argued that "there is no constitution but the will of the people" in regards to such matters. The bill passed the upper house on February 16, 1882.[40]

A month later the Edmunds bill was rushed through the House of Representatives as well. Although the time for debate was severely restricted, it was often marked with partisan comments. The Democrats again argued that the measure too severely threatened the Constitution, and several speakers openly accused the sponsoring party of special ulterior motives in seeking its quick passage. A. H. Buckner expressed his regrets that the bill was being pushed so rapidly "to foreclose the case of Cannon v. Campbell" and thus "give countenance to that great wrong committed against the right of suffrage" by Governor Murray at the behest of Utah Liberals. *Cannon vs. Campbell* referred to the Utah contest over the seat of the Utah delegate to Congress. Although Cannon had again received a majority vote, Territorial Governor Arthur L. Thomas certified Liberal candidate Allen G. Campbell as duly elected. Cannon was successfully contesting this election until the Edmunds bill appeared.[41]

Passage of the Edmunds Act was at least partly aimed at assuring that Cannon, an avowed polygamist, would not retain his position in the House of Representatives. He did, however, remain a frequent visitor at the nation's capital. Besides assisting his replacement, John T. Caine, a monogamist Mormon, he would still directly manage several of the steps toward eventual statehood.

While Cannon was yet in the East, he had occasion to converse with Edmunds and learned that the senator's efforts were not "seeking so much to put down polygamy as to break down the 'Mormon' system of theocracy," which he claimed was entirely in conflict with the institutions of the nation and therefore much more dangerous to the people than polygamy. This was but one of many such admissions during the era that the furor raised over plural marriage was but an emotion-laden pretext that could be effectively utilized to arouse the public clamor necessary to implement sufficiently stringent measures to curb the political influence of the Mormon hierarchy. They were undoubtedly correct that most Americans, including most congressmen, were more concerned about polygamy; however, it was admittedly the political involvement that the majority of the nation's anti-Mormon leaders most abhorred and aimed to eradicate.[42]

Despite public statements by Cannon and his contemporary Latter-day Saint leaders that they agreed with the principle of complete separation of church and state, they persisted in dominating political affairs in Utah.

Part of the justification was that most committed adult males held some lay ecclesiastical position and to prohibit all such from participation would eliminate most capable Mormons from active citizenship. And although the Constitution of the United States was revered as divinely inspired, the belief persisted that godless men had misinterpreted its provisions. This was particularly true of the right to freedom of religion as it applied to polygamy.[43]

Developments in the East and their implications for Utah notwithstanding, in February, 1882, the territorial legislature again launched an attempt to achieve the elusive goal of statehood. It resolved that it was the right and duty of Utah's people to plead for and demand a "republican form of government," so that they and their posterity could enjoy the blesings and liberties that the founding fathers had fought to secure for citizens of the United States. At the same time the Utah lawmakers adopted resolutions authorizing community gatherings to begin the process of selecting county delegates to attend the territorial convention.

This convention, comprised solely of Latter-day Saints, with the exception of two members of the law firm church leaders most often employed, gathered on April 10, 1882. Regular meetings continued for two weeks, with the delegates finally reluctantly abandoning some vestiges of the old state of Deseret, including the name. In mid-May the new constitution was submitted to the Utah voters, who cast over 28,000 ballots in favor and only 500 against its ratification. Although a committee was promptly dispatched to deliver the constitution to Congress, the matter of statehood was virtually ignored until February 23, 1883, when Wilkinson Call introduced a bill on the subject in the Senate. On December 11, Caine presented a similar bill in the House. Both bills were referred to the appropriate committees, where they were promptly and permanently pigeonholed.[44]

During 1883 Mormons and Gentiles in Utah jostled over what the Edmunds Act meant in actual practice. The duly appointed Utah Commission arrived and settled into its prescribed duties, but little was accomplished during the first year the law was in effect, except possibly to exacerbate the existing mutual antagonisms. Since the executive branch of territorial government was staffed with individuals anxious to enforce this law fully it must have been a disinclination among members of the Utah judiciary to implement the Edmunds Act that prevented immediate and strict execution of the new law. But the following summer President Arthur appointed Charles S. Zane as chief justice of the Supreme Court of Utah Territory. This selection was made partly through the influence of Senator Cullom, who as the appointee's law partner certainly knew Zane would interpret the Edmunds Act in the desired manner. None of the Gentiles so inclined would have cause for disappointment because soon the anti-polygamy crusade reached its highest pitch in fervor and effectiveness.[45]

Zane's extreme judicial program began even before the end of 1884. In one of the first cases, when the defendant affirmed higher allegiance to his family and religion than to the law in question, the chief justice replied, "If you do not submit, of course, you must take the consequences, but the will of the American people and the law will go on and grind your institution to powder." The territorial judges embarked on the "grinding" process by adopting a set of judicial tactics that included selecting grand jury members according to their stated biases against Mormonism, seating all-Gentile trial juries, imprisoning witnesses—including women—who refused to testify, denying bonds, and levying lengthy prison sentences on those convicted. This last matter was made even more harsh through the practice of segregation, in which additional sentences were allowed for each distinct period for which the defendant could be proved guilty of practicing unlawful cohabitation.

This anti-polygamy raid aimed specifically at the highest Mormon officials, all of whom were assumed to be polygamists. Some of these authorities, particularly the older men, had made sincere attempts to conform with the Edmunds Act as they understood it, by ceasing to live with more than one wife. But when the first prosecutions clearly indicated that harsh judicial treatment was intended for all, most church leaders went into hiding rather than be subjected to what they deemed to be a gross miscarriage of justice. Following the cue from their ecclesiastical superiors, most polygamous men throughout Mormondom "went on the underground," which was a rather elaborate network of hiding places, escape routes, warning systems, and support from much of the Mormon community in a concerted effort to avoid capture. And for those who were unfortunate enough to be apprehended, the church not only aided in supporting the family of the accused but also provided legal counsel for each trial. In spite of the relative ease with which unlawful cohabitation could be established during the era, more than a few cases ended in acquittal through the efforts of church-retained attorneys.[46]

A large force of deputy U.S. marshals, who well understood that increased arrests would enhance their salaries and expense accounts, scoured the territory in search of "cohabs." They often disregarded not only constitutional rights but even the canons of common decency as they insulted women and invaded privacy in the pursuit of their purposes. On several occasions the bitterness engendered by such tactics led to violence, with deputies killing one young Parowan polygamist and wounding another man angered by the Salt Lake court's treatment of his sister, who had been called to testify against her polygamist husband.[47]

As this crusade was getting under way, an important change was brought about on the national scene by the election of Grover Cleveland as president in 1884. This triggered an unprecedented celebration among the Mormons of Salt Lake City and other communities. On November 8, just after the victory was certain, amid bonfires, blaring bands, and fireworks, Delegate John T. Caine sent a telegram to the president-elect in behalf of the celebrants. It stated "ten thousand citizens of Salt Lake City tonight are enthusiastically celebrating your election. Their joy is as sincere and honest as the jollification is demonstrative." Caine affirmed that his people's confident hope was that Cleveland's administration would be as honest and fair-minded as his gubernatorial years in New York state had been.[48] Although Gentile Democrats in Utah also welcomed the new administration, they took no part in these jubilant proceedings. Some of these Utahans were apprehensive that perhaps Cleveland would be as lenient as some Mormons seemed to expect.

This was also the feeling of George L. Miller, one of the most consistent defenders of the Saints outside of Utah. A month before Cleveland was inaugurated, his private secretary and chief advisor, Colonel Daniel S. Lamont, received a letter from Miller, a longtime Democratic national committeeman from Nebraska, who had used the *Omaha Herald*'s editorial columns for many years to urge fair treatment of the Mormons. Miller enclosed a detailed memorandum on Utah matters for the president-elect. Explaining that he had spoken for the Mormons as their "recognized friend," Miller surveyed the background of polygamy and the hostile public opinion engendered thereby. Then, referring to the Edmunds Act, he warned of the distinct possibility that the prevailing methods of execution might well launch Cleveland's presidency with a violent conflict in Utah territory.

Although their defender, Miller had never condoned the Mormon's practice of plural marriage. And the most important portion of his memorandum to the man about to become president was advice to take a firm position on that issue. Miller warned that the Latter-day Saints probably assumed, or at least hoped, that the inauguration of a member of the more friendly Democratic party would mean more lenient treatment of polygamists. The Nebraskan suggested that Cleveland use an early speech to call for passage of an amendment to the Edmunds Act providing for "prompt and severe penalties" for church officials who performed polygamous marriages within any territory of the union. Miller concluded that if the president convinced the Mormon leaders that there was no reason to expect leniency from the Democratic administration, it would provide the "key that would unlock and solve the Mormon problem by causing the early surrender of the leaders of the church" and would thus be "the crowning glory" of Cleveland's public life.[49] In his inaugural address the president partially followed Miller's advice. He stated that "the conscience of the people" demanded that polygamy in the territories should be eliminated. With such apparent approval of their policies by the chief executive, the Utah territorial officials rejoiced. Governor Murray, in behalf of the "law-abiding citizens" of Utah, telegraphed the president to thank him for his "determination to suppress polygamy."[50]

Cleveland's message may also have prompted Cannon to draft a letter sent to the president several weeks later in which he submitted "the 'Mormon' side of the case." Cannon recounted at length the history of the church, including a frank exposition on the subject of plural marriage. He gave an account of the recent Mormon-Gentile conflict in Utah, laying the brunt of the blame for the hostility on a "class of men whose sole object was political and personal aggrandizement." Cannon charged that the concerted anti-Mormon activity in Utah had not really gotten under way until after the results of the recent presidential elections had become known. He told Cleveland that he did not believe "that the 'raid' now in progress was begun for any other purpose than to make it difficult for you to remove officers who were appointed by your predecessor." Cannon said that the instigators of the prosecutions had openly declared they would place the Cleveland administration in a position where it had to support them or appear to be soft on the Mormon question. Cannon then reported that it had required all of the influence that leading Mormons could muster to prevent violent resistance to the acts considered so outrageous. He expressed belief that in any other community federal officers perpetrating acts so abhorrent to prevailing sentiments would have been lynched. He confessed uncertainty as to whether the people could be permanently restrained if the anti-polygamy raid continued in like manner and pointedly reminded Cleveland that all of the territorial officials were appointees of the previous Republican administration and called upon him to put a halt to the actions that were aimed at least in part at embarrassing him.[51]

There was apparently no response to Cannon's letter, and certainly conditions did not change as a result of it. Six weeks later, with some instigation from church authorities at a general conference, heavily attended mass meetings were held throughout Mormondom. At many of these a "Declaration of Grievances and Protest" was read and approved. This lengthy document contained the historical explanation of polygamy and recounted the details of the conflict between Mormons and federal officials. It also included specific protests against the Edmunds Act as "special legislation" stemming from "popular prejudice" against the Latter-day Saints. As the Cannon letter had previously done, this document concluded by calling for President Cleveland to appoint a commission to "fairly and thoroughly investigate the Utah situation," and in the interim they petitioned against continuance of the "merciless crusade." Caine presented the protest document to Cleveland on May 13, 1885. After listening courteously, Cleveland ended the interview by stating that although he had no alternative but to enforce the Edmunds Act, he believed that the Saints were entitled to fair consideration. He promised that in his future appointments dealing with the Mormons, he would endeavor to select only men who would insure that the laws were impartially administered. The president expressed the wish that the Mormons "could be like the rest of us," to which Caine replied that all his people were asking for was fair-minded enforcement of the laws.[52]

At about the same time as the petition to President Cleveland was being formulated, Orson P. Arnold, a respected Mormon businessman, was complicating the polygamy situation by taking an alternative to submitting to imprisonment. When he was brought to trial on an unlawful cohabitation charge, instead of quietly accepting the sentence and enjoying the resultant hero's send-off from his brethren, he pleaded guilty and promised in court to obey the law on condition that he not be incarcerated. This was a shock to many Latter-day Saints and was much deplored by their leaders, indicating as it seemed a willingness to abandon what had been regarded as highly sacred commitments. But during the remainder of the year, at least one-fifth of the eighty-three men similarly indicted chose the same course.[53] Bishop John Sharp and S. W. Sears were among those who accepted this alternative to the difficult dilemma posed by the strict enforcement of the Edmunds Act. Although they were indicted in the spring of 1885, soon after Arnold, their trials were set for September, allowing them time to organize further efforts through Miller to influence the Cleveland administration in favor of their approach to the problem.

At the behest of Sharp, Sears, or their associates, Miller made a quick summer visit to Utah. He did so expecting to confer with Presidents Taylor and Cannon. But although he had been led to believe such a meeting would take place, Miller was disappointed when not even Cannon made an appearance. The Nebraska Democrat later stated that the church leaders' failure to meet with him was not only discouraging to himself but also caused embarrassment and concern among Mormon friends, who believed the church leaders should be anxious to meet with a man with close ties to the Cleveland administration.[54]

However, at the time there was a reward for the capture of both Cannon and Taylor, and since Miller had been recognized upon arrival by train, any of the dozens of deputies eager to collect the reward money would have had an easy time apprehending the church leaders had they agreed to a meeting under those circumstances. Also there would have been little inclination on the part of these highest church leaders to confer with Miller because they had no sympathy with the course Sharp, Sears, and Miller were advocating. They were also undoubtedly disappointed that the inception of the Democratic administration had not brought changes in Utah. This was made abundantly clear in a letter Cannon sent in early August to secretary of the Treasury Daniel Manning, another of President Cleveland's closest confidants. Cannon opened the lengthy letter by stating caustically that "if the purpose of the administration is to persecute the Mormons for their religion and to impress them with the idea that their object is to destroy them because of it, it would be difficult to adopt a better plan" than was being executed in Utah and adjacent areas since Cleveland's inauguration. Detailing the flagrant abuses of the crusading officers, Cannon affirmed a belief that the administration, engrossed in other matters, must not have been aware of how serious the situation was. Either that, or else there was a "disposition to allow the Republican policy to be carried out in all its severity and vindictiveness" to eradicate the objectionable portion of Mormonism or "compel the Mormons to surrender and conform to popular demands." The church leader stated that if the latter were the aim, it had failed because what had been regarded as persecutions had only strengthened the resolve of the people to resist. Cannon vented his disappointment at the course being taken by the Utah judiciary. He claimed that "no man, whatever the circumstances of his case may be, can expect mercy, or even fair treatment, in the courts as at present constituted." He also alleged an attempt to "frighten" men into promising to "put away their wives and to cease to regard them as objects of their care and protection."

Cannon was clearly aiming at raising the administration's political consciousness sufficiently to cause the removal of some of the crusading territorial officials. He again reminded Manning that with one exception the officers were Republican appointees of previous presidents and claimed that if their anti-Mormon measures succeeded, the Republican party would gain supremacy throughout the Rocky Mountain region. Cannon explained that the Democrats were simply generating the impression among formerly friendly Mormons that the party in power was quite willing to condone their destruction. He reported that some Mormons believed that the treatment they were then receiving was "worse than any ever extended to Utah under the most hostile Republican administration," and he predicted that unless corrected such would have a telling effect on future Democratic party fortunes in the West.

In addressing the partisan aspects of the problem, Cannon said, "I take it that the Democratic party is not so bigoted on this question of religion as, for the sake of appearing as reformers, to destroy its prospects for growth." And yet, he warned, the policy currently sanctioned by the administration "must act disastrously upon the future prospects of the party." Observing that the Mormons in the intermountain area numbered possibly a quarter million souls, Cannon stated that their vote was important. He pointed out that his people were "with very few exceptions, Democrats," who had the power to sway elections in Utah, Idaho, and Arizona along with a strength "not to be despised in Nevada and Colorado." Cannon predicted that the number of Latter-day Saints would increase and that some party, he hoped the Democrats, would eventually "appreciate their value" and seek to win Mormon favor by granting them rights free people were entitled to under the constitution. He admitted that the people had hailed the inauguration of a Democratic administration with genuine delight. This was not because they expected it to condone polygamy or "wink at its practice," but because they had been led to believe through the opposition of party congressional leaders to the Edmunds Act and other such issues that the Democrats would at least enforce such laws "in the spirit of humanity and not in the ferocious spirit of religious bigotry." There was no need for the party "to conceal its aversion to polygamy to secure the good feelings of the Mormon people." They did not expect the law to be ignored, but simply enforced fairly.[55]

Despite these strong words, there was no perceptible result from the letter, and Cannon would soon become even more disturbed at the course of events after Bishop Sharp, Sears, and several other prominent Mormons some weeks later took their controversial course before the Salt Lake courts. Aided by his son-in-law, Parley L. Williams, a Gentile attorney, Sharp made a formal statement in which he pledged to hold himself amenable to the laws of his country. Admitting that he had become husband of more than one wife when such had not been contrary to the law, he stated he understood that even the harsh Edmunds Act did not deem that he should disown the mothers of his children or abandon them to the charity of an unsympathetic world. While affirming his intention to continue to support them, Bishop Sharp satisfied Judge Zane that he intended to abandon all semblance of the practice of plural marriage. Sears, with less elaboration, followed a similar course, and both were freed with a fine but no prison sentence. Within a short time, they each resigned church-related positions, Sharp his ecclesiastical office and Sears the assistant superintendent's post in the cooperative department store, Z.C.M.I.[56]

In contrast, in the same court Bishop Hiram B. Clawson refused to make similar promises. Then, having changed his plea to guilty of unlawful cohabitation, Clawson was sentenced to the most severe fine and length of imprisonment allowable under the Edmunds Act. Clawson also took occcasion to state his position publicly. He explained that his wives of many years were too dear to be cast off and besides by doing so he would not only be false to covenants he had made, but would incur the scorn of those wives and others of his co-religionists. Clawson concluded there were only two courses, "one is prison and honor, the other is liberty and dishonor." For his course, Clawson was hailed as a martyr-hero among many of the Latter-day Saints.[57]

Although Miller returned to Omaha empty-handed, he kept in touch with Utah affairs through correspondence with trusted friends there. One such letter in late September so alarmed him that he forwarded it immediately to another Cleveland cabinet member, W. C. Endicott, with instructions that the president should be informed of the situation described therein. The letter was from Salt Lake merchant, C. R. Barratt, a non-Mormon Democrat who reported that the anti-polygamy raid was creating a truly dangerous situation. He was particularly concerned about a recent series of *Deseret News* editorials that openly suggested that Mormon resistance might soon include violence. The Salt Lake observer suggested a possible intention of church leaders to arouse resistance among their faithful against polygamists who, like Sharp and Sears, were contemplating a promise to obey the law. Barratt also lamented the honors heaped upon Clawson for his bold refusal to follow such a course.[58]

Within a month Cleveland wrote to Miller requesting his further views on the "Utah problem." Miller's response was essentially a repetition of his earlier advice that the Edmunds Act not only be strengthened but rigorously enforced. This time the Nebraskan placed more emphasis on fair execution of the law, as opposed to the bitterness accompanying its current enforcement at the hands of the Republican officials. The position was apparently in agreement with a statement Cleveland had made to the effect that he did not for a moment intend to execute any law unjustly even if good would ultimately result. Miller did reemphasize that in acting fairly there should not be the slightest hint that anything but the "absolute surrender of polygamy" could be accepted by the president.

Miller also divulged that negotiations were again in progress, through Caine, for a clandestine Utah conference with Cannon.[59] This meeting actually materialized. Miller took a westbound Union Pacific train and arrived as quietly as possible at Sale Lake City in late afternoon, probably on November 6, 1885. After being driven in Caine's carriage "by a circuitous route," he and Caine arrived at the designated meeting place. There Miller conferred until late in the night with Cannon. But despite earlier indications, nothing was accomplished as far as gaining official Mormon acquiescence to the concessions on polygamy Miller was seeking. Thus, upon returning home, he informed President Cleveland through Endicott that he had not seen nor heard anything on his visit that would cause him to alter any of his views.

Miller did, however, come away from Utah even more critical of the appointed officials there, whom he described as "Republican bandits who preach the gospel of hate from every federal office in the territory." He hoped Cleveland would not delay too long, particularly in replacing those controlling the courts and law-enforcement positions.[60] But Cleveland had espoused the relatively new civil service reform—including tenure of office based upon ability rather than political affiliation—which made him, to many Democrats, exasperatingly slow in replacing even blatantly partisan Republicans. This circumstance became particularly evident in Utah, where in the entire first year of the Cleveland presidency only Judge Orlando W. Powers was appointed to territorial office. And he was so totally unacceptable on several grounds that Mormon leaders fully supported successful efforts to prevent the requisite approval of his appointment by the U.S. Senate.[61]

Before any action could be taken on Utah matters in the direction urged by Miller, Cannon sent a letter to Miller that dashed hopes for concessions or even cooperation from Mormon leaders in the immediate future. Cannon stated that after conferring with other leading churchmen, he was convinced that any plans previously discussed between him and Miller were presently unworkable. This, he explained, was primarily because the bitter feelings still prevalent in Utah would prevent the kind of cooperation among all elements of the population essential to the success of such undertakings.

Cannon fully recognized the benefits to be derived through statehood and the infinitely greater protection his people could enjoy thereby. But, the church leader pointedly confessed, he and his associates did not believe that it would be granted even if "polygamy were waived or laid aside." The basis for Cannon's pessimism was the continued activity of territorial officials, particularly the Utah Commission, which he mentioned had recently recommended that all Mormons, not just polygamists, be disfranchised. To Cannon this was evidence that the "old mobocratic spirit," which had prevailed against the church even prior to the institution of plural marriage, still existed, and he predicted that his people would yet have to withstand such an onslaught until their God in His own due time relieved the pressure in His own way. The Mormon political strategist confessed that many had hoped for better treatment from the Democratic administration. But Cannon concluded, "It requires a courage, not to be found in a political party as a party to treat us with a moderate degree of fairness while such a torrent of misrepresentation concerning us sweeps over the land." The letter to Miller closed on an appreciative and friendly note, but the message it conveyed was undoubtedly a disappointment to its recipient and to Cleveland, to whom it was quickly forwarded.

Cannon's letter rejecting the indirect overtures from the Cleveland administration referred to the increasingly frequent negative references to the Mormon question in the nation's newspapers.[62] L.D.S. leaders were also aware of a proliferation of bitter comments by some of the most prominent ministers of religion in the country and the numerous petitions and resolutions sent to Congress by church congregations and women's and veterans' organizations. Members of the Mormon hierarchy often credited Utah Liberals and an associated territorial missionary organization with being the ultimate source of such negative sentiments.

The *Salt Lake Tribune* was viewed as being in the forefront of the crusade. This had been even more the case since Patrick Lannan and Charles C. Goodwin assumed control of the paper as publisher and editor, respectively, in 1883. But even prior to that a veteran *Tribune* employee, William Nelson, had played a significant role as the sole source of Utah news launched into nationwide circulation through his Associated Press dispatches. During his term in Congress, Cannon once noted that "the agent of the Associated Press in Salt Lake City is the champion liar of his class. Every day we have a batch of inflammatory and lying dispatches" to counteract. Cannon's successor, John T. Caine, made similar statements and was forced to act in a similar manner as an important adjunct to his congressional duties in the 1880s.[63]

Actually, it was at least partly Caine's use of a series of false Associated Press reports in 1886 that caused Cleveland to become sufficiently disenchanted with Governor Murray to remove him from office that year. But the president was probably inclined in that direction anyway because at the same time he was also acting to replace U.S. Marshal E. A. Ireland and U.S. Attorney W. H. Dickson with more moderate men, as Miller and others had been urging. This was even more apparent from the conciliatory efforts of Cleveland's gubernatorial appointee, Caleb W. West. One of West's initial actions was offering the ranking Mormon apostle, Lorenzo Snow, recently sentenced to prison for unlawful cohabitation, terms through which he could receive amnesty and release. This was conditional upon Snow's promise to obey the law henceforward, which, to West's disappointment, the apostle firmly rejected. But many, even among the Latter-day Saints, recognized the sincerity and anxiousness of the governor to alleviate the bitterness prevailing in the territory. Thereafter, discouragement at the rebuffs undoubtedly pushed the governor and other recent Democratic appointees closer to the Liberal camp, and the following October West urged Congress to enact more stringent legislation to resolve the Mormon problem.[64]

Although Governor West's proposals were not acted upon, there was at that time considerable legislation pending in Congress aimed at more successfully curbing Mormon polygamy and even more important, to the sponsors at least, the power of church leaders in secular affairs. Among these measures was an early version of the one destined to become the Edmunds-Tucker Act. This had been initially introduced even before the Edmunds Act had been in effect a year. Progress had been slow for the new bill because of the general disinclination of congressmen to crowd through a more stringent law before the one already enacted had sufficient time to work. But in early 1884 Edmunds's Senate Judiciary Committee favorably reported the new bill. It included amendments openly aimed at destroying the "temporal power" of the L.D.S. church by directing the U.S. attorney general's office to institute proceedings to forfeit and escheat to the United States all church property in excess of $50,000, which was claimed to be held in violation of the earlier Morrill Act. This bill was debated on several occasions early the following summer and was subsequently passed. But although the same measure was ordered printed when introduced in the House of Representatives, it then disappeared into committee for a year and a half. However, on December 8, 1885, Edmunds reintroduced his bill and quickly had it reported from the Judiciary Committee. In January, 1886, it was again debated on the Senate floor. There was considerable opposition due to its general restrictions on the rights of citizens, such as the abolition of women's suffrage, which had been enjoyed in Utah territory for more than a decade. Nevertheless, the bill passed by a vote of 38 to 7 with 31 either absent or abstaining. The bill again went to the House on January 12, 1886.[65]

This time there was more interest shown in the House Committee on the Judiciary, to whom it was assigned. Under the leadership of Chairman J. Randolph Tucker, the Edmunds bill was thoroughly scrutinized, and during April and May hearings were held. Baskin was again on hand to assist interested congressmen in favor of the bill, and Caine and several specially retained attorneys spoke for the Mormons. The House committee subsequently reported a substitute for the Edmunds bill, which, while omitting some harsh provisions, added others, including a section making unlawful cohabitation or "any polygamous association" a felony punishable by five years' imprisonment. It also provided for the appointment of many territorial officials hitherto popularly elected and added a test oath to exclude from voting, holding office, or jury service any who would not agree to obey the anti-polygamy laws. This bill did not reach the floor before the end of the session but was prepared for prompt action at the next session of Congress.[66]

During the same time Congress had also witnessed a flurry of legislative activity relative to statehood for many of the western territories. This was particularly important because it was an era in which the balance between Democrats and Republicans in both houses of Congress was so close that a few additional seats would give tremendous advantage to whichever party was able to gain the majority. As the debates of the decade make clear, and as several twentieth-century students have reaffirmed, Democratic and Republican leaders perceived the new states and their congressional seats as important matters of party interest.[67]

A case in point was Dakota Territory, which, because it possessed the largest population and was situated closest to the East, received the greatest share of attention. By 1884 the Republican-controlled Senate was prepared to admit the territory as two states. The Democrats, in control of the House, were hard-pressed to find legitimate pretext for refusing to concur. They argued weakly that there had been no general demand from the residents for division of the territory. A more effective strategy was that of William Springer, chairman of the House Committee on Territories, who for strictly Democratic party purposes reported a bill in late May, 1886, to admit Dakota as a single state. But by that time Springer and his associates realized that they might be permanently antagonizing the sizable Dakota electorate and thus they began seeking means through which they could allow admission of the territory and yet neutralize the anticipated Republican advantage by admitting territories more likely to elect Democratic congressional delegations at the same time. For this reason Springer began working on the "omnibus idea" through which he proposed to provide for an enabling act to include the territories of Dakota, Montana, Washington, and New Mexico.[68]

Thus, it was likely that the approaching second session of the 49th Congress would be an eventful one for several western territories. Concerned Utahans not only hoped for inclusion of their territory in the proposed statehood bill but also faced the probability that further anti-polygamy legislation would be attempted. Although in the previous four decades both subjects had arisen with notable frequency, this time there were particular grounds for anticipation—and apprehension.

NOTES

1. Dale L. Morgan, "The State of Deseret," *Utah Historical Quarterly* 8 (1940), 114–20.

2. Leland H. Creer, *The Founding of an Empire: The Exploration and Colonization of Utah, 1776–1856* (Salt Lake City, 1947), 333. Fillmore announced his appointments for Utah in Sept., 1850. They were as follows: Brigham Young of Utah, governor; B. D. Harris of Vermont, secretary; Seth M. Blair of Utah, U.S. attorney; Joseph L. Heywood of Utah, U.S. marshal; Lemuel H. Brandebury of Pennsylvania, chief justice of the Supreme Court; Perry E. Brocchus of Alabama, associate justice; and Zerubbabel Snow of Ohio, associate justice. Snow and the Utah residents were Mormons.

3. Brigham H. Roberts, *A Comprehensive History of the Church of Jesus Christ of Latter-day Saints*, 6 vols. (Salt Lake City, 1930), 5:295–301; Larson, "*Americanization*" *of Utah*, 37–52; Stanley S. Ivins, "Notes on Mormon Polygamy," *Western Humanities Review* 10 (1956), 229–39; Richard D. Poll, "The Mormon Question, 1850–1865: A Study in Politics and Public Opinion" (Ph.D. diss., University of California, Berkeley, 1948), 21–24; Jedediah M. Grant, *Three Letters to the New York Herald from J. M. Grant of Utah* (New York, 1852), 1–64.

4. Morgan, "State of Deseret," 133, states that the territorial legislature memorialized Congress to authorize state constitutional conventions in 1852, 1853, and 1854—finally deciding to hold such a meeting without outside authorization. Poll, "Mormon Question," 45–47, 54; *New York Herald*, June 17, 1856; *Ohio Columbian*, cited *Deseret News*, June 14, 1856; *New York Times*, June 7, 1856.

5. John A. Wills, "The Twin Relic of Barbarism," in *Publications of the Historical Society of Southern California* 1 (1890), 41; Kirk H. Porter and Donald B. Johnson, comps., *National Party Platforms, 1840–1952* (Urbana, 1956), 27.

6. *Congressional Globe*, 34th Cong., 1st sess., appendix, 636, 713, 1135, 1181, 1195, 1211, 1297.

7. Norman F. Furniss, *Mormon Conflict, 1858–1859* (New Haven, 1960), 45–60, 62–95.

8. William H. Hooper to George Q. Cannon, Dec. 16, 1860, copy in *Journal History of the Church of Jesus Christ of Latter-day Saints*, Feb. 1, 1868, Historical Department of Church of Jesus Christ of Latter-day Saints, Salt Lake City (hereafter referred to as H.D.C.). Correspondence from Washington, D.C., published in the *Deseret News*, Dec. 26, 1860, reported a definite improvement in public feeling toward Utah. Roberts, *Comprehensive History*, 5:5. Seward's speech was delivered in the U.S. Senate, Apr. 9, 1856.

9. *Congressional Globe*, 37th Cong., 3rd sess., 166; Orson F. Whitney, *History of Utah*, 4 vols. (Salt Lake City, 1892–1904), 2:59.

10. Poll, "Mormon Question," 146, 216, 218–19, 232–45; *Congressional Globe*, 36th Cong., 1st sess., 1410.

11. Poll, "Mormon Question," 246–47; E. B. Long, *The Saints and the Union: Utah Territory during the Civil War* (Urbana, 1981), 58–79. The Republicans in Congress had been struggling for legislation on banking, the tariff, homesteads, land grant colleges, and the transcontinental railroad for many years. With south-

ern Democrats no longer present to oppose such laws, some of which were also sponsored by Morrill, they were promptly enacted. Besides defining the crime of bigamy, the Morrill Anti-Polygamy Act also provided that no religious association in the territories could hold real property in excess of $50,000. *Congressional Globe*, 37th Cong., 2d sess., apendix, 385.

12. Long, *Saints and the Union*, 65, 84–86; Gustive O. Larson, *Outline History of Utah and the Mormons* (Salt Lake City, 1958; rpt. ed., 1961), 197–98.

13. Long, *Saints and the Union*, 94–124; Robert J. Dwyer, *The Gentile Comes to Utah: A Study in Religious and Social Conflict, 1862–1890* (Washington, D.C., 1941; rpt. ed., Salt Lake City, 1971), 1–28.

14. Poll, "Mormon Question," 174.

15. *Congressional Globe*, 38th Cong., 1st sess., 1170–73.

16. Whitney, *History of Utah*, 2:121–39.

17. Ibid., 173–77.

18. Hansen, *Quest for Empire*, 109–74; Eugene Campbell, "Governmental Beginnings," in *Utah's History*, ed. Richard D. Poll (Provo, 1978), 153–72, draws heavily on D. Michael Quinn, "The Mormon Hierarchy, 1832–1932: An American Elite" (Ph.D. diss., Yale University, 1976), which correctly assigns less power to the Council of Fifty after the first years in the Salt Lake Valley. Morgan, "State of Deseret," 132–55, uncovered the details of a "Ghost Government of Deseret," established in connection with the unsuccessful statehood attempt of 1862. Mormon delegates convened at the close of the regular territorial legislative sessions to approve the laws recently enacted. This unique practice continued at least until 1870. Young explained the purpose was to hold the "machinery of government" ready to function when Congress should finally recognize their state organization.

19. Robert N. Baskin, *Reminiscences of Early Utah* (Salt Lake City, 1914), 23–27, 32–35.

20. Larson, *Outline History*, 199–207; Roberts, *Comprehensive History*, 5:225–31.

21. Dwyer, *Gentile Comes to Utah*, 29–58; Baskin, *Reminiscences of Early Utah*, 5–27, 164–72, 198–208.

22. Baskin, *Reminiscences of Early Utah*, 23–27; Roberts, *Comprehensive History*, 5:259–67, 305–17.

23. Baskin, *Reminiscences of Early Utah*, 23–24; Mark W. Cannon, "The Mormon Issue in Congress, 1872–1882: Drawing on the Experience of Territorial Delegate George Q. Cannon" (PH.D. diss., Harvard University, 1960), 279; C. C. Goodwin, "The Political Attitude of the Mormons," *North American Review* 132 (Jan.-June 1882), 279.

24. Dwyer, *Gentile Comes to Utah*, 74–93; Roberts, *Comprehensive History*, 5:382–414; Larson, *"Americanization" of Utah*, 74–76; *Clinton v. Englebrect*, 13 Wallace (U.S.), 434 (1872).

25. James D. Richardson, comp., *A Compiltion of the Messages and Papers of the Presidents, 1789–1897*, 20 vols. (Washington, D.C., 1898), 7:203, 151; *Congressional Glove*, 42d Cong., 3d sess., 1780–81 Roberts, *Comprehensive History*, 5:435.

26. James G. Blaine, *Twenty Years of Congress: From Lincoln to Garfield* (Nor-

wich, Conn., 1886), 2:657–67; Edward Standwood, *James Gillespie Blaine* (Boston, 1905), 223–32; Roberts, *Comprehensive History*, 5:436–37; Cannon, "Mormon Issue," 51, 57–59, 288.

27. Cannon, "Mormon Issue," 51, 57–59, 288. As discussed in Chapter 3, Southern Pacific Railroad was always interested in maintaining cordial relations with Utah and the Mormons. Joseph B. Rosborough, "Biographical Sketch," 23–25, ms., Bancroft Library, University of California, Berkely.

28. *The National Cyclopaedia of American Biography*, 58 vols. (New York, 1898), 16:1918; Goodwin, "Political Attitude of the Mormons," 282.

29. Whitney, *History of Utah*, 2:691–704.

30. House of Representatives, *Miscellaneous Documents*, no. 208, 42d Cong., 2d sess., 1–82; Whitney, *History of Utah*, 2:704–5, 721.

31. Ronald C. Jack, "Utah Territorial Politics: 1874–1896" (Ph.D. diss., University of Utah, 1970), 274–310, 470–78; *Deseret News*, June 7, 1872; *Salt Lake Herald*, June 8, 1872; Roberts, *Comprehensive History*, 5:464–67.

32. Larson, *"Americanization" of Utah*, 92.

33. Cannon, "Mormon Issue," 64, 167, 291–92.

34. Whitney, *History of Utah*, 2:722–50.

35. Ibid., 3:45–56; Baskin, *Reminiscences of Early Utah*, 61–72; *U.S. Reports* 98 (Oct., 1878), 244–251; George Q. Cannon, *A Review of the Decision of the Supreme Court of the United States in the Case of George Reynolds vs. the United States* (Salt Lake City, 1879), 8–9.

36. Cannon, "Mormon Issue," 66–67, 334; Whitney, *History of Utah*, 3:51–55.

37. Whitney, *History of Utah*, 3:119–26.

38. Richardson, *Messages and Papers of the Presidents*, 10:4558, 4601, 4644.

39. *Congressional Record*, 47th Cong., 1st sess., 1152–53; Richard D. Poll, "The Twin Relic: A Study of Mormon Polygamy and the Campaign by the Government of the United States for Its Abolition, 1852–1890" (M.A. thesis, Texas Christian University, 1939), 187–230; Cannon, "Mormon Issue," 72–77.

40. *Congresional Record*, 47th Cong., 1st sess., 1152–62, 1195–1217; Whitney, *History of Utah*, 3:176–80.

41. Whitney, *History of Utah*, 3:130–94. Cannon, "Mormon Issue," 72–85, 161–74; *Congressional Record*, 47th Cong., 1st sess., 1866–67, 3068, 1214. Senator Joseph E. Brown said, "I cannot shut my eyes to the fact that this bill, if it becomes a law, will transfer the political power of this territory to the Republican party—a party which has 1,500 votes out of 15,000, and its friends know that fact full well."

42. Cannon, "Mormon Issue," 236; George F. Edmunds, "Political Aspects of Mormonism," *Harper's Magazine* 64 (Jan. 1882), 285–88. One of the era's leading anti-Mormon crusaders later admitted, "My entire thought was through my own political activities to destroy the political power of the Mormon church and in this way, as I view it, destroy polygamy. Those of us who understood the situation were not nearly so much opposed to polygamy as we were to the political domination of the church. We realized, however, that we could not make those who did not come actually in contact with it, understand what this political domination

meant. We made use of polygamy, in consequence, as our great weapon of offense and to gain recruits to our standards. There was a universal detestation of polygamy, and inasmuch as the Mormons openly defended it we were given a very effective weapon with which to attack." Louis J. Clements, ed., *Fred T. Dubois' The Making of a State* (Rexburg, Idaho, 1971), 48; *Journal History*, June 10, 1885.

43. Lyndon W. Cook, "George Q. Cannon's Views on Church and State" (M.A. thesis, Brigham Young University, 1977), 67–84; Cannon, "Mormon Issue," 176–217; Jensen, "Mormon Theory of Church and State," 87–119.

44. Whitney, *History of Utah*, 3:202–6; *Congressional Record*, 47th Cong., 2d sess., 3149; ibid., 48th Cong., 1st sess., 122; Poll, "Twin relic," 233.

45. Thomas G. Alexander, "Charles S. Zane, Apostle of the New Era," *Utah Historical Quarterly* 34 (1966), 291–314; Whitney, *History of Utah*, 3:282–3, states that Zane's predecessor, John A. Hunter, "was not altogether in harmony with the radicals, who had endeavored for that reason to procure his removal from office."

46. Eli H. Murray, "Report of the Governor of Utah," in "Report of the Secretary of the Interior," *House Executive Documents*, 12, 49th Cong., 1st sess., 1022, quotes Zane; *Deseret News*, Oct. 21, 1885; Whitney, *History of Utah*, 3: 287–341. Larson, *"Americanization" of Utah*, 91–206, is an excellent treatment of most aspects of "the raid" from the Mormon viewpoint.

47. Fae Decker Dix, "Unwilling Martyr: The Death of Young Ed Dalton," *Utah Historical Quarterly* 41 (Spring, 1973), 163–77; Whitney, *History of Utah*, 3:447–57.

48. John T. Caine to Cleveland, Nov. 8, 1884, copy in John T. Caine Papers, H.D.C.; Whitney, *History of Utah*, 3:263–64.

49. George L. Miller to Daniel S. Lamont, Jan. 26, 1885, Miller to Lamont, Feb. 7, 1885, Miller to Cleveland, Feb. 7, 1885, Miller to Cleveland, Oct. 27, 1885, Miller to W. C. Endicott, Oct. 30, 1885, all in the Grover Cleveland Papers, Library of Congress, Washington, D.C.

50. Richardson, *Messages and Papers of the Presidents*, 10:4887; Whitney, *History of Utah*, 3:349.

51. George Q. Cannon to Cleveland, Mar. 25, 1885, Cleveland Papers.

52. Whitney, *History of Utah*, 3:377–86.

53. Ibid., 357–58.

54. Miller to Endicott, Sept. 30, 1885, Miller to Cleveland, Oct. 27, 1885, Cleveland Papers.

55. Cannon to Daniel Manning, Aug. 7, 1885, ibid.

56. James B. Allen, "'Good Guys' vs. 'Good Guys': Rudger Clawson, John Sharp, and Civil Disobedience in Nineteenth-century Utah," *Utah Historical Quarterly* 48 (Spring, 1980), 148–74.

57. Whitney, *History of Utah*, 3:420–25.

58. Miller to Endicott, Sept. 30, 1885, C. R. Barratt to Miller, Sept. 27, 1885, Cleveland Papers.

59. Miller to Cleveland, Oct. 27, 1885, ibid.

60. Miller to Endicott, Nov. 9, 1885, ibid.

61. Allan Nevins, *Grover Cleveland: A Study in Courage* (New York, 1932),

198–201; John Beck to L. J. Nuttall, Mar. 11, 1886, Apr. 14, 1886, L. John Nuttall Papers, Harold B. Lee Library, Brigham Young University, Provo, Utah.

62. Cannon to Miller, Nov. 19, 1885, Cleveland Papers.

63. Roberts, *Comprehensive History*, 6:21–29, 169–72; Dwyer, *Gentile Comes to Utah*, 183–88, 204–10; Dennis L. Lythgoe, "The Changing Image of Mormonism in Periodical Literature" (Ph.D. diss., University of Utah, 1969), 37–41; O. N. Malmquist, *The First 100 Years: A History of the Salt Lake Tribune, 1871–1971* (Salt Lake City, 1971), 66–137; Cannon, "Mormon Issue," 139, quotes George Q. Cannon's journal entry for Feb. 11, 1873; see also p. 70 herein. Eventually Goodwin admitted in court that Utah statehood would substantially undermine his newspaper's financial position (which was actually a confession of ulterior motives in the *Tribune*'s longtime oposition to admission). *Salt Lake Herald*, Apr. 19, 1889.

64. Whitney, *History of Utah*, 2:363, 3:499–503.

65. Poll, "Twin Relic," 233–57; *Congressional Record*, 47th Cong., 1st sess., 4564–65.

66. *Congressional Record*, 47th Cong., 1st sess., 7; ibid., 49th Cong., 2d sess., 582–96.

67. Howard R. Lamar, *Dakota Territory, 1861–1889: A Study of Frontier Politics* (New Haven, 1956), 244–73; Frederic L. Paxson, "The Admission of the 'Omnibus' States," *Wisconsin State Historical Society Proceedings*, 49 (1911); Robert W. Larson, *New Mexico's Quest for Statehood: 1846–1912* (Albuquerque, 1968), 147–55; Robert E. Albright, "Politics and Public Opinion in the Western statehood Movement of the 1880's," *Pacific Historical Review* 3 (1934), 297–306.

68. Donald L. Kinzer, "The Congress and State Making, 1889: Centennials and Precedents," 3–18, paper delivered at the Twentieth Annual Conference of the Western History Association, Kansas City, MO., Oct. 17, 1980; Larson, *New Mexico's Quest*, 147–55.

2

Another Attempt at Statehood: A Year of Preliminaries

In 1887, for the sixth time in their history, Utah citizens sent a delegation east with a constitution and memorial petitioning Congress for statehood. But this time their pleas were not automatically rejected. In fact, there was significant support for Utah statehood from a segment of the nation's Democratic party leaders, including President Grover Cleveland and several of his chief advisors. They aided Mormon agents in drafting a Utah constitutional provision that, for the first time prohibited plural marriage. The Mormon question no longer appeared to be irreconcilable, and for a year there was a distinct possibility that hopes for statehood would at last be fulfilled. In the end Mormon leaders could not bring themselves to make the minimum of concessions regarding their unique marriage practices, but the avenues of communication with the government were broader than ever before.

In December, 1886, during the first week of the new session of Congress, William Springer reintroduced his Omnibus bill. Soon after, John Taylor, president of the Church of Jesus Christ of Latter-day Saints, sent letters to each of the Mormon agents then in the East, instructing them to watch for an opportunity to include Utah in future versions of that bill. Besides Delegate John T. Caine, the recipients were John W. Young, a son of Brigham Young, now a railroad promoter operating in New York, and Franklin S. Richards, the leading attorney for the church. They subsequently met to assess what could be done to secure admission of Utah into the Union.[1]

Young, a sometime general authority of the church, assumed the lead in these efforts and indicated good prospects could accrue through the close relationships that he had established with some of the foremost leaders of the Democratic party. Although his correspondence with church leaders at Salt Lake City always referred to these men through coded numbers—one through eight—the context of his letters reveals them to include President Grover Cleveland; Daniel Lamont, the president's private secretary and chief political advisor; William L. Scott, an influential member of the House of Representatives from Pennsylvania; and George A. Jenks, solicitor general of the United States.[2]

During the same early days of the new congressional session, the Utah Liberal party lobbyists, Robert N. Baskin and Charles W. Bennett, were successfully maneuvering to accomplish the long-sought revision of the anti-polygamy statute. In this they were materially aided by Territorial Governor Caleb W. West, then in Washington, whose influence with fellow Kentuckian, House Speaker John G. Carlisle, enabled them to secure time on the House floor for consideration of measures of particular concern to the Judiciary Committee. This guaranteed that Committee Chairman J. Randolph Tucker's version of the anti-polygamy bill would receive prompt attention and thus dashed the hopes of those who had been quietly laboring to thwart progress of such legislation.[3]

Caine had recently confessed to Mormon leaders that if the Tucker bill reached the floor, it would likely pass with little opposition. Mormon hopes of preventing this were frustrated at the last moment, Caine reported, through the influence of Carlisle. The speaker was chairman of the powerful House Rules Committee in charge of the legislative agenda and largely determined the subjects of discussion as well as who would participate in debate. The delegate explained that the same persons and methods that had "held matters in past years" were again utilized, but the severe illness of several "friends" had prevented the possibility of "holding old combinations or forming new." Implying that railroad lobbyists had previously been helpful in the Mormon cause, the church delegate mentioned that the sudden death of one of the key men in the operation had demoralized those forces. The Mormon lobby had thus been outmaneuvered, and a most serious crisis resulted.[4]

As it became obvious that there was no likely means of preventing the Tucker bill from coming before the House, Caine and his associates drafted a measure soon to be designated as the Scott Amendment. This was actually a resolution providing that the Tucker bill not go into effect until six months after it became law, thereby allowing Utah citizens time to call a convention that might frame and ratify a constitution including a provision specifically prohibiting polygamy. The intent of the amendment was to suggest that the Mormons might be willing to accede to the anti-polygamy pressures and make the necessary concessions to avoid the more stringent provisions of the Tucker bill. In light of persistent Mormon opposition to such actions in the past, there was little reason to hope Congress would support such an effort, but short of outright capitulation it was the only recourse Mormon agents had. And in the long run it did provide a basis for the next attempt at statehood.[5]

On January 12, 1887, the Tucker anti-polygamy bill was fully discussed in the House of Representatives. Caine and several other Democrats spoke in opposition, while Tucker led the proponents. Near the close of the debate, Scott attempted to get his resolution attached to the bill. But the strong objections of Tucker led to decisive rejection of the proposal. The bill quickly passed. Since Senator George F. Edmunds disagreed with the House counterpart to his bill, which had previously cleared the upper house, arrangements had to be made for a conference committee to attempt reconciliation of the differences.[6]

As Caine later recounted to Utah church authorities the steps he had been compelled to take, quickly and without the usual imput or consent from them, he stated that "high Democratic leaders" had approved of the Scott Amendment. He also reported that despite subsequent passage of the unamended Tucker Act, some party leaders were still committed to support an effort to have the conference committee incorporate the essence of the Scott proposal into the draft of the bill that would be sent back to both houses for final approval. The delegate, more candid and realistic than John W. Young, cautioned, however, that this prospect was not to be regarded as assured.[7]

There was also uncertainty concerning the reaction of Mormon church leaders to the Scott Amendment. When the first notice of it reached Taylor at his hiding place, his immediate response was negative. He was concerned that approval of the anti-polygamy constitutional provision might convey the impression that the Latter-day Saints intended to surrender the principle of plural marriage. With his fervent belief in the divine origin of that doctrine and in spite of the great suffering the forced exile was causing him, Taylor was not at first in favor of condoning provisions through which the state government could outlaw polygamy.

In the communications from Washington, D.C., to Salt Lake City, the church political emissaries attempted to persuade Taylor that the Scott Amendment need not be viewed as a compromise of the church position on plural marriage. Charles W. Penrose, a local church official then on leave from duties as editor of the *Deseret News*, was assisting Caine at the nation's capital. In an important letter also signed by Richards, Penrose argued that accepting such a constitution would be a purely political matter in which non-polygamist Mormons, the only ones who could vote, would be acting in their capacity as citizens. The polygamists, including virtually all of the general authorities, would therefore not be committing themselves on the matter. This was the first of several instances during the period when L.D.S. leaders distinguished between political and religious positions on the doctrine of polygamy. The apparent implication was that it might be possible to allow the world's standards to apply to non-polygamous citizens while permitting some to render obedience to the higher law by remaining aloof from the actual sanctioning of the consitutional concession. The letter also stressed a benefit the Scott Amendment approach to statehood would offer polygamists. Enforcement of the laws would be by officials chosen by the predominantly Mormon electorate rather than, as under territorial conditions, by hostile federal appointees.[8]

Young was similarly anxious for Taylor to approve the Scott proposal. After a private interview with President Cleveland on February 10, Young inquired as to what the administration could expect from the Mormons toward "satisfying public clamor" if the president were to interest himself in such a Mormon statehood effort. Cleveland wanted the question resolved before the opening of a new congressional session the following December. Upon receiving a telegraphic reply from church headquarters that there could be "no surrender of principle," Young rejoined that it was unnecessary to surrender anything. As he carefully explained, the question was simply that if Cleveland accepted the Penrose political definition of the Scott Amendment, could Taylor give any assurance that the church leaders were willing to allow Mormon citizens to follow such a course.[9]

Meanwhile, most of the House members of the conference committee rejected incorporation of the Scott Amendment in the final version of the law. After one meeting of the committee, Tucker had been summoned home by news of his daughter's death. In his absence Senator Edmunds was able to get provisions from his own bill inserted into the House bill in several crucial sections. On February 15, after more than a week of "protracted and stormy" meetings, the committee reported a bill that had eliminated some of the harshest features of the Tucker bill.[10] Mormon attorneys were relieved to learn that the portions of the bill making polygamy and cohabitation felonies, with continuance of such relationships being separate offenses, had been eliminated. This left the penalties for these offenses the same as they had been. The *Salt Lake Herald* later elaborated in a series of editorials on the positive alterations in the bill, at one point revealingly referring to the "fangs drawn from the Tucker Bill."[11]

As both branches of Congress were approving the compromise Edmunds-Tucker bill, Young was waiting impatiently for responses to his inquiries. On February 22 he telegraphed that he needed to call on President Cleveland, but dared not, knowing he would be asked for answers to the earlier questions concerning the willingness of church leaders to accept the Scott Amendment. He warned that they were losing valuable time and desperately needed an immediate reply. Apparently before any response came from Utah, on February 25 Young reported another conversation with Cleveland in which the president expressed himself as completely satisfied with the provisions of the Scott Amendment, saying no good man at the nation's capital could ask for more than it offered. Young reassured those at church headquarters that the question of cessation of marriages had not been mentioned in the presidential interview, implying there was no danger that such a retrocession was expected. He confidently predicted that following the course of accepting a Utah constitution officially prohibiting polygamy would "make us a state." [12]

Taylor finally replied. He said that if the Scott Amendment would satisfy President Cleveland it would be acceptable to church leaders and he could see no objections to the Latter-day Saints carrying out its provisions. But the dispatch sent to Young at Taylor's direction carefully advised that "we desire it distinctly understood we accept terms of Scott Amendment as a political necessity and that in doing so we neither yield nor compromise an iota of our religious principles." The church leader further stipulated that "if by consenting to its terms we should be understood as conceding anything religiously or giving up any doctrine or principle for which we have been contending we should recoil from it and emphatically reject it." As indication that Taylor had accepted the Penrose political interpretation of the Scott Amendment, he observed that "if a constitution should be adopted according to its provisions it would, at worst, only be punishing ourselves for what our enemies are now punishing us." [13]

Thus Cleveland and Taylor accepted a strategy for resolving the polygamy issue that appeared to be intentionally vague. Non-polygamous Utah citizens would approve state constitutional provisions prohibiting the practice, while the already disfranchised participants in plural marriage clearly intended to continue living as they had before. There was a tacit hope that statehood would mean that the new statutes would be enforced more humanely by friendly co-religionists. An accompanying understanding seems to have been that new plural marriages would only be contracted beyond the jurisdiction of the U.S. government under the assumption that despite subsequent return to Utah, if such were not discovered and proved through court proceedings within three years, the statute of limitations would free participants from further threat of prosecution. The Mormon leaders apparently distinguished between the actual marriages, which they defined narrowly as polygamy, and the subsequent cohabitation with such plural wives, which, according to their understanding of the Scott approach to the problem, would not be specifically prohibited by law. This policy also differentiated between the politically expedient stance of appearing to the outside world to be outlawing polygamy, while yet making no concessions in the realm of a belief still regarded as a fundamental tenet of the Latter-day Saint faith.

Though this conditional acceptance was undoubtedly communicated to Cleveland, the president did not commit himself to his intended action on the Edmunds-Tucker bill awaiting his signature. One of Caine's dispatches said he hoped for a veto, but had no assurance of one. In the next telegram he reported the bill had become law without the president signing it. Cleveland had some consitutional objections to the Edmunds-Tucker Act, but knowing the public clamor for such legislation, he allowed it to stand because he feared a new version would likely be even more disagreeable. Similarly, Mormon legal advisors understood that the Edmunds-Tucker test oath had been instituted to disfranchise fellow church members, and thus they urged monogamist L.D.S. men to subscribe to it—however questionable the constitutionality—in order to maintain their right to vote.[14]

At the end of March the Utah Commission sent a circular to voter registration officers throughout the territory explicitly stating that nobody entitled to vote under the law should be deprived of that right. This clearly angered some Gentiles, and in late April commission chairman Ambrose B. Carleton received drafts of registration oaths from Baskin, Bennett, and others of the Liberal party essentially proposing that it be made more difficult for Mormons to qualify to vote. When Carleton explained why under the existing laws and intents of Congress it was not feasible to comply with their suggestions, he opened himself to a series of bitter denunciations and much abuse from the *Salt Lake Tribune*.[15]

Carleton's lenient actions were in keeping with what L.D.S. leaders had been led to expect from the Democratic administration. Immediately after passage of the Edmunds-Tucker Act, Caine relayed an assurance from Cleveland that there would be no vindictiveness in the administration of the laws. John W. Young also advised the First Presidency at the time of the law's passage that the president of the United States had acted as favorably as he could under the circumstances of anti-Mormon pressure, adding significantly that the passage of the law had not interfered with the plan for statehood. This quite obviously was a reference to the intention to continue to pursue the course outlined in the Scott Amendment.[16]

Early in April Young sent church leaders a sketch of the mode of operation agreed upon in the East for framing the desired Utah constitution. Taylor and George Q. Cannon were inclined to approve it, but again repeated the reservations that there must be no compromise of religious principle or even the appearance of a "surrender of any doctrine, however objectionable it may be to the world," which formed a part of the plan of salvation they held to be divinely inspired. Speaking for their followers as well, they stated that "all the advantages which are likely to flow to us by obtaining a state government, if they were multiplied a million-fold, ought not to have any weight with us in the face of God's commands." The presidency concluded, however, that if it were God's Will that Utah become a state in the manner and by the measures they proposed, He would open the way for such to be accomplished.[17]

Exchanges during the late spring probed the possibility of reconvening the constitutional convention of 1882 and appropriately amending the constitution framed at that time. But too many of the key figures of that movement were polygamists then on the underground who could not participate without endangering the entire scheme. Church leaders decided that a new convention would be held with delegates drawn from the monogamist class. Church agents and members of the Democratic administration agreed that the central committee of the People's party and, if possible, the Liberal party should be persuaded to call for mass meetings throughout the territory to select delegates to a constitutional convention.[18]

Provision was also being made for officials appointed by Cleveland to insure the further cooperation of the Utah Commission, so that a vote for ratification of the constitution could be included on the ballot at the regular legislative elections in August. And there was some assurance that by that time the attorney general and solicitor general of the United States would have promulgated an official interpretation of the Edmunds-Tucker Act favorable to Mormon voting rights.

In early June, 1887, Young recounted the most important of the visits that he recently made to Washington, D.C. On May 26 he had called on Cleveland's secretary, Daniel S. Lamont, who consented to have Penrose accompany them to an appointment with Solicitor General Jenks. During that interview Jenks divulged he had discussed Utah matters thoroughly with the president and others close to him. The solicitor general had made a draft of constitutional provisions, leaving the practice of plural marriage, in Young's words, "as lenient as we could expect to get through Congress." Jenks, the administration's leading advisor on legal affairs, explained that he had taken pains to meet all the objections raised in the recent past and expressed confidence that he had "covered every point that might be assailed when the matter should come up for discussion," probably meaning during the expected deliberations in the next session of Congress.

Young expressed relief that in Penrose's presence Jenks openly conceded that he and his Cleveland administration associates regarded this plan "as purely a political settlement of the question" that had nothing to do with Mormon religious beliefs. With corroboration from Penrose Mormon leaders could assume assurance that the Cleveland administration was willing to accede to the distinction between a political and a theological concession embodied in the constitutional provisions, with only the political being expected.[19]

Soon after Young sent Penrose west to insure that events there proceeded as they had been outlined in conjunction with Cleveland officials. When Penrose arrived at Salt Lake City, the inner circle of available general authorities of the church learned that he recently "had interviews with some of the leading men of the nation" and that these men had helped amend the Utah constitution of 1882 and place it in a form that they hoped would enable the territory to enter the Union as a state. Penrose explained that these amendments proposed to make polygamy or bigamy a misdemeanor punishable by a fine of not more than $1,000 and imprisonment for not longer than three years. Faithful polygamists were pleased that unlawful cohabitation incurred no penalty at all.[20] The weeks surrounding Penrose's arrival were a highly politicized period among the Mormon hierarchy. In fact, public knowledge of the activities in the two months beginning in June would have proved most of the allegations that the church dominated Utah politics at the time. On June 1 church leaders met with a number of stake presidents and the People's party central committee to deliberate "upon men and measures" to be part of the next territorial legislature. In mid-month the People's party leaders issued a call for mass meetings to be held throughout Utah on June 25 to select delegates to a territorial constitutional convention scheduled for five days later. Special invitations were sent to chairmen of the Democrat and Republican parties—which were still merely the links between the Liberal party in local politics and the two national parties.

Democratic leader Joseph B. Rosborough's negative response was typical of the Gentile reaction and should have been predictable. His first reason for declining involvement was that notice was too short to give his committee a chance to act effectively. In addition, he argued that such action was unwise as long as Utah was a theocracy and there was a "spirit of opposition" to the federal laws. He also observed there was little assurance that the powers of state government would not be perverted and abused by the majority, with non-Mormon groups severely threatened by such a condition. And there was a strong implication that compliance with the invitation would lend credibility to the assumption that the movement was spontaneous, originating with the people. Rosborough did not want to aid in conveying such an erroneous impression.[21]

On the morning of June 20 George Q. Cannon explained to several available apostles that President Cleveland "was willing to sign a bill admitting Utah into the union," providing the stipulations outlined were adhered to. The church leaders were also reassured that their revered prophet, John Taylor, whose health was then rapidly deteriorating, fully understood and approved of the plans. Cannon emphasized that what they had embarked upon was "the most important political move since the church was organized."[22] In the afternoon of the same day, approximately fifty Mormon political-ecclesiastical dignitaries from throughout the territory gathered at church headquarters to discuss the impending constitutional convention. President Cannon outlined the undertaking, without any mention of input or cooperation from Democrats prominent in the federal government. Delegate Caine expressed confidence that complying with the projected course would settle the entire difficulty with the government and allow Utah to be admitted as a state. Apostle Heber J. Grant gave assurance that he and his colleagues favored the proposed move.

In the lengthy open discussion Mormon politicians emphasized the need to control events carefully in order to create the most favorable possibilities for the plan. John R. Winder, about to be announced as the new People's party chairman, deemed it necessary to have matters "prearranged" by nominating committees so that the "right men" for delegates and mass meeting chairmen would be chosen. Caine stressed the need for all men so designated to be in sympathy with the movement outlined. In order to prevent undue controversy, the question of whether some polygamists ought to be seated among those assembled was tabled, as was the issue of whether woman suffrage should be reinstated at that time.[23]

The convention, the sixth in Utah's long experience with such events, first met on June 30 and continued until July 7. This time, in addition to the typical provisions that had been a part of previous versions, one stood out as noteworthy. It stated that "bigamy and polygamy being considered incompatible with a republican form of government, each of them is hereby forbidden and declared a misdemeanor."[24]

This constitutional provision has been acclaimed as a significant turning point, signaling the beginning of the end of Mormon plural marriage. If this was in fact true, it was unintentional because the church hierarchy had taken great care to avoid anything they regarded as a doctrinal concession. It must be concluded that Latter-day Saint leaders and some members of the Cleveland administration were perfectly willing to allow the public to believe that the anti-polygamy provision had real substance. And in the long run it may have been influential in undermining support for polygamy among Utah's citizens. But such was certainly not in keeping with the strategy of those responsible for the Utah Constitution of 1887.[25]

As the constitution was being shaped along the lines previously agreed upon, the Mormon hierarchy took steps to generate favorable votes at the ratification election to be held August 1. On the day the convention adjourned, most of those who had participated in framing the constitution gathered quietly to a meeting called by the general church authorities. Cannon assured those present that their actions had the hearty approval of the general authorities of the church. He reiterated his statement that the actions recently begun were the most important political movement that had been undertaken in his long career in the church. Apostles Lorenzo Snow, Franklin D. Richards, Heber J. Grant, and Moses Thatcher also spoke approvingly of the entire constitution and urged the delegates to go home and quietly inform their friends that church leaders were in accord with the actions that had been taken.[26]

The next day Abraham H. Cannon, a son of George Q. Cannon and himself a member of the First Council of Seventy, noted that he had been assigned to visit Emery and Uintah Counties in east-central Utah. He was to see local church leaders and other influential Latter-day Saints and "urge upon them the importance of getting every possible vote cast at the coming election in favor of the constitution." Cannon had permission to let it be known that "the head authorities approve the measure." Those he was to visit were also to be instructed to oversee the details of registration and election procedures. Other apostles were similarly engaged in other parts of the territory.[27]

Meanwhile, the outside press, often commenting on information drawn from *Salt Lake Tribune* dispatches and editorials, reflected widespread doubts about the sincerity of Mormon anti-polygamy actions. With the help of the *Tribune*, two New York newspapers penetrated to what appears to be the heart of the church leaders' motives. The *New York Times* pointed out that the enforcement of the laws against plural marriage "would be in the hands of Mormon officials, Mormon courts, and Mormon juries" and questioned whether the prohibition could be carried out in good faith without federal authority on the scene. The *New York Evening Post* concluded that since the new sections of the constitution failed to condemn unlawful cohabitation, all the Mormon polygamist needed to do was to keep knowledge of his marriages from the friendly prosecuting attorney until the three-year statute of limitations was passed and he was beyond the reach of the law no matter how openly he associated with his wives thereafter.[28]

Yet, despite these widespread allegations of duplicity, L.D.S. leaders had some cause to hope for success. Throughout the first week of July, 1887, Utah was graced with the presence of an official visitor, George Jenks, who unbeknown to almost everyone was the real author of the anti-polygamy provision then being incorporated into the proposed Utah constitution. The *Tribune* boldly surmised the solicitor general's visit indicated an awakened interest among leading Democrats in "playing for the admission of Utah into the union." The paper alleged, with no concrete evidence, that the object of Jenks's visit was to "manage the necessary negotiations" for the admission of the territory.[29] Jenks consistently denied any interest in the convention proceedings. But actually he conferred frequently with Richards and offered valuable suggestions on the course to be followed to get the constitution ratified. Although he expressed an interest in meeting Penrose and Cannon, when he was informed they were hiding on the underground he decided it was not worth the risk to see them at that time.[30]

One of the most significant results of the improved relations between Mormon leaders and the Democrats was the effect on the minority of Utah Commission members who belonged to that party. Communications from Washington had already demonstrated the sympathetic stance the administration was taking in many Mormon concerns. In late August Carleton, the chairman of the commission, wrote a letter that found its way into the hands of Young. It confided his desire to "fully advise the President of the condition of affairs," saying that this could best be done in a personal interview with Cleveland.[31] Several weeks later Young was informed by Salt Lake City church leaders that one of their number, who had been at a mountain resort frequented by several Utah commissioners, had engaged in a private conversation with General John A. McClernand. This old veteran of Shiloh and former Illinois congressman was reported to be "friendly disposed to the people of Utah" and seemed to be "desirous that the forth-coming report of the Utah Commission should be as fair as possible." The general authorities relayed McClernand's suggestions that "proper steps should be taken to influence Judge Carleton . . . so that his influence might be in the proper direction to give the report the desired shape." The church leaders recommended that Young take the Mormon lobbyist, former Senator Joseph E. McDonald, to speak to Carleton, a fellow Indianan. It was suggested that "perhaps [McDonald] could bring proper influence to bear upon the judge so as to have him look at these matters in a proper light." They concluded that "the result might be of sufficient importance to repay the trouble and expense."[32]

Young later reported that they had visited Carleton. Although there is no evidence that money changed hands, there was a subsequent split in the commission, as reflected in their report. McClernand and Carleton refused to sign a document strongly questioning the sincerity of Mormon motives in the statehood movement. In an unprecedented action they issued their own minority report which advised that the Mormon efforts be taken at face value. This minority report has been cited by the closest student of the commission as the first official indication of its changing policy toward the Mormons.[33]

On August 1, 1887, the new constitution was ratified by a vote of 13,195 to 507. Soon after, the Mormon general authorities met to make further plans. Taylor had died the week before, and although Wilford Woodruff was not to be officially sustained as his successor for many months, the senior apostle now became virtual head of the church. On August 4 Cannon and Joseph F. Smith were nominated to act with Woodruff as a committee charged to continue direction of the statehood movement. Other church leaders expressed the hope that the committee would do all that was possible to make Utah a state. Thereafter, much of their time and attention was devoted to political and economic matters related to this goal. Often, when writing letters in behalf of this effort, the three signatures were bracketed and labeled "committee," meaning the committee on statehood.[34]

Despite these extensive efforts to attain statehood, one major obstacle still loomed insurmountable. The comments of the nation's press indicated that most Americans continued to hold serious doubts about the sincerity of the Mormon actions in regard to polygamy. Numerous editorials advocated a policy of moving slowly on the policy of statehood for Utah so that the true intent of the Saints could be ascertained through their actions as well as their public utterances.[35] There was indeed cause for doubt because the Mormons had not yet actually given up any aspect of their peculiar institution, although the raid had certainly forced them to be more circumspect in their practices. Even before passage of the Edmunds-Tucker Act, some who intended to continue as Utah residents journeyed to Mexico to enter into other plural marriages they deemed necessary. Some older brethren, such as Woodruff and Lorenzo Snow, had already concluded to live alone or with a single wife. But many others, particularly those of child-bearing age, continued to engage in all facets of what they considered to be their divine obligation.[36]

While Solicitor General Jenks was in Utah in early July, he suggested to Mormon authorities that all references to polygamy in their public addresses should cease. As evidence that this policy was quickly implemented, Abraham Cannon's journal entry at that time stated that "public talk on polygamy and against government is forbidden for the present, and only wise, discreet men are asked to speak publicly."[37] Such a course certainly did not mean that the private views of L.D.S. leaders had been altered. Speaking at a small private gathering on July 31, the day before the Utah constitution was approved, President Joseph F. Smith said that God honored those women who entered plural marriage and "the men who obeyed it occupied a higher plane than those who disregarded it." He did make a slight distinction, which was becoming a more marked difference from earlier preachings, when he stated that "this celestial law is permissive, just as other laws of the gospel are." This meant that entering into plural marriage was more voluntary than mandatory. But, Smith continued, "those who reject it would be damned," and those who rendered obedience to it should be saved and rewarded. The church leader meant those who rejected the opportunity to enter plural marriage were depriving themselves of exaltation in the highest realm of the Celestial Kingdom—the heaven of Mormon theology. Although it did not entirely preclude lesser Celestial glories to non-polygamists, they could not expect the rewards to be anticipated by those who had complied with the higher law.[38]

In mid-September, 1887, Abraham Cannon was interviewed by his father, Woodruff, and church attorney LeGrand Young. They queried him as to whether he would, if it were deemed necessary, testify in court that he would promise to conform with the letter of the Edmunds-Tucker law and not live with his plural wives. Even though there were several qualifications providing that churchmen would continue to acknowledge the correctness of their religious beliefs and that the law would only be binding until it was repealed or modified, Abraham Cannon replied that he could not comply with the request conscientiously. He said that he would feel condemned if not allowed to follow the command of God to increase and multiply the earth through procreation. In his diary, young Cannon reflected that it appeared that his questioners thought some such concession was necessary to convince Congress of the sincerity of their efforts to halt polygamy and thus to gain statehood.[39]

Later at an assemblage of apostles a document assumed by them to have been drafted by someone in the Democratic hierarchy at Washington, D.C., was read and discussed. It stated that unless the Mormons who were summoned before the Utah courts on the charge of polygamy or unlawful cohabitation "shall promise to obey the law against these offenses," it would be impossible to "bring the Congress of the United States to believe" that the church leaders had been "honest in adopting a constitution prohibiting polygamy." The apostles also considered a statement attorney Young had prepared in relation to the Washington document, which he proposed church members could use in court. This was similar or identical to the one previously submitted to Abraham Cannon. In the extensive discussion of the matter, the apostles expressed the opinion that "no Latter-day Saint could make such a promise and still be true to the covenants he had made with God and his brethren" at the time he was married. They therefore concluded "that if such a promise was necessary as a condition to our securing statehood that we at once give the administration at Washington to understand that we could not accept of it." It was further resolved that it was better to cease efforts for statehood rather than make such a promise.[40]

Despite these conclusions, the statehood movement continued. Although in light of the rejected Democratic demands this appears to have been a futile venture, church leaders may have decided that the admission efforts had progressed so far that they could not be halted abruptly without focusing undue attention on the reason why. They certainly did not wish to publicize the fact that they continued to condone the practice of plural marriage. Furthermore, a call summoning the constitutional convention to reconvene to consider a memorial to congress had already been issued. Without any known effort to stop this assemblage, it met on October 8, at which time the delegates approved this document, apparently drafted by Caine, who as the convention president was designated to head the delegation authorized to present the constitution and memorial to Congress when it started its new session.[41]

Soon after, the Mormon hierarchy's committee on statehood also urged Caine to present a handsomely engrossed copy of the constitution and memorial to President Cleveland. They explained this should be done as soon as possible so the president would have access to that material for consideration as he began drafting his annual State of the Union address. Within a short time, Caine met with the president, who informed him that the Saints had done all that anyone could reasonably ask in adopting the state consitution providing for punishment of polygamists.[42]

Young also sent word to the church statehood committee that Cleveland approved the Mormon efforts. Though probably picqued at not being given an official place in the delegation presenting the documents, Young, as head of the church lobbyists, moved to Washington, D.C., in late November to prepare the ground for the culminating effort that he and his associates had been aiming at throughout much of the year. His first step was to discuss matters with Cleveland's lieutenant, Daniel Lamont. He discovered that the president's annual message was not going to mention the Mormon question at all. Lamont confided that Cleveland would like to give favorable notice to the subject, but felt it best to say nothing on it. Until the message was delivered, probably only Lamont knew that the chief executive had concluded to depart from the usual format of including comments on a broad range of subjects needing congressional attention. The message was entirely devoted to the tariff, the most controversial national issue of the day.[43]

Soon thereafter, Young was granted a private interview in which, he claimed, the president was more cordial and less restrained with him than ever before. Cleveland confided that he had learned to view the Mormons in a different light than formerly and recognized that they were honest and sincere in their religious convictions—even on polygamy—and were entitled to fair consideration. According to Young, the president again expressed himself as highly pleased at the outcome of the Utah convention. As the twenty-minute visit came to an end, Young recalled a similar conference earlier in the year in which both had pledged to work "to bring about a better state of feeling" and do what they could toward admission of Utah into the union. He pointedly asked the president if he still held that same sentiment and reported that the reply was "I do and I will do all I can."[44]

Later in the month, after Cleveland's annual message had been delivered, a delegation of Mormon politicians was granted an audience with the president. During what was described as a pleasant interview, Richards remarked that "as the people of Utah had now placed themselves in harmony with the rest of the nation on the only question of difference between them," he hoped they would receive the favorable consideration they now in justice deserved. Cleveland's only recorded response was that he did not know what kind of a reception the Mormon effort would get "from those fellows at the capitol"—meaning Congress. At that point Caine rejoined that "in case of difficulty from that source" they might appeal to the Cleveland administration for help. The president replied that he would "try to hold things steady."[45]

Cleveland's indication of unsureness as to the attitude of Congress toward the Utah situation was well founded. In fact legislative developments soon made it clear that although the Mormon lobby had done well in cementing relationships with the executive branch and some other segments of the Democratic hierarchy, they had not been nearly as successful with either house of Congress. Despite the president's assurances, the hope Caine expressed that help could be expected from the Cleveland administration in winning congressional support proved to be vain. Not only were there indications that the legislative members among Young's original Democratic contacts, Representative William L. Scott and Senator Arthur P. Gorman, were increasingly uninvolved with the Utah effort, but it was also apparent that the reasons were at least partly related to the growing alienation between Cleveland and many of his own party in Congress. The faction these men represented was the one most shocked by the president's tariff message. And Cleveland's stubborn personality, along with the aloofness from legislative matters his conception of the office imposed, would do nothing to restore the lost harmony.[46]

When the Mormon political emissaries returned to Washington, D.C., prior to the convening of Congress in late 1887, they received letters from church leaders outlining a strategy recently adopted at the behest of advisors representing an established lobby network with which the church was becoming engaged. Alexander Badlam, the spokesman for the California-based section of this organization, maintained that the tactics previously utilized by the church agents had been wrong. He stressed that they should appear indifferent, with the matter of statehood treated "in the least important manner possible." The statehood committee quoted extensively from a letter advising this course, stressing that friends and agents should not be permitted to argue or talk of statehood publicly or in the press. Penrose, Young, Richards, Caine, and others were carefully instructed to give the impression that their people were thoroughly satisfied with the territorial status and conditions as they were.[47] However, this course did not preclude these men from engaging in numerous private discussions with members of Congress in an extensive effort to allay misinformation and secure support for the coming struggle. Both Young and Richards reported considerable approval among Democrats as to the justice of Utah's claims and disapproval of the fanatical manner in which anti-polygamy efforts were being pursued there.[48] Yet throughout the numerous visits the lobbyists were struck by the continued ignorance of their situation, even among some of the most friendly members of Congress. And the Democrats were clearly not united as to the best way to accomplish statehood. Comment was frequent among the church agents that although they were courteously received, there was still a perceptible lack of willingness for anyone among the Democratic legislators to come forward with advocacy or a public commitment to the Mormon cause. Despite earlier assurances from Cleveland, Jenks, and others in the executive department that such a course as they had followed would result in admission, it now became apparent that this sentiment was not shared in the legislative circles where it was most necessary.[49]

This particular Congress took an unusually long time in getting organized for its regular business. At that juncture those friendly to the church advised patience in taking even the first step toward getting the Utah statehood measure started through the legislative maze. But finally, in mid-December, several of the delegates selected to deliver the constitution and memorial concluded that they could no longer remain in the nation's capital and would therefore have to perform their task promptly. On December 17, 1887, Caine introduced his associates to president *pro tem-*

pore of the Senate, John J. Ingalls and Speaker of the House John G. Carlisle. Richards made the presentation of the documents, briefly explaining the action of the Utah people and outlining the important provisions of the constitution. Ingalls accepted the papers and graciously promised to present them to the Senate and lend his support to careful consideration. Carlisle explained that the rules did not permit him to introduce the documents himself, but he promised he would be pleased to recognize Caine for that purpose whenever he wished.[50]

When Senator Wilkinson Call, an associate of Young, introduced a resolution that the Utah memorial be printed in the *Congressional Record*, it met with immediate opposition from Senator Algernon Paddock of Nebraska, a former member of the Utah Commission. With this indication of the hostility with which the statehood movement would often be met by some members of the Republican majority in the Senate, the motion was tabled. When Call again brought up the matter, he and the church were subjected to a bitter verbal barrage from Paddock and the leading legislative opponent of the Mormons, George Edmunds, who was against printing the material on the weak grounds that it might contain "something disrespectful to Congress." Senator Call endeavored to disprove that point by reading the inoffensive memorial from the floor and having accomplished his original purpose of getting it into the *Record*, he then withdrew his motion. The Mormon agents, acting on good advice to allay partisanship by working first for passage of their measures in the Senate, had failed at the first step.[51]

Undaunted, Caine introduced a bill on January 10, 1888, in the more friendly House of Representatives, seeking the admission of Utah upon the constitution framed and ratified the previous summer. The bill was read by title and referred to the committee on territories for consideration.[52] That same evening, accompanied by Richards, Caine engaged in a two-hour interview with committee chairman, William Springer. The Illinois congressman had not even read the Utah constitution, but he listened patiently as its main points and the other essentials of Utah's case were elaborated. Springer offered Caine opportunity for prompt hearing before his committee, but the Utah delegate replied he would rather wait and have Utah's efforts joined in any combination that might be made for the admission of other territories later in the year.[53]

Although Springer assured Caine that he would cooperate in the Mormon statehood effort, church agents doubted his sincerity. They took occasion through a trusted Vermont newspaperman to have the chairman interviewed and queried as to the territorial question in general and Utah in particular. When the committee chairman was asked about Utah, he said he was friendly and that the administration and the party generally were much interested in fulfilling her claims. But, the congressman continued, he did not think the Democrats were able to "carry Utah" then and that the citizens of that territory would have to wait a while longer for statehood. These were unquestionably Springer's real sentiments.[54]

Springer was not at all unrealistic in his assessment of the Utah situation. Abundant evidence indicated that if the Mormons were left to themselves, polygamy would continue to flourish. For this reason Springer introduced a resolution proposing an amendment to the Constitution of the United States regarding polygamy. During his interview with Caine and Richards, the chairman assured his object was to meet the major objection raised to admission of Utah, which was that if statehood were granted, the clause of the state constitution providing for the punishment of polygamy would be a dead letter since public sentiment would be adverse to its enforcement. Springer's amendment provided that should a state fail to enforce its polygamy law, Congress could pass one for such a state and provide for its enforcement. The Springer Amendment had been submitted to Carlisle, David B. Culberson, chairman of the House Judiciary Committee, and other prominent Democratic members who gave their approval and said it was better than any that had yet been proposed on the subject. Some of the territory's best friends in the House thought the action would bring Utah much closer to admission.[55]

Mormon agents in contact with Democratic congressional leaders were fully cognizant of the need for further concessions on polygamy. Apparently Young had not been willing to give up after just one rebuff from the apostles on the matter. During a visit to Utah prior to the December opening of the congressional session, he brought the subject up again—this time to the church committee on statehood, the First Presidency. In their carefully considered response the committee members admitted they had been unable to formulate questions and answers that could be delivered by polygamists brought into court that would be satisfactory to both the Mormons and members of Congress. The presidency explained that such an attempt came too close to retraction of religious principle, and therefore they could not say what Washington officials desired "without saying too much." Young had no choice then but to accept these conclusions. But a month later he again mentioned similar pressures saying, "I am urged by our friends all the time to put ourselves into the shape that the party can handle us," which undoubtedly referred to abandonment of the practice of polygamy.[56]

The First Presidency also firmly restrained their agents from cooperating in drafting any kind of enabling act, informing Young that this approach might too closely specify requirements regarding a state constitution or statutory laws regarding plural marriage. While church leaders were undoubtedly correct in these assumptions, this was the commonly accepted method of admitting new states, and even some members of Congress known to favor Utah's admission insisted on an enabling act.[57]

In like manner, Caine acknowledged the church statehood committee's instructions that he and his associates should oppose any proposed amendment to the U.S. Constitution that aimed at regulating the marriage relation. These orders had probably been issued in response to Caine's report of the Springer Amendment in January, 1888. The delegate stated that it was his duty to inform the First Presidency of the "fixed determination among members of Congress to adopt a constitutional amendment upon the subject of polygamy." The delegate observed that this feeling was actually stronger among those generally sympathetic to Utah's admission, for these supporters believed that such an amendment would strongly enhance statehood prospects.[58]

Even after church leaders had again declined to support the measures clearly necessary for statehood to be granted, at least some Democratic congressional leaders continued to seek an acceptable basis for agreement. In February, 1888, Culberson, chairman of the House Committee on the Judiciary, reported a substitute to the Springer resolution. This proposed constitutional amendment omitted all mention of unlawful cohabitation and was thus expected to be more acceptable to defenders of L.D.S. polygamists. Yet when Culberson cautioned Caine "not to give it even a seeming approval," which might arouse anti-Mormon opposition, the delegate replied there was no such danger as he was opposed to the proposition and any other amendment "no matter how modified" it might be. Caine acknowledged Culberson's friendly intentions in attempting to make the amendment "as harmless as he possibly could" while still meeting the demands for an anti-polygamy amendment as a prerequisite to Utah statehood. But without Mormon support for any such restrictions on local lawmaking powers, neither the Culberson nor Springer resolutions progressed any further than being assigned to the sponsors' committees.[59]

The determination of Mormon leaders to resist even the most vague congressional limitations on the practice of polygamy virtually doomed this most concerted attempt at achieving Utah statehood. Without some positive assurances concerning the persistent overtures from Democratic congressional leaders, there simply was no basis from which those friendly to Utah's cause could begin to generate the support they would need among their more dubious colleagues. Thus the battleground was left, almost by default, to the long-time opponents of the Mormons, who could argue persuasively that the Latter-day Saints were insincere in their assurances that they had altered their unique marriage practices.

A Senate subcommittee had meantime begun considering the Utah constitution and memorial on statehood. On January 30, 1888, Republican subcommitteemen William M. Stewart and Shelby M. Cullom presented a report filled with anti-Mormon statements and denounced the entire statehood movement as a fraud on the part of the Saints. The Democrats opposed taking any action by the entire Committee on Territories until those favoring statehood could be heard in an attempt to refute the charges. Conceding the point, Committee Chairman Orville H. Platt asked Caine if any of the Utah men then at Washington desired to speak in behalf of admission at a hearing scheduled three days hence. This caused Caine serious concern, not only because he expected to be called upon to explain the complicated church position on polygamy and the law, but also because it gave him so little time to check further with church leaders back home on how they wished such questions to be answered. The delegate telegraphed church headquarters to inform his brethren that their spokesmen before the territorial committee would be questioned closely on actual Mormon intentions concerning the abandonment of polygamy. Caine revealed his own hesitancy to stand in the unenviable position of attempting to satisfy doubting senators without conceding more than church authorities would approve.[60]

Caine and Richards were encouraged to make whatever assurances they deemed necessary, although they were cautioned to carefully "preserve political as distinct from church attitudes." This recurring separation of the doctrinal position, still rigidly espoused by the Mormon hierarchy from the political stance, which the majority of Utah citizens were inclined to assume, may well appear to be a distinction without any substantive difference. But it was sufficiently reassuring to those involved in the delicate matter of seeking accommodation between the church leaders and their counterparts in the highest circles of government in the United States. While the Mormon hierarchy and other polygamists, already disfranchised by the Edmunds-Tucker Act, intended continued allegiance to what they considered laws more binding than anything emanating from Congress, they were no longer averse to non-polygamists complying with some carefully drafted restrictions that might accelerate the process of admission of Utah as a state. Caine and Richards were reminded that they were primarily the representatives of the monogamous class of Utah citizens and should act accordingly.[61] With this direction, Caine and Richards hastily prepared to face the Senate committee. They engaged prominent attorneys to assist them. Former Senator Joseph McDonald had been involved in Mormon affairs with the Democrats in the past and was well versed on their question. Republican Jeremiah M. Wilson, though he worked conscientiously to become prepared, needed more time and was granted a postponement of several weeks until February 18.[62]

While these spokesmen for Mormon statehood were busily engaged in preparing for their testimony before the committee on territories, John W. Young was further diminishing any chances that such efforts would be successful. On February 13 Young telegraphed church headquarters that he needed $15,000 "for Cullom and [Ezra] Davis," apparently meaning money to secure their acquiescence, if not cooperation in a favorable committee report. He added that he needed another $10,000 "to make sure of the majority of the committee." Young, who enjoyed the reputation of being heir to his father's vast fortune, had secretly expended church funds for such "retainers" throughout the year. When this request arrived, the increasingly apprehensive church leaders immediately replied that he should do nothing until he had consulted with other brethren, including Joseph F. Smith, who was already enroute to replace Young as head of the Mormon lobby in Washington, D.C.

Woodruff and Cannon informed both Smith and Young, that Young's actions had not only embarrassed them but also severely hampered other efforts, through their California friends, toward securing acceptable Senate treatment without resort to bribery. As the church committee members still in Utah informed Caine of Young's actions, they stressed that theirs was "not to be a moneyed fight" and that they had no inclination to "buy up Congress." They were convinced that such a policy would be bad for them, and while recognizing that some cash outlay would be necessary, they stressed a desire to achieve their ends only through legitimate methods that could be explained and defended to any fair-minded person.[63]

On February 18 the hearings before the Senate Committee on Territories commenced. Richards made the opening argument in favor of Utah statehood. Idaho Delegate Fred T. Dubois was the first to speak in opposition. He and the other major opponent, Baskin, reiterated their standard and not unwarranted argument that the Mormons were not sincere in their anti-polygamy professions. According to the Mormon accounts of the proceedings, Richards's enumeration of the outrageous miscarriages of justice under the guise of the anti-polygamy laws greatly impressed the Senate committeemen. And, they said, Baskin's lengthy excursion into the past, with detailed treatments of Mormon doctrine, so bored his listeners that, according to the Mormon version, they finally stopped him by requesting that his speech be printed for future reference. Ostensibly for the purpose of granting Wilson still more time to prepare his final arguments, the hearings were then postponed until March.[64]

In the ensuing weeks Penrose and his associates conducted further private visits to key senators and representatives. They attempted to voice the small extent to which polygamy was then actually practiced in Utah, the exclusion of polygamists from direct political involvement, and the intention of Utah citizens to enforce the provisions of their constitution in good faith. In some selected instances they also pictured the anti-Mormon crusade as an attempt to disfranchise Mormon Democrats so Gentile Republicans could gain control in Utah. They also emphasized to such partisans the sure Democratic ascendancy in the territory as compared with a rather discouraging comparable situation in most other potential states, including the need for a Democratic state like Utah to offset Republican Dakota, now almost certain to be admitted.

Church lobbyists also endeavored to impress upon all friendly senators the importance of preventing a report unfavorable to Utah statehood. If there could be no recommendation for admission of Utah, it was better to postpone any further action until a more opportune time the following session. Penrose reported having received assurances of such an understanding from members of both parties within the territorial committee. The Mormon agents assumed that the introduction of an enabling bill by Senator Matthew C. Butler on March 16 would aid in attaining that end. However, they once again stressed that "all want to be assured that polygamy is destroyed as a practice" since that was the clearly expressed will of numerous constituents.[65]

Ten days later, possibly out of anger at Young's failure to keep his financial commitments, Senator Cullom issued the type of report the church lobbyists most feared. The committee resolved that Utah should not be admitted into the union as a state until it was "certain beyond doubt that the practice of plural marriage, bigamy and polygamy" had been entirely abandoned and until it was similarly certain that the "civil affairs of the territory were not controlled by the L.D.S. church hierarchy." Joseph F. Smith confessed that after the assurances they had received, the committee report was "wholly unexpected" by the church agents.[66]

The report did not absolutely preclude reconsideration at a future date, and church leaders accepted that possibility philosophically. There was little interest exhibited by the Utah press toward admission during the spring of 1888, which was the very approach recommended by the California lobbyists. A *Salt Lake Herald* editorial in late March seemed to be following the expert advice closely when it stated that "there is less desire for a State government today than there was two years, or five years, or ten years ago, and as the improvement in the administration is noted the discontent with the territorial system is less pronounced." Besides, the editor reminded, under the present status, the federal government had to pay many of the expenses local taxpayers would be liable for under state government. It is doubtful if this was the true feeling of the majority of the Latter-day Saints, or their leaders, but it was the stance that had been counseled, and for the time being at least it was as effective as any other.[67]

There are indications that opposing forces had reached a stalemate on the Mormon question in Congress. Those in favor of Utah statehood clearly could not gain sufficient support to accomplish their aims. On the other hand, the fervent hopes of the anti-Mormon crusaders were also largely frustrated. At this time Senator Stewart was compelled to admit to an impatient Minnesota clergyman that he feared it would be impossible to get his territorial committee to do anything further concerning Utah "until the country stirs up Congress" again about the Mormons. With the presidential campaign approaching, there was little prospect for that occurring in the near future.[68]

One of the main obstacles to Utah statehood in 1888 was the general disinclination among Democratic party members to interfere with the existing Electoral College balance prior to Cleveland's run for reelection in November. They undoubtedly knew, as did the Mormon agents, that the Dakota territory had a better claim to admission and would, if admitted, likely vote Republican. In such a contingency Dakota would have at least one more electoral vote than Utah could offer. Besides, Young reported, the party leaders had not forgotten that Samuel J. Tilden's loss of the presidency to Rutherford B. Hayes in 1876 was partly because Colorado, admitted earlier that year, had cast its electoral votes for the Republicans.[69]

Also, neither Mormon nor Democratic politicians were slow to recognize the liability of Utah in a presidential election year. Young admitted that he could already see that the Republicans were prepared and "anxiously waiting for the opportunity to charge the Democratic party of admitting the Mormon church into the Union." He therefore advised working quietly to prepare the party for action in the early part of the following congressional session after the election was over.[70]

Thus, for a time at least, the statehood movement launched so optimistically by Young and members of the Cleveland administration over a year earlier had not attained its expected ends. Although it is apparent that Cleveland and Jenks were satisfied simply to have the anti-polygamy provision included in the state constitution, no matter what actual intentions were, it is also abundantly clear that this was not enough to win the necessary support for the Utah statehood movement in Congress. And since the leaders of the Church of Jesus Christ of Latter-day Saints rejected all overtures aimed at further limiting the practice of plural marriage, no further progress could be expected at that time. Nevertheless, both Mormon agents and some of their Democratic friends remained somewhat optimistic concerning future prospects and they continued to lay the groundwork necessary for the yet elusive goal of having Utah admitted into the union as a state.

NOTES

1. John Taylor to John W. Young, Nov. 29, 1886, George Q. Cannon to Young, Dec. 16, 1886, Taylor to Young, Dec. 22, 1886, John W. Young Papers, H.D.C.; Franklin S. Richards to Joseph F. Smith, May 3, 1887, Franklin S. Richards Papers, Utah State Historical Society, Salt Lake City.

2. Young to Taylor and Cannon, June 2, 1887, Young Papers, H.D.C., has the most extensive reference to Democratic party leaders by number. The context of this and other letters indicates that the other four were Chauncey F. Black, Senator Arthur P. Gorman, William H. Barnham, and Attorney General Augustus H. Garland. See also Charles W. Penrose to Wilford Woodruff and Joseph F. Smith, Dec. 27, 1888, Charles W. Penrose Papers, H.D.C.

3. *Congressional Record*, 49th Cong., 2d sess., 25–26, 503–7.

4. John T. Caine to James Jack [in behalf of First Presidency], Jan. 14, 1887, James Jack Papers, H.D.C.; Caine to Taylor and Cannon, Dec. 19, 1886, Caine Papers, H.D.C.; *Journal History of the Church of Jesus Christ of Latter-day Saints*, Jan. 12, 1887, H.D.C.; *Louisville Courier-Journal*, Jan. 5, 1887, contains an obituary of Charles H. Sherrill, described as a well-known lobbyist employed by Central [Southern] Pacific Railroad.

5. Caine to Jack, Jan. 14, 1887, Jack Papers; [William L. Scott], "Anti-Polygamy Bill," printed sheet, H.D.C.; Henry J. Wolfinger, "A Reexamination of the Woodruff Manifesto in Light of Utah Constitutional History," *Utah Historical Quarterly* 39 (Fall, 1971), 336–46, is an excellent treatment of the Scott Amendment.

6. *Congressional Record*, 49th Cong., 2d sess., 581–97.

7. Caine to Jack, Jan. 14, 1887, Jack Papers.

8. Young to Jack, Feb. 11, 1887, Young to Jack, Feb. 14, 1887, ibid; Penrose and Richards to Taylor, Feb. 16, 1887, Penrose Papers; Taylor and Cannon to Caine and Young, Jan. 27, 1887, Taylor and Cannon to Penrose and Richards, Feb. 19, 1887, John Taylor Papers, H.D.C. See also Taylor and Cannon to Caine and Young, Feb. 2, 1887, First Presidency Papers [Letterbooks], H.D.C.

9. Young to Jack, Feb. 11, 14, 1887, Jack to Young [care of Caine], Feb. 13, 1887, Jack Papers.

10. Young to Jack, Feb. 3, 1887, ibid; *Salt Lake Herald*, Feb. 5, 12, 13, 20, 1887.

11. F. S. Richards to Smith, May 3, 1887, F. S. Richards Papers; *Salt Lake Herald*, Mar. 9, 10, 13, 1887.

12. Young to Jack, Feb. 22, 25, 1887, Jack Papers.

13. Jack to Young, Feb. 27, 1887, ibid. James Jack, a trusted clerk in the office of the First Presidency of the church, carefully relayed the message he had received from John Taylor's "underground" hiding place in Kaysville, Utah, to John W. Young by telegram. Edward Leo Lyman, "The Alienation of an Apostle From

His Quorum: The Moses Thatcher Case," *Dialogue: A Journal of Mormon Thought* 18 (Summer, 1985), 69, suggests the possibility that Cannon made many decisions unilaterally. D. Michael Quinn, "L.D.S. Church Authority and New Plural Marriages, 1890–1904," *Dialogue: A Journal of Mormon Thought* 18 (Spring, 1985), 32, argues that Wolfinger and I "underestimated [Taylor's] enthusiasm for that compromise." In light of Cannon's July, 1887 statement that he had been essentially making church policy decisions by himself for the previous four months, there is serious doubt if this compromise is a reflection of Taylor's change of heart as much as it is the wishes of his nephew, George Q. Cannon. It must also be remembered that Cannon was virtually the only general authority in contact with the dying church president and all Taylor's statements were passed through him.

14. Caine to Jack, Mar. 1, 3, 1887, ibid.; John M. Whitaker Journal, Mar. 2, 6, 7, 1887, and John Henry Smith Journal, Mar. 7, 1887, both in Marriott Library, University of Utah, Salt Lake City.

15. Whitney, *History of Utah*, 3:580–83; *Salt Lake Herald*, Apr. 8, 20, 23, 29, 1887; Ambrose B. Carleton to Robert N. Baskin and John E. Dooley, Apr. 22, 1887; W. C. Hall to Charles W. Bennett, Apr. 23, 1887, copy in Cleveland Papers; *Salt Lake Tribune*, Apr. 25, 26, 29, June 9, 12, 1887.

16. Young to Jack, Mar. 4, 1887, Caine to Jack, Mar. 6, 1887, Jack Papers.

17. Taylor and Cannon to Young, Apr. 6, 1887, First Presidency Papers [Letterbooks].

18. Cannon to Young, May 9, 25, 1887, Young to Taylor and Cannon, June 2, 1887, Young Papers, H.D.C.

19. Young to Taylor and Cannon, June 2, 1887, Young to Jack, June 14, 21, 1887, ibid.

20. Abraham H. Cannon Journal, June 13, 1887, Harold B. Lee Library, Brigham Young University, Provo, Utah.

21. Franklin D. Richards Journal, June 1, 13, 16, 1887, H.D.C; *House Executive Documents*, 50th Cong., 1st sess., 10:917–19, 920–23.

22. Heber J. Grant Journal, June 20, July 6, 1887, H.D.C.; A. H. Cannon Journal, June 20, July 8, 1887.

23. Franklin D. Richards notes of meeting June 20, 1887, in Richards Family Papers, H.D.C., also listed names of those present. There is no implication of the Council of Fifty being at all involved in this era. On one occasion later in the year, John Taylor's son, Apostle John W. Taylor, suggested that the Council of Fifty direct the statehood efforts, but this was rejected by Wilford Woodruff. See Bibliographical Essay, pp. 303–4 herein.

24. Utah, Constitution (1887), Article 5, section 12, copy from the *Salt Lake Tribune*, July 10, 1887; Jerome Bernstein, "A History of the Constitutional Conventions of the Territory of Utah from 1849–95" (M.S. thesis, Utah State University, 1961), 63–73. Apostle Franklin D. Richards succinctly revealed the real intent of the entire movement: "Would it not be better to have these prohibiting laws administered by our own people in mediocre or minimum way than as now by our enemies and in the maximum method continually." F. D. Richards Journal, June 28, 1887. Heber J. Grant observed similarly that the statehood attempt "was the best thing we could do under the circumstances and that it simply meant

that in the future, should we get into the union, that we would be punished by our friends and not our enemies." Grant Journal, June 20, 1887.

25. Larson, *"Americanization" of Utah*, 217–19.

26. Grant Journal, July 7, 1887; F. D. Richards Journal, July 7, 1887.

27. A. H. Cannon Journal, July 8, 10, 14, 1887; Grant Journal, July 12, 14, 15, 19, 1887; F. D. Richards Journal, July 10–14, 1887.

28. *Salt Lake Tribune*, July 1–6, 1887; *New York Evening Post*, July 6, 1887; *New York Times*, July 7, 1887. See also n. 25 above.

29. *Salt Lake Tribune*, July 8, 1887.

30. C. Williams [underground code name for Penrose] to Young, July 6, 1887, Young Papers, H.D.C.; *Salt Lake Herald*, July 31, 1887.

31. Copy letter from Ambrose B. Carleton to unknown party, August 26 or 27, 1887, Young Papers, H.D.C. In late June Utah commissioner John A. Mc-Clernand began a series of letters to Grover Cleveland that indicated that "the work of reform in this territory has visibly and appreciably progressed . . . and, of course, the tenacity with which the institution and practice of polygamy was cherished has correspondingly relaxed." McClernand's main point was aimed at the potential effectiveness of the prohibition of polygamy incorporated into the Utah constitution. He stated that even though such a provision did not eradicate the problem, "the more often the Mormons commit themselves, whether regularly or irregularly, against polygamy, the more they will have increased the obstacles to a retreat from the path of reform." McClernand to Cleveland, June 30, July 5, 9, 1887, McClernand and A. B. Carleton to Cleveland, July 12, 1887, Cleveland Papers.

32. Woodruff, Cannon, and Smith to Young, Sept. 17, 1887, Woodruff Papers, H.D.C.

33. Stewart L. Grow, "A Study of the Utah Commission, 1882–96" (Ph.D. diss., University of Utah, 1954), 100–102.

34. J. H. Smith Journal, Aug. 13, 1887; Grant Journal, Aug. 4, 12, 13, 1887. See also Woodruff, Cannon and Smith to Young, Aug. 17, 1887, First Presidency Papers [Letterbooks].

35. *New York Times*, Oct. 4, 1887; *Chicago Times*, Oct. 1, 1887.

36. A. H. Cannon Journal, Jan. 4, 11, 19, 1887.

37. Ibid., July 8, 1887. Mormon leaders recognized the need to abandon such preachings in order to combat effectively the gravest threats from the anti-polygamy crusade, those related to blanket disfranchisement. In 1888 some church leaders in Idaho, where such a threat had become a reality, sought to get more favorable treatment by the courts through judicially establishing that polygamy doctrines were no longer openly preached. See William Budge to Wilford Woodruff, July 28, 1888, William Budge Papers, H.D.C.

38. A. H. Cannon Journal, July 31, 1887.

39. Ibid., Sept. 17, 1887.

40. Grant Journal, Sept. 29, 1887.

41. Judith Ann Roderick, "A Historical Study of the Congressional Career of John T. Caine" (M.A. thesis, Brigham Young University, 1959), 78.

42. Woodruff, Cannon, and Smith to Caine, Oct. 19, 1887, First Presidency Papers [Letterbooks]; Grant Journal, Nov. 14, 1887.

43. Young to Woodruff, Cannon, and Smith, Nov. 29, 1887, Young Papers, H.D.C.

44. Young to Woodruff, Cannon, and Smith, Dec. 1887 [letter 5, located in file folder between letter 4, Nov. 9, 1887, and letter 6, Dec. 18, 1887], ibid.

45. F. D. Richards Journal, Dec. 20, 1887; F. S. Richards to Woodruff, Cannon, and Smith, Dec. 17, 1887, F. S. Richards Papers, H.D.C.

46. Young to Taylor and Cannon, June 2, 1887, Young Papers, H.D.C. See also John R. Lambert, *Arthur Pue Gorman* (Baton Rouge, 1953), 114–44.

47. Maude [Alexander Badlam code name] to Allen [Woodruff], Nov. 15, 1887, First Presidency Miscellaneous Papers, H.D.C.; Allen to Maude, Nov. 28, 1887, Woodruff, Cannon, and Smith to Penrose, Nov. 22, 1887, Woodruff and Cannon to Young, Nov. 22, 1887, Woodruff Papers.

48. F. S. Richards to Woodruff, Cannon, and Smith, Dec. 17, 1887, Woodruff Papers.

49. Ibid.; Young to Woodruff, Cannon, and Smith, Jan. 23, 1888, Young Papers, H.D.C.

50. F. S. Richards to Woodruff, Cannon, and Smith, Dec. 17, 1887, F. S. Richards Papers, H.D.C.; Whitney, *History of Utah*, 3:607–8.

51. *Congressional Record*, 50th Cong., 1st sess., 85, 89, 118–21; Caine to Woodruff, Cannon, and Smith, Dec. 31, 1887, Caine Papers, H.D.C.

52. Caine to Woodruff, Cannon, and Smith, Jan. 7–21, 1888, Caine Papers, H.D.C.; *Congressional Record*, 50th Cong., 1st sess., 362; *House Miscellaneous Documents*, no. 104, 50th Cong., 1st sess., 3–14.

53. Caine to Woodruff, Cannon, and Smith, Jan. 7–21, 1888, Caine Papers, H.D.C.; F. S. Richards to Woodruff, Cannon, and Smith, Jan. 23, 1888, First Presidency Miscellaneous Papers.

54. Caine to Woodruff, Cannon, and Smith, Feb. 4, 1888, Caine Papers, H.D.C.

55. Ibid., *Congressional Record*, 50th Cong., 1st sess., 318.

56. Woodruff, Cannon, and Smith to Young, Dec. 7, 1887, Woodruff Papers; Young to Woodruff, Cannon, and Smith, Jan. 18, 1888, Young Papers, H.D.C.

57. Young to Woodruff, Cannon, and Smith, Jan. 23, 1888, Young Papers, H.D.C.; Caine to Woodruff, Cannon, and Smith, Jan. 7–21, 1888, Caine Papers, H.D.C.

58. Caine to Woodruff, Cannon, and Smith, Jan. 7–21, 1888, Caine Papers, H.D.C.

59. Ibid., Feb. 4, 1888; *Congressional Record*, 50th Cong., 1st sess., 1378; *House Reports*, no. 553, 50th Cong., 1st sess., 1–2.

60. Caine to Jack, Jan. 31, 1888, copy, First Presidency Papers [Letterbooks]; Richards and Caine to Jack, Feb. 1, 1888, F. S. Richards Papers, H.D.C.

61. Jack to Caine and Richards, Feb. 2, 1888, Jack Papers.

62. Caine to Woodruff, Cannon, and Smith, Feb. 4, 11, 1888, Caine Papers, H.D.C.; Young to Woodruff, Cannon, and Smith, Feb. 13, 1888, copy, First Presidency Papers [Letterbooks].

63. Young to Jack, Feb. 2, 1888, Woodruff Papers; Jack to Young, Feb. 13, 1888, First Presidency Miscellaneous Papers; Woodruff and Cannon to Jason Mack [code name of Joseph F. Smith] c/o John T. Caine, Feb. 16, 1888, First Presidency Miscellaneous Papers.

64. Mack to Woodruff and Cannon, Mar. 13, 1888, Penrose to Woodruff, Cannon, and Smith, Mar. 20, 1888, F. S. Richards to Woodruff and Cannon, Mar. 22, 1888, First Presidency Miscellaneous Papers.

65. Penrose to Woodruff, Cannon, and Smith, Mar. 20, 1888, ibid.; *Congressional Record*, 50th Cong., 1st sess., 2136.

66. Mack to Jack, Mar. 20, 1888, Richards and Penrose to Woodruff, Cannon, and Smith, Mar. 20, 1888, Mack to Woodruff and Cannon, Mar. 27, 30, 1888, First Presidency Miscellaneous Papers.

67. Maude to Allen, Nov. 15, 1887, ibid.; *Salt Lake Herald*, Mar. 27, 1888.

68. Allen to Mack, Apr. 10, 1888, First Presidency Miscellaneous Papers, stated, "It is now becoming difficult to get the attention of senators and members [of Congress] to our question; they have come to the unanimous conclusion that there is no possible show for us at this session and consider it a waste of time to stop to talk of Utah matters now." William M. Stewart to M. W. Montgomery, May 5, 1888, William M. Stewart Papers, Nevada Historical Society, Reno.

69. Young to Woodruff, Cannon, and Smith, Dec. 8, 1887, Young Papers, H.D.C.

70. Penrose to Woodruff, Cannon, and Smith, Dec. 10, 30, 1887, Penrose File, First Presidency Miscellaneous Papers; Young to Woodruff, Cannon, and Smith, Jan. 23, 1888, Young Papers, H.D.C.

3

An Unlikely Lobby: Mormon Public Relations Efforts, 1887–88

Along with extensive political activities, Mormon agents were preoccupied with molding public opinion. They had concluded that in many cases political figures would be willing to support the statehood cause if their constituents' attitude toward the Church of Jesus Christ of Latter-day Saints could be altered in a positive way. As the anti-Mormon raid had developed, with its flood of negative journalistic barrage, church leaders had become convinced of the need to exert their best effort to counter the press as well as the politicians and hostile clergy. Although the Saints were not complete novices in the art of presenting a favorable image to the world beyond their intermountain confines, involvement in these areas became more extensive than ever before as the new movement for Utah statehood got under way.

At the beginning of 1887 the public sentiment against the Mormons had risen to such a pitch that George Ticknor Curtis, a man of long experience in national affairs, observed that he had never seen such a phenomenon. As he explained to his associate, Franklin S. Richards, the leading Mormon attorney in the East, "You are a mere handful of people; 150,000 against 50 or 60 millions, and those millions have made up their minds that polygamy shall be exterminated *per fas ut nefas*" [completely].[1]

A major source of the Mormons' problems, as they had recognized for years, was the *Salt Lake Tribune*. That leading intermountain newspaper ably represented a growing body of Utah Gentiles, including many of the territorial officials, who were enjoying considerable power as the anti-polygamy raids continued. The *Tribune* was constantly embroiled in an editorial feud with the other Salt Lake dailies, the *Deseret Evening News* and the *Salt Lake Herald*, both considered organs of the Mormons. But even more galling to the Saints was that the nation's chief source of news from Mormondom was William Nelson, the region's Associated Press telegraphic correspondent, who was also a dedicated employee of the *Tribune*.

While the Edmunds-Tucker bill was still pending, a press dispatch reached the East from Salt Lake City, stating that a "strong Mormon lobby" had left Salt Lake City for Washington to work against the bill. Though the *Herald* and Delegate John T. Caine acted quickly to refute the statements made, Caine admitted privately that the report had seriously injured his efforts at the capital. He advised that influential Mormons be sent to see William Henry Smith, the general agent of the Associated Press, to "make charges against their Salt Lake agent on account of rabid partisanship and false telegrams which while it is injuring our people deceive the general public." The *Herald* charged, with some truth, that "we don't believe that during the last five years there had gone from the Salt Lake office a single Associated Press telegram that was not in some sense a lie." [2]

The Mormons had previously resorted to an arrangement with the *National Republican*, a formerly prominent newspaper published in Washington, D.C., which for a fee would print news items composed and submitted by church correspondents. Subsequent Nelson A.P. dispatches describing the Saints' supposedly bitter reaction to the yet unsigned Edmunds-Tucker bill forced Salt Lake church officials to attempt to alleviate the assumed damage. They telegraphed their own release to the *National Republican*, explaining that previous information had been intentionally misleading. They quoted from editorial comments in the *Deseret News* to show their more moderate feelings toward the bill. After the bill became a law, another telegram from church headquarters to the *Republican* reported that non-polygamous Mormons were being unfairly barred from jury duty by the overzealous U.S. district attorney, William H. Dickson, and Chief Justice Charles S. Zane. In spite of the fact that the church members were willing to take the prescribed oath affirming their intention to refrain from plural marriage, they were not allowed to be impaneled. The news item concluded that "this makes a test imposed entirely a religious one," with all jurors thus being drawn from a class hostile to most defendants. [3]

Yet matters may have begun to improve after passage of the Edmunds-Tucker Act. Curtis voiced optimism, saying that he thought he could see signs that he could "get access to public opinion" more easily than he could before President Cleveland took the course he did by not signing the measure. Although he was also seeking a substantial legal retainer,

Curtis did prove to be at least partially correct. Several important items written by him appeared that year in New York newspapers and magazines.[4]

The Mormon most involved in relations with the eastern newspapers, as well as with the Cleveland administration, was John W. Young. In March, 1887, he also noted that the nation's leading newspapers were printing fewer unfriendly articles and that the outlook for statehood was improving. He then queried church leaders, "Shall we begin to create a little public sentiment by gradually introducing friendly articles in the papers?" In the ensuing weeks he stressed the necessity of great caution in the selection and wording of news items, so that they might "strike the public mind in a manner favorable" to the church.

By June, Young thought he had made some progress in an effort to get the *Tribune*'s anti-Mormon A.P. correspondent removed and replaced with a more congenial man, possibly Byron Groo of the *Herald*. He also secured an arrangement through the New York City Press Association for favorable Utah news items to be published in several New York daily papers. Decrying the use of the "petty" *National Republican*, Young instructed that thereafter Mormon dispatches should be sent to C. A. O'Rourke of New York City, a press association manager.

Later that month reports of the impending Utah constitutional convention were telegraphed to New York in accordance with Young's directions. The *New York Star*, a minor paper Young was closely associated with, proposed that the Utah convention make the practice of polygamy impossible within the territory. Several dispatches were written so as to convey the impression of retreat and conciliation concerning plural marriage and the need for Utah to come into harmony with the rest of the nation. Young and others were careful to advise that the constitutional proceedings be conducted in a manner conducive to favorable newspaper comment. And they were not averse to generating their own occasions for such news releases.[5]

As Independence Day, 1887, approached, Young wrote to church leaders to suggest the need for the nation to see that the Mormons "revere that day even under such trying circumstances." He mentioned that an earlier episode in which some Mormons protested against the judicial crusade by lowering certain Salt Lake City flags to half-mast continued to generate unfavorable comments. Immediately after the suggestion, the First Presidency wrote to the People's party leader to set the machinery in motion for "honoring the Fourth of July by its celebration in proper form." They indicated that this would not only be welcomed by the people of Utah, but would likely "create the proper impression abroad." Such an

Independence Day celebration was arranged, and its success was widely hailed as an important step toward Mormon-Gentile reconciliation.[6]

After a July 4 recess, the Utah constitutional covention concluded its work, and outside press comments increased. These were almost unanimously critical of the Mormon effort, often repeating the *Salt Lake Tribune* allegations of insincerity about the provision banning polygamy. There was little evidence that Young's efforts did anything more than temper the tone of some editorials and possibly keep all mention of the convention out of a few others. The *New York Times* relied heavily on *Tribune* dispatches and was strikingly accurate in its criticisms of the Utah proceedings. On July 9, after notice that the Utah convention had finished its work, the *Times* challenged the veracity of the anti-polygamy provisions. An editorial asked why church leaders, who had so often in the past issued proclamations encouraging their people to stand firm against the onslaughts on polygamy, should now remain so strangely silent. The editor then specifically named each member of the First Presidency of the L.D.S. church and chided that their current opinions would make an interesting comparison with their earlier pronunciations.[7]

Soon after, Young wrote to John Taylor and George Q. Cannon to report on the reception the statehood efforts were getting. He warned that Congress was likely to focus on sincerity as one of its main questions. He observed that they could not determine the feelings of the public at large, and while many newspaper editors were also cautiously undecided, a few had begun to question the credibility of the Mormon actions; Young specifically referred to the *New York Times* editorial. Stressing the responsibility they had to answer proper inquiries to the subject at the proper time, Young proposed that something in the form of an interview with a respected newspaperman might be an acceptable solution.[8]

No such interview ensued. Taylor was on his deathbed and would die within two weeks, so it was already impossible to get more than the statement of his councilors, which would not carry the desired official weight. By this time the Salt Lake church leaders were becoming disenchanted with Young because of his failure to account for the considerable church funds sent him to aid in his endeavors. It may also have become apparent to Cannon, a former newspaperman himself, that Young's efforts had met with little success.

An examination of the coverage of the Utah convention by six of the most important New York newspapers yields only two items, one in the *New York Sun* and another in the *New York Herald* that could be construed as supportive, while there were at least a dozen negative or critical comments. These would culminate late in the month by the *Times* again alluding to the silence of the church leaders on the statehood question and warning that without some statement to the contrary, no one could expect them to regard polygamy as a crime. The final comment concluded that the silence of the general authorities was "full of meaning" to those who were certain the Utah movement was nothing but an attempt by the church leaders to escape enforcement of federal laws against their peculiar institution.[9]

Another important reason Cannon did not comply with Young's requests and advice was that by that time, in mid-July, 1887, overtures were being made from a more effective source. In the spring of 1887 several prominent Californians became involved in the Bullion-Beck silver mine at Eureka. Alexander Badlam, listed as president of the company, had family ties to the Mormons through his father and his uncle, Samuel Brannan, leader of the California Saints in 1847. When he arrived in Utah in mid-May, he was accompanied by a young former Utahan, Isaac Trumbo, who was to be his right-hand man and successor in many lobby-related enterprises. Trumbo, too, had Latter-day Saints in his immediate family background. His maternal grandfather, John Reese, was the Mormon colonizer of Carson Valley, Nevada, and his mother's cousin was Hiram B. Clawson, a Mormon bishop who was also at times manager of the Bullion-Beck properties. When Badlam and Trumbo visited the Eureka mine, Clawson accompanied them. These three were destined to be associated in many of the L.D.S. church's most crucial engagements during the ensuing years.[10]

On May 9, 1887, Clawson wrote to Young that his—Clawson's—influential California associates had powerful financial reasons, as well as personal friendship, for seeing that Utah received just treatment from the federal government. He reported that they were particularly concerned about who might soon be appointed to the territorial Supreme Court. The Californians had a candidate to suggest for such a judgeship, Harvey D. Talcott, who Clawson said would be eminently fair to the Mormons if he was appointed. These California friends would henceforth also be more interested in preventing press controversy regarding Utah; the *Salt Lake Tribune* and *San Francisco Chronicle* were specifically mentioned as papers they would attempt to pacify. This was the initial link in a complex undertaking that in 1888 would develop to amazing proportions.[11]

Just at the time Cannon was contemplating Young's reports from New York City, Clawson received a letter dated July 21, from San Francisco, apparently from Badlam; which alluded to the success of the recent arrangements made there to keep newspapers quiet. In a statement important enough to be extracted and cited in subsequent letters to several other Mormon leaders, it stressed "the securing the papers, that is the keynote and you are getting this advice from men who have had the experience."

Accompanying comments indicate that the parties referred to were officials of the Southern Pacific Railroad, Senator Leland Stanford, one of the company's four founders and directors, was specifically mentioned.[12]

Enclosed in the initial letter was a set of sketchy handwritten notes under the heading "memorandum-proposition-etc.," dated July 16, 1887. These proved to be details of a proposed association and a series of engagements and services of an extensive lobby organization that the railroad agents were willing to offer to the Mormon heirarchy. After inquiry as to the strength of the existing Mormon political movement, the memorandum strongly cautioned that if, with the assistance proffered, the Saints were not strong enough to secure statehood, then it was better not to waste the money to implement the plan. But if the church leaders decided to proceed with their efforts, the means here outlined were advised. These proposals related largely to the "keynote" mentioned in the cover letter—"securing" newspapers.

The notes implied a special arrangement with the A.P. network, said to represent 307 small daily newspapers and the National Associated Press, which involved twenty-six of the nation's largest papers. The notes further elaborated that if the proposals were carried out, it would be necessary to secure an even closer relationship with papers specifically listed including the *New York Times*, the *Philadelphia Times*, the *New York Evening Post*, the *St. Louis Globe-Democrat*, the *San Francisco Chronicle*, the *Chicago Times*, the *Alta Californian*, and "three southern papers." After discussing the discounted costs of sending dispatches, the memo mentioned that "the R-Co [Railroad Company] will try and arrange the terms with the papers satisfactorily, also with the Associated Press." The notes stress the necessity of "utmost secrecy," so that parties in the East would not know of the Mormon alliance with the lobby. (The explanation given was that if the connection were known, "those they want to use will want to be paid over again, whereas now they have already been paid for their services and S-[Stanford] and party do not want to have to pay them over again.")

The memorandum indicated several reasons as to why Southern Pacific officials would be interested in a closer relationship with the Mormon heirarchy. In fact, the first lines of the note stated cryptically, "One senator not averse to their interests—do not care whether he is Democrat or Republican." The officials also desired judges to be appointed who would be "favorable to them" and selectmen, "where their interests were concerned." Referring to railroad involvement in Utah since construction of the first transcontinental railroad, the notes said, "S——d [Stanford] wants to stand in with the people and wants them to stand in with him," which whatever it meant specifically implied a mutual need for the alliance offered.[13]

These propositions were undoubtedly submitted to the First Presidency. On July 27, 1887, two days after Taylor's death, his former councilors, George Q. Cannon and Joseph F. Smith, wrote a letter of introduction for Clawson to take to Stanford, assuring the senator of their high regard for Clawson. Stressing his tact and discretion, they clearly indicated he was their representative and worthy of complete trust.[14] These church leaders also sent Clawson a note, requesting him to journey to San Francisco to "endeavor to get from the principals whose names have been mentioned a full understanding of the propositions which they make." They stressed the importance of getting the information firsthand from the top men and determining exactly the "character of the work which they propose to do and the nature of our obligations that they expect us to assume."

Cannon and Smith specifically expressed concern over the mention of judges and selectmen favorable to railroad interests, noting they could promise nothing that would impair the integrity of the territorial judiciary. But they could see no objection to having men who were sufficiently favorable that railroad friends would be treated in all litigation "as friends should be." Listing each of the subjects mentioned in the initial memorandum, Cannon and Smith instructed Clawson to gather further details. They were particularly interested in having him assess what was expected and what it would cost. The church leaders wanted all of these items carefully spelled out, so there would be no grounds for misunderstanding.[15]

In the papers of the First Presidency are two brief telegrams Clawson sent from San Francisco during the early part of August, 1887. In the first, concerning his interview with Stanford, he reported that the senator would aid them "if press can be secured to help. Thinks that absolutely necessary." Clawson stated that they expected soon to have answers to inquiries regarding the papers. And several days later the other message to church headquarters reported simply, "Answer from East has come. The newspapers we want both East and here will work for us, if the price each names is satisfactory. Everything else alright."[16]

In the same church letter files containing the initial memorandum, are similar ones dated August 4 and 7, 1887, which are clearly Clawson's notes of his personal inquiries at San Francisco. Many of the same statements are repeated, along with much further elaboration on the agreements proposed. The first subject addressed concerned what was expected in Utah. Clawson's notes state that "on general principles they want fair and reasonable protection as a consideration." The question of costs was answered with a list of essentially the same newspapers previously named, with amounts of money ranging from $500 to $20,000 for each paper's services. The total cost was estimated to exceed $140,000, if statehood were achieved.[17]

Each of the memos mentioned the feeling that church agents—meaning mainly Young—had been spending too much money ineffectively. Stanford believed that the movement he was outlining was the "only way out" of difficulties arising from the prevailing impression among some elements of politicians that they could "get any amount of money" out of the Mormons if they only kept up the "pressure." The senator expected the situation to worsen unless the present statehood effort was energetically and properly brought to fruition. Clawson observed that Stanford was under the impression that recent difficulties had "nearly drained" the church of its cash resources, and he was even willing to offer financial aid if it were needed. Throughout their subsequent association with this syndicate, the church leaders appreciated the lack of pecuniary interest displayed.

The railroad representatives thought the final amount of money agreed upon by the press was moderate "when the services required were considered," particularly when compared with what others involved had previously paid. It was reported that some of the papers, when first approached in connection with the Mormons, "named exorbitant figures." But when the situation was explained to them that unlike their usual corporate clients, "those who now wanted their help were fighting for existence with comparatively a very small amount of means," lower fees generally prevailed.[18]

Within a week of Clawson's return from San Francisco, C. W. Penrose was sent to New York. Young received instructions to allow the Mormon editor free access to the New York newspapermen he had been working with so that ignorance and prejudice toward the church might be further dispelled. The Utah leaders admitted to Young that "fears have been expressed very freely that we are losing valuable ground, because of the attitude of the press, that it is becoming too far committed against our movement, and that it will be very difficult, if not almost impossible for some of the papers to be changed."[19]

Undoubtedly Penrose was also assigned the task of ascertaining what arrangements Young had made with the New York press and attempting to reconcile the self-assumed kingpin of the Utah statehood movement to the fact that other means than his might be utilized by church leaders in their quest for the coveted goal. Young had already been vaguely informed that assistance, which had access to both A.P. networks, had been offered. But, Penrose reported, his stubborn yet strikingly personable colleague could not imagine how anyone else could possibly obtain more influence over editorial policies than he could. However, Penrose determined that despite Young's jealousy of any outside effort, he had actually accomplished little of substance other than engaging several men of supposed influence who promised to see New York editors. Later, when the Mormon writer attempted to use those connections to get what he considered extremely conservative material published, Penrose met with almost constant failure and frustration. Before these details were elaborated by letter, Salt Lake authorities were telegraphed sufficient information in that regard to be decisive.[20]

On August 23, 1887, the church committee on statehood wired Clawson, who had returned to San Francisco, that after reading a recent dispatch from Penrose, they had decided to advise the bishop to proceed to make the best terms possible with the railroad lobby. The coded reply sent from California seems to indicate that the final arrangement with the Stanford associates turned out to be at least partly on a cash basis, although that does not necessarily mean the influence in Utah was discounted. Thus, an unlikely client engaged machinery capable of reaching a vast audience of newspaper readers in an effort to convince them that the Mormons were not as outrageously different as was previously reported.[21]

Although the existence of such arrangements has never been widely known, during this period they were not uncommon. And they were not as ethically questionable as might at first appear. In fact, it has been argued they were necessary. During the Gilded Age, officials of the national executive and legislative branches were often so complacent that it took special agents to represent private as well as some public interests. One student of the era, Wallace Farnham, has stated that "the defects in government gave rise to the lobby." Margaret Thompson prefaced her study of the role and process of lobbying in the second half of the nineteenth century by stating that such activities were "a prime contributor" to the national legislature's ability to function, despite "Congress's incapacity to effectually order its own policy priorities."

Thompson elaborated on the type of effort the Mormons were to become so deeply involved in—the attempt to generate a climate of favorable public opinion on a matter of concern to Congress. She explained that "the objective was to create the impression that a clientele's demand was also the will of 'the people.'" One way this was accomplished was "through the careful and sophisticated employment (or manipulation) of the not inconsiderable power of the press." Thus, the "third house" (the lobby) was often allied with "the fourth estate" (the press) in effective campaigns to create a public climate favorable to special legislation desired by sometimes hitherto unpopular clients.[22]

Farnham paid special attention to a Southern Pacific Railroad official, Collis P. Huntington, a "master in the use of docile government for private advantage." His primary responsibility was to represent and oversee corporate interests in the East. Heading an elaborate congressional lobby was one of the notably successful aspects of his job. Huntington's methods were well documented through a series of confidential letters made public during a bitter lawsuit in the 1870s. One of the favorite tactics, which Stanford outlined to the Mormon leaders a decade later, is illustrated in a letter Huntington wrote to an official at the company headquarters in San Francisco to advise that "if you could get some well-written articles published in the S.F. [San Francisco] papers showing up the great value of the S.P. [Southern Pacific]," he would get the articles republished in eastern newspapers. This was a "very effective and very cheap way of advertising." These suggestions allude to the fact that with the loose copyright laws of the day and the extensive exchange practices, once newsworthy items got into print they were likely to be widely disseminated throughout the nation's press. One can often find the same item reprinted from coast to coast the week after it first appears in a leading newspaper.[23] (In 1887 particularly, the Southern Pacific Railroad needed continued public relations work to counter complaints of unfair freight rates and questionable political manipulations. A decade of anti-railroad sentiment was culminating in the passage of the Interstate Commerce Act. Of even greater concern to the "big four" corporation heads was a special investigation by the Pacific Railway Commission, which threatened to generate considerable unfavorable public sentiment and corporate cost. The company's efforts to soothe negative public opinion was a natural consequence.)

The railroad lobby was already well established, with Trumbo and Badlam as part-time functionaries, before it was offered to the Mormons. A letter later in the year from Badlam to Wilford Woodruff contained many revealing bits of information. Badlam confided that they had "a great and powerful combination and can and will use them" for the benefit of the church. He noted that the Stanford group had "friends in the various rings and syndicates which almost sway the councils of the nation" and that their influence reached "into all of the states and are a small army." On another occasion when concern was expressed at agents being absent from Washington, D.C., Trumbo reassured Salt Lake church officials, "You need not worry about a single thing as they have, all told, over thirty people to watch their interests, which yours are tied to in every instance and they do it grand." In the same communication Trumbo divulged that others interested in the syndicate were Collis P. Huntington, Jay Gould, Western Union Telegraph Company, and Standard Oil Company, adding that "they are making an enormous pull." The corporations mentioned herein had compelling reasons for similar lobbying activities during this time, since each of them had legislation inimical to their interests proposed or pending before Congress.

One of the first undertakings this huge lobby started, upon confirmation of their alliance with the Mormons, was aimed at nullifying the influence of the *Salt Lake Tribune*. In San Francisco Clawson received a proposal to establish another non-Mormon Salt Lake City newspaper to undercut its prestige outside the territory. It was to be "made to appear strictly a Gentile" paper, but in contrast to the *Tribune*, it would be strongly for statehood. It was thought "it could be so managed as to become the accepted authority" on Utah affairs at Washington, D.C., and thus "paralyze" much of the *Tribune*'s power. These plans were not carried to fruition, but Badlam minimized the problem, assuring the Mormons that it was a "side issue" possibly helpful toward the statehood goal, but not essential to it.[24]

More important, Badlam advised church leaders to have the *Salt Lake Herald* and *Deseret News* ignore the *Tribune* and scrupulously avoid any mention of Utah's desire for statehood. The statehood committee members reported to the absent *Deseret News* editor, Penrose, that they had held private interviews with the key editorial formulators of both papers, determining that they would cooperate. Some time later, Badlam was not completely satisfied with observance of his advice and elaborated further on his policy of ignoring the *Tribune*. He cautioned church leaders to appoint a "censor" to scrutinize their daily press so that every item was precisely what was wanted. He wrote emphatically, "Allow the name of the *Tribune* never to appear in either of your papers. Don't allow one word to be said in either of your papers in favor of statehood." He wanted "no advocates from that quarter, they control no votes, and every word to be said in either *Herald* or *News* is an absolute injury." This time church leaders carefully heeded Badlam's exhortations.[25]

In the meantime *Tribune* editor Goodwin appealed to the press of the nation to "sound the alarm that in the movement for statehood for Utah there lies a mighty menace to the future peace of the Republic." He warned that a widespread conspiracy had been hatched at Washington and would "be urged by many men that no one not in the secret now suspects unless the press and pulpit of the country stamp it out and make it so unpopular that congressmen will not dare advocate it."[26] These statements contain the essence of the Goodwin-*Tribune* strategy, so successful in the past, which the Mormon lobby was threatening to undermine. A public aroused by the nation's newspapers could assure that Congress would not likely act with such political irresponsibility as to enact legislation favorable to Utah. On the other hand, if the anti-Mormon press did not renew its vigilance, public opinion might be altered sufficiently toward the Latter-day Saints that members of Congress could feel secure in voting in favor of Utah statehood.

Other aspects of the work involving newspapers went far beyond simply nullifying the influence of the *Salt Lake Tribune*. As previously stated, the original Clawson memoranda had several items concerning some of the most important papers in the country. One gave the weekly circulation of each. Another is reproduced herein.

New York Times	$10,000	$10,000 additional
New York Sun	10,000	15,000
New York Evening Post	5,000	5,000
Phila Times	5,000	10,000
Chicago Times	8,000	10,000
St. Louis Globe Democrat	20,000	10,000
San Francisco Chronicle	10,000	10,000
San Francisco Call	500	to remain quiet
do Bulletin	500	do do [ditto]
do Alta	2,500	do do do
do Evening Post	2,500	do do do
	$74,000	$70,000

Judging from arrangements entered into previously with other outside lobbyists, the first column refers to the amount to be paid initially to engage the desired services from each listed party. The additional amount is contingent on the success of the efforts at achieving statehood.

Bishop Clawson's notes referred several times to the Associated Press organizations. Information was given about the number of small and large daily papers involved with each wire service along with some details of the regular and reduced costs offered for Mormon use through their new arrangements. It is clear from these notes that the relationship with the newspapers mentioned in the lists is separate from the simple acquisition of access to the Associated Press news service. This aspect of the proposed scheme was undoubtedly aimed at bypassing William Nelson. Clawson's notes also mentioned the advice that a special outside correspondent be engaged to be "on the ground" to aid in shaping the policy of the press. His duties would also be to "attend to the correspondence by writing "one or more letters per week to each of the papers secured and also attend to the dispatches."[27]

There is evidence that such a policy was implemented. The best way to examine its workings is to focus first on two midwestern newspapers appearing on both lists and known to have been paid at least $8,000 each, the *Chicago Times* and the *St. Louis Globe-Democrat*. Both papers began the year 1887 by utilizing news dispatches, probably from the Associated Press, expressing consistent negativism toward the Mormon church and polygamy. On the day after the Tucker bill passed, both published at least two-column reports detailing and praising the provisions of that law. The next day the *Times* printed an interview with Utah Governor Caleb West, granted at House Speaker Carlisle's capitol office and highly laudatory of the Tucker bill. A week later, the *Globe-Democrat*, a Republican paper, editorialized that the Republicans had rid the country of slavery in its time and should now engage in similar services against polygamy—even if they had to fight the Democrats, as well as the Mormons. After passage of the Edmunds-Tucker Act, it ran a full column editorial lauding that law as the beginning of the end of the Mormon problem. At that time the *Globe-Democrat* published an interview with Goodwin, who was visiting St. Louis, giving him opportunity to denounce President Cleveland for lacking the courage to sign the bill.[28]

In July each newspaper again published negative dispatches about the Mormon statehood efforts. Both contained editorials closely resembling those appearing in the *Salt Lake Tribune*. The *Times* editorialized that the Mormons were wasting time and money on statehood. Both also derided the Utah Commission for condoning the proceedings by allowing use of the regular election machinery for a constitution ratification vote. The *Globe-Democrat* had editorials on the Mormons six days in succession, each critical of the Saints' political efforts. One followed the *Tribune* allegation that the Cleveland administratin was playing for the admission of Utah into the Union and that Jenks was in Salt Lake City to conduct the necessary negotiations to accomplish that as soon as possible.[29]

On July 22 the St. Louis paper published a full column of special correspondence from Salt Lake City headlined "the crafty Mormons." It detailed what was termed a "barefaced swindle" which the Mormons were undertaking to perpetrate on the country through their Utah constitution scheme. The piece included the not inaccurate allegations of an attempt under way to secure amnesty for John Taylor without his actually renouncing plural marriage. It also criticized the Utah Commission for not preventing the Saints from voting. This dispatch was signed with the letter "N," as close to a proof that it emanated from the *Tribune*'s Nelson as is possible. The next day the same paper called for Congress to investigate the supposed connection between the Mormon church and the executive branch of the government.[30]

At the same time the *Chicago Times* was beginning a direct editorial debate with Penrose and his defense of what it chose to call the Mormon "statehood fraud." Consistently using the term pettifogging, the Chicago paper denounced the entire Utah admission effort.[31]

However, by that time the influence of Badlam and his associates was about to become evident. On August 9, 1887, Apostle Franklin D. Richards noted in his diary a pleasant conversation he had that day with J. J. Jennings, a reporter for the *St. Louis Globe-Democrat*. The respected church leader had been given occasion to explain the principles of the Latter-day Saint religion. Jennings had already been in Salt Lake City several days because the following Sunday his newspaper contained his report of experiences the week previous at Mormon Sabbath services. This report was notably positive in tone throughout, not only describing the worshipers as more sincerely devout than most religionists of his experience, but carefully noting the intelligence, neatness, happiness, and health of those he observed. He commented significantly that there had been no mention of polygamy in the day's preachings.[32]

Similar articles appeared frequently during the ensuing month, each over the byline J.J.J. Together they carefully revised most of the negative aspects of the Mormon image as depicted in the press in the previous months—including the *Globe-Democrat*. Several articles were based on interviews with Mormon women. One detailed the views of those who shared their husband with others, emphasizing the difficulty of living in such a situation, for the men as well as the women, but also picturing the dedication of those involved and the love they shared. The other interview was with younger women who had rejected proposals to enter into polygamy. The main thrust of the message conveyed was that these Latter-day Saints believed they could be members in good standing in the church without becoming plural wives and that a growing number of the younger generation were determined not to get involved in that controversial practice.[33]

After September 10, J.J.J.'s dispatches to the *Globe-Democrat* ceased. Jennings may have remained in Salt Lake City to send unsigned correspondence to other papers or he may have been replaced by another individual. At least late in the month someone had a similarly lengthy and positive article ready to be published in the *Chicago Times* of October 1. It alluded slightly to the paper's former series of negative editorials and columns that had questioned the sincerity of the Mormon statehood effort. But this time there was a clearly recognizable attempt to soothe lingering doubts by reporting that the Saints appeared to have complied with all requirements demanded by the American people.

The *Times* dispatch also depicted the earnestness of the Utah statehood movement. This positive discussion was accompanied by a suggestion that it would be "proper to put the community on probation" to determine by the citizens' actions their sincerity. On the last day of the month a similar column in the same paper purportedly described an interview with a high Mormon official, who was quoted as agreeing that they "could not now look for popular acquiescence in the Saints' professions until the latter had proven their sincerity by something more substantial than words." This was a faithful rendition of the theme the lobby advisors often advocated.[34]

As a detailed mid-November letter Badlam wrote to Woodruff pointed out, that had become a major subject of concern to his organization. He told the church leader that they must "stoop to conquer," which proved to mean two things in particular. One was made clear elsewhere in the letter when Badlam said, referring to statehood, "I make it my practice, and you should make it yours; when you desire to accomplish a particular object, to treat it in the least important manner possible." This, he said, would throw the "unprincipled sharpers" who might oppose for personal gain off the track. The other meaning was that the church members should strike the appearance of having been brought to the point of submission by the concerted efforts of the anti-polygamy crusade in Utah. These messages were reflected during the remainder of the year in the *Chicago Times* and elsewhere.[35]

A special dispatch from Salt Lake City dated November 29 was published December 2 in the *Times* under the headline "The Latter-day Saints in Utah Dejected by the Action of the Government." It referred to threatened suits aimed at confiscation of church property under the Edmunds-Tucker Act. The lengthy article surmised that the dejection bore eloquent testimony to the fact that "the spirit of the Mormon has been crushed, and he has concluded to be as he was no more." In other *Times* Salt Lake specials in late December, Badlam's meaning about unconcern was an accompanying theme. Along with much discussion of the apathy, which was apparently rampant as the Saints began to recognize their political overthrow, there was a full column stating that there was "but little interest seemingly taken by the Mormons regarding the admission of Utah as a state." Besides the *Times'* own articles to this effect, it copied a similar one published December 23 in the *Louisville Courier-Journal*. Further examination of that respected southern newspaper indicated that the influential Henry Waterson's editorial stance regarding the Mormons had been similarly altered since the beginning of the year.[36]

While Badlam's behind-the-scenes work had been gaining in momentum, Penrose continued to labor, through more conventional means, at what was considered the vital center of the nation's news system, New

York City. Although he had full knowledge of the engagement with the Southern Pacific lobby, his regular correspondence to church leaders in Salt Lake City indicated no knowledge of efforts on their part in his field of activity. However, some of his early communications may have contained information useful in providing the Salt Lake brethren with a means for comparing the relative merits of the separate enterprises engaged in their cause.[37]

On August 27, 1887, Penrose assessed the Mormons' relationship with several of the New York newspapers. He said that the *Star* was "alright," the *Sun* "favorable," and the *New York Herald* was cooperative enough to publish an interview Penrose arranged in which Curtis Bean, Arizona's former delegate to Congress, favorably reflected on the Saints. And the L.D.S. newspaper agent reported vaguely, but meaningfully, that unnamed parties had informed him the *Herald*'s influence "could be had" at a cost of between $25,000 and $50,000.[38] Penrose also discussed their status with the *New York Times*. He said, "It is understood here that the *Times* cannot be engaged for any amount of money." But, he continued, the manager of the paper was favorable to the Mormons, and John W. Young had met with him several times. Unfortunately the editor, C. W. Miller, was not of the same mind, although Young still hoped to find a way to soften his position. However, in one of the October reports Penrose stated, "The *New York Times* is adverse to our cause," and in another, he confessed that the editor "is the strongest opponent I have met."[39]

Penrose was experiencing some difficulty with other papers as well. He had arranged for the *New York Tribune* to publish an interview with George Ticknor Curtis, but instead, he said, it merely incorporated a small amount of the information into an editorial in a manner not intended. On October 26 he told of replies he had recently written to negate articles appearing in the *World* and *Tribune*, but reported in disgust, "They don't want anything on our side of the Utah question." This confirmed his conclusion of earlier in the month: "It seems as though any influence down here on the press of New York that can be brought to bear in our favor is very feeble."[40]

But here, too, the tide was about to turn. In mid-November he reported that "public sentiment seems to have modified considerably and less bitterness appears in the press references to Utah." The next month he repeated essentially the same statement, adding that "every newspaper man I have met has received me very kindly and we have kept them quiet as to the wrong side if we have not made them say much on the right."[41] On December 10 he told of an acquaintance he had struck with Colonel Handy, sometimes a managing editor of the *New York World*. Handy told him he had already approached his publisher, Joseph Pulitzer, about the propriety of sending a man, possibly himself, to Utah to "write up" the statehood and Mormon questions. Although evidence is purely circumstantial, it is entirely probable that this man had already "been seen" by agents from the other organization. Penrose did not mention meeting Badlam and Trumbo until later in the month, but it is apparent that the favorable changes he had noted did not result as much from his efforts as from theirs.[42]

Wherever the credit resides, the results are evident, as an examination of the leading New York newspapers of November and December demonstrates. Whether the *World* was retained or not, the evidence here indicates it was at least approached. The *Evening Post* was on the original list that the Southern Pacific officials said were essential papers to be retained. Comparison of the two-column December 4 dispatch from Salt Lake City with the negative editorial of July 6 shows a definite about-face. The *New York Herald* had not been on the list in Clawson's memoranda, but the articles it published about Utah and the Mormons in November and December clearly fit Badlam's guidelines. The *New York Sun*, despite being named as essential for retention, was never unfriendly to the Mormons in its 1887 comments on the subject, but may have been subsidized nevertheless. The *New York Times*, also on the list of important papers, remained consistently opposed to the entire Utah statehood movement. And at year's end the *New York Tribune* published another negative editorial on the same subject.[43]

However, a closer look at the *Tribune* is of interest. The original Clawson memoranda implied that the widely respected *Tribune* editor, Whitelaw Reid, was not susceptible to the cash subsidies then under discussion. But, the notes stated, Badlam believed he could still secure the desired results, without cost, "through personal friendship." Although not evidence of the greatest substance, the *Tribune* index sheds some light. While each of the previous half-dozen years listed between six and twelve items under the headings of Utah, the Mormons, and polygamy, the year 1888 had none. Yet certainly there were no fewer newsworthy items emanating from that territory in that important year. Both sets of lobbyists had always been happy to accept silence when positive statements could not be elicited.[44]

The year 1887 closed amid optimistic reports of a more favorable attitude developing toward the Mormons. Trumbo confessed that "everything looks much better than we ever anticipated at this time of the game." On January 7, 1888, Trumbo sent an issue of *Public Opinion*, a journal containing excerpts from the nation's press, to show how well their "friends stood up." He pointed out that the newspapers secured had done very well and that even the papers making some negative comment were "not very strong and not very lengthy." Trumbo noted that Badlam and "all those others interested think that it is a very splendid showing."[45]

The successful arrangement with the first subsidized newspapers was soon expanded. In March, 1888, in a revealing passage, Badlam informed Bishop Clawson of some of his activities, saying he "was compelled to come here [from Washington, D.C., to New York City] and proceed to Boston and four or five other New York and New England cities to see some newspaper men and pacify them a little which I will do cheerfully for they have in almost every instance done handsomely with us, in fact I am proud of this branch of our labors as good results have come through from our efforts." He reported that "the puritanical and sectarian press here have been looked after and their material interest consulted in so handsome and economical a manner that you must pardon me for reference again to it. I have got to put up some more this week, but it will be well spent and in most cases final." Explaining that there "are so many of them and so many different circumstances and men to consult that my head just spins," Badlam concluded that "when a certain question comes up properly before Congress I am satisfied it will have strong support, where formerly enmity existed." As the last statement implied, Utah statehood was the ultimate goal. Earlier Trumbo had confided Badlam's contention that work with the newspapers was "where our strength lies." This presumably referred to the effort to alter public opinion in favor of the Mormons among congressional constituents because he also stated that if this was accomplished and congressmen were properly reassured concerning the future course of action of the church, getting sufficient congressional votes for Utah statehood would be an easy enough matter.[46]

One of Trumbo's letters advised the church authorities to "hurry and make stronger connections with all merchants possible," saying that there was great strength to be derived from such an endeavor. The First Presidency sent Robert Watson, the superintendent of the church-owned Salt Lake City department store, Z.C.M.I., on a tour to visit principal business houses, "appealing to them to use their influence with their representatives in Congress in favor of the state movement." In a portion of an ensuing letter of encouragement to their unique emissary, the church leaders summarized some principal aims of the efforts they had become so involved in: "We feel it to be our duty, at this time particularly to do all in our power to disabuse the public men from the prejudices which they have imbibed concerning us. The lies which are so commonly told about us are repeated so often that many people who have no opportunity of hearing the other side, never appear to think for a moment that there can be any other side to our question, and that we are all that we are reported to be." Visits such as Watson's should cause some individuals to "awaken the feeling within them that we are not such odious people as we are represented to be." [47]

Some of the era's most negative news stories concerning the Mormons had emanated from their missionary proselyting areas in the southern states. In the mid-1880s at least two L.D.S. missionaries and several of their associates had been killed by anti-Mormon mobs in Tennessee. Several Mormon agents had mentioned the distress this caused some southern senators and congressmen, who desired to support the Utah statehood movement, but were confronted with letters from constituents adamantly opposed to any aid to Mormons. The general authorities, after considerable discussion, explained the situation to the leader of their Southern States Mission. They instructed him to withdraw his workers from those districts where a threat of trouble or unfavorable publicity existed. A subsequent letter from Woodruff on the subject further justified such a retreat: "The present appears to be a time when it is wise for us to pursue a conciliatory policy and to do everything in our power to allay prejudice and to quiet down hostility." [48]

It is obvious that the connections utilized by Mormon agents included well-known figures of the political and business world. A letter from Trumbo to Clawson in March, 1888, mentioned some of these names: "I'm getting acquainted with all of the great big men and some of them seem to be a grand lot. We had a big dinner with [Roscoe] Conkling and senator [John P.] Jones of Nevada the day before yesterday." But he revealed some rather surprising associates as well when he commented that "yesterday afternoon we were at Bob Ingersol's house with Mark Twain, who is assisting Maude [Badlam] as regards some of the newspapers. He goes to Washington with us on Thursday and a jolly fellow he is too." Trumbo continued: "Cardinal [James] Gibbons has done a good deal more than ever was promised. Not a man in the city of Washington who is a member of that [Catholic] denomination has a word to say against. If they cannot say something for it they are silent." He then commented that the newly appointed U.S. attorney general, Don M. Dickinson, would "have to be looked after, as he is very bitter and so far they have not reached anybody who can seem to tame him down. In his mind nothing can be done too hard against them [the Mormons]." But he confidently affirmed that "President Cleveland, however, will take the task of softening him until someone else can reach him." [49]

Another name Trumbo could have added to his list was that of Susan B. Anthony, who was a leading organizer of several important woman's conventions held in late March, 1888, partly in commemoration of the fortieth anniversary of the first National Women's Suffrage Convention at Seneca Falls, New York. Mormon agents contributed something over a

$100 toward the expenses of the International Council of Women, one such meeting. Joseph F. Smith confided this had been "with the express understanding that they did not want to pay money to be misrepresented and maligned." They were particularly concerned that Dr. Ruth Wood, an associate of Mormon nemesis Angie Newman, might be given opportunity to deliver a bitter speech she reportedly had prepared. But the only mention of the church during the proceedings came in a report from the leader of the Utah delegation, Emily S. Richards, and the message communicated back to the L.D.S. heirarchy was that she and her associates had been well received.[50]

Unquestionably the greatest challenge to the church public relations efforts was convincing the people and their representatives that a change had indeed been made among the Mormons concerning plural marriage. All of the machinery had been set up for that purpose. Badlam, in one of his initial communications, advised church leaders to "do everything that is possible to convince your enemies of your sincerity in the abandonment of polygamy." Examination of articles in the newspapers he had helped to secure indicates that his organization was also taking great care in that direction. For example, a dispatch from Utah that was published in the *Lousiville Courier-Journal* depicted the polygamous Utahans as having lost their position of political dominance. It observed that "as polygamists could neither vote nor hold office, they were naturally and necessarily forced into the background." They were described as expecting to continue to "control the young officials and rule as formerly in fact, if not in name." But "powerful as was their ecclesiastical influence over their followers, it was not strong enough to destroy the ambition of the younger element," who had seized political control.[51]

The article suggested that the Edmunds and Edmunds-Tucker laws were having the intended effect. It recalled that Mormon polygamists had formerly assumed a defiant attitude, retaining a "powerful array" of attorneys to fight every case brought to trial. But as conviction consistently followed arrest and as the territorial penitentiary filled with polygamists, enthusiasm was described as waning. Citing the fact that only two out of 400 or 500 who had served sentences for polygamy had been reconvicted, it described a "general abandonment" of the plural wife system, adding that there was "reason to believe that the great majority of the Mormons rejoice rather than grieve over the downfall of the system. Truly has a wonderful revolution been brought about in a short time, and there is reason to believe that it will be permanent. Polygamy is truly a dead institution, in so far as it can be killed before the passing away of this generation." It went on to conclude that "a little longer and the regeneration will be complete, and then Utah will be great and prosperous."[52]

An earlier dispatch to the *Chicago Times* described a purported interview with a Mormon apostle, who was said to have assured the correspondent that the practice of polygamy would be discontinued, although belief in the principle would continue. The supposed interviewer pointed out that "for the first time was heard a high churchman declare the necessity for a law against plural marriage as a protection for society in general and the Mormons in particular." The *Times* article further observed that the apostle "uttered the sentiments of a controlling faction of his associates," who were depicted as anxious to "proclaim against the system."[53]

Despite these press articles, as discussion herein indicates, the church heirarchy had remained firm in their position on plural marriage. As they admitted to Delegate John T. Caine, who was preparing to answer questions on the subject at the congressional hearings on Utah statehood, they had been urged by Badlam and his associates to make strategic concessions through an amendment to the U.S. Constitution. This, the lobbyists promised, would be well received at the time by the American public at large. But, the Mormon leaders confessed, "it is hard for a people like we are to condescend to ask for a measure of this character when every feeling of our hearts revolts at it." They admitted that such action might well be necessary to gain Utah's admission, but, they continued, "up to the present we have not been able to bring our mind to that point."[54]

A rather complex episode illustrates the contradictory nature of the church position on plural marriage, while also showing how effective the public relations machinery had become in little more than a year. In April, 1888, the Church of Jesus Christ of Latter-day Saints held its regular semiannual general conference. Since President Wilford Woodruff was still hiding "on the underground," he issued the sixth of what had come to be called "epistles" to the Saints, which was subsequently utilized in the opinion-molding endeavors to show that the official stance on plural marriage had changed. A dispatch from church headquarters to the *National Republican* described the epistle in terms of contrast with the tone of Taylor's previous messages. The notice stated that Taylor had advocated and defended plural marriage with strong appeals to the Old Testament and recent revelations. But Woodruff's message differed markedly in tone and was actually not dissimilar to what any number of Protestant clergymen might write to their congregations. The news release suggested it was not known whether Woodruff merely thought an approach similar to Taylor's was impolitic for the present or, in the telegraphic language of the report, had "concluded day is past in this country to attempt convince American people that such system is defensible upon any such grounds." But, it was concluded, "it may be counted healthful sign Utah and her future that this distasteful doctrine is not flaunted in face of public opinion." A dispatch in essentially the same words also appeared in the *San Francisco Call*.[55]

However, the positive message delivered above was considerably complicated by several conference talks by prominent polygamists of the church hierarchy. On the first day of the session general authority Seymour B. Young alluded to celestial marriage pointedly enough so that one of the church agents felt constrained to telegraph that day from Chicago to complain that the speech was causing some damage to their efforts in the East and steps needed to be taken to suppress further negative comments. But on the next day Rudger Clawson, something of a hero in church circles because he had suffered patiently through the longest prison term yet levied against a Latter-day Saint for unlawful cohabitation, spoke in an almost boastful manner of his refusal in court to promise the judge that he would not return to living with his plural wife upon release. He stated, according to the *Deseret News*, "It is pleasing to God for men to go to prison under unjust law rather than act contrary to their covenants."[56]

The *Salt Lake Tribune*, which had already telegraphed a negative version of Young's speech, not only utilized Clawson's speech as a pretext for a vehement denunciation of church officials for duplicity, but also quickly disseminated telegraphic reports as widely as it could. The *New York Times* used such a dispatch for a front page article under headlines stating that the Mormons "won't abandon their faith"—in plural marriage.[57]

A clerk at church headquarters attempted to alleviate some of the ill effects by issuing the following statement to the *National Republican*: "I understand young Clawson, just released from penitentiary, delivered an address in Tabernacle in which he used some expressions favoring polygamy. But his remarks were viewed with much disfavor by leading elders." A similar dispatch in the *San Francisco Call* declared that "ever since deep indignation has been expressed by the public and interviews with leading Mormons prove that the young man's reckless and unauthorized remarks are as deeply chagrined by them as others." No such public disfavor is evident in any of the newspapers or diaries examined for such expressions. However, the church public relations agents were prompt in their protests against such developments.[58]

President Joseph F. Smith, who still headed the church lobbyists in the East, wrote to his brethren in the presidency to say that "remarks on polygamy at conference are reported in several New York papers in proof of the determination of the church to continue and extend polygamy. Very damaging to our cause. We understood such remarks were discouraged." Woodruff replied, "We meet on all sides expressions of regret at the utterances of the speakers at conference." He admitted significantly, "Our friends declare that great injury had been done by what was said, and they expressed a feeling of shame, because these utterances seem to put them in the position of having made false statements." The church leader confessed that "no one could have been more surprised at these utterances than ourselves and a number of the brethren of the Twelve, because it was understood that care would be exercised upon these points."[59]

In a similar explanation to Penrose and Richards, Woodruff and Cannon elaborated that it was supposed that the presiding authority at the session, President Lorenzo Snow, described as a very prudent man, had understood the policy of restricting discussion of controversial subjects at the conference. Woodruff explained he had cautioned his fellow apostle "that if anyone attempted to speak about polygamy, to throw his hat at him." The leaders repeated that they were as surprised and mortified at the remarks as anyone else. They did inform their brethren that they had attempted to alleviate the more serious repercussions by instructing the sending of an Associated Press dispatch "which would have the effect to counteract any wrong impressions that might have been made by the reports." They reiterated their belief that "it is our duty to avoid everything that would create unnecessary prejudice or that would excite hostility."[60]

It is doubtful if the church leaders fully comprehended just how completely the conference incident did what they had determined to avoid. Badlam had never been completely satisfied with their resolve to keep things quiet at home. In the same communication in which he reported greater success with the newspapers than had been expected, he again cautioned the church statehood committee to allow no local incident to mar continued progress. The conference statements and the resulting adverse publicity were exactly the type of reversal most devastating to the lobbyists' work. Woodruff's reply to Smith's complaint makes clear that the outside agents also had voiced dismay at the speeches that tended to destroy one of their most essential tools—credibility—without which a lobbyist is almost helpless. The church leaders confided to Penrose that Badlam and his associates "feel somewhat discouraged at our want of discretion and think their labors have been, to a great extent, nullified." They admitted that these outside associates were not consoled by the typical Mormon attitude that the storm caused by the conference talks would "blow over and the Lord will overrule all things for good."[61] In a letter soon after to Caine, the church statehood committee implied they had received reports of displeasure from another friendly Gentile source. They conceded many reasons to regret that Rudger Clawson had spoken as he had, continuing that "it is easy to understand how annoyed President Cleveland must have been at hearing about it."[62]

Joseph F. Smith sent his brethren the unfavorable newspaper clippings spawned by Clawson's remarks. After these and further reports from the East were examined, Cannon and Woodruff observed that "it seems that a great change had taken place within a brief period." They were not entirely prepared to admit that the conference utterances were the sole cause, but they understood that great damage had been done to the carefully implemented public relations work. In fact, as nearly as can be determined from the newspapers and correspondence of the church leaders, the elaborate effort they had been engaged in for most of the past year ended abruptly at this point. The conference statements played into the hands of opponents who had consistently maintained that the pretense of abandoning polygamy was a sham. They totally undercut the lobbyists who assumed that what they had been saying was true. Certainly thereafter, Badlam, the key figure in the initial contact with the lobby syndicate, would no longer be involved in the Mormon cause.[63]

It is impossible to assess the long-range success of the Mormons' attempt to alter public opinion in their favor. The self-serving nature of the contemporary reports church leaders received must be sufficiently discounted. Yet during an era in which the negative news coverage concerning the church and polygamy was clearly proliferating, the efforts to influence positive press treatment of the Mormons were at least impressive in extent and probably a necessary prerequisite to attainment of the ultimate goal of Utah statehood. Never again prior to Utah's admission as a state would there be any appreciable barrage of anti-Mormon press coverage, and that was certainly an impressive change from the previous situation.

NOTES

1. George Ticknor Curtis to Franklin S. Richards, Jan. 23, 1887, George Ticknor Curtis Papers, H.D.C. See also Richards to John Taylor, Feb. 9, 1887, F. S. Richards Papers, H.D.C.

2. *Salt Lake Herald*, Feb. 9, 10, 1887; Whitney, *History of Utah*, 3:405, 413, 487.

3. James Jack to *National Republican*, Feb. 21, Apr. 19, 1887.

4. F. S. Richards to Taylor, Feb. 9, 1887, Curtis to F. S. Richards, Mar. 8, 1887, F. S. Richards Papers, H.D.C.; *New York Evening Post*, July 14, 1887; *The Forum*, Nov., 1887; Charles W. Penrose to Wilford Woodruff, George Q. Cannon, and Joseph F. Smith, Oct. 11, 1887, First Presidency Miscellaneous Papers.

5. Young to Jack, Mar. 16, Apr. 29, May 28, June 17, 20, 29, 1887, Jack Papers.

6. Young to Jack, June 21, 1887, Taylor and Cannon to John R. Winder, June 23, 1887, Jack Papers. *Salt Lake Herald*, July 6, 1887; *New York World*, July 6, 1887.

7. *New York Times*, July 9, 1887. See also p. 50 herein.

8. Young to Taylor and Cannon, July 15, 1887, Young Papers, H.D.C.

9. *New York Evening Post*, July 6; *New York Herald*, July 1, 6–9; *New York Sun*, Aug. 9, 30; *New York Times*, July 3, 6, 7, 9, 25; *New York Tribune*, July 11; *New York World*, July 7, all for 1887.

10. *San Francisco Chronicle*, May 4, 1887; *Salt Lake Herald*, May 24, 1887.

11. Hiram B. Clawson to Young, May 9, 1887, Young Papers, H.D.C.

12. [Unsigned] to Clawson, July 21, 1887, First Presidency Miscellaneous Papers, which included enclosed "memorandum-proposition-etc.," July 16, 1887.

13. Ibid.

14. Cannon and Joseph F. Smith to Leland Stanford, July 27, 1887, Cannon and Smith to Clawson, July 27, 1887, First Presidency Papers [Letterbooks].

15. Cannon and Smith to Clawson, July 27, 1887, First Presidency Papers.

16. Clawson to Jack, Aug. 4, 7, 1887, Jack Papers.

17. Pencilled [Clawson] notes, Aug. 4, 7, 1887, First Presidency Miscellaneous Papers.

18. Ibid.

19. Woodruff, Cannon, and Smith to Young, Aug. 16, 1887, Wilford Woodruff Papers.

20. Williams [Penrose] to Jack [for Clawson], Aug. 22, 1887, Jack Papers; Williams to Woodruff, Cannon, and Smith, Aug. 24, 27, 1887, First Presidency Miscellaneous Papers.

21. Woodruff, Cannon, and Smith to Penrose, Aug. 20, 1887, Clawson to Jack, Aug. 22, 1887, Woodruff Papers; Woodruff, Cannon, and Smith to Clawson, Aug. 23, 1887, First Presidency Miscellaneous Papers.

22. Wallace D. Farnham, "The Weakened Spring of Government: A Study in Nineteenth-Century American History," *American Historical Review* 68 (1963), 662–69; Margaret Thompson, "The Spider Web: Congressional Lobbying in the Age of Grant" (Ph.D. diss., University of Wisconsin, 1979), 1–4, 24–25.

23. *Chicago Tribune*, Dec. 27, 1883, published extensive letters of Collis P. Huntington to David Colton from 1875.

24. Maude [Badlam] to Allen [Woodruff], Nov. 15, 1887, Caleb [Trumbo] to Lulu [Clawson], Dec. 19, 1887, First Presidency Miscellaneous Papers.

25. [Clawson-Badlam] notes, Aug. 4, 7, 1887; Dellie [Trumbo] to Clawson, Aug. 8, 1887, Maude [Badlam] to Allen [Woodruff], Nov. 15, 1887, ibid.

26. *Salt Lake Tribune*, Oct. 22, 1887.

27. [Clawson-Badlam] notes, July 16, Aug. 4, 7, 1887, First Presidency Miscellaneous Papers.

28. Clawson to Mr. Addy [Jack], Oct. 22, 1887, First Presidency Miscellaneous Papers; *Chicago Times*, Jan. 13, 14, 1887; *St. Louis Globe-Democrat*, Jan. 13, 22, 23, 30, Feb. 2, 19, Mar. 6, 8, 1887.

29. *Chicago Times*, July 3, 8, 13, 1887; *St. Louis Globe-Democrat*, July 6–11, 1887.

30. *Globe-Democrat*, July 22, 23, 1887.

31. *Chicago Times*, July 19, 21, Aug. 6, 1887.

32. Richards Journal, Aug. 9, 1887; *Globe-Democrat*, Aug. 14, 1887.

33. *Globe-Democrat*, Aug. 17, 20, 1887.

34. *Chicago Times*, Oct. 1, 31, 1887.

35. Maude [Badlam] to Allen [Woodruff], Nov. 15, 1887, First Presidency Miscellaneous Papers.

36. *Chicago Times*, Dec. 2, 22, 25, 1887; *Louisville Courier-Journal*, Jan. 13, 14, Nov. 18, Dec. 23, 1887.

37. C. Williams to Woodruff, Cannon, and Smith, Aug. 24, 1887, First Presidency Miscellaneous Papers.

38. C. Williams to Woodruff, Cannon, and Smith, Aug. 27, 1887, ibid.

39. C. Williams to Woodruff, Cannon, and Smith, Oct. 11, 17, 1887, ibid.

40. C. Williams to Woodruff, Cannon, and Smith, Oct. 11, 17, 26, 1887, ibid.

41. C. Williams to Woodruff, Cannon, and Smith, Nov. 16, Dec. 30, 1887, ibid.

42. C. Williams to Woodruff, Cannon, and Smith, Dec. 10, 30, 1887, ibid.

43. *New York Evening Post*, July 6, Dec. 4, 13, 1887; *New York Herald*, Mar. 22, Nov. 6, Dec. 4, 21, 1887; *New York Sun*, Aug. 30, Nov. 17, 1887; *New York Times*, Jan. 13, 14, Nov. 7, 8, Dec. 7, 21, 23, 1887; *New York Tribune*, Jan. 16, Feb. 1, 6, July 11, Oct. 16, Nov. 15, Dec. 27, 1887.

44. [Clawson-Badlam] notes, July 23, Aug. 4, 7, 1887, First Presidency Miscellaneous Papers; *New York Tribune Index*, 1881–90.

45. Dellie [Trumbo] to Lulu [Clawson], Jan. 7, 1888, First Presidency Miscellaneous Papers. *Public Opinion* devoted space to the Mormon and Utah questions in several weekly installments of its fourth volume. The issue of Dec. 31, 1887, was in all likelihood the one sent and discussed. However, to one not initiated as to exactly who was expected to "stand up" and how, the four pages containing thirty excerpts from papers throughout the country seem predominantly negative. Without an elaborate evaluation system, the tabulation would be twenty negative, seven positive (according to Badlam's advice of appearing indifferent as to statehood), and three noncommittal.

46. Alex [Badlam] to Hiram [Clawson], Mar. 5, 1888, First Presidency Miscellaneous Papers. At approximately the same time, church leaders expressed their own favorable opinion of the work: "It has been a great labor to keep the papers in line, and taking everything into consideration, we think the success has been very remarkable. To keep the papers quiet upon a subject of such interest is a wonderful performance in the excited state of feeling which prevailed in the public mind a short time ago. We think our friends have had a great labor to perform in accomplishing this, and that they have been so successful is very creditable to their efforts and an evidence to us that the Lord has favored us." Woodruff and Cannon to Smith, Feb. 28, 1888, Woodruff Papers.

47. Caleb [Trumbo] to Lulu [Clawson], Dec. 19, 1887, First Presidency Miscellaneous Papers; Woodruff, Cannon, and Smith to Penrose, Dec. 20, 1887, Woodruff, Cannon, and Smith to Robert S. Watson, Jan. 17, Feb. 4, 1888, Woodruff Papers.

48. Mack [Smith] to Jack, Mar. 20, 1888, Jack Papers; Woodruff and Cannon to Smith, Apr. 5, 1888; Woodruff to William Spry, June 15, 1888, Woodruff Papers.

49. Dellie [Trumbo] to Lulu [Clawson], Mar. 13, 1888, First Presidency Miscellaneous Papers.

50. Mack [Smith] to Woodruff and Cannon, Mar. 30, Apr. 6, 1888, ibid; *New York Times*, Mar. 26–30, 1888.

51. Maude [Badlam] to Allen [Woodruff], Nov. 15, 1887, First Presidency Miscellaneous Papers; *Louisville Courier-Journal*, Nov. 28, 1887.

52. Ibid.

53. *Chicago Times*, Oct. 31, 1887.

54. Woodruff and Cannon to Caine, Feb. 18, 1888, Woodruff Papers.

55. Jack to *National Republican*, Apr. 7, 1888, Jack Papers; *National Republican*, Apr. 8, 1888; *San Francisco Call*, Apr. 13, 1888.

56. *Deseret Weekly News*, Apr. 11, 1888.

57. *Salt Lake Tribune*, Apr. 7, 8, 1888; *New York Times*, Apr. 7, 1888.

58. Jack to *National Republican*, Apr. 7, 1888, Jack Papers; *National Republican*, Apr. 8, 1888; *San Francisco Call*, Apr. 13, 1888.

59. Mack [Smith] to Jack, Apr. 8, 1888, First Presidency Miscellaneous Papers; Woodruff to Smith, Apr. 19, 1888, Woodruff Papers.

60. Woodruff and Cannon to Richards and Penrose, Apr. 11, 1888, Woodruff Papers.

61. Woodruff and Cannon to Penrose, Apr. 20, 1888, First Presidency Miscellaneous Papers.

62. Woodruff and Cannon to Caine, May 9, 1888, Woodruff Papers.

63. Woodruff and Cannon to Smith, May 2, 1888, First Presidency Miscellaneous Papers. Belatedly, the brethren apparently implemented the advice given them by the Badlam group just prior to the conference incident—"to remove [their] question from public notice for a while," which might have meant cancelling the newspaper subsidizing effort. See Mack [Smith] to Woodruff and Cannon, Mar. 30, 1888, ibid.

4

Hopes and Disappointments

Throughout the so-called raid, Mormons and Gentiles had remained so separate in Utah that members of opposing elements seldom crossed the dividing lines. Yet if statehood were to be granted, national political leaders, including Grover Cleveland, required assurance that the mutual animosities were subsiding. After two decades of virtual segregation, in 1887 and 1888 there were several attempts to break down the barriers. But although these developments raised hopes that the divisive tensions were being alleviated, immediate results proved disappointing. The Mormon heirarchy remained stubbornly involved in politics and unwilling to make real concessions on plural marriage, and thus most Utah Gentiles and their friends in Congress remained unanxious to cooperate fully in admitting Utah as a state.

The first successful venture toward bridging the gulf between Mormons and Gentiles was among the more moderate members of the business community of Salt Lake City. Some of the long-time residents in the area had grown weary of the anti-polygamy crusade's detrimental effect on trade, property values, and ability to attract new investors and inhabitants. Such individuals were instrumental in forming the Salt Lake City Chamber of Commerce in April, 1887. Governor Caleb W. West was a leading figure throughout the formative phases, along with Gentile banker W. S. McCornick and several Mormon businessmen, including general authorities Heber J. Grant and John W. Young. Recognizing that aside from business concerns, the group was an experiment in harmonious Mormon-Gentile relations, members adopted the motto "no politics or religion in the chamber." This proved difficult to enforce, and in time the organization served as an important forum for discussing several crucial political matters.[1]

In Young's interviews with Cleveland, the president voiced continuing concern with the status of the Gentile minority should statehood grant the Mormons control of Utah's government. He expressed a strong desire to be able to assure those who had raised the concern previously that fairness would prevail. Certainly Young recognized the implication that further efforts toward Mormon-Gentile reconciliation would guarantee a favorable impression in the highest seat of national government. He soon wrote to church leaders to argue that "we of all people ought to show minorities by a practical demonstration in our policies that we firmly believe in minority representation," which he reminded his brethren they had scrupulously avoided in the past. Young recommended that in the approaching municipal elections of February, 1888, some of the "best non-Mormons" be offered seats on the Salt Lake City Council.[2]

After Gentiles initially rejected overtures that seemed too blatantly a gift from Mormon politicians, the territorial legislature enacted a uniform system of municipal and county government which provided for representation by ward in cities and commissioner districts in counties. Since non-Mormons predominated numerically in some sections of Salt Lake City, some moderate Gentiles reconsidered and consented to cooperate with the People's party in a Citizen's coalition slate for the elections. As the Mormon party convention ratified the combined list of candidates, church leaders confessed hope that it would "allay the great hostility between the Mormon and Gentile elements of the community."[3]

The coalition slate revealed division within the Gentile ranks as the issue was debated in a series of heated meetings. The more extremely anti-Mormon Liberals promptly denounced the actions of moderate Liberals and the Chamber of Commerce for cooperation with the Mormons' seemingly magnanimous offer, which chairman J. B. Rosborough charged was simply a ploy to further statehood aims in Washington, D.C. He and his fellows favored a "square-toed fight" in the municipal election and predicted that within two years the Liberals would control Salt Lake City elections. Governor West strongly endorsed the coalition movement. Speaking as a good Chamber of Commerce advocate, he stressed the positive value of such a course in inducing outside capital and attracting new residents. These, he argued, rather than further congressional action, were the best means of attaining the desired changes in Utah. He viewed the association of Mormons and Gentiles in the chamber as evidence of the progress for which he and his colleagues had been working. When the anti-fusionists denounced West and the four Gentiles on the coalition ticket as "traitors," the governor attempted to respond calmly, yet resolutely. But amid loud heckling, pandemonium reigned and violence seemed imminent. Order was barely restored when General P. E. Connor arose to stand at West's side. The ill feelings displayed certainly threatened a permanent split in the ranks of Utah non-Mormons.[4]

In mid-February, 1888, the Citizen's ticket, including Gentiles W. S. McCornick, John E. Dooley, M. B. Sowels, and Bolivar Roberts, was elected by a majority averaging about 860 out of just over 2,700 votes. After the clamor subsided, the church statehood committee confided to John T. Caine that they were gratified with the results. They expressed confidence that this and other similar actions would "soften" the respectable and law-abiding element of Gentiles. The church leaders also hoped that the actions might "lead to a division between the better class of non-Mormons and the howling rabble."[5]

However, before the fall elections most of the non-Mormon political activists closed ranks to resist an attempt by young Mormons to join their Democratic party convention. Governor West, who had so firmly defended the February coalition effort and who in his previous annual report to the secretary of the interior had been most optimistic concerning the Mormon statehood movement, was by the time of his 1888 report convinced that same movement was in fact a device to continue polygamy. He was again repeating the standard Liberal contentions that statehood would permanently enthrone "the Mormon political system" in power.[6]

There are several significant developments that might have been instrumental in altering the attitudes of the governor and other moderate Liberals. Disappointment at the outcome of the territorial legislative session was likely to have been the first. Or possibly some bit of information concerning the Mormon alliance with the Southern Pacific lobby might have leaked out to disillusion influential Gentiles. Undoubtedly the Saints' relationship with the Cleveland administration and the growing evidence of leniency of the latter were a disappointment. But in all likelihood the most important factor was the lack of any concrete proof of a change in the Mormon attitude toward polygamy and its practice that drove the non-Mormons back into a unified Liberal party.

When the territorial legislative session began in January, 1888, Governor West fervently pleaded for the lawmakers to codify separation of church and state. He was particularly desirous of implementing a free public school system, which he claimed Utah was one of the last to accept. The Mormon leaders had deliberated many times on what they felt the schools should be like but had always opted to retain church control. Although there was considerable desire to cooperate with the governor, they were still far from agreement with him on educational matters. Midway through the following month several lawmakers met with church leaders and concluded that "it was thought best to concede a few points to the governor if he will yield a little." But less than a week later a similar group reconsidered and concluded that no concessions would be made. Again in early March, during the crucial closing days of the session, seven of the apostles discussed the still-pending shcool issue and other questions. They too decided to refuse any compromise with the governor. Mormon lawmakers did offer a substitute for the education bill the governor preferred. It provided that private and denominational schools could share in the public school funds. West vetoed the rather blatant proposal, saying he regarded such a law as a blow to the American public school system, which should prevail in Utah as it did elsewhere. His strongly worded statement against the Mormon educational proposals revealed valid grounds for his immediate and long-term disgust with Mormon politics and the church leaders' seemingly unchanged attitudes toward government.[7]

A development that was particularly unsettling to Utah Gentiles was Cleveland's removal of Chief Justice Charles Zane, almost universally respected among non-Mormons. The president's associates had been promising Mormon agents that they would replace the Republican judge for a long time, but there had been difficulty deciding on his successor. Frank J. Cannon, the son of President George Q. Cannon, spent over two months negotiating a policy that he claimed would allow the government and the Mormons to settle outstanding difficulties over polygamy. Essential to the plan was the appointment of a judge who would allow Cleveland to pledge him "to show leniency to every man who should come in and make voluntary answer to process in court." It was understood that if a humane and just judicial policy were guaranteed, it would bring from hiding many Mormon polygamists who would "rather go to prison for a short time and then be free than to continue in their present unfavorable circumstances."

Through Frank Cannon's efforts, President Cleveland decided to appoint Elliot F. Sandford, who the Mormon emissary was convinced would follow the program of cooperative leniency. The New York judge received his appointment as Zane's replacement on July 9, 1888.[8] At about that time Congress created a fourth judicial district for Utah territory, which according to accepted practice enlarged the Supreme Court there to four members. Cleveland designated John W. Judd of Tennessee to fill this new position, and he received his appointment the same day Sandford was given his.

In early July, Caine recommended to the president and solicitor general that the new judges should be advised of the administration's policy regarding the Mormons. Caine emphasized that the apointees "should be made to understand that they were not going as missionaries to interfere with religion or politics, but were to administer the law in justice and in the spirit of humanity." The delegate was subsequently able to interview both Sandford and Judd and confided to his Salt Lake brethren that such a message had indeed been conveyed to them. Sandford was quoted as responding that he would not go to Utah if anyone expected him "to torture the law into an engine of persecution against any people or their religion." Judd pledged that he would administer the law "in a spirit of moderation and kindness." [9]

Several days before the new appointees were announced, a meeting was held at the Salt Lake City Chamber of Commerce to initiate a petition asking President Cleveland to reappoint Judge Zane. It can only be assumed that, as a chamber activist, Governor West was among those who agreed to sign such a plea. The document was still being circulated for further signatures when the telegraph brought word of Sandford and Judd's selection. This was undoubtedly a disappointment to many Utah Gentiles and would be even more so when evidence of the policy to be implemented became apparent. [10]

Even before the new judges arrived in Utah, Frank Cannon reported that President Cleveland and his acting attorney general, George A. Jenks, had assured him that if George Q. Cannon would surrender and submit to trial, he would be treated with fairness. Such arrangements were promptly made and on September 17, 1888, the church leader surrendered, was quickly brought to trial, pleaded guilty, and waived delay of sentencing. Judge Sandford pronounced such a light sentence that *Tribune* Liberals were noted to be "blue with rage." It was after this uproar that Governor West drafted his negative report to the secretary of the interior. [11]

Another development in mid-1888 demonstrated that political unity in Utah was yet illusory. It involved a group of young native sons of Utah who, though generally of Mormon parentage, were but nominally involved in the spiritual affairs of the church. Many had pursued their education outside the territory and had returned, often to practice law. This group had been growing restive under the local restrictions and contentions and had sought political means of alleviating the strife. Some concluded this could best be accomplished through the organization of Democratic clubs. These clubs, established between 1884 and 1887, espoused doctrines of states' rights highly critical of the Liberal party proposals that had urged Congress to dominate the local affairs of Utah.

On the other hand, they were equally opposed to the continued Mormon defiance of the anti-polygamy statutes then in force in the land and had little sympathy for the Mormon contention that such laws were unconstitutional.[12]

In the late spring of 1888 a Democratic territorial convention was called to elect two delegates to the party's national convention. Members of several of these dormant clubs selected representatives to attend. It was an open secret that any delegates holding ties to the L.D.S. church would not be seated, but four duly elected Mormons from as many different counties nevertheless attended the Ogden meeting. But a committee on credentials quickly excluded the Saints, and a resolutions committee soon decreed that membership in the Democratic party could not be given to anyone also a member of the Mormon People's party. The delegates in question refused to relinquish their seats until finally, amid an increasingly disorderly demonstration against them, they became convinced they had no chance to particpate. The four L.D.S. delegates withdrew, but they and their fellows would vocally reappear in the aproaching fall election campaign.[13]

The Mormon hierarchy and leaders of the People's party had been watching the Ogden proceedings with interest. Soon after news of the expulsion of the Mormon delegates reached Salt Lake City, Wilford Woodruff, George Q. Cannon, and six apostles met with People's party chairman John R. Winder. After some discussion, they concluded that "considering the fracas at the Democratic Convention in Ogden it was decided not to further organize politics among the Saints at present."

Despite disappointment with local Democrats, loyalty to the national party leaders continued. Deliberations among the general authorities indicated concern over what the Republican party national platform would say on the Mormon question.[14] The party, true to its lifelong anti-Mormon traditions, did devote a critical paragraph of the platform to the Saints. Noting the undue political power the church exercised in the territories, the Republicans pledged more stringent legislation not only to "divorce the political from the ecclesiastical power," but also to stamp out polygamy.[15]

Soon thereafter, Caine, who had previously expressed apprehension regarding both party conventions and platforms, noted the negative repercussions even upon the Democrats. Through the efforts of friends of the church, the Democrats had remained silent on the Mormon question. But Caine observed that Republican mention of the subject was a serious blow to their immediate prospects because "it will frighten the Democrats, who politically have not half the courage of the Republicans." The implication was that the statehood effort would receive no encouragement from even the supposedly friendly party during the difficult presidential election campaign.[16]

Nevertheless L.D.S. church leaders and their political assistants remained firmly committed to Cleveland's candidacy. In late July Caine said, "I believe his reelection will bring us some deliverance," though adding realistically that it would do neither the president nor anyone else any good to proclaim such sentiments "from the housetops." Upon request, church leaders sent $25,000 to assist in Cleveland's national campaign.[17]

Territorial status meant that Utah residents could not vote in the presidential elections. But after Cleveland was renominated by the Democrats, party members were encouraged to hold a territorial ratification convention to voice approval of the choice. Again the local party functionaries worded the call in such a way as to exclude Mormons from participation in the gathering to be held at Provo. The Gentile Democrats convened as planned. After endorsing Cleveland, the resolutions committee addressed the major local issue, stating that Utah's admission under existing circumstances would be "a lasting disgrace to the republic, because it would fortify behind state lines an ecclesiastical hierarchy whose principles are in favor of the domination of the church in the temporal, as well as spiritual affairs of men." The delegates further resolved it would still be impractical to place Democratic candidates in the field for local offices or delegate to Congress, which was an actual pledge of continued support for the Utah Liberal party.

The *Herald*'s account of the Provo proceedings was aptly headlined "Democrats desert their colors and become Liberals." In the same issue this organ of the People's party repeated the summons to its own territorial convention slated for October 8. But in the intervening days the established parties were compelled to share attention with a persistent effort by young Mormon Democrats to rejuvenate their partisan movement.[18]

That week was general church conference, when great numbers of Latter-day Saints from throughout the territory took advantage of reduced railroad rates to gather at Salt Lake City. An impromptu meeting of Mormon Democrats was called and approximately 100 individuals gathered for what proved to be a twelve-hour session. Amid numerous speeches, Samuel R. Thurman of Provo was nominated as a candidate for delegate to Congress. Fervent pledges were made to support him in the race against the Liberal and People's party nominees. For several days thereafter the press showed considerable interest in the fledgling party. The *Tribune* derisively labeled it the "Sagebrush Democracy." But the party members accepted the nickname with pride, citing the Utah truism that "noone ever knew sagebrush to grow on unfruitful soil." The *Herald* was initially supportive, but after Caine, one of the paper's owners, was renominated by the People's party as its congressional candidate, the paper cooled markedly toward Thurman.[19]

Two weeks later Thurman and several close supporters met with church and People's party leaders. The Sagebrush Democrats requested the meeting to explain what they thought was a misunderstanding regarding their action in forming the party. Referring to the ouster of their friends from the Gentile convention at Ogden the previous spring, they confessed one purpose for attempting the organization of a true version of the Democratic party was to divide the Liberal party. They denied any desire to harm the People's party. Woodruff and others expressed the opinion that a great mistake had been made. The church leaders did not wish to find fault with these brethren, but concluded that they "should not try to draw votes from the People's party but should get out of the mistake as best they could." Although Thurman and his associates continued to campaign, they garnered only 511 votes on election day. Caine had no trouble being returned for another term in Congress.[20]

The Latter-day Saints were not nearly as happy with the outcome of the national elections of 1888. Not only was Cleveland defeated by Republican Benjamin Harrison, but the Republicans gained control of both houses of the national legislature. This was met with considerable gloom among the Mormons, as Abraham H. Cannon reflected when he asked privately, "Does it not mean great oppression for the Saints?" He noted that anti-Mormon victory celebrations indicated a similar interpretation of the outcome.[21]

In subsequent days Caine was frequently asked what the election outcome had done to Utah's prospects for admission to the union. The delegate said he did not and could not know until he had consulted with Democratic leaders when the new session of Congress began the following month. But all discussions among the Mormon hierarchy reflected a strong desire for another concerted effort to achieve statehood before the Republicans took office the following March.[22]

Early in December Mormon agents C. W. Penrose and F. S. Richards returned to Washington, D.C., for a last-ditch fight. They met with the lame-duck president for a full hour, first conveying the regrets of their people at the result of the election. The main thrust of their visit was to apprise the titular head of the party of the political implications of the situation for the Democrats. They candidly explained the impossibility of church agents exercising maximum political influence in the West while Utah remained in its helpless territorial status. Cleveland was warned that there was a growing number back home who were "inclined to the belief that perhaps the Republican party would be more likely to accord them political freedom than the Democratic party," which was not living up to its principles by denying them local self-government. The president was reported to be favorably impressed by the suggestion that Utah should be joined to the other territories in the statehood attempt, and he promised to see Speaker John Carlisle on the matter and suggested northern Democrats who should also be visited.

Following this advice Penrose and Richards met with William S. Holman, who expressed himself as willing to vote for having all the territories enter the union at once. S. S. Cox, another congressman suggested by the president, was also contacted, but his response was far less encouraging. The venerable New York representative expressed himself as primarily concerned with the admission of Dakota as two states and thought Utah's effort should be kept separate. He was especially worried about Republican opposition to the Omnibus bill and other Democratic measures concerning the territories. He believed that the rival party was planning to take these matters into their own hands in a special session after their newly won congressional majority took office in March. However, he said he would comply with the decisions of his party caucus.

One of the most important visits the Mormon agents made was to William Springer. At first he had said Utah did not have a chance that session. But after the sponsor of the Omnibus bill had heard the views of the Mormon agents on the political situation and their "probable political influence in other territories" once statehood was obtained, Springer agreed to the proposition of admitting all the territories at once. He conceded that was the only way to get Utah admitted and mentioned that since the Democrats were going to make a concession to the Republicans in allowing two Dakotas, there was a chance for reciprocity concerning Utah. The chairman promised to present the matter at an upcoming party caucus.[23]

The outcome of the Democratic congressional caucus, held in December, 1888, was a great disappointment to the Mormons. Caine described the general feeling there as one of kindness toward Utah, with hardly a harsh word spoken concerning the territory or the church. But, he said, it was "very evident from the first that the members of the caucus had not the courage of their convictions. They were afraid to do for Utah what they felt in their hearts was their duty to do, and what they knew the territory was entitled to receive." The delegate was given a generous time allotment to present Utah's claims. He was followed by Carlisle, who admitted "the gentleman from Utah has made a very strong appeal in behalf of that territory." But, Caine reported, in spite of the justice of the claims for statehood, the Speaker was "not in favor of complicating the Omnibus Bill with any matter that would give the Senate a semblance of an excuse for rejecting it." Carlisle also added that he did not wish the Democrats to be open to the accusation by people of the other territories of encumbering the bill with a provision bound to induce a negative vote from the Senate. Caine felt the Speaker's comments carried great weight in the caucus. Carlisle's fellow Kentucky congressman, W. C. P. Breckinridge, followed with remarks that Caine considered very favorable. He called attention to the fact that "in leaving Utah out of the bill they were rejecting the claims of the only territory which was certain to come in as a Democratic state." However, the caucus voted to support the Omnibus bill as it was, without Utah. As soon as this vote was final, in the midst of confusion in which some members began to leave the hall, J. H. Blount made a motion that the caucus recommend at least a separate bill for the admission of Utah. J. H. Outhwaite spoke strongly in favor of Utah. Cox voiced himself in opposition, saying sponsoring Utah's admission would be "a fly in a pot of ointment." The recommendation passed for a separate bill.[24]

After the adjournment of the caucus, Penrose noted considerable dissatisfaction among prominent senators and representatives concerning the action taken toward Utah. He told the First Presidency that "they recognize the value of our influence to the party," and were aware of the threat of violent opposition if Utah had to stand alone in efforts for statehood. Several friendly members admitted to Penrose that "they could not afford to vote for Utah by itself because of the prejudices of their constituents, but would vote for a general bill" that would include Utah with the other territories. The most friendly senator, Wilkinson Call, thought Utah could be admitted alone, but it would be ten times more difficult than if the question were acted on in conjunction with the other territories.[25]

Though Caine had been particularly disappointed at Springer's lack of leadership in Utah's favor at the caucus and elsewhere the Mormons continued to work with him. They received a copy of amendments that Springer proposed to add to his Omnibus bill, which included a special proviso on polygamy for Utah. The alternative proposal of the Mormon agents simply added "and Utah" where appropriate to the original Omnibus bill, to tie the cause to the general statehood movement. Caine renewed his efforts to win the approval of the territorial committee members, and though there was again some progress, it was not enough.[26]

Amid these efforts, the First Presidency of the church received a document that they passed to the Quorum of the Twelve Apostles for discussion, saying only that it came from "friends in the East." Lengthy and full of quotations from the Mormon Doctrine and Covenants (although

Apostle Heber J. Grant observed that the scriptural citations were not correctly used), the document's main thrust was to ask Latter-day Saints to conform their lives completely to the laws of Congress and to have church leaders sign the paper. It was clearly written by individuals sympathetic to the statehood movement, probably by John W. Young at the behest of congressmen like Springer, who were still justifiably apprehensive about the polygamy situation. Some church authorities did not automatically reject the possibility of complying with the request, though none considered the benefits promised sufficient to justify the course. Others firmly stated they could accept such a change only if it came as "the Word of the Lord through the servant of God whose right it is to speak." That servant was Wilford Woodruff, who, though not formally installed as president of the church for several more months, was already president of the Quorum of the Twelve. At the conclusion of the discussion, Woodruff affirmed that "the Lord never will give a revelation to abandon plural marriage," noting that "we cannot deny principle." [27]

These conclusions, communicated east, were probably decisive in convincing key Democrats that the decision recently made at the caucus was still the proper course to follow concerning Utah. The disheartened Caine asked church leaders for advice as to whether to continue pressing for statehood with a separate bill. He expressed the opinion that such effort should be made if only to keep their claims fresh in the minds of congressmen and not lose the benefit gained in the previous months. Unless the agents received direction to the contrary, they would carry on for Springer had agreed that Utah's agents would be heard in committee hearings in January, 1889. The Mormons, with some hesitation, decided to make the best of it, especially when they learned the representatives of the Liberal party were also scheduled to be present. [28]

During the week of January 12th, 1889, extensive hearings on Utah statehood were held, with five persons on each side giving testimony. Richards and Caine led the proponents; Baskin, Idaho Delegate Fred T. Dubois, and Governor West were among those speaking against Utah's admission. Proceedings were lengthy, with the time equally alloted to each side. Thereafter, the House Committee on Territories took the matter under advisement. [29]

As a prolonged debate on general statehood questions progressed on the House floor, Congressman Charles Dougherty made a brazen attempt to improve the Democrats' position. Though Springer sought to block the move, Dougherty presented an amendment including Utah and Arizona in the Omnibus bill, saying that he did not see why a bill originating with the Democrats should admit all of the presumably Republican territories and keep out the Democratic ones. He did not see why

Utah should be excluded, since her people were fully qualified for statehood and were among the most reliable Democrats in the country. The reaction described in the *Congressional Record* as applause and laughter may have been closer to ridicule when he expressed belief "that it is bad politics for any party to admit territories in such a way as to increase the strength of their opponents and keep out territories which would add to their own strength." Arguing that party leaders should do "all that is honest and fair to strengthen their party," he said, "Let in Arizona and Utah; they will both be Democratic States. New Mexico will also be Democratic." The speech doubtless won few supporters and the proposal was quickly killed.[30]

Although the majority of the House committee would have been willing to report favorably a separate Utah admission bill, in the absence of real pressure from the Mormon emissaries they chose not to do so. Instead the subcommittee responsible for the matter weakly explained that owing to the lateness in the session, it was impracticable to secure passage of the bill, and therefore it was quietly ignored until the Democrats went out of power a month later.[31]

The House did pass a statehood bill for New Mexico, Washington, Montana, and Dakota. The Senate passed one too, dropping New Mexico from its version. The ensuing deadlock was finally broken when Cox offered an amendment abandoning New Mexico and favoring two Dakotas. Prior to a specific vote on whether or not to exclude New Mexico, Springer made an impassioned plea in favor of that territory. In that debate the major reason given for dropping the Democratic territory from the bill was that if the House did not give in to the Senate on that issue, it might endanger chances for admittance of the other territories included in the bill. Some congressmen actually stated that they were in favor of statehood for New Mexico but not at the expense of denying it to the Dakotas, Montana, and Washington.[32]

The Republicans held the Democrats in a hopeless position, especially with the threat of an immediate special congressional session to deliver statehood solely through Republican auspices if the Democrats failed to share the credit by cooperating. Realizing this, the Democrats surrendered. North Dakota, South Dakota, Washington , and Montana were granted enabling acts as President Cleveland signed the Omnibus bill on February 27, 1889. This was less than two weeks before the terms of the president and the Democrat-dominated House came to an end. It marked the close of Utah's sixth unsuccessful attempt at admission into the union.

Though finished, in Utah at least it was not forgotten. The next year, at a private gathering of leading Mormon politicians, Caine criticized Congress for not admitting Utah to statehood. He blamed the Democrats for not insisting that all the territories come into the union when the other omnibus territories did. The delegate pointed out that if all of the territories had been brought in together the Republicans would not possess the large number of western senatorial seats they had subsequently gained. In a letter of that year to George L. Miller, the prominent Nebraska Democrat who had once been an emissary to the Saints from the Cleveland administration, Caine even more candidly indicted his party: "I believe the Democratic party by its cowardice on the Mormon question through its refusal to admit Utah with an anti-polygamy constitution has lost the control of four states which the Mormon people could have given it, viz. Utah, Idaho, Arizona, and Wyoming." He recalled the argument of the recently deceased S. S. Cox in the House Democratic caucus that if they entertained the proposition to admit Utah with the territories then asking admission, "Utah would be a fly in the ointment," concluding that "in straining at the fly the party lost the ointment, pot and all. In rejecting the only certainly Democratic territory they lost all the new states and the control of the government, for many years to come." Caine further argued that the Mormons had "always been true to the Democratic party, but the party when in power, did not appreciate them and failed to take advantage of the strength which they could have given it." He observed that many congressional Democrats recognized and regretted "the short sightedness of their leaders." This was a prophetic statement as far as loss of party allegiance was concerned, and was partly true as to Democratic leadership.[33]

It is not certain whether Cleveland ever had the interview with Carlisle he had promised before the crucial December caucus. Carlisle was still a close political friend of Governor West, who was then becoming realienated from the Mormons and who had that month telegraphed the Speaker strongly opposing statehood. Other presidents at other times have certainly taken a more active role when party fortunes were at stake. However, Cleveland had already been repudiated at the polls and had long since lost much of his influence on Capitol Hill.

In an era when the party was notably deficient in leaders with foresight concerning party fortunes on a national level, there are other Democrats who could be singled out for a share of the blame for beginning the process of alienating a sizable segment of Latter-day Saint voters. The most powerful "friends" the Mormons had to depend on in Congress were William L. Scott in the House and Arthur P. Gorman in the Senate. According to the information reported back to Salt Lake City, Scott was apparently absent from Washington, D.C., most, if not all, of the decisive month when the fateful caucus was held. Gorman made some visits in behalf of Utah, but considering the power he wielded in the party, he was hardly valiant in the cause.[34] Yet it must be conceded that Speaker Carlisle and Congressman Cox were probably correct in the assumption that if party members attached Utah to the Omnibus bill they would bring about its defeat in the Senate.

When the session of Congress had ended, John W. Young, who had been a prime mover at the inception of the Utah admission movement two years previously, wrote to a friend to lament that the "campaign for statehood tapered out to a rather small point." He regretted that the plan originally formulated had not been followed and that in his opinion none had been instituted in its place. Actually, Young's overoptimistic dispatches may have been part of the problem. It is clear that some powerful Democratic leaders expected an adjustment of the plural marriage system in Utah. Although he, on occasion, commented that key Democratic contacts wished the Saints would conform to the standards of the nation, the Mormon emissary too often assured Mormon leaders that they could actually achieve statehood while evading real concessions on plural marriage. No such change had been forthcoming and thus there was no basis for persuading Congress to make the concessions necessary to implement the original plan.[35]

In March, 1889, when the Republican administration took office, the Latter-day Saints were almost entirely without means of airing their concerns within the highest circles of party power. Caine did his best, through regular channels, to prevent the most openly anti-Mormon aspirants for office from being appointed. Acknowledging a lack of influence with the Harrison regime, the delegate frankly asked church leaders, "Can you not ask your San Francisco friends [Badlam and Trumbo] to aid you with this administration." They certainly would do so—in due time.[36]

Meantime Democratic territorial officials were being promptly replaced. Utah Commission Chairman Ambrose B. Carleton was asked to resign, and a fourth Republican was added to the five-member body. Caleb W. West lasted but little longer before being removed in favor of Arthur L. Thomas, the long-time *Tribune* ring functionary and Utah commissioner. And most important, Chief Justice Sandford was removed with Zane replacing him. Although not marked by the bitterness of the previous anti-polygamy crusade, the new officials and their supporters would preside over difficult times for the Utah Saints.[37]

The era proved to be a transition. This was imperceptible at the time, but can now be recognized as significant in that a gradual shift in the political sentiments of some Mormons was beginning to take place. It would take several years before the mutual animosities between Mormons and Republicans would be sufficiently dissipated to allow any Latter-day Saints to consider entering the ranks of that party, but alienation from the Democrats was a necessary first step. And this was already under way.

In January, 1889, the *Salt Lake Herald* editor bitterly denounced the Democratic party for denying Utah entrance into the union. He particularly condemned the party congressional caucus for refusing "to be saddled with the responsibility" of advocating Utah statehood. Another editorial commented that the Republicans had been open and outspoken in the opposition to Utah's admission, while the Democrats "were sneaking about and dodging the question." The editor further argued the Democrats "didn't have the courage of the Republicans, though they were just as mean." If the Democratic party was not solely responsible for disappointments, including the failure of statehood, during the year 1889, it certainly seemed to some L.D.S. observers to lack willingness to stand by the Mormons in time of adversity.[38]

By that time the Mormon hierarchy was increasingly disappointed with local Democratic politicians who had been instrumental in causing important issues in Utah and Idaho to be decided against church interests. Besides passage of the anti-Mormon test oath, framed by a Democrat and enacted with aid from that party, democratic Governor Edward A. Stevenson cooperated in calling for an Idaho state constitutional convention which promised inclusion of the oath. Democratic Judge Charles H. Berry had recently upheld the test oath in the territory. A case involving the test oath had been appealed to the U.S. Supreme Court, and the outcome was among the gravest worries in Mormondom.

Concerning Utah, the national Democratic leaders had similarly assured Mormon authorities that they intended to be lenient in carrying out the economic mandates of the Edmunds-Tucker Act. But even before the end of Cleveland's administration, it was increasingly difficult to recognize fulfillment of the promises, mainly because the law had so clearly aimed at destroying the temporal power of the Mormon church. The Democrat-dominated territorial courts had affirmed that the defunct corporation of the church did hold property in excess of the legal limit. And when the excess was confiscated and placed in the hands of receiver Frank H. Dyer, also a Democrat, it was consistently reported as being squandered and poorly administered. This case too had been appealed to the highest court in the land and that forthcoming decision was also a source of great apprehension at the beginning of 1890.[39]

Besides the anxiety over these court cases, one of the most upsetting developments of the year was the loss, for the first time, of control of municipal governments in the two most populous cities in Utah, Ogden and Salt Lake City. Territorial officials and Liberal campaign directors may have generated more bitterness and desperation among the general body of Latter-day Saints at this time than had been felt even at the most difficult part of the anti-polygamy raid.

In Ogden the influx of non-Mormons into this important railroad center had been marked, and the number of L.D.S. voters on the registration lists had been considerably reduced through the Edmunds-Tucker Act, which barred all women and polygamists from voting. There was also a rift among People's party forces over whether candidates should be selected in advance by the central committee or nominated directly by the party convention. Some local church leaders resented the "hoodlum" defiance through which the party membership chose the candidates. But the major contributor to the defeat was election fraud and the inability of the Mormons to obtain redress of grievances related thereto.[40]

Predictably, those who lost the closely fought election alleged irregularities. Registration lists indicated a Liberal party advantage, but even before the election the Mormon politicians were claiming a majority of legitimate voters, despite the fact that some Saints, barred from registration, had appealed to the Utah Supreme Court, which on the eve of the election denied a rehearing of the lower court decision. When the election results were announced, the People's party newspaper, the *Ogden Standard*, reported that Mormon poll watchers had been consistently frustrated in their efforts to prevent non-resident Gentiles from illegally voting, since "the challenges were rapidly made and as rapidly over-ruled." The party spokesman minced no words in stating that "there was every appearance of fraud being practiced," referring to the large influx of residents from Utah mining camps and Wyoming railroad sections present on the streets of Ogden on election day.[41] Bernard DeVoto has depicted the scene more vividly than pages of more scrupulously accurate documentation could. He said that after the Mormons had voted all day long in Ogden "the polls closed. Then, out of nowhere, came rigs galloping; hard men descended on the polls, lifted the ballot box. . . . Down the Weber and Ogden rivers flowed streams of ballots sanctified by the Lord's chosen. . . . An hour before the polls closed all the locomotives in the railroad yard began to whistle. Two specials roared in from Echo, Wasatch, Evanston, and points east. How many Irish clambered down from cars and roofs and tenders history does not estimate. But they streamed uptown and began to vote. They voted the payrolls of the U.P., the registers of the Chapman House and the Broom Hotel, the tax-lists of Evanston, and every other document that bore names. Then reversing first and last names, voted again." The author knew whereof he wrote because his father was one of the half-dozen anti-Mormons blamed by L.D.S. leaders for masterminding this important Liberal victory, which they had good reason to conclude had been gained through illegal means.[42]

Soon after the Liberal mayor Fred Kiesel and his associates took office, marked changes began in the metropolis. Liquor laws were relaxed, and the supervision of vices was considerably slackened. The reputation of Ogden's 25th street red-light district began at that time. There was apparently even some Gentile concern about the changes brought about by the leniency of the new city government. Judge H.P. Henderson of the Federal District Court called the attention of the Ogden grand jury to the fact that gambling and prostitution were against the laws of the territory. When that jury ignored the situation, Arthur Pratt, the U.S. marshal in charge of the Ogden region, notified the parties involved that if they did not cease these illegal practices, he would prosecute them himself. The *Salt Lake Herald* eagerly kept tabs on these developments in an effort to discredit the Gentile government of the sister city to the north.[43]

By this time interest in the municipal elections of Salt Lake City was gaining momentum, even though the most crucial contest was still six months away. School trustee elections at the time indicated greatly increased Gentile voting strength and, conversely, apathy on the part of Mormon voters. Church authorities recognized this danger and commenced laying groundwork fo r what some recognized would be perhaps the greatest municipal election struggle in Utah territorial history. Besides calling on their most astute politicians for advice on how to conduct the campaign and encouraging People's party recruitment efforts, church leaders relieved two of the most popular young apostles from all traveling assignments to make them available for political speeches in the community until after the February, 1890, elections.[44]

One of the concerted efforts launched was to increase the number of potential Mormon voters within the city. On October 7, 1889, at the close of the semiannual general conference, members of the hierarchy met with stake presidents from throughout Mormondom. The imminent danger, including the probability that the Liberals intended to bring in all the miners, railroad graders, and every other available man to vote at the February election, was carefully depicted. The brethren were told that it would take their best efforts to foil the plan. According to the newly sustained Apostle Abraham H. Cannon, "It was proposed that those stakes who could spare young men to come to this city and acquire residence so as to be able to vote, do so, and that we here provide employment and pay for such."

Several days later, the Quorum of Twelve Apostles decided that members of the People's party in the city council should be approached to see if they could do something "to give employment to a lot of new voters." The next day Abraham Cannon and others met with those men, and it was agreed "to employ on city business a large number of workmen."

The compliant city leaders decided that the emergency was sufficient reason to begin building the joint city and county building, which had been discussed and planned for some time. The city already had some 330 men installing sewer lines and related projects and Mayor Francis Armstrong hesitated to enlarge its undertakings. But upon investigation some interested councilmen discovered that the treasury contained approximately $100,000 unencumbered dollars, which the Gentiles would certainly spend if they won. Thus the way was cleared for extensive street paving and developing the water supply in City Creek Canyon, with the city council quietly resolving to employ immediately between 200 and 400 additional men "on public improvements until after the election."

Meantime, individual church members were asked to help in similar ways. For example, John W. Young consented to furnish work for 100 men hauling rock from his quarries. Some consideration was also given by George Q. Cannon and others to the erection of church college facilities and a long-contemplated, Mormon-owned first-class hotel. And the need for work projects was one of the circumstances that led to the demolition of the old Endowment House, where polygamous marriages had reportedly taken place.[45]

Although only part of the employment projects materialized, there was a considerable influx of new potential People's party voters. Joseph Christensen, a Gunnison resident recently returned from an L.D.S. mission to Sweden, was probably representative of those who came to Salt Lake City at this time. In his diary he states that he was "called on a political mission" to the city to vote and thereby help prevent anti-Mormons from obtaining political control of the area. Much of the scheme was eventually thwarted by Liberal voter registrars, who barred these new residents from the polls, even though they had technically complied with the election laws.[46]

Church leaders also encouraged their sizable number of unnaturalized adult males to qualify for citizenship in time to be legal voters by election day. But this effort was also resisted by Liberals, who recognized the threat to their interests. In November the matter of Mormon naturalization was investigated at special sessions of the district court in Salt Lake City. Associate Justice Thomas J. Anderson, a Democrat appointed during the last days of Cleveland's administration, directed the proceedings. Not only did Judge Anderson bar confessed polygamists from the polls, he even denied the franchise to church members who did not believe in plural marriage. In his most important decision in late November, 1889, Anderson argued that since the aims and practices of the church were "antagonistic to the government of the United States, utterly subversive of good morals and the well being of society," aliens who were members of the Mormon church were unfit to be made citizens of the United States.[47]

While the hearings in Judge Anderson's court were still pending, Young came to Salt Lake City and took occasion again to argue to President George Q. Cannon that it was an opportune time for the First Presidency to make a statement in court that instructions had been given that no more plural marriages would be solemnized. Cannon did not favor such action but said that President Woodruff was the only one who could make such a decision. Young approached the venerable president, who, according to his secretary, L. John Nuttall, made the question a matter of prayer. As a result of such inquiry, Woodruff received what he claimed to be divine revelation. The essence of the message, as recorded by Nuttall on November 24, 1889, was that the presidency should not deny God's Word and Laws concerning salvation of men and they should make no pledges or concessions in court or elsewhere at that time. Even if these men had, it is doubtful if the court could have been swayed.[48]

Reversals in the Salt Lake City election campaign continued to be of grave import to many Latter-day Saints as 1890 began. Because of Judge Anderson's recent decision, hope had vanished for increased People's party voters through naturalizing immigrants. But greater expectations prevailed over efforts to insure that all current Mormon citizens were properly registered and eligible to vote. The day Anderson announced his decision, church party committeemen Heber M. Wells and Richard W. Young appealed to Utah Commission Chairman G. L. Godfrey to convene the commission because of the importance of the approaching municipal election and especially because of the questionable actions of Salt Lake voter registrars.[49]

The Utah Commission's primary responsibility was to oversee voting in the territory, and it had seldom become directly involved in municipal contests. The members did recognize the probability that the Salt Lake campaign would be heated, and prior to adjournment of their regular session in 1889 they had restructured the city's election machinery. A new chief registrar and five deputies were appointed, all of whom were Gentiles the commission considered competent and of good repute. They also carefully outlined the registration procedures through a detailed circular. However, upon receiving allegations against the appointees, Colonel Godfrey called a special meeting of the Utah Commission for December 10, 1889, at Salt Lake City, directing Wells and Young to prepare their charges against the registrars.[50]

The People's Party representatives alleged the registrars were conducting their tasks in a highly partisan manner. The charges consisted mainly of the ease of registration Liberals enjoyed as compared to the inconveniences experienced by People's party registrants. When the Utah Commission pressed for fuller substantiation Attorneys Young and James H. Moyle called a large number of witnesses. The accused were able to justify some of their actions, but serious allegations of preferential treatment for non-Mormon voters stood unrefuted. Although on December 19, 1889, the Utah Commission reiterated the duty of the registrars to enroll all applicants fairly, there was a notable exception. If the registrar had evidence of the falsity of an affidavit or oath required by law, he was justified in refusing the entry of the applicant. This essentially nullified the Mormon contention that if a prospective voter could prove compliance with the citizenship and residence requirements, and was willing to take the required oath, the registrar had no authority to refuse registration. Although the Utah Commission exhorted the registrars to conduct themselves without bias, both sides in the conflict understood the real implications of the decision.[51]

The image of both Utah commissioners and voter registrars was further tarnished a few weeks later when the Liberal party nominated four of the registrars as candidates for municipal office. The *Deseret News* charged that this was a reward for "notoriously unfair manipulation" of supposedly nonpartisan duties. As evidence, the paper stated that during the Liberal party proceedings, opposition to E. R. Clute's candidacy for assessor was quieted by reference to his heroic party service as registrar. The paper also denounced a situation in which the candidates themselves were the very persons empowered to judge cases of challenged voters.[52]

As testimony at the hearings made clear, the registrars were particularly on the look-out for would-be Mormon voters who had recently "colonized" in the city. Even those who had technically fulfilled the minimum requirement of six months' residence in the community prior to election were judged unacceptable. The *Herald* admitted that many newcomers might be temporary, but, as the newspaper correctly observed, "many of them are in every particular qualified voters" who could only be excluded from the polls through violations of the canons of justice. There is no doubt of intentional Mormon colonizing; however, in balance this was in every sense more legal than the methods used by the Liberals.[53]

While People's party colonization efforts were being frustrated by the biased registrars, their opponents were similarly engaged, but meeting with more favorable treatment from the territorial officials. According to People's party spokesmen, Liberal agents were traveling in the rural areas and along the railroad lines "drumming up men" to come to Salt Lake City to vote their ticket. It was reported in mid-December that an employment bureau had been established to provide work for the Gentile recruits. A sample of these tactics, which the *Salt Lake Herald* chose to reprint daily on its masthead, was a note from John Whitbeck at Nephi to Liberal campaign chairman Orlando W. Powers, stating that "the bearer of this wants to vote, look after a job for him."[54] Soon the People's party paper was detailing even more outrageous incidents.

One chain of circumstances embarrassing to the Liberals unfolded in the Salt Lake press in late January. Ernst F. Warner, a young tuba player in one of the Liberal campaign bands, died suddenly. His obituary naturally appeared in the *Tribune*, including the date of his recent arrival in the city. The *Herald* immediately called attention to the fact that the deceased's name was on the voter registration lists, without the requisite length of residence in the territory or the city. The Liberal organ futilely tried to explain and to turn attention elsewhere by denouncing the *Herald* for defaming a dead man. But the facts were irrefutable.[55]

The most sensational revelation appeared in the January 31, 1890, *Herald*. Gross Liberal registration irregularities had been documented by private detective John Bonfield. Recently retired from the Chicago police department, where he had previously achieved national fame as a witness and prosecutor in the Haymarket bombing affair, Bonfield had been employed by the People's party and had dispersed agents throughout the non-Mormon communities of Utah. The boldest scheme that he discovered was of a small train chartered from the Denver and Rio Grande Railroad, purportedly to transport a small deer hunting party. Actually the several passengers carried the Salt Lake City voter registration book of registrar Clute. According to the Bonfield report, the train stopped at the sections along the railroad line where dozens of workmen were engaged in grading. At each stop, according to notorized statements published in the *Herald*, the men were invited to enter a car, nicely fitted as a saloon at one end and a voter registration table at the other. Those who agreed to enter their names and come to Salt Lake City on a free train to be provided at the proper time were offered liquid refreshment.[56]

After the January revelations, the *Herald* noted a "wholesale weakening and wavering" among those who knew that with detectives on the prowl voting fraud could now bring a jail sentence. The paper predicted that "a large number of Liberal voters will therefore not appear on election day." It sarcastically reprinted Liberal Chairman Powers's warning that those who had not been residents for the requisite period and were "wrongfully on the lists" should definitely not vote. In response to continued People's party allegations of "packing the registration books," Powers offered to have any illegally entered names stricken, if they could but be pointed out to him. But Mormon party strategists discerned an ulterior intent to discover which voters were endangered and which were yet safe. There was no such cooperation from the People's party headquarters.[57]

Both camps of political contestants worked diligently to generate voter enthusiasm. Each expended great sums of money on uniforms for their extensive marching clubs and bands. The Liberals held more rallies and especially torchlight parades midway in the campaign, but the People's party culminated its crusade by staging the greatest demonstration of its kind yet held in Utah. Despite a heavy snowstorm on January 10, at least nine different bands and drum corps converged on the Salt Lake Theater. Over 3,350 marchers were counted, many in uniform and thoroughly drilled. During a considerable portion of the proceedings, the air was said to be full of the finest fireworks display many had ever seen. Even Chief Justice Zane, then an admirer of few things Mormon, was impressed with the costly display and public participation.[58]

Finally, after the longest and most bitter campaign—some said—in the history of the West, election day arrived on February 10, 1890. Both parties carefully watched each polling place. Numerous People's party members were barred from voting, although some won their cases upon appeal and were allowed to cast ballots. The *Herald* reported that during the day several Liberals were arrested for illegal voting, but as soon as they appeared before the magistrate, bonds were posted by party bondsmen already available for such contingencies.[59]

There was no question of the outcome: the Liberals won all offices. Church leaders had concluded that if the margin of victory was less than 500, they would contest the results vigorously, assured they could document that many fraudulent voters. But the opposing candidates, with only one exception, garnered 510 to 808 more votes than their Mormon opponents. The Liberal celebration was even more boisterous than usual, as could have been expected of the most important victory the party ever won.[60] C. W. Penrose of the *Deseret News* editorialized that "it was not a victory gained, but a robbery consummated, which has given to the Liberals the majority they claim." The *Salt Lake Herald* agreed. On the day after the election, its editors had stated, "We do believe there was rarely if ever a more crooked election." Undoubtedly some Gentiles expected and hoped for a mass exodus of Mormons to the safer hinterlands they still controlled, but the Saints made it clear that they were firmly resolved to remain in their homes and make the best of a bad situation.[61]

The annual report of the Utah Commission commented on the high-pitched partisan spirit rampant during the contest and also enumerated the charges and counter-charges. The commissioners excused themselves from further involvement, stating that they "did not deem it proper to pay heed to articles appearing in partisan newspapers unless some definite and important charge should be made." Although they followed this policy as far as the *Herald* was concerned, they did mention a similar *Deseret News* account of the registration of Rio grande work crews. On February 7, 1890, Godfrey wrote a letter to Penrose inquiring into the basis of the allegations that Salt Lake City registration officers had actually made the "deer hunting" registration trip. Penrose answered that although he took responsibility for the article, he had not written it and had no direct evidence to prove the allegations made. Conscientious investigators may have obtained better information from Bonfield or the *Herald*, but Penrose's disclaimer allowed the Utah Commission to conclude that the Salt Lake City election of Feb. 10, 1890, was legitimate and that "the Liberal party fairly won the day." There was probably not a Latter-day Saint in the territory who agreed, but the experiences of the past six months had made it clear there was nothing they could do.[62]

The traumatic experience of seeing their beloved city pass into the hands of men widely regarded as enemies was only the first in a series of ill effects the Mormons perceived as being ushered in by the election. As some Liberals had confidently predicted, the inauguration of the new non-Mormon city officials produced a considerable boom in real estate in Salt Lake Valley. Property that had sold for $300 per acre three years earlier brought $2,000 or more. When the inclement weather subsided in late March, real estate sales reached over $1 million per week.[63] Throughout the spring there was such extensive construction in the area that available residential property was almost nonexistent and builders seemed hard-pressed to keep up with demand. There were also many new business establishments being erected in the central portion of Salt Lake City. The building boom had little general planning or direction from municipal authorites, and what there was did not have any input from Mormons. Undoubtedly the fact that the face of the center of Zion was being transformed without its builders and previous governors having anything to say about the course it was taking was a source of great frustration.

In the past, under church rule, city improvements had been so few as to verge on negligence. The friendly press, before and after the Liberal takeover, had advocated numerous essential improvements. One such paper, in a two-month period, editorialized for more and better sidewalks, a more extensive waterworks and improved water quality, street signs, sewer system extension, street sprinkling (to eliminate dust), and better street paving. The city council made real efforts to implement programs in most of these areas, but it would cost much more money than the citizens were accustomed to paying.[64]

Taxes were a serious concern. Many old residents fully expected an increase when the new assessments were released in mid-summer. To the notoriety newly elected assessor Clute had gained in the municipal election frauds was added the knowledge that under the prevailing ordinances he could keep 2.5 percent of all funds collected, a built-in motivator to raise taxes. Besides, assessments were made on the basis of the inflated property values, a situation few taxpayers uninvolved in the boom could be expected to understand.[65] When the tax notices were released in late June, the Mormon press described the reaction as one of consternation and indignation. Valuations had been increased 400 percent. Throughout the summer the *Herald* and *Deseret News* argued that the assessor had made a huge mistake and that the city council should move to countermand it. Large numbers of taxpayers from all classes complained at the county court. A massive petition was presented to city council members, some of whom allegedly treated it with contempt. Despite the loud and varied protests, little was accomplished. The Mormon citizens could only resent their new position of helplessness.[66]

The newspapers opposing the current municipal regime also noted that since the inception of Liberal rule there had been an alarming increase in gambling, prostitution, and Sunday saloon activity. L.D.S. spokesmen voiced disgust at these developments but expected little to be done. In early May non-Mormon citizens, including some clergymen, held meetings to protest the spread of vice. At one gathering Judge O.W. Powers attempted to justify the leniency of law enforcement, and he was backed in this by the *Tribune*.[67]

By the beginning of summer the city was filled with a tough, lawless element, which brought on a marked increase in robbery, burglary, and assault. The *Herald* stated that "there never was a time when the criminal element in the city was more numerous, more vicious, more daring or more desperate." The *Tribune* agreed, concluding that "matters have reached a crisis" in that regard. Both papers were especially concerned at that time because of several near tragedies in which armed citizens almost shot men seen lurking in the shadows of night, who turned out to be policemen watching for "footpad" criminals. Despite the fact that the Liberal government had almost doubled the number of policemen, there was little hope, as the Mormons saw the matter, for alleviation of the problem as long as Gentiles ruled.[68]

Besides these municipal matters at the center of Mormondom, there was a host of varied troubles bombarding Mormon consciousness from abroad. The *Deseret News* claimed that the Mormons were currently the target of more plots and conspiracies than any other group in the nation. The immediate concern was a proposition of certain government officials, reported in New York newspapers, that 270 Latter-day Saint immigrants from Germany and Scandanavia be barred from entry. The crisis was averted through the foresight of church leaders and their friends, but there is evidence that further emigration to Utah was discouraged until the crisis subsided.[69]

During what could aptly be called "the year of shocks," the Mormons were faced with numerous causes for concern. There were several questions pending before the U.S. Supreme Court, including the right of "illegitimate" children of polygamists to inherit portions of their fathers' estates, the Idaho test oath, and the disposition of church funds confiscated under the Edmunds-Tucker Act. And related to the church property suits was a change in the Utah public school system finally forced upon Mormon legislators by Gentile Clarence E. Allen. This law would be implemented in Salt Lake City by a school board in which the Saints held only minority membership, and since it appeared likely that much receiver-held church property would ultimately be diverted into the school system, this was a matter of particularly grave moment.[70]

Thus, from the perspective of an unremitting chain of negative developments from the beginning of 1889 into mid-1890, the future looked truly ominous. Church leaders had recently recognized that future outcomes were beyond their control and proposed that a day of fasting and prayer be set aside, "that the Lord may interpose in behalf of His people and preserve them from the power of their enemies and incline the hearts of the rulers of the nation" to look with more favor upon the Latter-day Saints. The special day exhibited more participation than expected, but no immediate changes were noted.

However, by mid-1892 the same church leaders issued another proclamation, calling for their people to voice prayers of gratitude for deliverance "from the evil which environed [them] and which threatened [the Mormons'] overthrow." They admonished the Saints to recall how gloomy prospects had been for the church and how much conditions had improved.[71] The most decisive factor in bringing about such change was a series of concessions that the Mormon leaders made during the last half of the year 1890. Newly sustained church President Woodruff noted in his diary January 1 that 1890 would be an eventful year. At the time there was no hint that he understood how truly crucial it would be, nor was there any evidence that he was yet contemplating the important decisions he would be instrumental in making that year regarding plural marriage. But his "Manifesto" and some earlier commitments on polygamy were close at hand.

NOTES

1. Whitney, *History of Utah*, 3:609–14.
2. Young to Woodruff, Cannon, and Smith, Dec., 1887, [letter 5 located between one dated Nov. 29, 1887 and another Dec. 18, 1887], Young Papers, H.D.C.
3. Caine to Woodruff, Cannon, and Smith, Jan. 28, W. W. Ritter to Caine, Feb. 7, 1888, Caine Papers, H.D.C.; A. H. Cannon Journal, Feb. 4, 1888.
4. Whitney, *History of Utah*, 3:617–23.
5. Ibid., 623; Caine to Woodruff, Cannon, and Smith, Feb. 18, 1888, Caine Papers, H.D.C.
6. *House Executive Documents*, 50th Cong., 2d sess., 3:867–72.
7. Caleb W. West, *Message of His Excellency Governor Caleb W. West and Accompanying Documents*, 28th session of the Legislative Assembly of the Territory of Utah, Salt Lake City, 1888, 6–11; Grant Journal, Jan. 7, 23, Mar. 5–7, 1888; F. D. Richards Journal, Mar. 5, 6, 1888; John Henry Smith Journal, Feb. 10, 16, Mar. 6, 1888; Legislative Assembly of the Territory of Utah, 28th Sess., *House Journal*, 1888, 342–343.
8. Frank J. Cannon to Woodruff, July 1, 1888, Woodruff Papers; A. H. Cannon Journal, May 8, 12, 1888. Frank J. Cannon and Harvey O'Higgins, *Under the Prophet in Utah* (Boston, 1911), 53–81.
9. Caine to Woodruff, Cannon, and Smith, July 2 or 7, 28, Aug. 10, 1888, Caine Papers, H.D.C.; A. H. Cannon Journal, July 22, 1888.
10. Whitney, *History of Utah*, 3:632–33; *Salt Lake Tribune*, July 10, 1888, says petition originated with a Democrat.
11. A. H. Cannon Journal, Aug. 2, Sept. 8, 11, 14, 15, 17, 1888; Whitney, *History of Utah*, 3:634–36; Grant Journal, Sept. 16, 1888; L. John Nuttall [secretary to First Presidency] to Caine, Sept. 25, 1888, Caine Papers, H.D.C.
12. Roberts, *Comprehensive History*, 6:278–81; Alta R. Jensen, *The Unfavored Few: The Autobiography of Joseph L. Rawlins* (Monterey, Calif. 1965), 154–59, 166–70; Scipio A. Kenner, *Utah As It Is* (Salt Lake City, 1902), 137–41.
13. Kenner, *Utah As It Is*, 144–147; *Salt Lake Herald*, May 6, 1888.
14. F. D. Richards Journal, May 7, June 12, 1888, H.D.C.
15. Porter and Johnson, comps., *National Party Platforms*, 79–81; Jason Mack [J. F. Smith] to Caine, June 15, 1888, Caine Papers.
16. Caine to Woodruff, Cannon, and Smith, June 21, 1888, Caine Papers.
17. Caine to Jason Mack [Smith], July 28, 1888, ibid.; William H. Barnum, Calvin S. Brice, and Chauncey F. Black to Young, Sept. 1, 1888, Barnum to Young, Sept. 6, 1888, Young Papers, H.D.C.; Grant Journal, Oct. 15, 23, 24, 1888; J. Mack [Smith] to Caine, Oct. 19, 1888, Caine Papers.
18. Hadley D. Johnson to Caine, Sept. 22, 1888, Caine Papers; *Salt Lake Herald*, Oct. 3, 4, 1888.
19. Kenner, *Utah As It Is*, 137–41; Roberts, *Comprehensive History*, 6:281; *Salt Lake Herald*, Oct. 5–7, 9, 1888.
20. Grant Journal, Oct. 8, 22, 1888; *Salt Lake Herald*, Nov. 1, 1888.

21. A. H. Cannon Journal, Nov. 7, 10, 1888.

22. Grant Journal, Nov. 13, 1888.

23. Penrose and Richards to Woodruff and Smith, Dec. 7, 1888, Penrose Papers.

24. Caine to Woodruff, Cannon, and Smith, Dec. 27, 1888, Caine Papers; *Washington Post*, Dec. 14, 1888.

25. Penrose to Woodruff and Smith, Dec. 19, 1888, Penrose Papers.

26. Penrose to Woodruff and Smith, Dec. 19, 1888, Penrose File, First Presidency Miscellaneous Papers; Caine to Woodruff, Cannon, and Smith, Dec. 27, 1888, Caine Papers.

27. Grant Journal, Dec. 20, 1888.

28. Caine to Woodruff, Cannon, and Smith, Dec. 27, 1888, Caine Papers.

29. Penrose to Woodruff, Cannon, and Smith, Dec. 27, 1888; *House Reports*, 50th Cong., 2d sess., III, no. 4156, 83–295.

30. *Congressional Record*, 50th Cong., 2d sess., Jan. 18, 1889, pp. 948–49.

31. A. H. Cannon Journal, Feb. 7, 1889.

32. Larson, *New Mexico's Quest for Statehood*, 152–155.

33. Caine to Dr. W. W. Woodring, Apr. 21, 1892, Caine to Frank J. Cannon, Apr. 21, 1892, Caine to George L. Miller, Oct. 26, 1890, Caine Papers.

34. Penrose to Woodruff, undated fragment with Dec. 1889 papers, First Presidency Miscellaneous Papers.

35. Young to C. W. Nibley, Mar. 5, 1888, Young Papers, H.D.C.

36. Caine to Smith, Apr. 13, 1889, Caine to Woodruff, Cannon, and Smith, Mar. 20, 1889, Caine Papers.

37. Whitney, *History of Utah*, 3:667–72.

38. *Salt Lake Herald*, Jan. 25, Feb. 7, 1889.

39. E. Leo Lyman, "A Mormon Transition in Idaho Politics," *Idaho Yesterdays* 20 (Winter, 1977), 9–10; Merle W. Wells, *Anti-Mormonism in Idaho, 1872–92* (Provo, 1978), 133–54; William Budge to Jeremiah Wilson, Oct. 21, 1890, Budge Papers; Orma Linford, "The Mormons and the Law: The Polygamy Cases" (Ph.D. diss. University of Wisconsin, 1964), 397–412.

40. Richard E. Kotter, "An Examination of Mormon and Non-Mormon Influences in Ogden City Politics, 1847–1896" (M.A. thesis, Utah State University, 1967), 100–110; Henry J. Middleton, "The Life of Charles Franklin Middleton: A Man and His Times" (M.S. thesis, Utah State University, 1965), 81.

41. *Ogden Standard*, Feb. 12, 1889.

42. Bernard DeVoto, "Ogden: The Underwriters of Salvation," in *The Taming of the Frontier*, ed. Duncan Ackman (New York, 1925), quoted in Kotter, "Ogden City Politics," 152–53; A. H. Cannon Journal, Oct. 19, 1889.

43. Kotter, "Ogden City Politics," 109; *Salt Lake Herald*, July 10, Aug. 3, 1889.

44. *Salt Lake Herald*, July 10, 1889; A. H. Cannon Journal, July 9, 1889; *Salt Lake Herald*, Aug. 6, 1889; H. J. Grant Journal, Aug. 6, 1889; Caine to Cannon, Aug. 15, 1889, Caine Papers.

45. A. H. Cannon Journal, Oct. 7, 17, 1889; Grant Journal, Oct. 12, 17, 18, 1889.

46. Joseph Christensen, "Life and Ancestry of Joseph Christensen," *Utah Geneological and Historical Magazine* 28 (Oct., 1937), 148.

47. *Salt Lake Herald*, Nov. 1, 8, Dec. 1, 1889.

48. L. John Nuttall Journal, Nov. 24, 1889, Lee Library, Brigham Young University, Provo, Utah.

49. *House Executive Documents*, 51st Cong., 2d sess., 13:398–99.

50. Ibid.; Utah Commission Minutebook D, 302–4, Utah State Archives, Salt Lake City.

51. Utah Commission Minutebook D, 307–11, 313–21, 323–28; *House Executive Documents*, 51st Cong., 2d sess., 13:399–406; *Deseret Weekly News*, Dec. 28, 1889.

52. *Deseret Weekly News*, Jan. 25, 1890.

53. *Salt Lake Herald*, Dec. 21, 1889.

54. Ibid., Dec. 15, 1889, for example.

55. Ibid., Jan. 24, 1890; *Salt Lake Tribune*, Jan. 25, 1890.

56. *Salt Lake Herald*, Jan. 31, 1890.

57. Ibid., Feb 2, 1890; *Deseret Weekly News*, Feb. 8, 15, 1890.

58. *Deseret Weekly News*, Jan. 18, 1890; Charles S. Zane Journal, Jan. 25, 1890, Illinois Historical Society, Springfield.

59. *Salt Lake Herald*, Feb. 11, 1890.

60. A. H. Cannon Journal, Feb. 10, 1890.

61. *Deseret Weekly News*, Feb. 22, 1890; *Salt Lake Herald*, Feb. 11, 1890.

62. *House Executive Documents*, 51st Cong., 2d sess., 13:409–12.

63. *Salt Lake Times*, Mar. 22, May 6, July 17, 1890; *Salt Lake Tribune*, May 2, 1890; *Salt Lake Herald*, July 20, 1890.

64. Baskin, *Reminiscences of Early Utah*, 26–27; *Salt Lake Herald*, May 10, 1890; *Salt Lake Times*, May 6, 12, 13, 14, 21, 23, 28, 30, June 7, 1890.

65. *Deseret Weekly News*, July 5, Aug. 16, 1890; *Salt Lake Herald*, Aug. 31, Sept. 2, 1890.

66. *Salt Lake Herald*, June 18, 27, Aug. 9, 31, 1890; *Deseret Weekly News*, July 5, Aug. 16, Sept. 6, 1890; A. H. Cannon Journal, Sept. 1, 1890.

67. *Deseret Weekly News*, May 3, 1890; *Salt Lake Tribune*, Apr. 14, 1890.

68. *Salt Lake Herald*, July 15, 1890; *Salt Lake Tribune*, July 15, 1890; *Salt Lake Times*, July 16, 1890; *Deseret Weekly News*, July 26, 1890.

69. *Deseret Weekly News*, May 24, 10, June 14, July 26, 1890; A. H. Cannon Journal, June 12, 19, 1890; Woodruff, Q. Cannon, and Smith to William Spry, Sept. 29, 1890, First Presidency Papers [Letterbooks].

70. *Congressional Record*, 51st Cong., 1st sess., 6823–24; *Deseret Weekly News*, July 12, 1890.

71. Edward Leo Lyman, "The Mormon Quest for Utah Statehood," (Ph.D. diss. University of California, Riverside, 1981), 265–89.

5

The Crucial Year: 1890

Even though the Mormon practice of plural marriage had become less open and was no longer publicly discussed, the several attempts by officials of the U.S. government to secure concessions from the church hierarchy had been consistently and decisively rebuffed. It is well known that this situation changed in 1890, but why Mormon resistance ended then has not been sufficiently explained. Treatments of Utah-Mormon history of the last half of the nineteenth century almost unanimously agree that the decisive turning point in alleviation of the conflict between the Church of Jesus Christ of Latter-day Saints and the government came with the Manifesto issued by Wilford Woodruff in late September, 1890. However, little attention has been focused on other important developments occuring that year that place the announcement in a clearer perspective. By the time the Manifesto was issued, the Republican party was fully entrenched in Washington, D.C., and was gaining ground in Utah as well. At least some members of the Grand Old Party were no longer as hostile to the Mormon cause as theretofore. In fact, the mutual friendship beginning late in the spring is essential to understanding many subsequent events. Possibly related to this budding relationship were some quiet restrictions placed on the practice of plural marriage even prior to the public announcement. Without question, the series of blows inflicted on the Mormon church from many directions during the previous year predisposed many church members to recognize the need for changes.

The most ominous of all setbacks suffered in early 1890 was the decision of the U.S. Supreme Court upholding the Idaho test oath. This action was particularly serious because it made the subsequent threats of blanket disfranchisement of Mormons through the Cullom-Struble bill possible. The fateful *Davis vs. Beason* decision, written by Stephen J. Field and announced February 3, 1890, fully upheld the Idaho lawmakers' prerogatives as well as the constitutionality of the test oath. The influential justice denounced bigamy and polygamy as crimes against civilization that tended to destroy the purity of marriage while degrading and debasing men and women. And not only practice, but also teaching or advising this practice was a proper subject for punishment as aiding and abetting crime. He had no sympathy for the defense that such activity was entitled to the constitutional protection given to freedom of religion, saying that "crime is not the less odious because sanctioned by what any particular sect may designate as religion." On the main question of the constitutionality of the Idaho test oath, the Supreme Court observed that the law simply excluded from voting or holding office those who have either been convicted of actual offenses or those who advocate resistance to territorial law and approve of commission of crimes forbidden by those laws. The highest tribunal shattered the Mormons' last hopes of further legal contest for their rights when it declared that the test oath was "not open to any valid legal objection to which our attention has been called."[1]

The year 1890 also ushered in further partisan congressional infighting regarding statehood for other western territories. Although Utah did not play a prominent role, the subject was nevertheless of serious concern to the Latter-day Saints. The Republican party made it abundantly clear that it intended to enhance its majority in each house by admitting Idaho and Wyoming. The Democrats continued to advocate the simultaneous admission of those territories along with Arizona and New Mexico. On March 26, Democratic spokesman William Springer expressed regret that the Republicans were unwilling to follow the Democratic precedent of the last Congress and "treat all these territories fairly" by furnishing equal facilities for each of them to come into the union.[2]

Since early in the year, Delegate John T. Caine, attorney Jeremiah Wilson, and the leader of the Idaho Mormons, William Budge, had been working to prevent the admission of Idaho under a constitution that included the test oath. They had carefully prepared arguments to make before the congressional committees on territories, but there was no realistic hope of accomplishing their purpose even before the Supreme Court cut the ground from under them. Republicans controlled both houses, and they encouraged Delegate Fred T. Dubois and his allies at every step of the way. Budge did not even remain in the East for the final outcome, and Caine later reported to him in disgust that the statehood bill would soon pass in both houses "not because the members, even Republicans believe it is right, but because it is a party necessity."[3]

The Democrats continued to oppose the Idaho test oath and were also unimpressed with Wyoming's provision allowing for woman suffrage, believing that these provisions were being implemented for partisan reasons. Springer asked why the Republicans were so firmly opposed to Mormon voting in Idaho, and yet unconcerned with the significant number of such voters in Wyoming. He correctly pointed out that the Wyoming Latter-day Saints mainly voted the Republican ticket, while in Idaho they had for years been unanimously Democrat. Springer alleged that his political rivals "want separate bills to treat these two cases according to the different conditions existing." He further charged that "it appears that Mormonism is objectionable only when the person entertaining that belief is suspected of a desire to vote the Democratic ticket."[4]

Caine reflected similar sentiments along with a more ominous warning in a letter to F. S. Richards. The "Idaho test oath decision threatens to affect our people in all the territories. The Republicans want to make it applicable to every territory in which the Democrats with Mormon votes have a majority."[5] He well understood that such test oaths were not unique to Idaho. Nevada and Arizona legislatures had passed them once, and Republicans in Arizona were even then mounting another major effort in that direction.[6] Caine, who had fought hostile Republican actions throughout his eight years in Congress, feared a similar test oath law would soon be aimed at his territory "and thus saddle that outrage upon Utah for all time." The purpose was obvious to the fervent Democrat, who predicted "the Mormons disfranchised, the territory could very easily be secured and brought into the union as a Republican state." He was convinced the Republicans would "resort to any means" to garner further senate seats for their party.[7]

On April 10 Senator Shelby Cullom introduced just such a bill. It provided that "no person belonging to a church organization teaching or practicing polygamy shall be permitted to vote." The next day a similar bill was introduced in the House of Representatives by Isaac N. Struble. Caine immediately conferred with Wilson about how to counter the onslaught. They concluded that since the test oath had so recently been unsuccessfully opposed before committees of both houses, there was nothing further they could say that would have any positive effect. Caine confided that the distinction that in Utah the disfranchised would be a majority was not sufficient reason to fight the measure openly.[8]

For a time the Mormon representatives hoped the Cullom and Struble measures would meet the same fate as a similar proposal introduced earlier in the session. That one, authored by Robert N. Baskin, who had also written the currently pending bills, had died quietly in committee. But unfortunately for the Mormons, this time their opponents had gathered firm support to help them accomplish their purposes—"to wrest from the hands of the priesthood the political power which it had so long wrongfully usurped and shamefully abused."[9]

The Mormons desperately sought to counter the legislative attack. Caine first suggested encouraging Mormon businessmen to "make a strong and earnest appeal to the firms from whom they purchase goods, to have them use their influence with the members of Congress from their respective districts to defeat this measure." Representatives from a dozen different merchandising and professional enterprises were immediately sent east to generate letters to Congress protesting the economic implications of the Cullom and Struble bills. A considerable amount of mail was forthcoming, though it is impossible to measure its impact.[10]

There is no question, however, of the positive effect of protests from different segments of the Utah Gentile community. Petitions from non-Mormon businessmen in Salt Lake City and Ogden, probably concerned about the adverse economic affect of the measure, more than countered those of the Liberals, which favored passage of the bills. And resolutions passed by the revived Democratic party strengthened the resolve of congressional party members to resist the anti-Mormon onslaught.

On April 22 a group of about 100 men, described as "mostly newcomers," met in Salt Lake City to organize a Democratic club. The gathering was called to order by Colonel T. B. O'Brien, who had only been in the territory a few months. He stated that though it was "something out of the routine to have a Democratic party" in Utah, there were many present who agreed it was necessary. There was evidence at the proceedings that these outsiders considered themselves rivals of the predominantly Republican Liberal party. One of the statements made at the meeting referred indirectly to the Cullom-Struble scheme, saying that "we don't propose to have this great state of Utah pocketed by the Republican thieves."[11] Although the majority attending this meeting were non-Mormons, there were several Saints, like S. A. Kenner, who helped bridge the gap with "sagebrush" Democrats, still nominally in existence. And the party war-horse of former days, Hadley D. Johnson, encouraged further cooperation with the "sagebrushers" in one of his numerous letters to the *Salt Lake Herald* editor.[12]

Three nights after the initial meeting, the Democrats again convened to outline formally their purposes for existence. The preface to the by-laws affirmed that it was time that the "abnormal political distinctions which exist in Utah should be obliterated," and believing that the best interests of the territory were "coupled with the supremacy of pure Democratic doctrine," a formal party structure was established. The article on club membership stated significantly that all male citizens of Salt Lake County who pledged that in secular and political matters their only allegiance was to the United States would be eligible to become Democrats in good standing "without any other or further test" except for regular induction fees and dues.

At this organizational meeting Colonel O'Brien introduced a lengthy resolution protesting the admission of Idaho and the Cullom bill, which was said to be designed to disfranchise innocent American citizens. According to the Republican *Salt Lake Times*, these proposals were not met with universal approval of the participants. After some heated discussion, the matter was tabled for a week.[13] By then it was too late to prevent the Struble bill from being reported favorably out of committee, and the opposition in Utah soon centered on a petition drive. Yet, Caine reported, the formation of the Salt Lake Democratic club had been favorable to the Mormon cause and even the little that had been published of the proceedings had "strengthened the Democrats" in Congress. Springer offered an amendment to the bill providing "that no person shall be deprived of the right to vote, hold office or sit on a jury on account of his religious belief or opinions," but it was voted down by the Republican majority.[14] Struble's committee reported favorably on his bill on April 29, noting that the Edmunds laws had not accomplished the purposes for which they were enacted because the Mormon leaders had advised their people to take the oaths prescribed and continue participation as active citizens. The report appended numerous published statements, mainly from Utah territorial officials, to bolster their contentions that the Edmunds-Tucker Act "had no effect" and was in fact a "dead letter."[15]

Progress of the Cullom and Struble bills stirred considerable controversy in the Salt Lake Chamber of Commerce. It was known that Governor Arthur L. Thomas and former Governor Caleb W. West were both in Washington, D.C., at the chamber's expense, ostensibly in the interest of promoting allocations for a federal buildings program in Utah. But their names were so linked to Baskin's in the anti-Mormon legislative effort that the *Salt Lake Times* felt constrained to disavow any responsibility for sponsorship of the measures by the chamber of commerce.[16] As criticism of Thomas and West's activities continued, a significant number of chamber members "winced under the censure heaped upon its representatives and indirectly upon itself" for apparent violations of its cardinal rule against political or religious involvement. At a public meeting of the chamber, on May 5, 1890, Elias Morris, a respected Mormon manufacturer, addressed the group concerning the need for unified business efforts. He challenged those present that if they were indeed advocates of Utah prosperity, they should raise their voices against disfranchisement. This placed chamber vice-president Fred Simon, a Jewish clothing merchant, in a difficult position. He acted immediately to declare the speaker out of order. Morris incurred the chairman's warning by pursuing the subject, even alluding to West and Thomas's activities. Simon's statement that "the gentleman shall confine his remarks to manufactories or take his seat" was widely applauded as Morris resumed his seat.[17]

It is difficult to ascertain if this incident began the series of steps subsequently taken by the chamber of commerce against the Cullom-Struble bill. An indication that the key figure in those developments had not yet become convinced of the ill effects of the measure is that Simon's name appears on a petition being circulated in early May favoring passage of the bill. However, Simon soon reconsidered and became the leading sponsor of an even larger list of names of Gentile Salt Lake businessmen who were opposed to passage of that law.[18] In a letter dated May 23 to West, his longtime associate in the chamber of commerce, Simon sought to explain his reasons for opposing the controversial law. He reminded the former governor that the small body of Mormons most active in their chamber of commerce had been "the balance wheel" that kept that organization from becoming just another political clique of businessmen. He pointed out that the anti-Mormon measure was "conceived in hatred and vindictiveness," and "the moment the Cullom Bill passes, every Mormon who has worked hand in hand with us in the past in the building up of our city and territory must from that moment take an opposite direction." He continued that if the measure were passed non-Mormons must thereafter regard every Latter-day Saint as a conspirator. To attempt to build a commonwealth with more opponents than supporters in Utah would be like building upon a foundation of sand.[19]

In a similar letter to Thomas, Simon recounted efforts of the anti-Mormons to induce withdrawal of his signature from the petition against the disfranchisement bills and to prevent these documents from being sent to the Senate. He recognized that his course was political suicide to a career which had already included a term as deputy U.S. surveyor general for Utah. Possibly the discrimination he had felt himself because of his religious beliefs helped strengthen him as he courageously stood his ground.[20]

Several other factors helped to divide the Gentiles over the Cullom-Struble bill. The *Salt Lake Herald* editors warned that should the law be passed "the commercial unity" developed during the past several years would disappear and the deep-seated prejudices would reappear. The paper also called for non-Mormon citizens to speak out against the pending legislation and applauded those in Ogden who were doing just that.[21]

Franklin S. Richards wrote to Caine and George Q. Cannon at the nation's capital, saying that after overseeing the preparation of protests from among the Saints, he had concluded it was imperative that attention be directed to an effort at securing "remonstrance from non-Mormons." In his first interviews with what he termed some of their fairest friends, he found considerable hostility toward Mormon political methods and little sentiment against the disfranchisement measures. But when he adopted the argument that such laws would retard economic growth in the territory, he struck a more responsive chord. Soon, he said, a number of men representing different elements of the Liberal party were influencing their friends to oppose the Cullom-Struble bill. While much of Richards's initial success was in Ogden, he also mentioned the success he had through personal contact with O'Brien. Simon's name did not appear in the letter, but it is easy to see how Richards's efforts could have had some influence upon him, too.[22]

Early in 1890 Wilford Woodruff sent Cannon to Washington, D.C. After a month of disappointing struggle there, L. John Nuttall, a trusted assistant who had just discussed the political situation with Cannon, reflected some discouragement with the old party allies when he confided that "the Democrats should not see us used up in Utah, Arizona, Idaho, and New Mexico for then they lose four states." He added that Cannon and Budge had gone to confer with Arthur P. Gorman on such matters. The Maryland senator was still leader of the Democrats in Congress, and the Mormon leaders were seeking the highest authorities the party had. Later that evening Budge left for New York to determine when he and Cannon could confer with Calvin Brice, chairman of the Democratic National Committee.[23] Obviously satisfactory response from Democratic leaders was not forthcoming at these interviews, because a few months later, when Cannon returned to the East, he began a long association with similarly prominent Republican party leaders. With the aid of Isaac Trumbo, the California lobbyist helpful to the church authorities in the past, Cannon allied with important members of the Republicans in the fight against the Cullom-Struble bill.[24]

During his several years of intermittent service in behalf of the Mormons, Trumbo had enlisted the cooperation of several prominent Republicans. His sometime employer, Leland Stanford, had been urged to discuss the Mormon question with the intolerant Benjamin Harrison. Morris M. Estee, who had been chairman of the Republican National Convention that nominated Harrison for the presidency, became involved in lobbying activities in behalf of the Saints through Trumbo. As the legislation to disfranchise the Mormons was being discussed in congressional committees, Trumbo also appealed successfully for help from the chairman of the Republican National Committee, James S. Clarkson.

Clarkson soon became a leading advocate of the viewpoint that if the Mormon citizens were treated more fairly by the party, favorable political results were likely to occur. As Clarkson willingly embarked on his labors with Trumbo, they approached Secretary of State James G. Blaine, the most influential of all Republicans, and secured his influence in behalf of the Mormons. Clarkson claimed that Blaine's powerful appeal at a private congressional committee hearing successfully stemmed the anti-Mormon tide of legislation. Defeat of the Cullom-Struble bill was certainly a complex operation, but in fact Trumbo had engaged the aid of some of the most powerful Republicans in the country.[25]

In mid-May prospects for passage of the Cullom-Struble bill seemed bright. The bill had been reported favorably in the House and was apparently following a similar course in the Senate. In desperation, Caine called on one of the few Utah Mormon Republicans, his former assistant, Frank J. Cannon, to speak before the Senate Committee on Territories.[26] In Cannon's lengthy remarks, the young Ogden newspaper editor emphasized that the Cullom-Struble bill punished a "class of people who have obeyed the laws, who have avowed that they are willing to continue to obey the laws, and who swear that they will not aid or abet anybody else" in the practice of polygamy. He argued that polygamists had already been disfranchised and therefore it was only those who were willing to swear to the Edmunds-Tucker oath who were now to be so barred. He testified that to his knowledge polygamy was a dying institution and that the younger generation had little sympathy for it. Making clear his Republican preferences, he expressed regret that his party, recognizing it could not secure a majority of votes outside the metropolitan centers in Utah by respectable means, would resort to other methods. Following the lead of friendly Democratic Senator Matthew C. Butler, Cannon explained that the doctrine of plural marriage could only be nullified by what Latter-day Saints considered divine revelation through the designated prophet—a matter over which church members had no control. He concluded, "Our parents were punished for an act, but this bill proposed to punish us for a thought." Influential as this testimony was, what the young emissary stated behind the scenes was even more effective.[27]

Although Caine introduced Cannon as having been in the East by chance, he was actually summoned at the behest of his father, George Q. Cannon. After arriving there he held a crucial interview with Blaine, a friend of his father's from their earlier congressional years. The secretary of state told Frank Cannon to make personal pleas to individual members of the congressional committees on territories, with Blaine offering his quiet aid with hesitant members. He also stated significantly that while the Mormons would not be harmed "this time," permanently preventing disfranchisement would only be possible if the Saints would "get into line." [28]

When he reported Blaine's comment to George Q. Cannon, Frank Cannon claimed his father informed him that "President Woodruff has been praying. . . . He thinks he sees some light. . . . You are authorized to say that something will be done" in regard to the retrocession on polygamy. Frank Cannon visited members of the Senate committee and informed them confidentially of pending concessions by the church concerning plural marriage. With this he claimed to have prevented the Cullom and Struble bills from progressing any further. [29]

Cannon's account is essentially corroborated by the author of the bills, Robert N. Baskin, who later wrote that the Senate committee had decided to report his bill favorably. Then he was informed by Senator Cullom that "he had been assured by a delegation of prominent Mormons, that if further action on the bill was delayed for a reasonable time, the practice of polygamy would be prohibited by the Mormon church." The Liberal lobbyist was informed that the church delegation "had requested that further action on the bill be temporarily delayed." Explaining that Struble was told the same thing, he recalled the delay was granted, but with the clear understanding that if polygamy was not prohibited within a reasonable time, vigorous action on the pending bills would be resumed. Though his disfranchisement measure never became law, Baskin credited the threat of it with being "the last straw" which forced the issuance of the subsequent Woodruff Manifesto. [30]

In the month following the Senate hearings, Frank Cannon's brother Abraham was in New York City for medical treatment. While visiting with his father there, he was shown a paper drafted by Blaine, who expressed hope that church authorities would accept it. Young Apostle Cannon described the document as making "a virtual renunciation of plural marriage." The dedicated polygamist said his feelings revolted at the prospect of signing such a promise. [31]

When George Q. Cannon arrived at Salt Lake City, he reported to fellow church leaders on the political outlook, saying prospects were brighter for Utah than they had been in many years. That he had alluded to some tantalizing possibilities with Republicans is indicated from a later conversation on the subject in which he is quoted as saying that "we would doubtless have been disfranchised by the Struble Bill if the Republican leaders in Washington had not been given to understand that there were Republicans in Utah and that a wise course on the part of the Republicans would doubtless make more." Cannon was also quoted by his son Abraham as being optimistic that despite continuing anti-Mormon activity, "the Republican party are [sic] becoming more favorably impressed with regard to the importance of securing Mormon votes and influence." In reflecting on the political discussions he had heard that day, Abraham Cannon stated "the Democrats might have won several states had they but possessed sufficient courage when Cleveland was President to admit Mormons to political power, but they failed to do so and now realize their loss."[32]

Undoubtedly George Q. Cannon's recent experience in the East had great influence on the crucial decisions made in a meeting of July 31, 1890. At that time Cannon and Woodruff met and discussed politics with at least four prominent Mormon Democrats, Apostle Heber J. Grant, F. S. Richards, C. W. Penrose, and Richard W. Young. It was reported that the Democrats of Montana, Idaho, and Wyoming were anxious to "get Mormon votes" and had approached church members for that purpose. After some discussion it was decided not to help Democrats in any of these states, but to aid Wyoming Republicans "as a reward to Delegate [Joseph] Carey and his party for getting Wyoming admitted as a state without anti-Mormon legislation." Abraham Cannon's detailed account of this meeting includes the telling observation that "the Democrats when they had the power to do us good were afraid, and betrayed us so that now we feel as though the Republican party should be tried to see if they will be fair to us." The contrast between Idaho, where the Saints had voted Democrat, and Wyoming, where they voted Republican, was on the minds of those present. Abraham Cannon, usually an avowed nonpartisan, concluded that "self-protection demands that we look to the Republicans for relief, now that the Democrats have proved themselves cowards on our question."[33]

Abraham Cannon had recently noted the private reading of an important First Presidency resolution in regard to plural marriage made on June 30, 1890. It was to the effect that no such marriages would be permitted to occur "even in Mexico unless the contracting parties, or at least the female," was resolved to remain in the Mormon colonies recently established there, largely by polygamists.[34] This is a most significant announcement, as it is the first mention of the concession on plural marriage made that year. Though the Woodruff Manifesto issued almost three months later has usually been emphasized as the most important step, it was merely the public announcement of the policy previously implemented. This earlier change of position came soon after Cannon's visits with Blaine and his Republican associates and whether intended to do so or not, at least partially fulfilled the promises the Cannons had made.

Further insight into the new church policy may be gathered from a letter that President Joseph F. Smith wrote to his good friend and fellow church leader Charles W. Nibley, dated July 18, 1890. Nibley had inquired about the possibility of a mutual friend (possibly himself) then taking another plural wife. Smith replied that he approved of the idea in principle but confessed that "times have changed, the conditions are not propitious and the *decrees* of the powers that be" are against the move. He explained that he was referring to powers within the church, though prudence dictated they also defer to governmental authority. Smith further stated "the *decree* now is that there shall be no p———— m————s [plural marriages] in the United States, and that there should be none anywhere else—unless *one* or both of the parties remove beyond the jurisdiction of the government to make their home." He did not profess to know how long this condition would prevail, but what he described as an almost "absolute prohibition" was for the present the law of the church. He spoke discouragingly of the prospect that the family of the woman in question would allow her to live in Mexico, alone much of the time, and attempted to convince the applicant that he was already involved enough in plural marriage to satisfy any requirements of God's law on the subject. But he did assure Nibley that "should the clouds roll by and the gloom pass away . . . it would be altogether a different matter."[35]

While word of the church position quietly spread through Mormon circles, Gentile territorial officials were not informed and continued to seek further legislative measures to pressure the Saints into submission. The most active agency was the Utah Commission. At the August 7, 1890, meeting of the commission, R. S. Robertson was assigned to gather the material for the annual report to the secretary of the interior. The commissioners agreed that a special object of the report should be to present a full and accurate statement of the "existing status of the polygamous question—including such facts and statistics as may show, or tend to show the increase or decline of the practice." After Robertson's subsequent draft was considered and to an extent altered, it was adopted and forwarded to Washington, D.C.[36]

The Utah Commission report, made public soon after, charged that forty-one males had entered polygamous relations in the territory since the previous annual report. There was substantial evidence of one well-publicized case, but documentation of the other forty marriages was extremely dubious, much of it coming from reports of voter registration officers, which gave no details. The obituary columns from Mormon newspapers noting the deceased had left more than one wife was the only evidence presented to bolster the charges. What was being reported seems to have been older polygamous relationships only recently discovered by territorial officials and therefore treated as new marriages.[37] In the ensuing months, during discussions mentioning the Utah Commission report, Mormon leaders referred to the alleged new plural marriages as a blatant falsehood. These denunciations were not made for public consumption, but appear to be the candid and spontaneous expressions of church authorities who had banned further polygamous marriages in Utah and were angered over what they considered an unmerited indictment.[38]

Late summer was a busy time for the First Presidency. As soon as they returned from a short trip to New Mexico, the men embarked for San Francisco. It has been implied that their purpose was to confer with national political leaders; however, there is little evidence for this supposition, and Abraham H. Cannon specifically stated that the purpose of the California visit was that the presidency wished to absent themselves to avoid being subpoenaed as witnesses before the court in matters related to the church property suits.[39]

In their absence hearings were commenced before Colonel M. N. Stone, a special commissioner appointed by the Utah Supreme Court to review the accounts and actions of Frank H. Dyer, the former receiver of escheated church property. A primary purpose of the proceedings was to determine if an earlier decree of the Supreme Court had prevented further government efforts to secure church property not already in the hands of the new receiver, Henry W. Lawrence. The U.S. attorney for Utah, C. S. Varian, indicated a special interest in the Utah temples located in St. George, Logan, Manti, and Salt Lake City. The main criticism of Dyer was that he had allowed a compromise between government and church attorneys enabling the four Utah temples to remain in Mormon hands. Varian appeared to be probing for an opening through which the church suits could be reopened sufficiently to allow government confiscation of the temples. Varian wished the hearings to remain in session until Woodruff could be compelled to testify, but on at least one occasion the official summons-server was unable to locate that gentleman. The presidency out-waited their would-be inquisitor in California. However, as soon as they returned, church attorneys undoubtedly warned of the danger to church property, including temples.[40]

Within a week after his return Woodruff confided in his diary his oft-quoted observation, "I have arrived at a point in the history of the Church of Jesus Christ of Latter-day Saints when I am under the necessity of acting for the temporal salvation of the church." He referred to government attempts to suppress polygamy as the main reason for making his declaration, but "the temporal salvation of the church" could easily have also referred to the temples.[41]

Apostle Marriner W. Merrill, then specifically in charge of the Logan Temple, discussed the impending announcement with Woodruff as it was about to be released. He commented in his journal that the Manifesto "seems the only way to retain the possession of our temples and continue the ordinance work for the living and dead which was considered of more importance than continuing the practice of plural marriage for the present." This was later corroborated by other statements, including some by Woodruff.[42]

Moses Thatcher, another apostle who had occasion to speak with Woodruff just before the announcement was made public, found the president anxious about false statements published about the church by the Utah Commission. Woodruff feared "great trouble was coming unless something was done to offset their publication." Thatcher also noted Woodruff's apprehension that Congress was about to enact further legislation inimical to church members.[43]

These were worries pressing upon the prophet. But none of them was new. Pressures at least as serious had been withstood in the past. Even if the church was figuratively backed to the wall and practical considerations demanded concessions, that does not necessarily deny the possibility of the divine inspiration Woodruff and his associates claimed as his ultimate motivation. George Q. Cannon later told of the numerous earlier suggestions from within and outside the church that such action be taken. He explained the time chosen in terms easily understood by fellow believers by simply saying that "at no time has the Spirit seemed to indicate that this should be done. We have waited for the Lord to move in the matter." Finally, he said, on September 24, Woodruff felt what he deemed to be spiritual direction, and the Manifesto was the result.[44]

On the afternoons of September 24 and 25, 1890, the First Presidency and several apostles met and considered the text of the momentous announcement Woodruff had drafted. After careful examination and discussion they agreed with its contents as worded. With such approval, what became known as the Woodruff Manifesto was released to the Associated Press and forwarded to Delegate John T. Caine at the nation's capital.

Upon receipt later that day, Caine arranged to have the announcement printed for distribution to the leading men of the government and the press. Publication of the document labeled "An Official Declaration," dated September 25, appeared in the *Washington Evening Star*. It was accompanied by a letter from Caine to the editor, which criticized the Utah Commission report. Charging the commission's object was to bolster chances for passage of pending legislation, particularly that to disfranchise non-polygamous Mormons, the delegate expressed hope this announcement would thwart the attempt. Caine's actions, undoubtedly in accordance with instructions, suggest that countering the Utah Commission report was a primary purpose of the Manifesto.[45]

The opening paragraph of the Manifesto indicates the same intent, with the one following being an answer to the specific charge that a plural marriage had taken place under church supervision within the past year. After reference to the court decisions upholding the laws prohibiting plural marriage, Woodruff affirmed his intention to submit to those laws and to use his influence with church members to do likewise. He pointed out there was nothing in his recent teachings that could be construed as encouragement or even mention of polygamy. He concluded, "I now publicly declare that my advice to the Latter-day Saints is to refrain from contracting any marriage forbidden by the law of the land."[46]

Press coverage of this announcement was extensive. The *Salt Lake Tribune* automatically doubted its veracity, saying that it did not come "in the authoritative manner in which orders of the church are generally clothed" and that Woodruff spoke "merely as an individual." Placing emphasis on the term "advice," the *Tribune* claimed that he "does not speak as though that advice had come authoritatively by revelation." When the *Salt Lake Herald* retorted that no one except the *Tribune* had ever claimed the Official Declaration was a revelation, the latter editor rejoined, "If the Saints do not understand it as a revelation, but simply as the words of a weak old man then it will not count as against the former declaration which all Saints have been taught to understand was a revelation."[47]

Although word of the Manifesto spread quickly throughout the Mormon communities, most general authorities withheld comment until the regular quorum meetings beginning September 30. There they freely expressed their impressions regarding it, recorded in considerable detail in the journals of Heber J. Grant and Abraham H. Cannon. They exhibited awareness of the need for the announcement to alter the increasingly negative public opinion regarding that aspect of the church. Several apostles agreed with Grant who, referring to the ban within the United States, stated that "President Woodruff had simply told the world what we had been doing and if there were any advantages to secure by the Manifesto I feel that we should have them."[48] The most striking aspect of the apostles' comments at this time was the indication that as far as they were concerned personally the declaration hardly applied at all. It was merely a ban on contracting new marriages in the United States. Several expressed their intention to continue their present marital arrangements. John Henry Smith pledged that the only thing that would restrain him from living with all of his wives would be incarceration in prison. His close associate, Francis M. Lyman, endorsed that sentiment: "I design to live with and have children by my wives, using the wisdom which God gives me to avoid being captured by the officers of the law."[49]

At the time the Manifesto was released, President Joseph F. Smith wrote to his plural wife Sarah, then residing in Nephi, that she would soon likely hear of a "pronunciamento by Prest. Woodruff in relation to our political and domestic status" that would "no doubt startle some folks." He assured her that "it will not startle *you*, neither will you be worried about it for you and the rest of us are all right." He explained that it was only "those who could and would *not*, and now can't, who will be affected by it. *They* may growl and find fault and censure, but *not those* who have done their whole duty."[50] Here it is abundantly clear that those who had already been obedient to the divine injunction to enter plural marriage were considered beyond the sweep of the declaration. It was more an announcement of the fact that other Latter-day Saints had procrastinated too long and would not now be able to enter into living the declared higher law.

Another reason for the pronouncement of the Woodruff Manifesto can be proposed. In the early summer of 1890, at the time George Q. Cannon was in the East fighting the Cullom-Struble bills and negotiating with Blaine, his fellow counselor in the First Presidency confided to Nuttall, "We are making a strong effort to *do something* in defense of the rights of our '*monog*' brethren. I hope we can do as much in their behalf as they have done in ours."[51] It is entirely possible that the intention of the Mormon hierarchy was to absolve the formal church organization of responsibility for the continuance of plural marriage. This being accomplished, those charged with polygamy or unlawful cohabitation might then be prosecuted as individuals, without their cases directly implicating the Church of Jesus Christ of Latter-day Saints as a whole. Under such circumstances monogamist Mormons could not justifiably be disfranchised, and the continuing efforts for statehood would be less encumbered by plural marriages of some who happened to be church members.

In further discussions among the general authorities there was some question as to what additional action was needed regarding the Manifesto. During general conference the first week of October, 1890, this question was resolved by a telegram from Caine, who reported that the secretary of interior had informed him he could not recognize the official declaration unless it was formally accepted by the conference. Consequently the church leaders decided to present it immediately.[52] The next day one of the church's most popular orators, Orson F. Whitney, addressed the huge throng at the Tabernacle. He prefaced his remarks by reading the tenets of the L.D.S. religion as summarized by Joseph Smith's "Articles of Faith." There was probably special attention given to the one which states: "We believe in being subject to kings, presidents, rulers and magistrates, in obeying, honoring and sustaining the law." After Whitney had read the text of the Manifesto, President Lorenzo Snow made a motion that it be accepted by the congregation, which was done apparently without dissent.

These actions were followed by important contemporary justifications for the declaration, by Woodruff himself and his counselor, George Q. Cannon. Cannon recounted an instance from Mormon history when a Missouri mob had prevented the Saints from carrying out what they considered a divine injunction to build a temple at Jackson County. He followed by reading what was accepted as a revelation to Joseph Smith relieving them of their divine charge, with condemnation laid on those preventing completion of the task. Cannon then stated that it was on the same basis that Woodruff felt justified in issuing the Manifesto.[53]

President Woodruff followed, reminding all that, given his age, he was not long for this world and soon expected to meet his predecessors and his God. Claiming the Manifesto had not been issued without earnest prayer, he testified, "For me to have taken a stand in anything which is not pleasing in the sight of God, or before the heavens, I would rather have gone out and been shot." Woodruff explained that it was not his purpose to "undertake to please the world," but with laws enforced and upheld by a nation of 65 million people, reality must prevail. "The Lord has given us commandments concerning many things and we have carried them out as far as we could, but when we cannot do it, we are justified. The Lord does not require at our hands things that we cannot do."[54]

Throughout this time, the leading opponents of the church continued to criticize the Manifesto. Among these was an interview by Governor Thomas in the *San Francisco Chronicle*, pointing out that the declaration "in no way asserts that polygamy is wrong or the law right." The *Deseret Weekly News* replied "There is nothing in President Woodruff's declaration in regard to faith, or doctrine, or tenets, but it contains a volume in a few words as to practice." It was only with practices, not beliefs, that laws and governments were empowered to impose conformity. The *News* editor commented in disgust that the demands involving limitations on beliefs carried matters further than church leaders had thought they would need to go in their concessions.[55]

That was the problem. Possibly some national government officials had indicated that something like the Manifesto would suffice, but it was now certain that territorial officials and their newspaper allies would not let the Mormons off easily. The L.D.S. hierarchy obviously did not intend to disrupt present polygamous marriages or renounce belief in plural marriage. But if they had possessed assurances that they had done all that was necessary, further requests for the government to clarify their present status would not have been so promptly forthcoming.

Such an appeal was sent by Woodruff to E. C. Foster of the U. S. Department of Justice less than a month after the Manifesto. After acknowledging Foster's previous letter, which had expressed concern for the humane treatment of those still imprisoned for unlawful cohabitation, Woodruff stated that his people would gladly avail themselves of any clemency the government saw fit to grant. He hoped that a "better understanding would be reached as to the treatment that can be lawfully extended to the women who have entered into plural marriage and their offspring." He explained that some of his brethren's continued hesitation to make court promises to obey the law was because judges had construed unlawful cohabitation laws in such a manner that many felt it would be "dishonorable in them, and would amount to an entire repudiation of past obligations" if they were to promise obedience to laws so interpreted. He gave an example of a man who had visited the home of a plural wife to see his sick child and had been sent to prison on unlawful cohabitation charges. Making his plea specific, Woodruff said that "having acceded to the requirements of the law, it has seemed to us that a more lenient interpretation of what constituted unlawful cohabitation might now be rendered and enforced." After voicing confidence that action would be taken that would be satisfactory to all concerned, he concluded, "The practice being now stopped, those who have innocently entered into this relation should not be made to suffer more than absolutely necessary." [56]

This request for a more acceptable legal definition of unlawful cohabitation and clarification of the rights of plural wives and their children was not met. At the next general conference in early April, 1891, George Q. Cannon described the continuing dilemma of women bound to their husbands with ties as sacred as if they were the only wife. He asked what should be done with them, then expressed a continued hope that the question would be resolved by the action of the government. He significantly stated that he thought this would occur when the government became "convinced of our sincerity in issuing this Manifesto declaring that plural marriages should cease." He implied that they were not yet convinced, undoubtedly because of the negative reports sent to the East by the press and territorial offiials. He therefore admonished the Latter-day Saints to take one more step toward abandoning plural marriage. President Cannon recalled that he had testified of his belief in plural marriage to a president of the United States and that such a faith was embedded into his very being. Yet, he added, he had consented to obey the law. He appealed to each individual to seek spiritual guidance to reconcile this seeming contradiction with formerly held ideas, encouraging all to "trust in our God for the results." Cannon then proclaimed, "I say now publicly that it is the intention of the Latter-day Saints to obey the law and leave the results with the God of Heaven."

The respected church leader was close to asking husbands to avoid even the appearance of cohabitation with plural wives when he stressed that each must "accommodate himself to affairs so that we shall not create a feeling that will be a continuation of the antipathy manifested through the doctrine." Further enjoining the Saints to live so that the world could recognize their sincerity in the matter, Cannon candidly defined what the presidency now felt constrained to adopt as the church's difficult compromise position regarding existing polygamous relationships. He explained, "We have made covenants it is true, but each man must arrange his affairs so that he would not violate those covenants, thereby bringing down the displeasure of God"; at the same time, he added pointedly, each man must also honor the law of the land.[57]

Later in the year Woodruff appeared to go even further toward discouraging any form of cohabitation. By that time church leaders had been given some hopes of recovering confiscated church property in the hands of a government receiver if they could convince certain officials that it would never be used to help promulgate polygamy doctrines. The First Presidency therefore consented to appear in court before Master-in-Chancery Charles F. Loofbourow. In conferences with their attorneys prior to the court appearance, the general authorities agreed "that polygamy had ceased in good faith, and as to the course we will take if it is ever revealed anew, we cannot say, though there is no human probability of its restoration." Although at that time non-Mormon counsel W. H. Dickson stated that law officers had no intention of preventing a man from providing for his family, his former law partner, U.S. Attorney C. S. Varian, sought to elicit testimony to the contrary.

Placing Woodruff on the stand, Varian asked, "Do you understand that the Manifesto applies to the cohabitation of men and women in plural marriage where it already exists?" The witness replied he could not say for sure but thought that "the effect of it is so." Continuing, Woodruff stated that he did "not see how it can be otherwise," adding the prohibition of polygamy was intended to be universal, in foreign countries as well as in the United States.[58]

It was obvious from subsequent private discussions among the general authorities that Woodruff was not satisfied with the impression he had conveyed when placed in a position where he could see no alternative to the testimony he had given. He said that if a man deserted or neglected his plural families he would likely be disfellowshiped from the church. It is clear from this discussion that church leaders continued to advocate the policy enunciated earlier in the year by George Q. Cannon.[59]

An accurate picture of this position can be gained from two letters Joseph F. Smith wrote to concerned polygamists. In one dated December 15, 1891, to Elder Warren M. Johnson of Arizona, he explained God did not require them to put away plural wives, neither did the law say they could not support these families. "What the Lord requires is that we shall not bring upon ourselves the destruction intended by our enemies, by persisting in a course in opposition to the law." Smith expressed the same point in terms of a commandment: "thou shalt keep thy covenants with thy family but thou shalt not break the law of the land." Just as Cannon had commented publicly earlier in the year, Smith said that every man would have to determine for himself how best to do that.

In the second letter, dated December 21, 1891, addressed to I. E. D. Zundell at Deming, New Mexico (the gateway to the Mormon colonies in Mexico), Smith essentially repeated the instructions given in the previous letter in regard to supporting polygamous families. But since the recipient of this communication actually resided beyond the boundary of the United States, Smith's comments in this regard are of additional importance. "The Manifesto is not more severe than the *law*, nor does it apply anywhere except where the *law* applies, only in regard to *polygamy*. The U.S. laws do not apply in Mexico: *there* you must be governed by the Mexican law. The Manifesto applies there only to marriages and nothing more." The implication seems to be that living with plural wives was still more permissible for Mormons in Mexico than for those in the United States. And there the matter was to stand for an indefinite, but lengthy period of time.[60]

Despite the subtleties of private interpretation, the Woodruff Manifesto was sufficient to produce government concessions gradually. A directive was soon sent out from the U.S. attorney general that the law should be enforced in Utah so as to "maintain the status quo and not alienate Mormon citizens." Amnesty for a great number of Latter-day Saints indicted for polygamy or unlawful cohabitation was already being promised by members of the Harrison administration. And the beginning of an amazing transfer of a majority of Utah voters into the ranks of the formerly hostile Republican party, brought about, partly at least, through the evidences of friendship exhibited by party leaders at home and beyond, was not far behind.

As these events transpired, the rival Democratic party, the more friendly of the two to the Mormons for forty years, could only lament the course of developments. The Democrats had consistently sought the kinds of concessions on polygamy finally made in 1890–91. But in the years that party was last in power they had not backed the requests with the kind of pressures the Republicans eventually brought to bear. Ironically, the party using the heaviest hand ended up benefiting the most politically from the transition so rapidly taking place in Utah.[61]

NOTES

1. Linford, "Mormons and the Law," 397–411, 433–35; Wells, *Anti-Mormonism in Idaho*, 138–43.

2. Wells, *Anti-Mormonism in Idaho*, 133–54; *Congressional Record*, 51st Cong., 1st sess., 2701–12.

3. Lyman, "Mormon Transition in Idaho Politics," 24–25; Caine to William Budge, Apr. 1, 1890, Caine Papers, H.D.C.

4. *Congressional Record*, 51st Cong., 1st sess., 2701; *House Reports*, I, no. 39, part 2, 51st Cong., 1st sess., 1–7.

5. Caine to Franklin S. Richards, Mar. 26, 28, 1890, Caine Papers, H.D.C.

6. *Deseret Weekly News*, May 17, 1890.

7. Caine to Richards, Mar. 26, 28, 1890, Caine Papers, H.D.C.

8. *Congressional Record*, 51st Cong., 1st sess., 3227, 3327, 4000, 6654, 10211; Caine to Woodruff, Cannon, and Smith, Apr. 12, 1890, Caine Papers, H.D.C.

9. Caine to Woodruff, Cannon, and Smith, Apr. 30, 1890, Caine Papers, H.D.C.; Baskin, *Reminiscences of Early Utah*, 184. The Caine letter reported to church leaders that while members of the Utah Commission were in the nation's capital, there was a "meeting held at the Riggs House, attended by Governor Thomas, West, Commissioners Godfrey, Robertson, and Saunders, Baskin, Dubois, and some members of the House Committee on Territories, Struble and Dorsey being among the number. The disfranchisement bill was discussed and agreed upon, and it is believed, that Struble then committed himself to the measure."

10. Caine to Woodruff, Cannon, and Smith, Apr. 30, 1890, Caine Papers, H.D.C.; Spencer Clawson to Woodruff and Smith, June 11, 1890, Woodruff Papers; George T. Odell to Caine, June 12, 1890, William H. Lowe, Leonard W. Jennings, and Spencer Clawson to Caine, May 23, 1890, E. C. Simmons to Charles H. Mansur, May 16, 1890, copy, Caine Papers, H.D.C.

11. *Salt Lake Herald*, Apr. 23, 1890; *Salt Lake Times*, Apr. 23, 1890; *Salt Lake Tribune*, Apr. 23, 24, 1890.

12. *Salt Lake Herald*, Apr. 25, 1890.

13. Ibid., Apr. 26, 1890; *Salt Lake Times*, Apr. 26, 1890.

14. Caine to Woodruff, Cannon, and Smith, Apr. 30, 1890, Caine Papers, H.D.C.; *Salt Lake Herald*, Apr. 29, 1890.

15. *Congressional Record*, 51st Cong., 1st sess., 4000; "Hearings Before the House Committee on Territories on H. R. 9265," *House Reports*, 51st Cong., 1st sess., 6, no. 1811, 1–24.

16. *Salt Lake Herald,* Apr. 18, 19, 29, 30, 1890; *Salt Lake Tribune,* Apr. 30, May 1, 1890; *Salt Lake Times,* Apr. 29, 30, 1890; *Deseret Weekly News,* May 31, 1890.

17. Whitney, *History of Utah,* 3:734–35.

18. *Senate Miscellaneous Documents,* 51st Cong., 1st sess., 2, no. 156, 1–3. Because Simon's name is misspelled in the petition urging passage of the Cullom-Struble bill, it is possible someone else added his name to the petition.

19. Fred Simon to Caleb W. West, May 23, 1890, copy in Whitney, *History of Utah,* 3:737–39.

20. Ibid.; Simon revealed some sensitivity stemming from his Jewish background, noting that "the Cullom Bill looks to me more like a 'Ukase' conceived in the mind of the Czar of Russia than a bill framed under the government that is supposed to be built upon the broadest platform existing upon the face of the earth." Earlier in the year it was reported that the Alta Club, to which many leading promoters of the Cullom bill belonged, had adopted a policy of excluding Jews from membership. *Deseret Weekly News,* Jan. 4, 1890.

21. *Salt Lake Herald,* May 11, 1890.

22. F. S. Richards to Caine and G. Q. Cannon, May 22, 1890, Caine Papers, H.D.C.

23. Nuttall Journal, Feb. 14, 1890.

24. A. H. Cannon Journal, May 2, 1890; Cannon and O'Higgins, *Under the Prophet in Utah,* 85–88.

25. Woodruff Journal, Apr. 16–24, 1889; James S. Clarkson to Woodruff, July 11, 1894, copy in A. T. Volwiler Papers, Lilly Library, Indiana University, Bloomington. Clarkson recalled that at the time he and Blaine "were studying the elements of voters in the United States to try to secure a majority for the political principles in which [they] believed." The Republican leaders were impressed as they "learned of the magnitude of the Mormon people, the greatness of their development in many states besides Utah, and the large part that they were sure to bear, for good or evil, in the destiny of this republic." Clarkson explained that Trumbo "came upon the scene and gave to Mr. Blaine and [me] such a practical and accurate knowledge" of the past and present situation regarding the Mormons that they were thereafter able to devise an effective strategy in their behalf. The key event recounted was of Blaine appearing before a congressional committee considering the Cullom or Struble bills, "protesting against such an outrage upon any portion of a free people, asserting that no republic of free men could tolerate such a wrong and live." The writer concluded his typically overlaudatory account of this event by saying to the Mormon leader, "Of course, your people know something of the courage and loyalty of Mr. Blaine towards you in oppression; but the summit and sublimity of it all was reached when he stood in this small committee room and smote down with the giant strength of his indignant wrath this further attempt—in a free government to degrade still further a people already wronged too much." See also Whitney, *History of Utah,* 3:743, an account by a contemporary with access to church general authorities, which also credits Blaine with stopping the Cullom and Struble bills.

26. *Hearings Before the [Senate] Committee on Territories in Relation to the Exercise*

of the Elective Franchise in the Territory of Utah, 51st Cong., 1st sess., microfilm copy, Lee Library, Brigham Young University, Provo, Utah. (These papers may have been privately printed with church funds as had the 1887 Utah commission minority report.) Those present to hear Frank J. Cannon were Senators Platt, Cullom, Stewart, Butler, Payne, Jones (of Arkansas), and Blackburn. Cannon alleged that "the purpose of the bill is clearly to disfranchise us, for the sole reason that being in the majority in the Territory of Utah, it is desirable to our opponents that we should lose the franchise."

27. The final exchange of the hearings was as follows: "Senator Payne: One question more—if in your opinion the young Mormons of whom you have spoken disavowed polygamy, and would have it disavowed by the church if they had the power? Mr. Cannon: They do disavow it two or three times a year, usually. Every time they take this oath [provided for in Edmunds-Tucker Act] they disavow it. Senator Payne: I understand you; but would they have the power to amend the creed of the church? Mr. Cannon: They have not the power. Senator Payne: If they had the power would they do it? Mr. Cannon: I think so. The Chairman: They have not the power because it is a revelation." Ibid., 14.

28. Cannon and O'Higgins, *Under the Prophet in Utah*, 85–91; G. Q. Cannon to Woodruff and J. F. Smith, May 24, 1890, Woodruff Papers, contains a comment possibly of great importance. Cannon, then in Washington, D.C., said, "We shall have time to get in some work and I favor the proposition which Tobias [Trumbo] submitted to you, and which you referred to me, if the party [Republican?] will now accept the business on those terms. I shall do all I can while I am here, and I feel that the Lord has been with us, and that our efforts have been blessed. Tobias has seen Basil [Blaine?] today and he feels all right. Looking over the whole field I think it looks encouraging." Scott Kenney, a knowledgeable scholar on the subject, has suggested that "the proposition" could have been the promise to halt plural marriages within the United States if Republican leaders would halt the anti-Mormon legislation.

29. Cannon and O'Higgins, *Under the Prophet in Utah*, 85–91. Cannon told of conferring with Orville Platt, chairman of the Senate Committee on Territories, and then with other members of the committee. He claimed to have "told them that the Mormon church was about to make a concession concerning the doctrine of polygamy."

30. Baskin, *Reminiscences of Early Utah*, 183–86.

31. A. H. Cannon Journal, June 12, 1890.

32. Ibid., July 10, 1890; Richard W. Young to John Henry Smith, Feb. 6, 1892, and accompanying notorized statement by Young dated Feb. 7, 1892, John Henry Smith Papers, Marriott Library, University of Utah, Salt Lake City; Whitney, *History of Utah*, 3:743, states that one of the arguments used to appeal to Blaine and his associates was that "Utah was not 'hopelessly Democratic' that many of her people were indoctrinated with Republican principles—notably [tariff] protection—and that it was suicidal to antagonize the element that might make Utah a Republican state."

33. A. H. Cannon Journal, July 31, 1891. Republican delegate to Congress Joseph Carey of Wyoming had won Caine's full political support for election to

the U.S. Senate from the new state. He recounted Republican service at the recent Wyoming constitutional convention, where they had "knocked down" the "Mormon Question" raised there by a Democrat. While further describing the political situation in his state, Carey alluded to the test oath controversy in a manner certain to ingratiate himself to the Saints when he declared that his party wanted "no ostracized class in [their] state." See Carey to Caine, Aug. 6, 1890, Caine Papers, H.D.C. See also Edward Leo Lyman, "The Elimination of the Mormon Issue from Arizona Politics, 1889–1894," *Arizona and the West* (Autumn, 1982), 213–15.

34. A. H. Cannon Journal, July 10, 1890; F. D. Richards Journal, July 10, 1890. Quinn, "New Plural Marriages," 40–41, while unfairly stating that I am "unaware of the demographics of polygamy," draws rather heavily on a preliminary draft of this study. He disagrees that the June 30 resolution is particularly significant for two reasons: first, there had been a prohibition on plural marriages in the United States and Mexico in 1889, but these had soon been nullified and essentially disregarded; and second, Quinn observed "a decision cannot be regarded as a concession if it is not announced to those who expect or demand it." It is true that the June policy did not immediately come to the attention of hostile territorial or federal officials, but there is every reason to assume that James G. Blaine and the other friendly Republican leaders who were interceding in the Saints' behalf received notice of the changes more promptly.

35. Smith to Charles W. Nibley, June 20, 1890, Joseph F. Smith Papers [Letterbook], H.D.C.

36. Utah Commission Minutebook D, Aug. 7, 22, 1890, 461–81.

37. *House Executive Documents*, 51st Cong., 2d sess., 13:414–20. The report elaborated on the details of the Hans Jesperson case of Utah County, in which the defendants' own testimony incriminated them of a polygamous marriage in Apr., 1889. The report cited newspaper interviews with church officials indicating confusion and dismay over the case. Woodruff, in an interview in the *St. Louis Globe-Democrat* of Oct., 1889, stated, "I do not understand it at all. It is giving us a good deal of trouble. . . . It seems incredible. If it is true it is against all of my instructions."

38. Caine to George L. Godfrey, Nov. 11, 1890, Caine Papers. Caine asked Godfrey to furnish him any evidence of those entering the polygamic relation since June, 1889. He received no answer. See Caine to Charles W. Penrose, Dec. 19, 1890, Caine Papers. J. F. Smith to L. John Nuttall, Sept. 22, 1890, Joseph F. Smith Papers [Letterbooks], mentions that "the recent bold efforts of the [Utah] Commission and the [*Tribune*] ring to create a furor by falsifying the statements of the Presidency in relation to polygamy may cause a statement of the facts to be made by them, or at least President Woodruff." Smith was probably referring to George Q. Cannon's earlier interview published in the *St. Louis Globe-Democrat*, which the Utah Commission report cited extensively as incriminating evidence. The report clearly misconstrued statements intended to show that while the Mormons continued to believe in polygamy, they were prepared to "bow to the law" and obey it outwardly in their actions.

39. Gordon C. Thomason, "The Manifesto Was a Victory!" *Dialogue: A Journal of Mormon Thought* 6 (Spring, 1971), 37–45; Woodruff Journal, Sept. 16, 17,

1890; A. H. Cannon Journal, Sept. 3, 1890; Woodruff, Cannon, and Smith to
J. A. Fillmore, Sept. 23, 1890, Woodruff, Cannon, and Smith to A. N. Towne,
Sept. 23, 1890, First Presidency Papers [Letterbooks]. These letters make clear
that the First Presidency received the lavish hospitality of Southern Pacific Railroad officials, along with mutual friends Trumbo, Badlam, and Estee. Although
Clarkson was somewhere in the West at the time on U.S. Post Office business,
there is no direct evidence of the church leaders conferring with him or any other
national Republican leader in California. F.D. Richards Journal, Sept. 23, 1890,
indicates that more than one of the presidency were "laid up a few days" with
colds while at San Francisco.

40. *Deseret Weekly News*, Sept. 13, 20, 27, 1890.

41. Woodruff Journal, Sept. 25, 1890. The entry continues from what is
quoted in the text to state that "the United States government has taken a plan and
passed laws to destroy the Latter-day Saints upon the subject of polygamy or pa-
triarchal order of marriage. And after praying to the Lord and feeling inspired by
His Spirit, I have issued the following proclamation which is sustained by my
counselors and the twelve apostles." For the text of the Manifesto, see Appendix 1.

42. Marriner W. Merrill Diary, Sept. 24, 1890, H.D.C. After listening to
Woodruff, Cannon, and others discuss the Manifesto on Apr. 2, 1891, Heber J.
Grant noted in his journal: "If it had not been for the Manifesto, all the work for
the living and the dead in our temples would have had to stop." Later that year at a
Logan stake conference, Woodruff said, "The Lord showed me by vision and revelation exactly what would take place if we did not stop this practice [of plural
marriage]." He explained that if polygamy did not cease, the brethren who offici-
ated at the local temple would not be needed to help perform the vicarious work
for the dead which was an important tenet of the L.D.S. faith because "all ordinances would be stopped throughout the land of Zion." Woodruff said that although he foresaw exactly what would happen if changes were not made, he
would have allowed the temples to be confiscated, and many more priesthood
holders to be sent to prison, "had not the God of Heaven commanded me to do
what I did do." Speech published in *Deseret Weekly News*, Nov. 21, 1891, and
G. Homer Durham, ed., *The Discourses of Wilford Woodruff* (Salt Lake City, 1946),
213–16. Woodruff made similar comments at the dedication of the Salt Lake
Temple in Apr., 1893: "I saw by vision and revelation this temple in the hands of
the wicked." See notes, Manifesto File, Woodruff Papers.

43. Grant Journal, Sept. 30, 1890. In his recollections as an old man, church
attorney Franklin S. Richards stated that the imminent danger of passage of the
disfranchisement bills was the immediate cause of the issuance of the Manifesto.
He recalled that he was at the president's office on the morning of Sept. 25, 1890,
"when President Woodruff came in and stated that the Lord had made manifest to
him, after much prayer and supplication, that our people must submit to the law,
inasmuch as they had exhausted every legal means of showing its unconstitu-
tionality." Address given Nov. 13, 1932, copy, F.S. Richards Papers, H.D.C.

44. *Deseret Weekly News*, Oct. 18, 1890. There is a relevant bit of "reliable
heresay" involving a member of the L.D.S. Church Historical Department staff
who told this writer of a church general authority who had recently read the en-

Political Deliverance

try in George Q. Cannon's diary (which is presently unavailable for use by scholars) regarding the Manifesto. He reportedly said that Woodruff had received divine prompting to write a draft of the statement, which the first counselor claimed to have proofread. Cannon stated he was glad to know the Lord's Will on the matter of plural marriage.

45. *Washington Evening Star*, Sept. 25, 1890. W. B. Dougall [telegrapher for First Presidency] to Caine, Sept. 24, 1890, Caine to Woodruff, Sept. 26, 1890, copy, Caine Papers. Dougall reported, "President Woodruff wishes the widest circulation possible given to his dispatch [containing the Manifesto]."

46. The Doctrine and Covenants of the Church of Jesus Christ of Latter-day Saints (Salt Lake City, 1981), 291–93. This latest edition for the first time includes the additional page entitled "Excerpts from Three Addresses by President Wilford Woodruff Regarding the Manifesto." These include his remarks at General Conference, Oct. 6, 1890; at Cache stake conference, Nov. 1, 1891; and a discourse at the sixth session of the dedication of the Salt Lake Temple, Apr., 1893. A preliminary version of this chapter entitled "Woodruff Manifesto in the Context of Its Times" (including citations of Woodruff's speeches, see n. 42) was presented at the Mormon History Association session in conjunction with the American Historical Association meeting at San Francisco in Apr., 1979. A commentator's copy of the paper was subsequently loaned by the Church Historical Department to persons from the First Presidency's office. See also Appendix 2 for these new notes.

47. *Salt Lake Tribune*, Sept. 26, Oct. 10, 1890; *Salt Lake Herald*, Oct. 9, 1890.

48. A. H. Cannon Journal, Sept. 30, Oct. 1, 1890; Grant Journal, Sept. 30, Oct. 1, 1890.

49. A. H. Cannon Journal, Sept. 30, Oct. 1, 1890; Grant Journal, Sept. 30, Oct. 1, 1890.

50. Smith to Sarah E. Smith, Sept. 24, 1890, Joseph F. Smith Papers [Letterbooks].

51. Smith to Nuttall, May 7, 1890, ibid.

52. Caine to Warren [Woodruff], Oct. 4, 1890, Caine Papers. A. H. Cannon Journal, Oct. 5, 6, 1890; *New York Herald*, Oct. 7, 1890, contains interviews with the secretary of the interior and the attorney general on their reaction to the Mormon Conference proceedings and the need for the same.

53. *Deseret Weekly News*, Oct. 18, 1890. Quinn, "New Plural Marriages," 47–8, convincingly questions the unanimity of the conference vote.

54. Ibid.

55. *San Francisco Chronicle*, Sept. 27, 1890; *Deseret Weekly News*, Oct. 18, 1890. Zane Journal, Oct. 7, 1890, noted, "In naturalizing an alien this morning, I took occasion to say that I would take judicial notice of the Manifesto of the President of the Church of Jesus Christ of Latter-day Saints and adopted by the conference declaring the Manifesto to be authorized and binding on the members of the church and that I would record the church as opposed to polygamy hereafter, unless something happened to change my opinion as to the sincerity of the church in adopting the resolution."

56. Woodruff to Foster, Oct. 23, 1890, First Presidency Papers [Letterbooks].

Foster had visited Utah the previous spring to inspect the territorial judiciary and had subsequently issued a report. See Caine to Woodruff, Cannon, and Smith, June 17, 1890, Caine Papers, H.D.C. See also Zane Journal, Apr. 7, 13, 1890. Thomason, "Manifesto Was a Victory," argued it was a victory because the church leaders had gained assurance of security and sanctity for existing plural marriages before they made their concessions. In light of the letter to Foster, there is serious doubt about that being the case.

57. *Deseret Weekly News*, Apr. 11, 1891.

58. Ibid., Oct. 24, 31, 1891. A. H. Cannon Journal, Oct. 12, 1891, recounts a meeting of L.D.S. general authorities with their attorneys in which the attitude to be expressed toward plural marriage was discussed.

59. A. H. Cannon Journal, Nov. 12, 1891.

60. Smith to Warren M. Johnson, Dec. 15, 1891, Smith to I. E. D. Zundel, Dec. 21, 1891, Joseph F. Smith Papers [Letterbooks].

61. Victor W. Jorgensen and B. Carmon Hardy, "The Taylor-Cowley Affair and the Watershed of Mormon History," *Utah Historical Quarterly* 48 (Winter, 1980), 4–36. This excellent article explains correctly that "the Manifesto was incomplete and begged amendment if Gentile demands for a cessation of all polygamous activity were to be met." The authors then proceed to trace the "amendment" of the official church position on plural marriage in the post-Manifesto years of the early twentieth century.

6

The Emergence of the National Parties in Utah

Utah's unique political divisions, based primarily on religious affiliation, were incompatible with mainstream American politics. Previous efforts to organize the national parties in the territory had failed, but finally in 1891, with decisive stimuli from non-Mormon sources, the permanent formation of national parties occurred.

At the beginning of the year, Morris M. Estee, who had maintained a steady correspondence with the First Presidency since congratulating them on the Manifesto, explained that effective public relations work was needed to convince the nation that the L.D.S. church had indeed changed political as well as marital practices. It had to be shown that "Mormons are at liberty to vote according to their political convictions and not according to the dictates of the priesthood." Estee also counseled that harmony in local affairs was needed—undoubtedly a reference to the long-standing bitterness between the Liberal and People's parties. The Mormon authorities who heard the letter resolved to seek "to establish greater harmony between Mormons and Gentiles in Utah." There was no immediate effort in that direction, but the church hierarchy became more disposed to work with non-Mormon Utahans when the opportunity did arise.[1]

Contemporary Utah historian Edward Tullidge uncannily predicted that after the Liberal party had won control of the government of Utah's two largest cities, territorial politics would "become reconstructed under the regular organizations of Democrats and Republicans." He further anticipated that Weber County would set the example for Salt Lake. He was correct in both instances.[2]

Even before Estee's letter, some outraged Ogden citizens began moving to overthrow the Liberal political clique controlling their municipal affairs. On January 16, 1891, more than 100 Gentiles convened to consider improvement of city government in the approaching local election. The *Ogden Standard*, spokesman of the interested but uninvolved People's party, noted such action was a rebuke to the reigning administration, delivered by its former supporters. It was, the paper said, not that they "loved Liberalism less, but good government more." Some non-Mormons had been angered by the undemocratic machine methods of selecting Liberal party candidates. Much of the criticism focused on pharmacist (and alleged liquor dealer) J. W. McNutt, the incumbent city treasurer, who emerged as Liberal candidate for mayor.[3]

Near the end of January another faction of Ogden Gentiles calling themselves the "Anti-ring Liberals" also held a convention and discussed alternative candidates. Some of the participants were current Ogden city officials excluded from the new Liberal ticket headed by McNutt. A committee was appointed to approach the Citizen's party to see if they could unite on an acceptable list of candidates. After careful negotiation, the parties emerged with a coalition slate, which also included several People's party members. With Mormon candidates Frank J. Cannon and Thomas D. Dee listed among the city council aspirants, the People's convention also chose to support the Citizen's ticket rather than nominate its own.[4]

The *Ogden Daily Commercial*, organ of the regular Liberal party, echoed its Salt Lake City counterpart, the *Tribune*, by erroneously suggesting that the opposing fusion party was Mormon-controlled. The *Tribune* alleged that it was merely "the People's party with a change of name." Both papers appealed to advocates of good government to retain the true Liberals in power and confidently predicted that the McNutt ticket would win.[5]

When opposition forces coalesced, both the Citizen's and the anti-ring candidates for mayor stepped aside, and the party united behind a popular new standard bearer. W. H. Turner had been the only incumbent city councilman renominated by the regular Liberals. At that time he was conceded by all sides to be capable, honest, and popular. When he bolted to the opposition, accepted the Citizen's principles, and consented to take the proferred place as mayoral candidate, it proved a blow McNutt could not withstand. Although Turner was elected, neither side could claim a complete victory. Of the twenty offices, the regular Liberals won thirteen. But among the seven Citizen's victors were Cannon and Dee. The *Standard* lauded the outcome as ushering in a new era in "which religious prejudice will cease to be a figure." The paper hoped that recent events would prove Ogden "first to avail herself of the disposition of just men to divide on the broader issues."[6]

The Ogden election was important in the larger sense of stimulating the birth of the first permanent organizations of the national parties in Utah. Even during the campaign there were hints of nationally based partisanship. The *Commercial* denied that the Republicans were aggrieved because most of he nominees on the regular Liberal ticket were Democrats. However, there is evidence that the anti-ring faction was motivated partly by that fact.

The anti-ring Gentiles had a voice in the columns of the *Ogden Daily Union*, headed by the erratic editor of Utah's first Liberal newspaper, Charles S. King. On election day King's open letter to the editor of the *Standard* recounted instances in which McNutt had treated him—King—so shabbily as to force him to become one of the original anti-ring Liberal opponents. Referring disparagingly to McNutt as a southerner and an "ex-rebel majah, suh," he said, "The time has at last arrived in Ogden when self-respecting, radical Republicans can and must draw the line against contemptible, sneaking Copperheads." When the first Republican party organization was effected, King was among the participants and expressed the opinion that the "city had been too long dictated to by a bad Democratic ring." The Republicans, he said, had been too timid and had been imposed upon.[7]

On February 11, two days after the election, a petition circulated calling for Republican signatories to meet "for the purpose of consultation and organization." The list of over fifty participants at the meeting, held the next evening at the federal court house, contained almost no Mormons. The keynote remarks were delivered by Judge Allen Miller, who pointed out that Utah was the only place in the Union where national politics were not the rule and proposed that it was time party lines were drawn here, too. Some speakers voiced mild distrust of Mormon voters, but the consensus of the gathering was that party organization should begin anyway, under the assumption that the Gentiles could quickly re-form Liberal ranks if the need recurred. One Mormon in attendance, David Kay, assured his listeners that they were mistaken if they believed he and his fellows were "dictated to in politics," swearing he had never been so commanded. The meeting adjourned with a general summons of all Weber County Republicans to attend a mass meeting on February 16.

At the appointed time the court room was filled with interested citizens. After D. H. Baldridge was elected permanent chairman, the Mormons present were tacitly welcomed into the movement when Frank

Cannon was chosen vice-president. Completing the club organization, those present adopted a series of traditionally Republican resolutions and, prior to adjournment, approved a motion by Ben E. Rich that an appeal be made to Republicans throughout the territory to organize similarly.[8]

With prods from *Standard* editorials and talk of Republican success, Ogden Democrats gathered at the Grand Opera House to organize on February 21. They selected recently retired Utah Supreme Court Judge Henry P. Henderson as president. Not to be outdone by the Republicans, they also selected the son of a Mormon apostle, Charles C. Richards, as vice-president. Among the significant speeches was one by H. W. "Kentucky" Smith, author of the Idaho test oath and strategist of the initial Liberal election victory in Ogden, who said he saw no reason why all could not forget and forgive all that had occurred previously. None of the Mormon speakers disagreed. Other important remarks foreshadowed the partisan battles, which would divide the Mormons politically for the first time. Visiting Salt Lake Mormon Democrat, Scipio A. Kenner, sharply took issue with a *Standard* editorial by Cannon, which had lauded Republican party achievements. This tended to prove what the *Salt Lake Herald* had predicted that day, that Ogden citizens no longer fought politically as churchmen and anti-churchmen, but would thereafter contest as Democrats and Republicans.[9]

The initiative in the Ogden movement was taken by the Gentiles, with Mormon political activists invited to participate only after the organization was under way. On the morning after the Republican mass meeting, members of the Weber stake presidency, L. W. Shurtleff and H. H. Rolapp, accompanied Cannon to Salt Lake City to receive counsel from the First Presidency. They reported that the Liberal party of Ogden had broken up to allow members to choose between the national parties. The Ogden L.D.S. leaders reported Gentile associates were encouraging the People's party to do likewise. The presidency took the matter under advisement and two days later decided to encourage Ogden Saints to combine with the national parties.[10]

Within the week the presidency showed what would continue to be a major concern throughout the period, by advising Ogden church authorities to use their influence to keep the parties about equal numerically. The next month other high church officials were informed that this political movement should extend no further than Weber County. The situation was considered experimental, and the First Presidency wished to examine developments closely before advising adoption of a similar course elsewhere. As late as April, 1891, George Q. Cannon counseled some of his brethren to repress any inclination on the part of their people to divide along national party lines, unless they were in a minority in the area and invited to do so, as they had been in Ogden. He did, however, acknowledge a belief that the "Lord's Hand" was in the political movement there.[11]

As the division movement spread, the *Salt Lake Tribune* was hard-pressed to prevent further erosion of the Liberal ranks. When its Weber County counterpart, the *Commercial*, conceded the Ogden Mormons were sincere in their actions, the skeptical *Tribune* editor charged a church attempt to capture both parties in Utah. As spring approached, many *Tribune* editorial columns were devoted to answering letters from Liberals throughout the territory who ventured to express a degree of trust in the Latter-day Saints. Calvin Reasoner, a non-Mormon resident of Payson, even accused some fellow Liberals of being unable to think independently from the *Tribune*, saying there was a "portion of the reformation that needs to be reformed." The *Salt Lake Herald* naturally joined the opposition, encouraging other fledgling division movements, such as Provo's. It reached into the old *Tribune* files to document C. C. Goodwin's long-standing bitterness, particularly in his advocacy of confiscation of church property and denial of the vote to all Mormons. The *Herald* encouraged non-Mormons to repudiate the "disfranchisement and robbery doctrine" and also laid a major portion of the blame for Utah's political backwardness upon the *Tribune*.[12]

Newspapers were recognized by the Mormon hierarchy as essential in any effort to transform the political scene. When Weber County church leaders approached the First Presidency about division, Ogden papers were discussed. In considering the future political complexion of the *Standard*, in which the church and its members held substantial stock, Joseph F. Smith argued that since the *Herald* was such an influential Democratic paper, "the Republicans should have the *Standard*." Within a few days Frank J. Cannon resumed the editorship of that paper, which adopted a Republican stance. Upon the request of Democratic club president Henderson, church leaders consented to John Q. Cannon, also George Q.'s son and an experienced editor, taking a similar post with the Democratic *Commercial*.[13]

Church leaders were even more preoccupied with the recognized influence of Salt Lake newspapers. On March 16 they received a report that a majority of stock in the *Salt Lake Times*, a Republican daily they considered to have treated them favorably, was on the market for sale. Three days later the matter was discussed at considerable length among the authorities. The newspaper was incorporated for $30,000, and it was understood that if the church or some of its members took stock shares worth $12,000, that an additional $3,500 would be placed in escrow and thus guarantee them a controlling interest. As a result the editorial policy and management would be decided by Mormons whose aim would be to have the *Times* "work against the *Tribune* and try to break its influence, and to sustain Republicanism." Church leaders decided to make the transaction, but to keep it quiet under the correct assumption that the *Times* could be more effective if it were not widely known that church interests controlled the paper.

In April members of the Quorum of the Twelve were asked to consider the possibility of John Henry Smith accepting the position of president of the *Ogden Standard*, which was rapidly becoming a major Republican organ. The consensus of the discussion among his fellow apostles was that although Smith held strong Republican sympathies, leaders of the church should "hold themselves aloof from politics."[14] But the next day their superiors in the First Presidency advised Smith to go ahead and become affiliated with the paper. President George Q. Cannon, whose political background and recent visits to the East more fully enabled him to appreciate the need, appeared to be the leading proponent of the move.[15]

Smith's involvement with one of the leading Republican newspapers was only the first phase of his extensive political activity. His open partisanship became a source of controversy throughout the crucial formative period of the national parties in Utah. At the same time that he received encouragement to associate with the *Standard*, it was decided that he should not take a more direct role in politics. Yet just over a month later, Smith was meeting leading Gentiles who favored immediate organization of the Republican party, and he noted in his diary that Cannon and Woodruff had approved his actions.[16]

There were several reasons why the highest church leaders permitted Smith to play the part he did in organizing the Republican party. One of these was the action taken by Gentile Democrats in freely opening their party organization to Mormon participation, in contrast to the continued opposition by a large proportion of Liberal Republicans toward the division movement. When a Liberal party committee arranged the itinerary of a brief visit by President Benjamin Harrison, it demonstrated that the antagonism toward the Mormons yet persisted. It was abundantly clear that if Latter-day Saints were going to join both major parties, a more cordial Republican organization would need to be fostered.

On the eve of the presidential visit, church officials discussed the necessity of the Saints honoring and impressing Harrison. They made assignments that appropriate preparations be carried out in several communities along the railroad route. Arrangements included decorating business buildings and encouraging large throngs of people to turn out to welcome the chief executive. But the Gentile committee planning the program for the distinguished visitors convinced church officials of an intention to prevent the Mormons from showing Harrison their loyalty and progress.

The presidential party had only the morning of May 9 to be in Salt Lake City before resuming its journey.[17] It was difficult to select from many suggestions the most appropriate means of allowing the people to view the president. There was little complaint about a parade and serenade of patriotic songs by the city's schoolchildren or of the program wherein Harrison and several cabinet members could make a few remarks. But the selection of the less-than-verdant Liberty Park instead of the more appropriate Tabernacle for the program appeared to be an intentional slight to the Mormons, especially since it was known that Mrs. Harrison and her daughter wished to see the building and hear the famous choir and organ. The *Herald* accused the arrangements committee of trying to show Utah through the perspective of former conditions rather than present ones. The *Deseret News* alleged the purpose to be "to keep the virtues and progress of the Mormon people as far as practicable in the shade."[18]

Even before Harrison's visit the momentum of the movement for division along national party lines gained impetus from the revival of the Salt Lake Central Democratic club. On May 5 they met at the office of club president Frank H. Dyer and adopted resolutions that the time had arrived when the political parties of Utah territory "should be formed upon the lines of national politics leaving each individual citizen to choose for himself his affiliation with one or the other" of the major parties. The membership, which included many recently active Liberals and no Mormons, resolved that "we are unalterably opposed to the disfranchisement of any citizen except for crime, whereof he shall have been first duly convicted." As news of the organizational movement spread, prominent Gentile Democrats and People's party leaders voiced hearty approval.[19]

The *Tribune* expressed distrust of the entire proceedings, alleging that a "secret understanding" had been made between the Democrats and the authorities of the L.D.S. church. The paper claimed that the Mormon people still voted exactly as they were instructed by their leaders. The *Tribune* promised that when those leading the church announced in an authoritative manner that the mission of the People's party was completed and encouraged members to choose their own places in either of the political parties, then the Liberal party would be "willing to accept it to be true and to adjust things on that line."[20]

The *Deseret News* applauded the Democrats' action, particularly the denunciation of blanket disfranchisement. When the call was subsequently issued for a Democratic mass meeting to ratify the club's resolutions, editor C. W. Penrose encouraged People's party members to attend in order to study the issues from at least one national party's perspective. He also anticipated the next step, cautiously observing that "it appears to us only self-preservative for the Republicans to announce where they stand on the issues presented by their political opponents," so that the citizens who were contemplating a new political affiliation could more intelligently make a choice of party.[21]

The *Salt Lake Times* prodded local Republicans to action. On May 13 it observed that since the Democrats had determined to withdraw from the old Liberal organization and establish their own party, there could be no reason for Republicans not doing the same. With political interest at a high level and statehood on the horizon, the *Times* said, "It would be almost criminal on the part of the Republicans if they should neglect to prepare for it." For several days the theme continued that Republicans could not sleep while the Democrats mustered forces.[22]

Amid the volatile situation, those who would be instrumental in bringing forth a "straight" Republican organization in Salt Lake City were quietly making preparations. On May 12 John Henry Smith visited one of the most respected Gentile Republicans, Territorial Chief Justice Charles S. Zane. Confessing his Republicanism, Smith stated that since the Democratic party was organizing, "if the Republican party does not, it will be in a minority when it does." He said that many Mormons were Republicans at heart and asked Zane if he was in favor of a division along national party lines. The judge responded that although his position precluded active involvement, he felt that the Republican party ought to be organized. As the apostle later confided to a relative distant from the scene, with the judge's approval Smith promised he would "go into the movement with the determined purpose of making Utah Republican." It is apparent that Zane, the leading crusader against church involvement in politics and polygamy, did not believe that Smith was acting in his ecclesiastical capacity. Shortly thereafter, the judge recorded in his diary that the "Mormons have abandoned politics as an organization and that they will hereafter cooperate with the other political parties."[23]

Smith also conferred with Gentile banker William S. McCornick, who would soon take the chair at the first meeting of regular Republicans at Salt Lake City. And on May 14 they and several former Liberal Republicans held an interview in the First Presidency's office with Woodruff and George Q. Cannon. With Woodruff and Smith exchanging statements of personal preference for the Republican party, it was concluded best "to go ahead and organize" it. Woodruff instructed Smith to select such men as he wanted to assist in this effort.[24]

Meanwhile, the Salt Lake Democrats staged their mass meeting on May 15 at the Salt Lake Theater. The *Herald* reported some 1,500 enthusiastic participants attended. After announcing their purpose to prepare for the permanent organization of the Utah Democratic party, club president Dyer nominated Samuel A. Merritt, a former Liberal party leader, as chairman. Upon election, Merritt summarized the principles of the Salt Lake Democrats in a manner certain to ingratiate himself to the Mormons present. After Judge John W. Judd spoke in a similar vein, the new chairman asked for remarks from prominent members of the People's party. The audience first called for John T. Caine, who enthusiastically endorsed the new platform and pledged himself to be a Democrat in local as well as national politics. Similar responses followed from former People's party chairman, John R. Winder, Judge Elias A. Smith, and several L.D.S. attorneys. There were enough other Mormons in attendance to lend credence to the *Tribune's* allegation next day that "the marriage of the Democratic party of Utah and the Church of Jesus Christ of Latter-day Saints took place last night at the Theater."[25]

By this time some Republicans were finally ready for an attempt to prevent the People's party members from rushing by default into the Democratic party. The day after the Democratic mass meeting, Republicans set to work to arrange their own organizational meetings. A hastily arranged, informal gathering was held in the Salt Lake Mining Exchange. After McCornick was selected as chairman, Judge C. W. Bennett offered a resolution that the Republican party should be organized. Liberal party chairman Ricketts and several of his associates objected strenuously as long as the People's party continued. But Liberal central committeeman Arthur Brown countered that the Mormon party could not be expected to disband "as long as there was no place for it to go. It is waiting to be swallowed up, and the Republican party should swallow its share." Other leading Gentiles spoke similarly. John M. Zane said, "The Democrats were organized ready to take the People's party in, and the Republicans were in duty bound to meet them on their ground." The president of the Young Men's Liberal Club, E. B. Critchlow, angered his former allies by saying that the Liberal party was a "bastard" and could not and should not be longer maintained. When the vote was taken, those favoring party organization held a clear majority. They signed the call for a general Republican meeting and designated a committee to work out the details and name a suitable meeting time.[26]

It was also decided that another meeting should be held sooner for the purpose of forming a Republican club to be affiliated with the National League of Republican Clubs of which James S. Clarkson was president. Though the purpose of such clubs was strictly to educate members on party principles, the *Tribune* opposed any such organization. The paper appealed each day for Liberal members to be present to defend the anti-

Mormon viewpoint at the impending meetings. Possibly sensing difficulty, proponents of the Republican club postponed organization until after the approaching mass meeting. Since friends of the club movement received word of the delay and did not attend the organizational meeting, it was consequently packed with anti-club Liberals. At the appointed time on May 18, Chairman Nick Treweek read a call for the mass meeting for two nights hence. Then, after announcing to those present the decision to delay club organization, he declared the meeting adjourned.

This did not suit the rather hostile audience, which proceeded to hold an impromptu anti-organization "revival." As the meeting continued, amid emotional speeches by prominent leaders, from the first Liberal party chairman, Patrick Edward Connor, to the future party congressional candidate, Clarence E. Allen, some in the audience discovered the supposed traitor, Critchlow, seated in the rear. Upon being invited to speak, he calmly explained his reasons for believing it time to organize the Republican party. He observed that the Democrats had taken a step they would never retrace, leaving "only the Republicans masquerading under the name of the Liberal party" to receive the odium, so far as the Mormons were concerned, for all former and present party activity. Other speakers expressed strong disagreement with Critchlow's position, but they treated him courteously. There were, though, considerable denunciations of other former members who had defected into regular Republican ranks. The speeches and reactions generally bolstered enthusiasm to renew efforts aimed at preventing contamination of effective political association, which contact with Mormons was said to threaten.[27]

In spite of rain, the Republican mass meeting held May 20 in the Salt Lake Theater was well attended and very vocal. The *Tribune* again insured that an outspoken contingent of Republican Liberals would be present. Arrangements committeeman John Zane began proceedings by stating that his group recommended that Bennett be selected as chairman and despite Liberal opposition, Zane declared him elected by voice vote. Proponents of party organization were given the floor first, with Zane and Critchlow repeating their arguments that given the fact of Democratic organization, Republicans had no realistic alternative but to organize. Allen warned that political enlightenment had not extended beyond Salt Lake and Weber counties and to fragment political strength in those urban areas would guarantee inundation by the Mormon-dominated "cow counties." W. H. Dickson contended that in fact the Democratic organization was not formidable and reiterated the standard Liberal contention that Mormons could vote only as their leaders dictated.

The decisive moment came when Bennett invited John Henry Smith from the audience to the speaker's rostrum. Heber J. Grant, a skeptical spectator, later confessed that he thought Smith was making the worst mistake of his life, assuming the Liberals would shout down and humiliate his fellow apostle. But though all accounts depict the meeting as generally rowdy, they also agree that Smith was given careful attention. He defended previous efforts of the People's party, then declared that he was as free to vote his own mind and conscience as Judge Dickson or anyone else. He claimed many Mormons would never again hold allegiance to the People's party and pleaded for a place in the Utah Republican ranks. Smith and Grant both felt that the speech had been effective. The *Times* had "no hesitation in asserting that it cleared away doubt from the mind of every man who was at all inclined to be just." [28]

The real purpose of the meeting had been, as resolutions Judge Bennett read stated, "that political parties in Utah should be organized with reference to the national questions and politics" and that as chairman he should appoint committees to perfect Republican organizations throughout the county and in conjunction with other county committees throughout the territory. Weber County representatives Frank Cannon and Ben E. Rich spoke briefly in support of this motion. There was loud opposition, but when the vote was taken the motion carried. The *Tribune* claimed that it had actually failed by a considerable margin. The *Times* termed that assertion a "shame-faced falsehood" and agreed with the *Herald* that the vote had been two to one in favor of carrying out Republican party organization. [29]

The Liberal party and its *Tribune* organ continued their bitter opposition. Their main contention was that with recent Liberal victories in Ogden and Salt Lake City and with the Mormon vote divided control of the next territorial legislature was within their grasp. With a chance to enact the reforms Mormon legislators had so long opposed, it would be tragic to dash hopes for the "regeneration of Utah" through a premature effort to bring the Republican party to dominance. [30]

The possibility that the anti-Mormons might be correct in anticipating control of the coming territorial legislature helped to convince some within the Mormon hierarchy that they could not safely hold themselves "aloof" from active politics. The very week, in early April, when Smith's quorum advised him not to take an active part in territorial politics, Penrose, an advocate of division along national party lines, predicted an effort would be made by the Liberal party to "capture the legislature, and then pass laws to disfranchise all Mormons." He warned of the need to arouse their people and prepare them politically to withstand that threat. At that same time George Q. Cannon had spoken approvingly of the division movement at Ogden and warned that if the Saints "remained as an uncertain element in politics," they would be "liable to disfranchisement." [31]

Developments during the ensuing two months, particularly Liberal opposition to division, reinforced these beliefs and convinced others among the church authorities of the correctness of the assessment. Entries in Abraham Cannon's diary of late May reflect the thinking among the hierarchy by that time. After attending the Republican mass meeting, Cannon commented that the "Tribune gang" had been out in force to thwart all Republican organization efforts. A week later he gave vent to further suspicions, alleging that the "ring" was "laboring very energetically to prevent the division of the people in this territory on party lines. They desire to continue the old antagonisms until the 'Mormons' are robbed of every vestige of right, and the control of the territory is given into their corrupt hands." Cannon expressed a hope that their "vile schemes" would be thwarted.

By that time the church leaders had decided to approve the next decisive step in Utah's political regeneration. On May 25 the First Presidency and several other church leaders met at the Gardo House to discuss the advisability of summoning the county and territorial People's party officers to consider the current political situation. Those present concluded, according to Abraham Cannon, that the national party organization taking place in their midst would eventually bring them great relief, whereas if they did not support it, "the Liberal or Tribune gang will finally rule and ruin in our fair country." [32] As calls went out for People's party committees to convene, word spread that the Mormon party was about to be abolished.

On May 28, 1891, the First Presidency met with People's party territorial committee chairman Franklin S. Richards, his predecessor, John R. Winder, and several other experienced Mormon politicians. They approved resolutions previously drafted by party central committeemen. The next day, in accordance with an earlier summons, the governing officers of the party in Salt Lake County met and heard the proposed decree. It was adopted without dissent, and the document was then published in the *Deseret News*. Stating that since there was a disposition on the part of both Democrats and Republicans to dissolve their "unnatural union" of affiliation with the Liberal party, the necessity that had existed for the maintenance of the People's party seemed to have passed. It was therefore resolved that the People's party machinery for the county be disbanded and its members be "left free to ally themselves with the respective national parties, according to their individual preferences." [33]

At that time the First Presidency divulged part of their thinking on political matters in a letter to John W. Young, their long-time contact with national Democratic leaders. Informing him of the impending dissolution of the People's party, church authorities described the Utah political field as "ripe ready to harvest." Reporting the general impression that the Mormons were Democrat in their sympathies, they indicated serious concern that there would be "a general rush into the Democratic ranks." The presidency expressed their view that it was "of the highest importance that this should not be the case." Then disclosing what would continue to be their policy, they admitted they were "exceedingly desirous that the Republicans should on the start find sufficient encouragement to enable them to make the struggle for Territorial supremacy a close and interesting one." The church leaders reasoned that if the two parties were "evenly balanced," Mormon citizens would be more secure in their liberties. Subsequent events would further illuminate the thinking on these matters by the highest council of church authority and show considerable foresight in such an approach.[34]

Comments in the *Times* and a resolution presented at their mass meeting indicated that Salt Lake Republicans contemplated using their club as a base from which to spread similar party organizations throughout Utah. Apparently when the movement got far enough along, they expected a convention to be called to organize the territorial party formally. Bennett assumed authority as chairman of the mass meeting to appoint a committee to engage in organizing clubs in Salt Lake County and beyond. Apostle Smith, along with two young charter members with prominent fathers, John Zane and George M. Cannon, were assigned to this task. Between this appointment on May 26 and the legislative election on August 3, Smith participated in Republican organizational meetings in over thirty different locations outside Salt Lake City.[35]

Typical of these was the formation of the club in Provo. In accordance with the call from Smith, Zane, and Cannon, citizens interested in Republicanism met at a courtroom there on May 28. A Mormon was elected chairman, and a Gentile, secretary. Smith occupied most of the time dwelling on local and national history from a partisan viewpoint. He urged his listeners to make Utah County Republican as he believed Weber and Salt Lake to be. Several dozen members were enrolled in the club, including Mayor John E. Booth. Booth, also a Mormon bishop, was to take the lead as a featured speaker several nights later when the infant local party staged a rally, which had been planned at the initial meeting.[36]

This second gathering was watched with interest by the long-time editor of the *Provo Enquirer*, John C. Graham. He complimented the Republicans for the orderly, dignified, and instructive nature of their rally and heartily encouraged participation in such efforts to prepare Provoans for more active citizenship. When the editor, a self-confessed opponent of division in Provo, announced it was time for Utah County to fall in with the national party movement, it marked the conversion of a formerly vocal opponent to the Republican party. Graham had long been opposed to protective tariffs, including the McKinley Act of 1890. As recently as January 29, 1891, the *Enquirer* had waxed critical on the subject under the heading "Evils of High Tariff." However, by the second week of June, there had been a complete about-face. One of several tariff editorials at that time was entitled "Benefits of a High Tariff." Although this switch did not go unnoticed, especially by the *Tribune*, the editor was undoubtedly sincere in his conversion, remaining a dedicated Republican from then on. He was soon spreading the doctrines of the party at county rallies, including one at the sugar factory town of Lehi, where no opponent of protection would have dared to venture.[37]

Since the division movement began, leading non-Mormon Democrats had been negotiating with Mormon stockholders to secure controlling interest in the *Salt Lake Herald* and transform it from the People's party organ into one for the Democratic party. This was accomplished in May, 1891. As the People's party was disbanding in the Salt Lake area, the *Herald* was increasing its efforts to shepherd Mormon voters into the Democratic fold. In an editorial on June 3, the paper claimed that "a member of the People's party is not required, in order to become a Democrat, to abandon or modify a single doctrine he previously held," since the basic tenets of both creeds were said to be the same. In an adjoining column, the *Herald* editor stretched his point in an attempt to show, on the other hand, that the beliefs and policies of the Liberal and Republican parties were essentially "identical." The next day the paper discounted the idea that it would "look badly if all the Mormons join the Democratic party," saying it would appear much worse "for any of those who are Democrats to join any other party." The *Herald* article assured readers that such an occurrence was unlikely and in subsequent days reported confidently that Mormon communities in southern Utah and elsewhere would soon be Democratic.[38]

Church authorities were becoming increasingly apprehensive about such an eventuality upon disbandment of the territorial People's party. In a June 9 discussion of politics, Abraham Cannon reported that "the danger of our people all becoming Democrats through the influence of the *Herald*, which is widely circulated, is feared." The First Presidency concluded that if but one party gathered strength from among the Saints, "the results of such a course would doubtless prove most disastrous," assuming that the same kind of persecution they had been forced to endure during the previous half-dozen years would be repeated by the slighted party, which happened to be the one then controlling the national law-enforcement machinery. The church leaders present at the meeting concluded that "efforts should be made to instruct our people in Republicanism, and thus winning them to that party," and that once the negative Republican influence of the *Tribune* were broken, good would accrue from the more equitable political division of the people.[39]

Salt Lake newspapers also carried a summons by territorial committee chairman Richards for his fellow board members to gather on June 10, 1891. In a letter to the committeeman from San Juan County, Stake President Francis A. Hammond, who lived in the most remote region of Utah, Richards divulged that the increasingly well-known purpose of the meeting was to put an end to the People's party. Upon receipt of this communication, Hammond commented on the political situation and indicated that the move was also aimed at forcing the break-up of the Liberal party, despite the continuing efforts to the contrary by *Tribune* editor Goodwin and his "small clic of anti-Mormon fanatics."[40]

Thus, by the eve of the day the Mormon political party would be dissolved in Utah, considerable insight can be offered into what brought about that important event. Estee's advice had certainly remained in the minds of the general authorities who backed dissolution. And encouragement brought about by the initial efforts at dividing along national party lines, with Mormons accepting invitations from the spearheading element of Gentiles to join them as Democrats and Republicans, was of great moment. It is striking, in reviewing the most detailed accounts of political discussions among Mormon leaders at the time, how often mention was made of the *Salt Lake Tribune*. As the most consistent voice of opposition and distrust of Mormon intentions, the Latter-day Saint leaders clearly reciprocated those feelings. Their preoccupation with the evil intentions of the Liberal-*Tribune* clique to harm their people and the consequent hopes that Mormon countermoves might further reduce their enemy's influence must be placed high on a list of causes for bringing about the dissolution of the People's party.[41]

June 10 was the day Richards had designated for the territorial central committee to convene at the Social Hall in Salt Lake City. Since disbandment of the local party had already occurred, little notice was given of the event by the friendly newspapers. They briefly noted that resolutions to that effect had been adopted and that though successful in the past, the People's party was no longer necessary.

Another meeting later that day at the Gardo House was even more important in the People's party demise. Several dozen party leaders gathered there to hear each member of the First Presidency endorse disbandment of the Mormon party. The thrust of the messages conveyed can be gathered from the accounts of three other general authorities who attended. Franklin D. Richards recorded that "the policy of the present political move" was explained and cheerfully accepted by all. A. H. Cannon noted that those present were informed that though the First Presidency "desired the Saints to join the different [national parties], they did not want them to go *en masse* into either side." John Morgan added that they were "advised that the present Democratic tendency was not what it should be" and that an equilibrium between the major parties should be sought.[42]

Recollections of the Gardo House meeting by James H. Moyle, an influential Utah Democrat for more than half a century thereafter, made an important point concerning reaction to George Q. Cannon's advice on division. In regard to most Mormons' natural inclination toward the Democratic party, Moyle recalled that this could push the non-Mormons into the Republican camp and perpetuate the political division along religious lines. At the meeting, Moyle raised the question of his well-established preference for the Democrats and was told by Cannon that feeling as he did he should definitely ally with that party. Those who had not yet formed such preferences were the only ones encouraged to consider joining the Republicans. Observing that there had been no objections to the suggestions, Moyle reflected no resentment at the advice detrimental to his party, and he observed that it did not seem to be a "church fiat" either that the People's party disband or that the striving for equal alignment be fully carried out. Whether such was the case or not, the divisions proceeded rapidly.[43]

The situation in parts of the territory farther removed from the metropolitan centers may be illustrated by reference to diary accounts of councilors to stake presidents in Coalville in Summit County and Beaver in Beaver County. Coalville resident Alma Eldridge had participated in the June 10 meetings that disbanded the party. The day he returned home he found the Democrats not only fully organized but also actively campaigning. The contingent already making partisan speeches included his Summit Stake President W. W. Cluff and Delegate John T. Caine. It was almost a month later before Eldridge and others even issued a call for a Republican county convention, and by that time the legislative elections were only weeks away.[44]

Two hundred miles to the south, John F. Tolton observed that from present indications in his hometown of Beaver "it would seem that the people who are afflicted with political itch in any manner are almost unanimously Democrats. No move has yet been made by the Republicans to organize, and encouraging and flattering reports come from the lower settlements that the masses of people are there Democrats as well as in Beaver." This condition was observed several days later by Apostle Francis M. Lyman, who had embarked on a tour of southern communities after the Gardo House meeting.

Lyman's activities upon arrival at Beaver probably became a basis of the well-known legend arising from this era that as church authorities preached in the various congregations, they divided the people politically according to which side of the meetinghouse they happened to be sitting on at that particular time. Tolton, who several years later would lend credence to such stories by swearing in a negatively worded affidavit that Lyman had approached him about being a Republican, more accurately noted at the time that "Apostle Lyman was surprised to see such a political craze as had apparently struck us." The visiting church leader inquired why there were so many Democrats and stated that the "authorities desired us to divide about equally on national party lines in order that we could receive favors from whichever party was in power." He advised that "those who had not already declared themselves Democrats and could conscientiously do so, should ally themselves with the Republicans."[45]

These comments had reference to a private political conference attended by the entire Beaver Stake Presidency and members of presidencies from neighboring Millard, Panguitch, Parowan, and Kanab stakes. As Lyman later commented, his purpose at the time was to give church authorities in the southern region "the key note from the First Presidency upon party lines so that it should be known that it was not wrong to be a Republican." The apostle would feel compelled to solicit recollections from others present to discount Tolton's allegation of extreme partisanship in his remarks. The resultant evidence indicated that despite Lyman's personal preference for the Republican party he did make a reasonably unbiased presentation of the position his ecclesiastical superiors wished local leaders to take in explaining and encouraging equitable division. As the meeting ended, the brethren were advised to keep the source of their counsel secret so that the advice would appear to stem from more local initiative.[46]

Tolton's charges of extreme partisanship on Lyman's part, while stemming from 1891 activities, did not surface until the heated campaign of 1895, when it was a part of the most widespread protest by Mormon and non-Mormon Democrats against church interference in politics in favor of the Republicans. But a lesser undercurrent of discontent may be discerned in the midst of the initial division movement. In late May, 1891, the *Salt Lake Herald* criticized John Henry Smith's sometimes offensive partisan activites, especially pointing to his distortions of facts as the Democrats saw them. A few days later, on June 3, Smith noted that F. S. Richards, C. W. Penrose, and Provo Democratic leader William H. King were "getting concerned" about his proselyting converts to the Republican cause. The next month, as Smith began a six-day campaign tour in Weber County, Richards's brother Charles C., an Ogden party leader, went to church headquarters and insisted that some Democratic apostle spend a week lecturing in the same area.[47]

Shortly thereafter the Twelve Apostles gathered for their regular quarterly quorum meeting. Their quorum president, Lorenzo Snow, an ardent seeker of harmony among his brethren, recognized growing internal differences and expressed hope that political dissension would not overflow into the ecclesiastical realm. He opened the meeting on July 7 with the observation that some were finding fault with Smith because of his recent political activities. Conceding that he had at first been displeased with Smith's course, Snow concluded that it had been approved by the First Presidency and thus he had come to feel it was "all right" for him to continue. As Snow finished his own remarks, he encouraged each of his associates to openly express their views.

Moses Thatcher first took occasion to express his opinions in a more critical manner. He recalled that at the last council meeting they were "united in saying John Henry Smith should not actively engage in politics," and yet, it was pointed out, he had done so, "doubtless with the sanction of the Presidency." Thatcher continued, "If he goes into politics I do not know why other apostles should not seek to make converts to their principle." He strongly reiterated his opinion that church leaders should not be actively involved in politics, adding there should certainly be no committee assigned to change the views of the people.[48]

In the ensuing discussion each apostle present expressed his views. Although there was a consensus that political division of the Saints was good, the opinion was almost unanimous against Smith or any other general authority actively engaging in partisan politics. The four present who would eventually align most definitely with the Democrats were outspoken against Smith's course of action. One of them, Heber J. Grant, described his dilemma. He had been active in past People's party campaigns and said, "His Democratic friends could not understand what was the reason he did not come out and work for them." He said several prominent Gentile Democrats had alleged that the church authorities were restraining him from making political speeches so that the Republicans could get a better foothold in the territory. He expressed the opinion that possibly it would be better if he and Thatcher made some speeches for the Democrats.[49]

Two days later the apostles met with George Q. Cannon and Joseph F. Smith to try to clarify the situation. John Henry Smith apologized for recent absences, then elaborated on his reasons for political involvement. He stated that after the two past chairmen of the People's party, John R. Winder and Franklin S. Richards, along with Delegate Caine and other prominent brethren, had declared themselves Democrats, he felt it was "necessary for him and other leading men who were Republicans to come out and work for their cause or the people would all go with one bound into the Democratic party." He said, "I have tried to disprove the theory that this Territory belonged to the Democrats by divine right." Apostle Smith said that the only counsel he had received from the First Presidency was to do as he felt best, and in the turbulence of the first Republican mass meeting he had decided to participate and felt good about having done so. He expressed as his main purpose "to get out of the minds of the people" the idea "that it would be a crime to become a Republican." [50]

Apostle Smith was followed by President Joseph F. Smith, who confessed that the presidency had been at times less than open with the apostles in political matters at the insistence of outside friends who wished to remain anonymous. He admitted there had been a committee proposed to prevent the Saints "from going overwhelmingly in either direction. But, he continued, it was not "to influence or coerce them contrary to their desires." He said it had been intimated by some of their best friends that it would be injurious to the people if they were all to join the same national party. Elaborating further he stated, "As the leanings of the people seemed to be to join the Democrats it seemed absolutely necessary to have some one high in authority who was a Republican to come out and labor for that party." Cannon spoke similarly of Apostle Smith, saying that "while the Presidency did not call him to labor as he has at the same time they had felt that what he had done and was doing was for the best interests of the people and he had had their full approval." Cannon mentioned that their friends had advised that their "political affairs should be so managed that we would have friendship if possible of both the political parties." [51]

Presidents Smith and Cannon explained that since the majority of Mormons as yet had no real party preferences, there would be a good chance for equitable division—except for one problem. "With the impression all over the land that it was almost a crime to [be] a Republican there would not be a division, as the people would become Democrats if they thought their duty was to join that party," even if in their hearts they felt that the principles of the Republican party were more appealing. The apostles were repeatedly assured that "it was not the intention to convert one man to be a Republican who was a Democrat." [52]

There were several less-then-veiled references by the presidency to the advice of friends. Indications are that they were carefully considering the counsel and wishes of national Republican leaders. Abraham Cannon quoted President Smith as saying that "we have received the strongest admonition from our Republican friends that we must not allow this territory to go strongly Democratic." After voicing confidence in that party and its future in Utah, he contrasted Republican loyalty to their friends with that of the Democrats and said he knew many prominent men of the former party who were "today our friends and are working in our interests," but he did "not know a single Democrat who is helping us." He mentioned Estee, Stanford, Blaine, and Clarkson as being "deeply interested in [our] affairs and desirous of doing [us] good."

Throughout the discussions, the ultimate benefits anticipated from following the course outlined were clearly amnesty and statehood. President Smith advised that if they wished to accomplish those ends, there could only be hope through the party then in power in Washington. Both Smith and Cannon were lavish in their praise of Estee and Isaac Trumbo, Cannon stating that Trumbo had "done more in time and in money for us than any man among the outsiders." He continued, "It was due to Trumbo to say that he had done as much if not more for us than any man in Zion" and the people were "under deep obligations" to him and his associates. Estee, who credited Trumbo for his own interest in the cause of the Saints, was reported to be in Salt Lake City laboring among Gentile Republicans in an effort to get them to petition Washington for amnesty.[53]

Church authorities were at least partially aware of the benefit national Republican leaders expected to gain from friendship with the Mormons. At the subsequent quarterly meeting of the Council of the Twelve, George Q. Cannon read a copy of a letter from Estee to Clarkson in which the latter was reminded that "if the Mormons are now properly handled they will make of Utah a Republican state." In light of the closeness of the balance between the two parties in Congress, the benefits of gaining additional states for the Republicans was clearly worth courting Mormon favor.[54]

In spite of the obvious interest the First Presidency had in the outcome of the political situation during the summer of 1891, there is a complex question of how much they did to influence it. Shortly after the dissolution of the People's party, the management of the *Salt Lake Times* submitted a series of questions to Woodruff and George Q. Cannon. These and the carefully considered answers thereto were published as the "Times Interview" on June 23. The prefatory comments by the newspaper reveal a tone of warm sympathy toward the church authorities. In fact the secret financial support and resultant Mormon control of the paper's editorial policy had more than accomplished its intended purpose. Hardly a day went by between April and August, 1891, that the *Times* columns did not engage in direct battle with the *Salt Lake Tribune*. In this it was considerably more active than either of the other Salt Lake dailies also friendly to the church.

The stated purpose of the *Times* interview was to destroy the *Tribune's* favored contention that the church authorities continued to direct the political activities of their people. The paper claimed to speak for thousands of Gentiles who did not believe that the charges had any current basis. The newspapermen asked such questions as "does the church claim the right to dictate to its members in political matters?" and "is it your wish that the Republican and Democratic parties should organize and present their principles to the Mormon people, and that they should unite with them according to their honest convictions?" Woodruff and Cannon replied in a manner that caused the *Times* to conclude that it was evident they were "deeply interested in securing the establishment of conditions that would forever remove" the Church of Jesus Christ of Latter-day Saints from politics.[55]

In light of the previously discussed activities and the ones that followed, it is difficult to take these disclaimers and declarations literally. They illustrate the dilemma of Mormon authorities during this difficult transition phase in the roles they perceived for themselves and which their followers accepted, from the multifaceted one involving all aspects of the people's lives toward one more strictly ecclesiastical. Despite their stated desires and the undercurrent of Democratic criticism, they obviously had a difficult time giving up the temporal—including political— power they had wielded for so long. One recent scholar, Michael Quinn, has commented on these problems. Specifically on the context of the *Times* interview, he described their dilemma thusly: "On the one hand, political issues that were regarded as crucial to the church's interests could fail without active support of the hierarchy. On the other hand, any time the Mormon hierarchy became involved in a political issue, both Mormon and non-Mormon partisans of the contrary view would become alienated and accuse the hierarchy of violating promises concerning the separation of church and state." To further elaborate on the point, Quinn cited the general assessment of Jan Shipps, who was referring not only to the *Times* interview but also to subsequent similar declarations. Concerning the choices between standing above politics and continuing to direct such affairs, she concluded that the general authorities of the church chose neither alternative. "Instead a vacillating course between the two was pursued. Denials of the use of ecclesiastical influence followed hard upon decisions announcing the Will of the Lord concerning political matters. The consequent confusion gave credence to the earlier charges of duplicity." There are indeed subsequent instances that appear to make the *Times* statement deceptive.[56] The interview in its broader context seems to be more an affirmation of a position strived for than one consistently maintained.

Yet it can be argued that at the time the First Presidency was sincere in these statements. Close examination of the questions and answers of the *Times* interview indicate no intentional falsehoods. Reference to previous treatment of the two main concerns—of having initiated the division into Democrat and Republican parties and the disbandment of the People's party—shows that in both cases the movements were already under way before those involved made any contact with the presidency. The Mormon leaders never denied approving the actions after they were in progress, and they were technically accurate in what they did deny. In fact, there is some indication that the subsequent Utah campaign and election of 1891 were quite displeasing to the First Presidency, and had they been actively involved in directing political affairs, they could undoubtedly have swayed the outcome more in accordance with their wishes.[57]

Meanwhile, further political complications developed in Salt Lake City. When the Liberals accelerated their activities, former People's party members had second thoughts as to the wisdom of the recent decisions to disband and divide. On the evening of June 30, 1891, over a dozen leading Salt Lake Mormon political activists met at the office of ex-People's party chairman Richards to discuss the propriety of returning to some kind of fusion ticket for the local elections. But when reminded of the harm the action might cause to the division movement, this was apparently reconsidered. Heber J. Grant, who had been in favor of such a coalition, concluded that "if we were to have a fusion ticket it would give our enemies a chance to say that we were not really Democratic or Republican in our politics." Maintaining the straight party tickets would in the long run offset the undesirability of immediate election successes by the Liberals.[58]

However, this was not the final word, as other Mormons, with less experience and prestige, did just what their leading brethren had decided against. In early July, as the Liberals intensified efforts to control the outcome of a supposedly nonpartisan Salt Lake school board election, Mormon opponents gathered under the label of the Citizen's ticket. This was a rather unorganized venture, and the Liberal candidates were victorious. The *Times* attempted to argue that the smaller margin of victory indicated erosion of party strength, but more realistic observers conceded that a voter turnout similar to that of the crucial municipal contest of 1890 could not be expected in this election.[59]

By that time, though, the more important campaign for the territorial legislative seats was also reaching its peak, and additional complications were developing that would lead to an apparent decline in support from what the *Times* and other Republican spokesmen expected for their party. In a mid-July column the *Herald* told of a prominent Salt Laker who expressed preference for the Republican party but had concluded that since the Liberal party was a foe to both Democrats and Republicans, and since "his vote would be most effective in killing that enemy if cast for the Democratic ticket," he would defer his support for the weaker party until after the immediate crisis had passed. The Democratic paper pointed to this situation as an expression of a broader public sentiment and a portent for coming party success.[60]

Two days before the August 3 election, the *Tribune* charged that in case of emergency it was understood that church members were to be available to make support of the Salt Lake County Democratic ticket substantially solid. Such an emergency, the paper alleged, was that the Liberal party had not yet fallen apart. In an adjoining column the *Tribune* claimed to have witnesses to statements Frank J. Cannon made while drunk at an Ogden saloon, disclosing that orders had come from Salt Lake City for Republican activists like himself not to oppose the Democrats any more at this time. Whatever credence can be placed in the *Tribune* comments, it is true that part of the Mormon motivation in disbanding their own party and in strengthening the national parties in Utah had been to bring about the destruction of the Liberal party. When that did not occur, the disappointment could easily have led to a re-forming of old ranks.[61]

The outcome of the election gave the Democrats exactly two-thirds of the seats in each house of the territorial legislature, with the Liberals garnering one-third. Although the total Republican vote was not far behind that of the Liberals, 6,397 to 7,411, the Republicans had reason for disappointment. The *Times* explained the results in terms of a Mormon reaction to "bitter assaults" again launched by the Liberals on the Latter-day Saints and their church. "Human nature led them to cooperate in the election with the party that promised to make the greatest headway against Liberalism and their votes went to the Democracy." The Republican paper also criticized Democratic spokesmen, especially the *Herald*, for unprincipled attempts to link Liberalism with the Republican party in the public mind.[62]

The *Salt Lake Tribune*, seeking to show betrayal by Mormon voters, hypothesized what a typical party leader might surmise after the election. Using the name of Salt Lake Republican club leader Nick Treweek, without an actual interview or—probably—even permission, the paper pictured him as musing over the fact that at the last club gathering there were over 700 "true Republicans" ready to support the party. Since, the paper claimed, 150 of these were certainly Gentiles, it had been the Mormon Republicans who had defected, leaving only 365 total Salt Lake Republican votes.[63]

Naturally the *Herald* saw the matter differently. It took specific issue with those charging bad faith on the part of Mormons in the recent elections, saying that "the non-Mormon Republicans, almost to a man, had returned to the Liberal fold and voted the Liberal ticket." The Mormons who had declared their allegiance to Republican principles were said to have voted a straight ticket for that party. The *Herald* charged that "the playing false in the late election was by the Liberal Republicans and their victims were the Mormon Republicans."[64]

Though each of the newspapers exhibited strong biases, they agreed that Republican strength had not been what there had been reason to expect. Probably the best insight into what happened came from one of the first Mormons to break with the People's party and become an insider among the Democratic leaders, S. A. Kenner. He admitted that in the face of a dogged and disciplined onslaught by the Liberals, Democrats and Republicans "were brought measurably closer together than would otherwise be the case." He elaborated that they did not oppose each other as strongly as usual elsewhere or as they would be expected to do in Utah under different circumstances. Instead of aiming their entire campaign effort against each other, they "expended a part of their ammunition unitedly upon the common opponent." In the midst of a family fight, he said, the Liberal "wolf" still had to be kept from the door.[65]

One of the most recently sustained general authorities, Apostle Anthon H. Lund, was a direct participant in the election. As a respected resident of Ephraim, Sanpete County, local Republicans placed his name on their ballot as candidate for the upper house of the Utah territorial legislature. There is no evidence in his journal or the local newspapers that he campaigned actively, and though he received the majority vote in his own and several neighboring communities, he was defeated at the polls by the Democratic candidate from adjacent Millard County. In his election day diary entry, Lund described George Q. Cannon as rather disgusted that the apostle could not be elected to the legislature. This entry also recorded other significant comments by Cannon and Joseph F. Smith.

Smith undoubtedly was referring to his own support for the Republican party when he stated the view that he had taken the only course open to "make the Democratic party believe that we were in earnest." Prior to the election, Smith had expressed the wish that more of the apostles belonged to the Republican party. Yet Lund, John Henry Smith, and Lyman were the only members of the twelve who exhibited any noticeable preferences in that direction. For this reason Lund's account of his election day conversations also divulged that Cannon was displeased with other apostles for not sustaining the First Presidency's policy of equal division by joining the Republican party in greater numbers.[66]

Some time thereafter, as the general authorities discussed the continuing accusations that they were directing political affairs in the territory, President Woodruff reflected disappointment that Lund could not have been elected. Woodruff commented sarcastically, 'As evidence of his interference in politics he could say that he had very much desired to see some Republicans sent to the legislature, but not one had been elected." If the First Presidency had taken the direct role in Utah politics that they were so often accused of, neither these statements nor the lamented outcomes would have occurred. The inner circle of church leaders knew of the presidency's preferences regarding politics, but with the exception of John Henry Smith and to some extent Lyman and Lund, most general authorities continued the position of remaining above partisanship in direct dealings with their people.[67]

As the August election results were totaled, Salt Lake Republican leaders were reported to be disappointed and bitter. But each day thereafter brought a recovery of better feelings, and it was soon generally conceded that they should move onward in their efforts to organize the party. Working mainly through the Republican League of Clubs, a territorial convention was called for early September. League president Arthur Brown, in calling the delegates to order, designated the gathering as the "convention that will lay the cornerstone of the party in the territory." In his keynote address Brown was critical of the office-seeking Liberal Republicans and called for formation of a party territorial committee independent of the anti-Mormons. This was quickly carried into effect, with formal organization of a regular Republican party, including committeemen representing nineteen of the territory's twenty-five counties. The proceedings and resolutions reflected strong opposition to the Liberal party and the intention to carry their contest for legitimacy to the Republican National Committee.[68]

James S. Clarkson, who was just then becoming chairman of the National Republican Executive Committee, had been expending great effort to convince national committeemen as to the wisdom of supporting and fostering regular Utah Republicanism. The first fruits of the effort came in late November, 1891, when Clarkson announced the regular faction's delegation had been recognized as the legitimate party organization in Utah. The Liberals put up a concerted fight in opposition, but the national committee directly repudiated them in resolutions demanding local party harmony under the leadership of non-Liberals.[69]

In late August Lyman embarked on his annual tour of the stakes in the south-central portion of Utah with Lund as his traveling companion. They went by train as far as Sevier County, where they were met by horse-drawn conveyances to carry them farther south. After preaching visits at Panguitch and Escalante, Garfield County, they moved southward over the mountain divide into Kane County accompanied by local church authorities. Throughout the journey days were spent meeting on church matters with ward and stake leaders, with sermons delivered to specially convened congregations almost every night. By the second week of September the party was in Washington County, where in addition to ecclesiastical duties, the visiting authorities added a political theme.[70]

In the recent elections the citizens of extreme southwestern Utah did not even have a choice of casting votes for Republicans because none appeared on the ballots. Washington was by far the most populous of the Utah counties unrepresented at the recent Republican territorial convention. After mentioning this situation in several outlying towns, the visiting authorities arrived in St. George, the largest of the county's communities. There, at a priesthood meeting on Sunday, September 11, Lyman laid before the local brethren the political situation as he perceived it. Lund quoted him as saying that "there are too many Democrats here. We were told to divide but here in St. George you have turned in a body from People's party to Democracy." He explained that since the Republicans then dominated the national government, "they can do something for us the Democrats can't at least not until the fourth of March next!" On several occasions Lyman advised that when a person had not yet taken sides in the political realignment, it was wise to consider the Republican party in order to "court the side that is in power." Such discussion fully amplifies the policy outlined by the First Presidency to the apostles earlier in the summer of 1891.[71]

Later in the year L.D.S. leaders once again became embroiled in political controversy through the release of the Utah Commission's annual report to the secretary of the interior. This report was the commission's first official response to Woodruff's Manifesto of 1890, and the church authorities were particularly angry over allegations that plural marriages had continued to be contracted. They also emphatically took issue with what they considered further allegations of their interference in politics.[72] The report was released the first week of October, coincidentally the time of the church's semiannual general conference. General authorities discussed the commission report at length and listened to a rebuttal drafted by C. W. Penrose. But deciding better results would accrue from a protest rising from the thousands of Saints assembled, they allowed it to be mounted in that manner—with Penrose on the committee drafting a protest statement. Among other things, the resolutions adopted by the conference said, "We deny most emphatically the assertion of the commission that the church dominates its members in political matters and that church and state were united."[73]

This declaration was received by Gentiles at home and abroad in the same dubious manner as the statement published in the *Times* interview a few months before. But if the Mormon leaders' denials were essentially ignored outside the territory, the Utah Commission report was not. Late in the year President Benjamin Harrison's annual message closely reflected its sentiments. He credited congressional enactments with being the sole cause of the repression of polygamy. Throughout his discussion of the Mormon question, the president exhibited doubt as to the church members' and their leaders' sincerity in adhering to promises they had made. As the *Salt Lake Times* observed at the time, the Saints still had to accomplish the task of convincing the people of the nation that they did intend to abide by their promises. To those outside of Utah, little of what Estee had advised at the beginning of the year had been accomplished.[74]

However, those who had closely observed political developments within Mormondom in 1891 could see that great strides had indeed been taken along the path of conforming with the normal patterns of American politics. If the repeated disclaimers of political involvement had little effect outside the church, they were falling upon more receptive ears among those predisposed to believe the statements of L.D.S. leaders. That church authorities denied political dominance tended to promote permanent political independence among a people who had never previously valued such a right. As the Utah election campaigns of the following year made clear, the Mormon brethren, accustomed to rather unrestrained bitterness toward their Liberal political opponents, were too harsh with each other in their initial contests after the division along national party lines. This was even true of general authorities who espoused opposite parties. The political activities of 1892 also made abundantly clear that such church leaders were having considerable difficulty, and sometimes inability, restraining themselves from direct partisan involvement.

In March, 1892, a seemingly insignificant municipal election at Logan became a hotbed of political controversy. The contest was initially of significance chiefly because it was among the first instances in which a predominantly Mormon electorate would be able to show its preference between two fully organized national parties. The Democrats had reason for confidence because seven months previously they had carried the city by 100 votes in the legislative elections. Just before election day the *Salt Lake Herald* urged Logan Democrats to exert special efforts in getting out their vote: "A splendid victory in Logan will have its effect in every county and city in Utah, spreading encouragement everywhere and giving strength all along the line."[75]

However, after the ballots were tallied, the *Herald* was forced to concede that the Republicans had carried the Logan election by a majority of seventy-seven votes. The first reaction was aptly described as "puzzlement." A *Herald* dispatch laid some of the blame on C. C. Goodwin, Jr., the registrar, for allowing Republicans of questionable qualifications to vote, while refusing to register legitimate Democratic voters. A less emotional aspect of the explanation cited Goodwin, a former leader of the Logan Liberal party, as authority for the fact that of the eighty who had supported the Gentile ticket the previous year, all but two voted Republican in the recent election. The *Herald* still called the outcome "mysterious and unaccountable," noting that while the Democrats made some numerical gains over previous elections, the Republican vote increased from 207 to 400. The report significantly commented that in contrast to the active Democratic contest "no open campaign was made by the Republicans of a nature that would be calculated to convert any voters." It was ominously suggested that outside Republican workers, like George F. Gibbs, a clerk in the office of the First Presidency of the church, had conducted "some kind of a still hunt on the part of the Republicans."[76]

Within a week, Democratic leaders had pieced together an explanation of the victory, with alarming implications of church interference in the election. On March 16 Mormon and Gentile Democratic leaders of the territory confronted church leaders at Woodruff's office. Statements and affidavits from more than twenty Logan voters alleged that people known to be in close contact with church headquarters had stated to individuals in the city that the First Presidency wished the election to go Republican. Abraham Cannon's account of the meeting observed that "all denounced the using of church influence in political matters," noting that "some of these remarks were not mild."[77]

Though preceded by half dozen others, mostly non–Mormon, one of the most outspoken Democrats was Franklin S. Richards, the long-time church legal and political advisor. His father, Apostle Franklin D. Richards, a nominal Democrat himself, was apparently the notetaker at the meeting who recorded the essence of young Richards's remarks. He predicted "far-reaching mischief" if the activities being protested were allowed to proceed without correction. Reflecting on his extensive experience as emissary for the church among Democratic leaders at the nation's capital, Richards observed critically that "Congress admits we are honest and sincere in our religion, but in politics we are *harlots*." The staunch adherent of the L.D.S. faith stated that he had always defended the sincerity of church leaders when it had been questioned, but now, sensing his own word was also in doubt in some circles, he fervently pleaded for his ecclesiastical superiors to clear the record regarding political loyalty.

After another Mormon attorney, LeGrand Young, had seconded Richards's remarks, the delegation prepared to withdraw and leave the matter for the general authorities to resolve. But Woodruff urged them to remain. The aged church leader stated that "he had no word with Br. Gibbs about politics or voting—had no word to anybody about using influence." He reminded those present that the presidency's influence could not have been very great since no Republican was elected to the legislature, adding that he had not even been successful in convincing his own sons concerning party preference, they being divided about half-and-half on the matter. Joseph F. Smith also denied having authorized the use of his name, though he was described as not particularly sorry for Gibbs's actions. The other member of the Presidency, George Q. Cannon, was in Washington, D.C., but his son Abraham defended him and told those present that his father was sincerely for division.

In further exchanges during what turned out to be a three-and-a-half-hour meeting, Gibbs was called upon to explain his actions. He admitted that he had intended to convey the impression that the presidency did wish that the "Republicans gain ground and preponderance" at the election, though he denied that he had acted in the specific manner alleged by the affidavits. Under close cross-examination by Joseph L. Rawlins and others, he specifically disclaimed any right to use the names of the presidency.[78]

The same day, the *Herald*'s story "Church Influence at Logan" stopped short of accusing the First Presidency of any wrongdoing. This undoubtedly led to the signed statement of denial by Woodruff and Smith, which soon appeared in the *Deseret News*. The disclaimer noted that George Q. Cannon was absent, but that if he were available, "he would sign this declaration with us."

The *Tribune*, obviously enjoying the controversy between the Mormon and Democratic leaders, suggested in an editorial that since Cannon was the politician of the group and had made promises in the East, he might well have wished to bolster statehood efforts among majority congressmen. The editor freely surmised that "it would be good to show in Washington that the tendency of the territory was toward Republicanism, by showing that Logan, which was Democrat last summer, was Republican this spring." While not directly accusing Cannon of assigning Gibbs to his political mission, the *Tribune* contended, "It is the most natural suggestion that could possibly come to any one's mind who knows anything of the workings of George Q. Cannon's mind."[79]

There is no direct evidence to refute the allegation—and some that bolster the *Tribune* contention. Abraham Cannon, who did not specifically deny his father's implication in the Logan affair, had noted in his diary on February 9, 1892, prior to Cannon's departure for the East, that "Geo F. Gibbs and Robt. Campbell were selected to go quietly to Logan and work to make the Republican ticket successful in the approaching city election, which takes place on the 1st of March." Whether Gibbs had been "called" on a political mission to Logan or not, he (and others) at least surmised what was desired. The First Presidency had certainly not yet withdrawn from a preoccupation with the political situation.[80]

If no other harm was done by the Logan election furor, it considerably exhausted the patience of Democratic leaders toward the clearly biased members of the First Presidency. Possibly the church leaders could still claim they were abiding by the principles set forward in the *Times* interview—as far as active involvement in directing political activities was concerned—but there was no longer any question about the personal party preferences of all three members of the presidency. And activities of Joseph F. Smith in the ensuing campaign were entirely inconsistent with the professions in the *Times* statement of 1891 (which he had not signed himself). The persistent allegation of church interference in politics justifiably recurred throughout the year.

Another serious consequence of the Logan affair was the reaction of the apostle residing there to the seeming interference of outside persons in local affairs. Soon after, at a quorum meeting, Moses Thatcher described the unity that had once existed in his home valley and decried the fact that presently "politics have so divided the people that one can scarcely tell Saints from sinners, and we are calling each other all the vile names we can think of." He did not know what the future result would be but strongly protested against church interference in politics, warning that continued involvement would "bring irretrievable trouble upon ourselves." At that time Thatcher elaborated on the principle of separation of church and state, a subject that would several times bring him into serious conflict with the First Presidency and one to which he did not strictly conform on all occasions.[81]

In fact, the next important incident of 1892 in Utah occurred when Thatcher was invited to speak at the Territorial Democratic Convention at Ogden on May 14. The speech was lengthy and packed with partisan statements. One of the most controversial portions of it was construed by some opponents to imply that the speaker had claimed Jesus Christ had been a Democrat and Lucifer, a Republican. Thatcher later claimed that both Ogden newspapers had been inaccurate in their reports of the speech, but in the meantime the reaction to it was strong among some fellow general authorities.[82]

Several days later John Henry Smith discussed the Democratic convention, including Thatcher's speech, with the First Presidency. When recounting the day in his diary, he specifically referred to the "satanic part" of his fellow apostle's remarks. The presidency decided that a response was necessary to Thatcher's message and enlisted Frank Cannon to assist Smith in the matter. In subsequent days Cannon and Smith conferred several times at Salt Lake and Ogden on the subject of a reply to Thatcher's speech. Finally, an open letter signed by John Henry Smith and Joseph F. Smith was published in Cannon's *Ogden Standard*. To their protest against reference to Jesus in a political context in favor of the Democratic party, the Smiths added that to so connect the Savior might also make Him "accountable for the innocent blood of our martyred kindred"—a reference to the murders of Joseph and Hyrum Smith in 1844—because this took place, they claimed, in localities where Democrats predominated.[83]

Thatcher answered through a letter to the editor of the *Salt Lake Herald*. He clarified the points that had been misquoted, upon which the Smiths' response had been based, and expressed regret at the "intense partisan feeling" pervading their open letter. Throughout his correspondence, Thatcher exhibited a conciliatory spirit, saying he earnestly desired to be one with his brethren in religious matters. But he reaffirmed his independence in political affairs, especially "in reference to the fundamental principles dividing Democracy and Republicanism." Referring to recent Republican actions relative to tariffs, bounties, and the Force bill, Thatcher declared them "oppressive and harmful to the masses." And yet even here he declared a willingness to encourage others to entertain and maintain opposite views.[84]

By the end of May the Thatcher-Smith exchanges had ended, but undoubtedly not before engendering considerable concern among members of the Church of Jesus Christ of Latter-day Saints. At a July 12 apostles' meeting, quorum president Lorenzo Snow admitted that the political positions taken by Thatcher and John Henry Smith had caused him much serious thought. He expressed his firm determination not to allow such matters to divide the quorum. Comments by the combatants indicated no hard feelings toward each other, though neither made any political concessions.[85]

The entire episode seemed to reflect the inexperience of the Saints in differing from each other in political matters. It also exhibited the need for restraint in resorting to personality and religion on the campaign stump. Heber J. Grant observed that "the little tilt of Bros. Smith and Moses Thatcher in the papers will do more towards satisfying the people of the world that we are sincere [in having divided along national party lines] than a great amount of talk would do."[86]

Utah's socio-political structure had been for years perhaps the most completely divided of any area in the United States. While the groupings were not the pietistic-liturgical ones carefully deliniated in recent years by scholars, there was no doubt that religious preference—at least either favoring or opposing Mormonism—was the decisive factor in the party divisions. It was probably unique that the territory's Catholics and Protestants were so largely able to subordinate their differences as they struggled together against the Mormon majority, although as they began the process of normalizing the party alignments, internal strife within the Liberal party became more noticeable.

The political division of the Latter-day Saints, largely accomplished in 1891, was essentially artificial. It is probably not possible to differentiate between the ethno-cultural background of the church members who remained Democrats and those who became Republicans. Those Mormons who became Republicans did find ideological compatibility with the party once its outright hostility toward them ceased, but the real impetus for the growth of Latter-day Saint membership in Republican ranks was almost entirely pragmatic. That party was perceived by church leaders as able to deliver substantial aid in the struggle for Utah statehood, and thus they successfully persuaded many of their fellow religionists to follow them into the Republican fold. It can be observed that most of the men in high church positions who had been most politically active in the 1880s remained Democrats, while many of the church hierarchy new to political activism espoused the Republican cause. Thus the number who made the abrupt switch of parties, such as George Q. Cannon, was relatively small. Nevertheless, without the conscious efforts of the Mormon First Presidency, nothing approaching equitable division of the Utah electorate would have been likely in that generation.[87]

NOTES

1. Wilford Woodruff Journal, Oct. 14, 1890, H.D.C.; Woodruff, Cannon, and Smith to Morris M. Estee, Dec. 3, 5, 9, 1890, First Presidency Papers [Letterbooks]; A. H. Cannon Journal, Jan. 30, 1891.

2. Edward W. Tullidge, *Tullidge's Histories: Containing the History of All the Northern, Eastern and Western Counties of Utah; Also the Counties of Southern Idaho*, 2 vols. (Salt Lake City, 1889), 2:112–13, 249, 319.

3. *Ogden Standard*, Jan. 15, 1891; *Salt Lake Herald*, Feb. 11, 1891; *Ogden Daily Commercial*, Jan. 15, 1891.

4. *Ogden Standard*, Jan. 29, 1891; *Salt Lake Tribune*, Jan. 29, 1891; *Ogden Daily Commercial*, Jan. 30, 1891.

5. *Salt Lake Tribune*, Jan. 28, 1891; *Ogden Daily Commercial*, Feb. 3, 4, 1891.

6. *Ogden Standard*, Jan. 31, 1891; Feb. 10, 11, 1891.

7. *Ogden Daily Commercial*, Jan. 30, Feb. 13, 1891; *Ogden Standard*, Feb. 9, 1891.

8. *Ogden Daily Commercial*, Feb. 13, 17, 1891; *Ogden Standard*, Feb. 17, 1891.

9. *Ogden Daily Commercial*, Feb. 22, 1891; *Ogden Standard*, Feb. 20, 1891; *Salt Lake Herald*, Feb. 21, 1891.

10. Nuttall Journal, Feb. 17, 19, 1891.

11. Ibid., Feb. 25, 26, 1891; A. H. Cannon Journal, Apr. 2, 7, 1891.

12. *Ogden Daily Commercial*, Feb. 17, 18, 19, 1891; *Salt Lake Tribune*, Feb. 18, 20, Mar. 4, 6, 9, 16, 1891; *Salt Lake Herald*, Feb. 26, Mar. 18, Apr. 7, 9, 1891.

13. Nuttall Journal, Feb. 19, 26, 1891; J. Cecil Alter, *Early Utah Journalism* (Salt Lake City, 1938), 177.

14. A. H. Cannon Journal, Mar. 16, Apr. 1, 2, 1891.

15. The actual decision was that for the convenience of the *Standard* board of directors, Smith would accept the position as president, then resign. But he did remain on the board. See John Henry Smith to Ben E. Rich, Apr. 8, 1891, John Henry Smith Papers; J. H. Smith Journal, Apr. 3, 1891.

16. J. H. Smith Journal, Apr. 1, 2, May 14, 1891.

17. A. H. Cannon Journal, May 5, 8, 1891; J. H. Smith Journal, May 5, 1891. This was one of the last stops on a lengthy Pacific coast tour by Harrison and some of his family and cabinet members. See *New York Times*, Apr. 22, May 5, 6, 1891.

18. *Salt Lake Tribune*, May 7, 8, 10, 1891; *Salt Lake Herald*, May 10, 1891; *Deseret Evening News*, May 9, 1891; *Deseret Weekly News*, May 16, 1891.

19. *Salt Lake Herald*, May 7, 8, 1891.

20. *Salt Lake Tribune*, May 11, 13, 1891.

21. *Deseret Evening News*, May 8, 13, 1891.

22. *Salt Lake Times*, May 13, 15, 1891.

23. J. H. Smith Journal, May 13, 1891; J. H. Smith to Joseph Smith [III], Jan. 14, 1892, copy, John Henry Smith Papers; Charles S. Zane Journal, May 12, 15, 1891.

24. J. H. Smith Journal, May 14, 15, 1891. The later entry said, "I spent most of the day buttonholing men to find out what their politics were if they had any. President Woodruff told me to select such men as I wanted to go with me in this work."

25. *Salt Lake Herald*, May 16, 1891; *Salt Lake Tribune*, May 16, 1891.

26. *Salt Lake Herald*, May 17, 1891; *Deseret Evening News*, May 18, 1891.

27. *Salt Lake Herald*, May 19, 1891; *Salt Lake Times*, May 19, 1891; *Salt Lake Tribune*, May 17, 1891.

28. *Salt Lake Tribune*, May 20, 21, 22, 1891; *Salt Lake Times*, May 21, 1891; *Salt Lake Herald*, May 21, 1891; Grant Journal, May 20, 1891; A. H. Cannon Journal, May 20, 1891; J. H. Smith Journal, May 20, 1891.

29. *Salt Lake Herald*, May 21, 1891; *Salt Lake Tribune*, May 21, 22, 1891; *Salt Lake Times*, May 21, 1891.

30. *Salt Lake Tribune*, May 22, 23, 1891.

31. A. H. Cannon Journal, Apr. 7, 1891.

32. Ibid., May 20, 25, 27, 1891.

33. *Salt Lake Herald*, May 26, 31, 1891; *Deseret Evening News*, May 28, 29, June 1, 1891; F. D. Richards Journal, May 28, 1891.

34. Woodruff, Cannon, and Smith to John W. Young, May 29, 1891, copy, First Presidency Papers [Letterbooks].

35. *Salt Lake Times*, May 22, 23, 25, 26, 1891; J. H. Smith Journal, May 22, 26, July 31, 1891.

36. *Salt Lake Times*, May 30, 1891; *Deseret Evening News*, June 2, 1891; *Provo Enquirer*, June 4, 1891, Aug. 5, 1890; Robert D. Anderson, "History of the Provo *Times* and *Enquirer*, 1873–1897" (M.S. thesis, Brigham Young University, 1951), 83–88, 90–91.

37. *Provo Enquirer*, June 4, 1891, Jan. 29, Aug. 5, 1890, May 18, June 5, 10, 11, 16, 18, 1891; *Salt Lake Tribune*, June 26, 1891.

38. Grant Journal, May 1, 4, 1891; *Deseret Evening News*, May 25, 1891; *Salt Lake Times*, May 25, 1891; *Salt Lake Herald*, May 26, June 3, 4, 1891.

39. A. H. Cannon Journal, June 9, 1891.

40. *Deseret Evening News*, May 29, 1891; Francis A. Hammond Journal, June 3, 1891, H.D.C.

41. See p. 161 herein.

42. F. D. Richards Journal, June 10, 1891; A. H. Cannon Journal, June 10, 1891; John Morgan Journal, June 10, 1891, H.D.C.

43. James H. Moyle, *Mormon Democrat: The Religious and Political Memories of James Henry Moyle*, ed. Gene A. Sessions (Salt Lake City, 1975), 178–81.

44. Alma Eldridge Diaries, June 10, 12, 13, 15, July 10, 1891, H.D.C.

45. John F. Tolton, "Memories of the Life of John Franklin Tolton," ms., June 18, 20, 1891, H.D.C. . See also J. D. Williams, "The Separation of Church and State in Mormon Theory and Practice" 1 *Dialogue: A Journal of Mormon Thought*, (Summer, 1966), 37.

46. A. H. Cannon Journal, June 21, 1891; Francis M. Lyman Journal, Nov. 1, 1895, H.D.C.

47. See pp. 269–72 herein; *Salt Lake Herald*, May 27, 29, 1891; *Salt Lake Times*, May 27, 1891; J. H. Smith Journal, June 3, 1891; F. D. Richards Journal, July 2, 1891.

48. Grant Journal, July 7, 1891; A. H. Cannon Journal, July 7, 1891.

49. Grant Journal, July 7, 1891; A. H. Cannon Journal, July 7, 1891.

50. Grant Journal, July 9, 1891; A. H. Cannon Journal, July 9, 1891.

51. Grant Journal, July 9, 1891.

52. Ibid.; A. H. Cannon Journal, July 9, 1891.

53. A. H. Cannon Journal, July 9, 1891.

54. Ibid., Oct. 15, 1891.

55. *Salt Lake Times*, June 23, 1891.

56. Quinn, "Mormon Hierarchy, 1832–1932," 240; JoAnn Barnett Shipps, "The Mormons in Politics: The First Hundred Years" (Ph.D. diss., University of Colorado, 1965), 215.

57. See pp. 173–74 herein.

58. Grant Journal, June 30, 1891.

59. *Salt Lake Times*, July 14, 1891.

60. *Salt Lake Herald*, July 11, 1891.

61. *Salt Lake Tribune*, Aug. 1, 1891.

62. *Salt Lake Times*, Aug. 4, 1891.

63. *Salt Lake Tribune*, Aug. 5, 1891.

64. *Salt Lake Herald*, Aug. 9, 1891.

65. S[cipio] A[fricanus] Kenner, *The Practical Politician* (Salt Lake City, 1892), 148, copy, Lee Library, Brigham Young University, Provo, Utah.

66. Anthon H. Lund Diary, Aug. 3, 1891, H.D.C.; Grant Journal, July 9, 1891, had noted President Smith saying that "personally I wish we had more Republicans among the leading brethren so that our people would not think that it was wrong for them to join that party."

67. A. H. Cannon Journal, Oct. 6, 1891.

68. *Salt Lake Times*, Sept. 2, 3, 1891.

69. Clarkson to Woodruff, July 11, 1894, Volwiler Papers; *Salt Lake Times*, Nov. 24, 25, 1891; *Salt Lake Herald*, Nov. 25, 1891.

70. Lund Diary, Aug. 25, Sept. 8, 1891.

71. Ibid., Sept. 11, 18, 1891.

72. *House Executive Documents*, 52d Cong., 1st sess., 16:422–29.

73. A. H. Cannon Journal, Oct. 6, 1891.

74. Richardson, ed., *Compilation of the Messages and Papers of the Presidents*, 12:5641; *Salt Lake Times*, Dec. 10, 11, 1891.

75. *Salt Lake Herald*, Mar. 3, 1892.

76. Ibid., Mar. 8, 9, 17, 1892. See p. 230 herein for definition of a "still hunt."

77. A. H. Cannon Journal, Mar. 16, 1892; F. D. Richards Journal, Mar. 16, 1892.

78. Notes of meeting Mar. 16, '92, Prest's Office, 1–30 P.M. (7 notepad pages stapled together), Richards Family Papers, H.D.C.

79. *Salt Lake Herald*, Mar. 16, 1892; *Deseret Evening News*, Mar. 17, 1892; *Salt Lake Tribune*, Mar. 19, 1892. ,

80. A. H. Cannon Journal, Feb. 9, 1892; *Salt Lake Tribune*, Nov. 2, 3, 5, 1895; *Salt Lake Herald*, Nov. 3, 4, 1895.

81. A. H. Cannon Journal, Apr. 1, July 13, 30, 31, Aug. 2, 4, 1892.

82. *Salt Lake Herald*, May 15, 1892; *Salt Lake Tribune*, May 15, 1892.

83. J. H. Smith Journal, May 17, 20, 23, 1892; *Ogden Standard*, May 23, 24, 1892. In his journal, June 16, 1892, Lyman stated that he "had a visit with John Henry [Smith] and learned from him that the open letter answering Bro. Moses Thatcher's political oration at Ogden was written at the wish of Pres. Woodruff."

84. *Salt Lake Herald*, May 28, 29, 1892.

85. Grant Journal, July 12, 1892; Lyman Journal, July 12, 1892; A. H. Cannon Journal, July 12, 1892.

86. A. H. Cannon Journal, July 12, 1892.

87. It is not just the Utah L.D.S. who seem not to fit the standard pietistic-liturgical mold of political preference in the decade prior to 1900. Members of the Roman Catholic faith remain frequently enough in the Republican party not to fit the patterns, so seemingly consistent in the Midwest, of scholars Paul Kleppner and Richard J. Jensen. See note 8 in the following chapter.

$800 REWARD!

JOHN TAYLOR.   GEORGE Q. CANNON.

To be Paid for the Arrest of John Taylor and George Q. Cannon.

The above Reward will be paid for the delivery to me, or for information that will lead to the arrest of

JOHN TAYLOR,

President of the Mormon Church, and

George Q. Cannon,

His Counselor; or

$500 will be paid for Cannon alone, and $300 for Taylor.

All Conferences or Letters kept strictly secret.

S. H. GILSON,

22 and 23 Wasatch Building, Salt Lake City.

Salt Lake City, Jan. 31, 1887.

Reward poster encouraging highest church leaders to remain in hiding "on the underground" even when nationally prominent emissaries, such as Dr. George L. Miller, were in Utah to confer with them. Marriott Library, University of Utah.

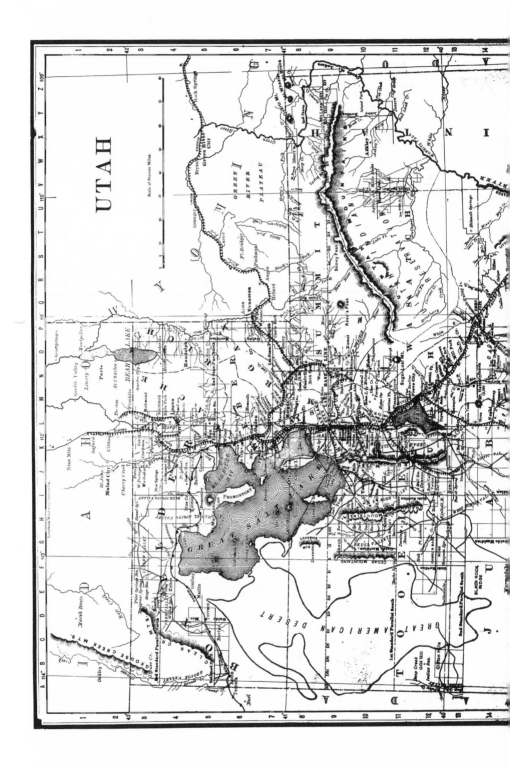

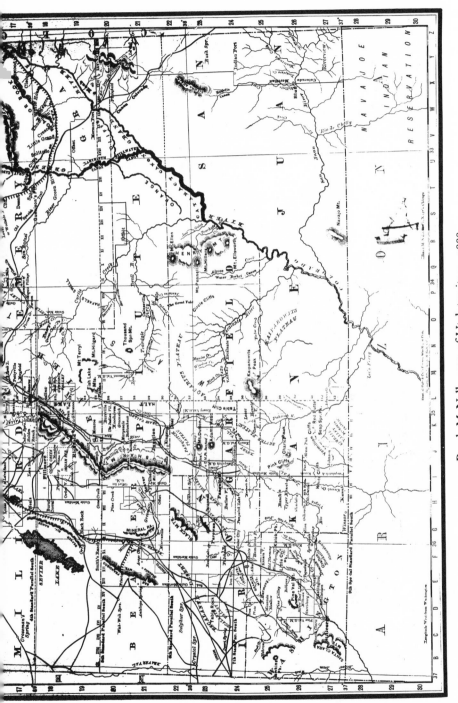

Rand, McNally map of Utah territory, 1888.

Railroad promoter and sometime general authority John W.
Young, lobbyist for the Mormons with Democratic party
leaders in the late 1880s.
Utah State Historical Society.

The Mormon delegation stationed at Washington, D.C., in 1887. Front row, left
to right: John T. Caine, Mrs. Caine, Joseph F. Smith, Emily S. Richards, and
Franklin S. Richards. Back row, left to right: John Irvine, L. John Nuttall, and
George F. Gibbs. Historical Department, Church of Jesus Christ of Latter-day
Saints.

The First Presidency of the Church of Jesus Christ of Latter-day Saints from 1889 to 1898 was also designated a committee to seek Utah statehood in August 1887. Left to right: George Q. Cannon, Wilford Woodruff, and Joseph F. Smith. Historical Department, Church of Jesus Christ of Latter-day Saints.

Looking northward on Main Street, Salt Lake City, including a street sprinkling wagon, circa 1890. Keystone-Mast Collection, California Museum of Photography, University of California, Riverside.

General James S. Clarkson of Iowa, the key intermediary between the Mormon lobby and the Republican party during the final struggle for statehood. Iowa State Library and Archives.

Colonel Isaac Trumbo at the height of his brilliant career as the lobbyist who did the most to achieve Utah's entrance into the Union as a state. Leila T. Ethington, niece.

Bishop Hiram B. Clawson of Salt Lake City, a church representative far more influential in helping achieve Utah statehood than has ever before been credited. Historical Department, Church of Jesus Christ of Latter-day Saints.

Rare photograph of general authority and diarist Abraham H. Cannon, whose candid and insightful journal was the most valuable source of information for this book. Historical Department, Church of Jesus Christ of Latter-day Saints.

Salt Lake City and County Building constructed partly to create employment for Mormon voters imported into the city to counter the "colonized" Gentile voters prior to the heated 1890 municipal election; it was also the meeting place of the first state legislature. Utah State Historical Society.

The Gardo House, once a home of Brigham Young and official residence of the church president John W. Taylor, was the site of the actual disbanding of the People's party in 1891. Utah State Historical Society.

Don't Be a "Bastard"

Election, Monday, Aug. 3, 1891.

Let Honest Men TAKE CARE How They Vote.

The LIBERALS have unjustly raised our taxes.
The LIBERALS have piled up houses of ill fame.
The LIBERALS have poisoned the earth and air.
The LIBERALS have open saloons all day Sunday.
The LIBERALS have heaped up unnecessary offices.
The LIBERAL "four boodlers" should be voted down.
The LIBERALS have ruined the fair name of our city.
The LIBERALS have given the gamblers a carte blanche.
The LIBERALS have recklessly squandered the people's money
The LIBERALS have made our citizens politically dishonest
The LIBERALS have given Salt Lake work to Omaha workmen
The LIBERALS have given Salt Lake work to Denver workmen
The LIBERALS **have not** given Salt Lake work to Salt Lake workmen.
The LIBERALS have caused property values to decrease since they have been in the city government.

A Democrat Votes the Democratic Ticket;
A Republican Votes the Republican Ticket;
What is he who VOTES A "BASTARD" TICKET?

VOTE EITHER THE DEMOCRATIC OR REPUBLICAN TICKET.

Don't Vote the "Bastard."

Keep the LIBERAL Imported Tramps from Voting and thus neutralizing honest men's votes.

VOTE AS AN AMERICAN!

Political campaign broadside utilizing the label former party activist E. B. Critchlow had placed on the Liberal party in 1891. Utah State Historical Society.

Saltaire resort on Great Salt Lake, one of the properties of the short-lived Utah Company, was a popular scene for celebrations, including the first one recognizing passage of the Utah Enabling Act in the summer of 1894. Keystone-Mast Collection, California Museum of Photography, University of California, Riverside.

Salt Lake City street scene during informal parade celebrating arrival of statehood proclamation on snowy day, January 4, 1896. Historical Department, Church of Jesus Christ of Latter-day Saints.

Interior view of front of Salt Lake Tabernacle showing electrically illuminated star installed to commemorate Utah's addition to the union as the forty-fifth state. Keystone-Mast Collection, California Museum of Photography, University of California, Riverside.

7

Steps toward Statehood

With polygamy supposedly abandoned and the major national political parties fully organized, the main obstacles to Utah statehood had disappeared. There was still intermittent opposition to admission from some Utah Gentiles, but this too was dissipating. Yet before the achievement of statehood finally came in mid-1894, additional political developments occurred: the demise of the Liberal party, two territorial elections, several unsuccessful attempts to get Utah admission bills passed in Congress, and the further high-level lobbying still considered essential to gain an enabling act. Finally, the House of Representatives approved a statehood bill, and prospects brightened concerning similar favorable Senate action.

L.D.S. leaders hoped the Manifesto would alleviate much of the opposition to Mormon causes. Less than a month after its issuance, Joseph F. Smith expressed the conviction that it had already prevented a new Edmunds bill from being enacted. And at about the same time Frank J. Cannon reported from Washington, D.C., that the feeling there was noticeably more friendly toward the church and its members. Even President Benjamin Harrison, though clearly against giving the Saints any more voice in the conduct of Utah government, at least did not favor legislation against a mere belief in polygamy.[1]

The anti-Mormon reports, influential with the president, must have generated some apprehension among outside church friends as well because in early December, 1890, George Q. Cannon felt constrained to reassure M. M. Estee that there was no foundation for allegations that no steps had been taken to show their sincerity in the action concerning plural marriage. He charged that claims to the contrary were a trick by enemies determined that the Mormons should not have the benefits they expected from the Manifesto. Cannon affirmed that the announcement was "a truthful and sincere expression of our willingness to conform to the requirements of the law," further attesting that plural marriages had ceased. This was sufficient assurance for the chairman of the Republican National Convention and several of his prominent associates.[2]

In late January, 1891, a letter from Estee was discussed at a gathering of general authorities of the church. It reported that Harrison was still opposed to them, though not as much as formerly. Friends had arranged with the president's private secretary, Elijah Halford, to keep "all improper matters concerning the Mormons away from the President as much as possible." It was also noted that other influential men were working in their interest.[3]

One of those specifically mentioned as inclined to help the Mormons was W. H. H. Miller, President Harrison's attorney general and personal friend. In November, 1890, the attorney general informed James S. Clarkson that he had advised the Idaho district attorney that state officers should be "exceedingly careful not to do anything that may look like persecution" of the Mormons, encouraging them to maintain an easy status quo while awaiting developments. Miller also divulged in the letter—a copy of which eventually ended up in the files of the First Presidency— that he had given similar advice to Utah law-enforcement officials and had caused several cases pending before the territorial supreme court to be postponed.[4]

In the months following the Woodruff Manifesto, Republican leaders requested information from the Mormons that could be used to show church members in a favorable light. One aspect of this was to compile information on who maintained the gambling houses and saloons as compared to who built the miles of irrigation canals and roads in Utah. They were also interested in literacy rates and schools maintained, and particularly in relative crime rates (other than cohabitation) of Mormons compared with Gentiles. The stated purpose was to show "that the morality of the Mormon people is equal to if not superior to that of the older states of the union."

Even more important was a set of population statistics requested by Isaac Trumbo, Clarkson, and Estee, which would eventually be utilized to win much wider Republican cooperation for the Mormon cause. Church leaders immediately engaged their assistants to compile such information, asking one, "Have you any data at hand to show what the number of our people is in Idaho, Montana, Wyoming, Colorado, Arizona, New Mexico, and Nevada?" And W. W. Cluff, the stake president presiding over some of the Latter-day Saints residing in the new state of Wyoming, was asked specifically for the current population of his people there, particularly those who might be so isolated from organized wards and branches as to not appear on the relatively accurate semiannual stake reports. Requesting prompt response, the First Presidency advised Cluff not to underestimate their numerical strength in his reply.[5]

During the first week of December, the church leaders informed Estee that the approximate number of Mormons in adjacent states was Idaho, 25,000; Arizona, 10,000; Colorado, 4,000; Nevada, 1,500; New Mexico, 1,000; and Wyoming, 300. Within a month, the Californian, still prominently mentioned as a candidate for Harrison's cabinet, attempted to use the newly acquired population figures. In January, 1891, Mormon leaders discussed a recent Estee letter that recounted that when the president was told of the Mormons' political power in Utah, Wyoming, Colorado, Arizona, and Idaho, Harrison replied, "Such people should be checked." Instead of desiring to gain L.D.S. favor, the rigid Presbyterian expressed the opinion that they should "be disfranchised for thirty years." Despite this setback, these arguments concerning potential Mormon voters were more persuasive with other key Republicans.[6]

This was just one example of the general difficulty Republican leaders were having with the titular head of their party. The congressional and state elections of the previous year had been one of the most disastrous repudiations of the party in power in American history, and the outlook was not good for the future. Clarkson labored faithfully to bolster party fortunes, and by mid-1891 he headed both organizations responsible for conducting the campaigns of the following year—the Republican National Committee and the Republican League of the United States. In these capacities he corresponded frequently with Halford and Harrison, freely giving and soliciting advice and information. The elections at year's end were not as disastrous as those of the year before, but were still disturbing to campaigners as perceptive and experienced as Clarkson. Clearly the party had lost and was losing ground in states that had recently been considered impregnable bastians of Republican strength.

By this time the Republicans had essentially given up on any realistic possibilities of winning electoral support below the borders of the South.[7] The alternative strategies of playing for allegiance and support of electoral majorities in the newly admitted western states had paid large dividends, including eleven out of twelve seats in the U.S. Senate. But even there and in the previously secure farming regions of the Midwest, instability was recognized. For this reason a western delegation argued successfully in late 1891 that the next year's national convention should be held in Minneapolis because the "doubtful states are now to be found in the West and Northwest owing to the flocking in of the foreign population and the growth of the Alliance movement."

This statement reflects the growing awareness among the politicians of the day of the cultural sensitivities that modern students have found to be so important in determining political preferences and shifts in electoral behavior.[8] Clarkson, who had long been cognizant of these considerations, had them further imbedded into his consciousness as he attempted to undo the damage done to his party in his home state of Iowa, where a combination of an ill-fated prohibition crusade and the growing appeals of the Farmers' Alliances, alluded to above, had brought an unprecedented Republican defeat.[9]

After several years of frustration and disappointments, the party chairman vented his feelings to Halford in a letter dated December 5, 1891. Lamenting the recent electoral disasters in Wisconsin and Illinois, largely related to Republican attempts at eliminating foreign languages from use in public schools—much to the resentment of German-Americans and others—Clarkson blamed the "moral spasms which periodically come over the Republican party." He continued with an important observation: "The trouble is that as a party we are too missionary and too sympathetic and take up with too many isms and hobbies. Like some children we catch all the diseases that come into the neighborhood." Suggesting that "if we could unload all the hobbies and moral reforms, the efforts to make a police sergeant out of the party and centralize ourselves on the great national issues of tariff reform and reciprocity, sound money and an honest ballot, we would find a great majority of the country in our support." Clarkson argued that the Republicans needed to unload prohibition, anti-foreign language legislation, and crusades against lotteries and other moral reforms, warning that "if we try to carry an ism in one state, and a hobby in another, and a moral idea in some other place, we are constantly sheared of our strength locally and left without a majority nationally." He observed that the party had too large a burden: "We are trying to make the Republican party better than the churches and society. It is all God's service of course, but we shall die in trying to do it." Predicting that the next year's presidential race would be "the most desperate fight that American politics has ever known," he called for new methods of approaching and winning over of the voters. The party chairman concluded that if Republicans did not summon up all the energy and resources the party possessed, they were going to "get whipped" the next year and the party would not be back in power in their active lifetimes.[10]

Whether these observations and warnings got through to the consciousness of the stubborn Benjamin Harrison is not known, but Clarkson undoubtedly had better success among party leaders in the states and with fellow members of the national committee. Although the Mormons and the anti-polygamy crusade were not mentioned in this letter, those matters clearly fit the framework of the concern expressed therein. There certainly had been an element within the Republican party that had labored long and hard to force an unwilling segment of the Mormon population to conform to more acceptable standards. But as they became more cognizant of the L.D.S. influences particularly in areas outside of Utah, Clarkson and other Republican associates became anxious to alter the prevailing party attitude toward the Latter-day Saints.[11]

As the party chairman later recalled, "It took a year of patient effort, of direct personal appeal to almost every member" of the national committee to win them over to such friendship. The reason for the apprehension, Clarkson explained, was the knowledge that "the Republican party had enacted and enforced the severe laws against Utah," and there was apprehension that to allow political power to the Mormons might invite some form of revenge. With the aid of Trumbo, Clarkson finally convinced a majority of the committeemen that since the Saints believed "in protection of American interests and industries" most compatible with Republican tariff doctrines, and imbued as they were with a unique sense of patriotism, they "would be found and indeed would be forced by their own destiny as a people to gravitate toward the underlying principles of Republicanism." Probably more persuasive with some Republicans was Clarkson's detailing "the fact that this was not merely a Utah question but that the Mormon people were spread through the valleys of eight or ten western states, and that sooner or later they would hold the balance of power in the election of every senator and of every electoral vote for President in these states." Clarkson made these assumptions the foundation on which he centered his efforts to "change the Republican party from being a party of opposition . . . to one of friendship and support" among the Latter-day Saints. These arguments, seemingly inflated at every telling, were repeated often in party circles when Utah and the Mormons were discussed.[12]

Besides the prospect of Utah statehood, Republicans also courted Mormon favor by promising to restore full-fledged citizenship to polygamists through amnesty. Despite Harrison's continued coolness to the Mormons, other party leaders, particularly Estee, expended great effort seeking general amnesty for those previously indicted for polygamy and unlawful cohabitation. In mid-July, 1891, the Californian was in Salt Lake City conferring with leading Gentiles of Republican leanings in a quiet attempt to solicit their support for the requests needed to secure this presidential concession. At that time he gained the cooperation of C. W.

Bennett and several other non-Mormons who were already inclined to cooperate with L.D.S. Republicans in the attempt to get their party established in Utah. It was Estee's plan to generate petitions at the local level, after which the National Republican Committee could exert pressure on President Harrison to act on the requests. There is some indication that Estee's secretive campaign was temporarily thwarted by the resurgence of Liberal party activity in late July and August, because after the elections were over he urged Clarkson to use his influence to check the power of the uncooperative Liberal Gentiles.[13]

Progress was slow, but by mid-December, 1891, an amnesty petition had been prepared to be sent to President Harrison. On December 19 John Henry Smith and Presidents George Q. Cannon and Joseph F. Smith met with Judge Charles S. Zane and Governor Arthur L. Thomas at the latter's residence. They discussed amnesty, and the Gentiles present agreed to endorse the petition. During the next two days, Thomas and Zane drafted a cover letter to Harrison. In it these two chief presidential appointees of Utah Territory said of the petition signed by the church leaders that "we have no doubt of its sincerity, and no doubt it is tendered in absolute good faith." They recommended favorable consideration of the petition, stating that "we believe it will be better for the future if the Mormon people should now receive this mark of confidence." On December 22 these papers were given to C. C. Goodwin, who forwarded them to General George B. Williams, described as a personal friend of Harrison.[14]

As other general authorites of the church were informed of the extensive cooperation offered by their former opponents toward what was termed their "emancipation," some expressed astonishment that the mainstays of the so-called *Tribune* ring were taking the lead in seeking amnesty. The details of how this was accomplished were not divulged, but copies of Estee's correspondence with Governor Thomas convinced the Mormon brethren that in the California lobbyist they had an influential advocate.[15]

These developments necessitated some quick changes of course by the representatives of the regular Republicans of Utah. Two party leaders, Mormon John Morgan and Gentile E. B. Critchlow, were then in Washington, D.C., to "secure harmony in the ranks of the Republicans by asking for the removal of Governor Thomas and Mr. Varian," the U.S. attorney for Utah. When John Henry Smith returned to Salt Lake City after a brief absence, he found it necessary to telegraph Morgan and have C. W. Bennett do the same to Critchlow to have them halt those efforts. Apparently the desired harmony was in prospect even while Liberal Republicans remained in territorial office. In mid-January, 1892, Apostle Smith noted that Zane, Thomas, and Goodwin were now in favor of

Utah statehood. Shortly thereafter the *Salt Lake Tribune* declared for statehood, and Smith noted that accompanying developments included the possibility that the Liberal mainstays connected with the newspaper were about to withdraw from the anti-Mormon party.[16]

By February, 1892, the *Tribune* was consistently advocating amnesty for Mormon polygamists, repeating that it would be better for Utah's future for the Mormons to receive that mark of confidence from the government. When some concern was raised within the Harrison administration about the president's power to act, Utah Gentiles called upon their friend Senator Algernon Paddock to introduce appropriate legislation. The resultant bill provided for repealing a section of the 1882 Edmunds Act so as to afford the president ample power to exercise executive clemency and grant amnesty to Mormons who had been convicted since passage of the anti-polygamy law. Utah detractors argued that if Harrison desired to act, he did not need the Paddock bill, and soon after Attorney General Miller agreed that the president already possessed sufficient power in these matters.[17]

Although assurances persisted that Harrison had decided to comply with the Utah requests, the announcement was not forthcoming. Paddock and other senators favoring the move conferred with the president, and in late March Cannon and Trumbo confidently predicted that an amnesty proclamation would be made within a few days. But it did not occur. The president was still hesitant to offer a general amnesty, which might include non-Mormons also convicted under the anti-polygamy act.[18]

The delays were embarrassing to Utah Republicans. The *Herald* and other Democratic spokesmen alleged that the entire matter had been promoted for the benefit of the rival party. On March 23 the newspaper suggested that Harrison lacked the courage necessary to carry out the plot Utah Republicans had hatched to win the territory to that party. Although there were later reports that the president was impressed with the plea of church leaders in behalf of their people, and a considerable number of individual amnesties were granted, the general amnesty failed to materialize.[19]

Another matter concurrent with amnesty, also influential in helping force the *Tribune* associates' abrupt reversal of position on statehood, was the action of Utah Democrats. Late in 1891 the party's territorial central committee sent copies of a "Home Rule Bill" to John T. Caine, which he and Senator Charles Faulkner introduced in their respective houses during the first week of 1892. The legislation aimed to abolish the Utah Commission and to allow the people a larger voice in their government by providing for popular election of territorial judges, the governor, and other officials. At the time the bill was first announced, the *Herald* conceded the party was not demanding immediate admission into the union, but was realistically advocating an acceptable interim situation until a more opportune time for statehood arose. As Caine confided to a Utah editor shortly after, his party assumed that Harrison and his administration were still absolutely opposed to Utah's admission. The delegate also mentioned a political motivation for their bill, when he disclosed to Franklin S. Richards the central committee's thinking that "it would be an excellent political move for the Democratic party to advocate such legislation and leave upon the Republicans the responsibility of defeating it if they chose to do so." [20]

Contrary to Democratic hopes, introduction of the Home Rule bill almost proved to be the impetus needed to unite all Utah Republicans and to help destroy the Liberal party. The *Salt Lake Tribune*'s first comment on the measure called it a "stupid document," saying it accomplished the only real objection to statehood, which was local control by Mormon majorities. The paper then significantly stated, "If we are going to have statehood in fact we want statehood in name," including voting for representatives in Congress. During the next several days some Liberal and regular Republicans conferred and decided to send John M. Zane and Frank J. Cannon to the east to ask for the admission of Utah as a full-fledged state. Within a week these men joined John Morgan, already in Washington, D.C., and, after making copies of a hastily prepared statehood bill, arranged with a long-time friend of Utah, Henry M. Teller, to sponsor it in the Senate, with C. W. Clarke agreeing to do the same in the House. The Teller bill was introduced immediately, although there were ominous indications from Senate Territorial Committee Chairman Orville Platt that the measure was still premature. [21]

Caine appeared incredulous at the actions of Senator Teller and his Utah Republican associates. On several occasions immediately thereafter he felt constrained to recall past Republican actions to prove that the Republican party was not Utah's best political friend. As the delegate wrote to one Utah Democratic activist, he expected the Republicans to be put to an embarrassing test with their statehood bill. He observed that the Democrats were certainly willing to grant Utah's admission into the union, provided that the Republicans offer a detailed and acceptable enabling act instead of "a skin and bones affair like the Teller Bill." Caine's personal hope was that Congress would pass both the home rule measure for immediate relief and an enabling act that could, in the absence of the Utah Commission, more fairly and gradually inaugurate actual statehood. He predicted, however, that for the present the Utah Republican delegation, lobbying at the nation's capital, would have to accept home rule or nothing and he confidently assumed their choice would be for the partial measure.[22] But by the time the extended congressional hearings on the subject began in mid-February, Utah Republicans had sent two of their chief spokesmen, party chairman C. W. Bennett and Apostle John Henry Smith to Washington, D.C., for the specific purpose of opposing home rule. Smith, assuming that the home rule measure would delay actual admission, told the congressional committee that he preferred Utah to remain in her present inferior condition if statehood could not be attained. These hearings exhibited the political diversity still prevailing in Utah. Besides the Republican viewpoint voiced by Smith and Bennett and supported by C. C. Goodwin of the *Tribune*, those Liberal Republicans not yet prepared to accept statehood were represented by Clarence E. Allen, who was backed by Liberal Democratic spokesman O. W. Powers. By far the largest Utah contingent was of regular Democrats who favored home rule. This group included Gentiles Frank Dyer, Caleb West, J. W. Judd, Joseph Rawlins, and H. W. Smith, along with Mormons F. S. Richards and C. C. Richards. Although the home rule advocates occupied most of the time before the committees, their results were not entirely favorable, largely because of criticisms they leveled at present and former territorial officials, who had many friends in Congress. Some previously receptive lawmakers withdrew support from home rule because its passage would reflect unfavorably on these officials, particularly on members of the Utah Commission.[23]

The *Salt Lake Herald* continued to be optimistic that the Home Rule bill would pass, and finally in late March it was reported favorably by the House Committee on Territories. But the paper noted that Orville Platt, chairman of the comparable committee in the Senate, had vowed that he would not allow similar legislation to be called up, much less reported. Although the Democratic newspaper expressed hopes that sufficient Republican committee members could be persuaded to support the Home Rule bill, it continued to languish. Caine eventually succeeded in getting the bill passed in the House, despite Republican obstruction tactics, but the measure died without progressing further.[24]

Notwithstanding the cooperation of Utah Republicans in opposing home rule, predictions and hopes that this would be the basis for further harmonious association among Mormon and Gentile members of the Republican party proved premature. The evident interference of the L.D.S. church in the Logan election campaign may have sparked renewed doubts among those associated with the *Salt Lake Tribune*. Or possibly Harrison's failures to grant general amnesty to the Mormons might have encouraged the Liberal ring members that their hold on territorial offices was yet more secure than they had previously assumed (or had been told by Trumbo and Estee). And many die-hard Liberals had not forgotten their setback the previous December when the Republican National Committee recognized what they termed the Mormons' "bogus Republican party." For whatever reasons, the energetic effort Liberal Republicans made in May and June for recognition by the Republican National Convention proved conclusively that they were far from prepared to disband their party or cooperate with the other faction of Utah Republicans.[25]

By the beginning of 1892 President Harrison had alienated many national committeemen and most of the state party bosses who could most effectively guide the Republicans to victory in the crucial November elections. Aside from the president's personal iciness, opposition stemmed to a large degree from fear that he would lead the party to further defeat if he remained the standard bearer. Republican professionals and masses of party faithful turned almost by reflex to James G. Blaine, still by far the most popular man in the Republican party and certainly the only one who could wrest the nomination away from an incumbent president. Blaine, Harrison's secretary of state, was not openly hostile to the president and took an ambivalent course concerning the possible submission of his name as a candidate. He had been deeply hurt by the personal abuse characteristic of his 1884 presidential campaign and had no desire to face even a small amount of it again. He had been ill the previous summer and while in Europe thereafter had publicly announced that he would not be a candidate for the presidency. But that did not stop many Republicans from looking to him as the only alternative to the Democrats gaining control of the executive branch of government as well as both houses of Congress.[26]

Clarkson played a prominent part in the movement to draft Blaine. He too was not as much disloyal to the president as he was concerned about maintaining the Republican party in power. Clarkson's committee had carefully analyzed the situation and discovered a widespread and deep-seated dissatisfaction in the West that would lead to the formation of the Populist party later that year. The members concluded that "any Republican candidate who cannot carry the western states cannot be elected" and were convinced Harrison could not possibly win in Ohio, Indiana, and Illinois, which were known to be pivotal. As party chairman he wrote to Blaine in January, 1892, in an effort to convince him to make a run for the good of the party because he was the only man "who can draw from the Farmer's Alliance the necessary votes to keep the party in power in the northwestern states." Besides possessing widespread support among farmers, party leaders expected him to have a wider appeal among the Knights of Labor than anyone else in the party. By late spring the sentiment in his favor in the Far West was reaching almost frenzied proportions.[27]

In the midst of these developments, the regular Utah Republicans began organizing early and called for their convention to be held at Provo on April 1, to select two delegates to the Minneapolis convention. Amid much celebration, noise, and electioneering, Frank J. Cannon and O. J. Saulisbury were selected. Cannon was a logical choice as one of the first Mormons active in the party and with a strong base of support in Weber County. The non-Mormon Saulisbury was described—even by the *Tribune*—as a great favorite among Republican leaders throughout the West, a status that may have been partially enhanced by the fact that he was married to one of Blaine's nieces. Since a short time later the Liberal Republicans selected a separate pair of delegates, C. C. Goodwin and C. E. Allen, there was sure to be a contest at the Minnesota convention as to which Utah Republican organization would be recognized.[28]

The regular Republicans, probably assisted by Clarkson and Trumbo, went to considerable effort to gather support for their cause at the approaching convention. This was particularly evident from their work in Idaho. Conferences and correspondence with Idaho Attorney General George H. Roberts made him an ardent advocate in favor of the regular Republicans. In a circular letter drafted in behalf of seating Cannon and Saulisbury, he argued that over two-thirds of the 6,000 Mormon voters in his state would be Republican if they were properly treated by the party at that crucial time. He cited an extravagant version of Clarkson's voting figures, saying that "there are about 200,000 Mormon voters in the United States. They are the balance of power in California, Colorado, Montana, Arizona, and possibly in Illinois and Missouri." Besides the circular letter, Roberts wrote to members of his state's congressional delegation, arguing that the Utah Liberals represented "the still life of a Dead Sea in politics" and could never pass a satisfactory examination as legitimate claimants of the territory's convention seats.[29]

On June 1 Cannon, Saulisbury, and a group of over thirty regular Republicans from Utah took a special Union Pacific Railroad car to Minnesota. Upon arrival, they embarked on a predetermined program of contacting other delegations in an effort to secure promises that they would stand with the regulars when the decisive vote on seating came up. A major aspect of the effort was distribution of a fifteen-page pamphlet, which, besides defending the rights of Cannon and Saulisbury to the Utah seats, reiterated the oft-used argument of Mormon voting strength. According to a *Tribune* report, the question of recognizing Utah delegates was a matter of "more than local significance, as other states and territories named have 460,000 Mormon population, all of which will feel aggrieved if the Liberal Republicans are accorded full or even partial recognition." The closely printed pages ended with the affirmation that it was in the interest of Republicans generally and especially the party in the Rocky Mountain region that the regular Utah delegates retain their seats at the convention.[30]

When the Liberal Republicans arrived to present their credentials at the convention, they found that the party secretary had already entered the names of their rivals on the roster of recognized delegates. But after the way the National Committee had treated them the previous year, this was expected. The Liberals understood that their best hopes for recognition lay in waiting to get beyond the biased committee's preliminary machinery to the main body of the convention. In the meantime the national committee assigned a subcommittee of Garrett A. Hobart of New Jersey, Charles Warren of Montana, and C. M. Leland of Kansas to investigate and conduct hearings on the contested seats. These meetings convened on June 5, and even in the presence of the national committeemen the animosity between the rival factions was pervasive. The Liberals represented themselves as the long-established legitimate Republican organization, denying any need for the usurping faction of regulars ever to have organized. But pointed questioning by Hobart and an animated response from Frank Cannon regarding his futile early attempts to identify with the Liberals soon proved that they did not welcome Mormon Republicans or their sympathizers.[31]

The next day the national committee met and accepted a unanimous subcommittee report in favor of seating Saulisbury and Cannon. A *Tribune* editorial of June 7 reassured readers that this was expected and would not be the final outcome, and that all of these proceedings were merely preliminary. The editors explained that after the convention got under way, a credentials committee would pass final judgment on seating matters; patience was advised. They believed it unimaginable that the Republican party could act so irresponsibly as to accept the Mormon church as an ally and simultaneously refuse to recognize their long-time associates as the legitimate holders of the convention seats.[32]

The *Tribune* proved to be correct. In subsequent days, as the Blaine boom faded, the prestige and power of Clarkson and his associates, which had favored the regular Utah delegates, dissipated as well. The credentials committee and the convention as a whole were in no mood for further delays, which Harrison's forces had blamed on the president's opponents. The outcome was undoubtedly influenced by the fact that Cannon and Saulisbury were quite clearly supporters of Blaine and their rivals were almost as surely for Harrison. When a recommendation carried that the rival claimants divide the votes Utah was entitled to and both be seated, the regulars protested. But more important business was pressing, and the appeals were ignored. As the tide turned, Utah's Blaine supporters were caught in the backwash and had to accept half-recognition or nothing.[33]

There was one final facet of the regular-Liberal feud at Minneapolis. Speaking for the regular delegation, Frank J. Cannon proposed the name of Arthur Brown for Utah's member of the Republican National Committee. The outgoing member, Judge J. R. McBride, no longer a resident of the territory, also campaigned in his behalf. But C. C. Goodwin let it be known that if the name were submitted, the Liberals would fight to prevent his approval. However, they conceded that they would oppose only Brown and McBride, both of whom they considered traitors to the Gentile cause. Brown subsequently allowed his name to be withdrawn in favor of Saulisbury, who was then proclaimed acceptable to all Utah Republicans.

As the rival delegations returned from Minnesota, each claimed to have gained the greater victory. The Liberals alleged that the regular Republican claims of getting their man on the national committee was an odd kind of victory in light of the fact that Brown had been their first preference. When Brown, who claimed to have made the selection of Saulisbury, was asked by the *Herald* why he had withdrawn from the contest, he explained that it was because at that point the Liberals abandoned any pretext they had to a separate organization. He did it "to unite the party" if possible. Many hoped that the Liberals were in fact finished, but the *Tribune* denied it vociferously.[34]

However, a simiar contest at the Democratic convention did seem to bring the Liberal party close to its end. At the Chicago convention, the Utah Democrats faced a fight strikingly similar to the one their counterparts had recently encountered. But in this case the Liberal Democrats, nicknamed the Tuscarora club, had several added handicaps. The regular Democratic party had been organized longer than the Republicans and had a more impressive recent vote-gathering record than either the Republicans or the Liberals. Besides, Powers and his associates apparently had fewer friends and supporters in positions of national power than did their Republican Liberal counterparts. Since the Democratic national convention had fewer disputed delegations and was more certain of who their presidential nominee would be, it was more likely that the Utah contest would get a careful hearing.

The Tuscaroras received considerable attention from the press and spectators because their brilliantly uniformed marching corps, over 100 strong, was the first to appear at the convention city. But the rival Democratic faction had gathered more effective support. As the convention prepared to open, a group of leaders of the national Democratic clubs, including Senator Faulkner and national club president Chauncey F. Black, released a statement concerning their visit to Utah the previous year. They attested to the fact that the regular Democratic organization was literally the party in Utah and that delegates Henry P. Henderson and John T. Caine were entitled to the territory's seats.[35]

Another of the signatories to the statement was Congressman W. D. Bynum, who also accompanied several Utahans in testifying before the convention credentials committee. After stating that if there were other Utah Democrats he had not seen them on his visit, he warned that if the forces working against the regular delegation were recognized, it would take many years for the party in Utah to recover from the blunder. The congressman also played on a familiar theme when he said that their actions would "be felt in the adjoining states and territories." Bynum concluded with the pledge that "a Democratic Congress stands solidly behind the Democratic power in Utah."[36]

One of presidential nominee Grover Cleveland's congressional floor leaders, William L. Wilson, also offered to appear in behalf of Caine and Henderson if necessary. This proved to not be needed, but thereafter Delegate Caine gratefully acknowledged the full measure of support he had received from his colleagues in the House of Representatives. The *Salt Lake Tribune*, speaking for the defeated Tuscaroras, also bitterly conceded the powerful influence of Black, Faulkner, and their associates.[37]

Amid subsequent discussion, including some by the *Herald* predicting the demise of the Liberal party, the *Tribune*, with its usual narrowness, commented that Liberals who had journeyed to Minneapolis and Chicago possessed no desire to advertise Utah's unique troubles and they were not interested in personal gain. Resorting to the old stereotypes, the paper continued, "They went there believing they represented the only American people in Utah; they went there believing that the men on the other side represented a people whose best allegiance was not to the United States but to an alien power." The *Tribune* could not yet see, it claimed, any evidence that the Mormon church had relaxed its assumption of "universal sovereignty" in the territory. Editor Goodwin had some legitimate basis for his conclusions regarding continued church activity in politics, but at the national conventions, especially Chicago, it was the activity of non-Mormons that persuaded national party leaders that the old Liberal claims of Mormon domination were no longer true.[38]

After the disappointing conventions, the Liberal party regrouped its forces, with Powers as chairman and Allen as secretary of the territorial organization. But when the party delegates convened in mid-July to decide the party's future, only eight of the twenty-five Utah counties were represented. Although a poll of the central committee indicated that the majority wished the party to remain active as a distinct political movement, one of the minority, C. S. Varian, offered a resolution favoring dissolution. Part of his argument was that in view of recent actions at the national conventions, they had no choice but to consolidate with the national parties and continue their efforts from within that structure. Varian's associate, W. H. Dickson, also advocated this position. In a *Herald* interview he admitted that he was opposed to the division along party lines, but he conceded that as the movement had progressed so far, it was unrealistic to oppose it further. He then said, "We might as well accept the inevitable and make the best of the situation." Nevertheless, those Liberals who disagreed would continue their separate efforts for another year, although there were numerous defections during that time. In August the *Herald* observed that the Liberal party was "going to pieces" throughout the territory, except for Salt Lake and Summit counties, where local election victories had bolstered party membership.[39]

An illuminating example of the thinking of former Liberals in other portions of Utah is found in a letter Charles Crane of Kanosh, Millard County, wrote to his Liberal party county chairman as he declined to be a delegate to the party convention. This Civil War veteran, who had become one of the foremost sheepmen in the West, recalled he had been a Liberal when such meant a social ostracism that Gentiles in the northern part of the territory knew nothing of. He voiced great concern that with the recent division of Mormon voters on party lines, the Democrats had gained the ascendancy in the legislature and from there could pass measures to enhance their party's interests. Yet, he observed, "Utah should naturally and geographically be Republican," and when the people properly understood tariff protection and other Republican positions, he was confident they would become members of that party. Crane then stated that "by longer adhering to the Liberal party, we are giving the Democrats an open field," and when the former party is disrupted "which it surely must be, we will be found with the bag to hold, the game having long since been captured." While he did not blame Salt Lake Liberals for maintaining their party, he expressed confidence that he could help elect a Republican representative from his county district to serve in the next Utah legislature and stated that was his intent. Before the end of the summer Crane was to become chairman of the Territorial Republican Committee, charged with direction of the entire Republican campaign.[40]

Another interesting but somewhat ambivalent position was taken by Arthur L. Thomas. Following the Republican National Convention, the Utah territorial governor showed willingness to lead the attempt to reconcile the rival branches of his party. Soon after, he appeared on the same speaker's platform with Frank Cannon. Later in the summer, Thomas called at the L.D.S. church offices to see Joseph F. Smith. Since Smith was not available, the governor confided to Francis M. Lyman that the *Deseret News*'s advocacy of home rule and Utah statehood was actually serving to help hold the Liberal party together. Lyman reported that the governor was of the opinion that if the church paper would refrain from its course, the Gentile party would soon disband, and its members would take their places among the regular Democrats and Republicans. Thomas affirmed his intention to work for the Republican party in the coming campaign. However, before he could carry out his promise, something drew him back into the anti-Mormon ranks—perhaps the influence of his close friend, Patrick Lannan, the *Tribune* publisher, or possibly the subsequent course of the Utah Republican nominating convention.[41]

This convention, held in mid-September, did prove to be a considerable detriment to party unification and harmony. Bitterness first surfaced in a dispute over whether proxy delegates could represent counties in which they had never resided. Rival delegations seemed particularly determined not to allow Salt Lake City residents to use the proxy mechanism to dominate matters more than their superior population merited by having city dwellers serve in place of absent delegates from outlying areas. A decision against the Salt Lakers indicated that their preferred candidate for delegate to Congress, C. W. Bennett, would not garner sufficient votes for the nomination. The Weber County contingent, supporting Frank Cannon for that honor, was jubilant at this test vote, which it considered to bode favorably for their man. After a third indecisive ballot, Bennett withdrew and attempted to shift his support to the Utah County candidate, future justice of the U.S. Supreme Court, George Sutherland, but Cannon came up with the requisite number of votes and was nominated. Analysts later credited his victory to the fact that his county's forces were so much better organized and unified than were those from Salt Lake.[42]

Newspaper accounts of the Cannon nomination clearly indicated disillusionment and resentment among a significant portion of Gentiles who had recently repudiated Liberalism and expressed confidence in the Republican party. The *Tribune* was glad to note the words of disgust uttered by former Liberals, who were said to have assumed that the "Gentiles were to have a show in the convention," but found the Mormons dominated it completely. The *Herald* cited Judge Powers as authority that Cannon's nomination was worth over 2,000 votes for his opponents.[43] Actually, the matter was not so simple. There were significant numbers of L.D.S. politicians who favored and worked for the nomination of

Bennett, including Cannon's cousin, George M. Cannon. Apostle John Henry Smith was perhaps Bennett's foremost campaign manager. In fact, even the First Presidency of the church was less than enthused about young Cannon's candidacy, although this was at least partly because they were of the opinion that no Republican could yet win such an election in Utah.[44]

Seeking to capitalize on the growing dissension in the Republican ranks, some Democratic leaders were reported to be determined to nominate a Gentile instead of a "scion of a royal family of the Mormons." John T. Caine had expressed a desire to retire after ten years as delegate, feeling that the first congressional election under the new party alignment was a good time for him to step down. Amid what appeared to be a completely harmonious association between Gentiles and Saints, Joseph L. Rawlins, son of a Mormon bishop, but not himself affiliated with the church, was chosen as the Democratic party candidate for Caine's congressional seat.[45]

True to their promises, the Liberals also held a nominating convention. After apostate Mormon Henry W. Lawrence and O. W. Powers declined to have their names submitted, C. E. Allen was selected as what turned out to be the last Liberal candidate for Congress. Although the Republicans' nomination of a Mormon generated more Liberal support than had been anticipated, in contrast to the preceding congressional campaign, little major party attention was aimed at Allen. By this time the Utah Democrats and Republicans were prepared for a head-on contest.[46]

The most notable feature of the fall campaign was the bitter pamphlet barrage. This began with a dozen-page broadside entitled *Nuggets of Truth*, which the *Herald* stated was authoritatively linked to the Republican territorial committee. Its purpose was essentially to prove, with statements drawn from the men themselves, that all four Latter-day Saint prophets had professed political views that would place them squarely in the Republican camp. The *Herald* charged that "a more miserable demagogic attempt than is made in this scandalous pamphlet has never been known in politics." The Democratic paper argued that since Frank Cannon was the chief beneficiary of the pamphlet, he must be blamed for its dissemination. Several days later the *Herald* admitted that the Republican candidate, for whatever reasons, had ordered it to be withdrawn from circulation. Although Cannon later stated he had abhorred the blatant attempt to use the prestige of the current and former church presidents to his advantage, Democrats believed that he stopped the pamphlet only upon discovery that church members resented its use.[47]

Whatever the candidate's true feelings, by that time President Joseph F. Smith, who had also been quoted in *Nuggets of Truth*, had prepared his own extremely partisan booklet entitled *Another Plain Talk: Reasons Why*

the People of Utah Should be Republican, in answer to a *Herald* column by
Penrose under a similar heading about why Utah citizens should be
Democrats. In his pamphlet Smith recounted Utah's history in a most biased manner, questionably concluding, among other things, that the only
two Democratic presidential administrations during the past thirty-one
years, those of Buchanan and Cleveland, "stand out as the blackest pages
in American history, so far as the treatment of the people of Utah is concerned." President Smith's comments called forth several broadsides full
of refutations, including one by Penrose. Since the church leader had paid
little attention to historical facts, the Democrats made considerable political capital in correcting what they could legitimately term "errors and
misstatements."[48]

Another feature of the campaign, also involving President Smith, was
the so-called bishop's recommend. Aparently some Democrats had
launched a whispering campaign in portions of the territory, recounting
facts and rumors of Frank Cannon's past moral indiscretaions. In response, the Republicans circulated a two-page statement denouncing and
denying the allegations. More important, Joseph F. Smith rather unwisely secured a letter from Bishop Thomas J. Stevens of Ogden's 5th
Ward, which conceded that Cannon had transgressed, but had made complete amends and was presently considered a member in good standing
among his fellow church members.[49]

As the campaign reached its final week, the *Herald* observed that the
pamphlets and bishop's recommend were acting as a "boomerang" with
reference to the perceptions of Liberal and ex-Liberal voters toward the
activities of the Mormon authorities. The *Tribune* admitted that it was
"delicious" to see such a quarrel going on between so-called Democrats
and Republicans over the real position of their prophets in politics. The
paper expressed firm belief that the church was using a good deal of influence in the campaign, and this could not be denied.[50]

Even in the more ordinary aspects of the contest between Cannon and
Rawlins, including a series of debates in the last days prior to the election,
the presence of the church authorities was noticeable. Cannon's constant
theme was tariff protection, supposedly as taught by Brigham Young,
and certainly as embodied in the McKinley Act. For the present at least,
Rawlins and his party were able to blame recent economic ills on the 1890
tariff. But obviously two of the highest Mormon leaders had taken
the other side on the most widely discussed issue of the day. In the recent
semiannual church conference both Joseph F. Smith and George Q.
Cannon strongly stressed the need to foster home industries. The former
called this "the gospel of temporal salvation," and the latter agreed.[51]

By this time Cannon and Smith were making no pretense of neutrality or nonpartisanship in their personal political views—at least among trusted church members. They had definitely concluded that Utah's best interests politically and economically were intimately associated with Republican success. On several occasions serious disappointment continued to be expressed that the policy of equal division had not been more conscientiously carried out. At the end of general conference on October 10, priesthood leaders from throughout the church were informed that if they would follow such counsel on political division, they would "soon see a bright day dawn upon Utah" and their "deliverance," presumably meaning statehood, would be promptly accomplished. Later in the month, Abraham H. Cannon overheard his father pointedly tell general authority John R. Winder, a loyal Democrat, that he believed the Mormons' safety and political prosperity depended on Mormons voting Republican. Young Cannon described the comments as kind and yet forceful.[52]

In the final days of the campaign a committee of prominent Gentile Democratic leaders, including territorial judges Henderson and Judd and ex-Governor West, called upon the First Presidency to complain about continued church interference in political affairs and to ask for a reaffirmation that they had withdrawn from politics. Several days later the *Salt Lake Herald* disavowed any implications that the First Presidency had officially sanctioned use of their names in the campaign, though there was a question why a denial from the church leaders had not been given sooner. The paper told of the recent interview in which fellow Democrats had been assured by the presidency that they had publicly expressed no preference and had not authorized anyone else to speak for them. Although not so stated, the presidency's answer obviously resorted to a narrow distinction between public, collective counsel and private, individual advice. The *Herald* must have understood this to some extent because a week previously it had recounted a statement from Joseph F. Smith's Logan conference address in which he had refused to limit himself and other church authorities to strictly spiritual concerns and opinions. Yet despite the First Presidency's obvious concern, they had not intervened, as they could have done, to turn the election in Frank Cannon's favor.[53]

It proved to be fortunate that church authorities had not been more insistent in this regard because, as the *Herald* observed after Rawlins's decisive victory, it would have looked suspicious for Utah to have been the glaring exception to the overwhelming Democratic electoral landslide of November, 1892. Cannon's *Standard* rightly stated that there should have been no realistic expectation of victory yet. The newspaper was full of enthusiasm at the tremendous inroads Republicans had made into the Democratic majority and waxed optimistic about the future of Cannon and his party.[54]

In 1892 more than in the previous year it is difficult to see how the church presidency could claim to be uninvolved in politics, although it can sometimes be argued that technically it was as private individuals rather than as church officials that they participated as political activists. An example of this individual activity involved a continuing controversy over the office of U.S. marshal for Utah. In late August, 1892, the *Tribune* and other opponents of the relatively lenient Marshal Eli H. Parsons finally convinced President Harrison that a change was required. Attorney General Miller's call for Parsons's resignation caused serious concern among the Mormon leaders, who expected a Liberal attempt to get someone appointed who would rejuvenate the old anti-polygamy crusade.[55]

On September 1, John Morgan, a member of the First Council of Seventy, met at the office of Republican leader C. W. Bennett, where it was decided that the Mormon general authority and Willey L. Brown, a Gentile, would go east to lobby concerning Parsons's replacement. On the way Morgan, a decorated Civil War veteran, stopped at his (and President Harrison's) old home in Indiana, where he secured letters of introduction to men prominent in the Republican administration. When the Utahans got to Washington, D.C., they first met with Clarkson, who assured them that he would do all he could in their behalf. Thereafter, their chief conferences were mostly with an influential group of Indianans, including Miller, Elijah Halford (Harrison's private secretary), personal friend and presidential political advisor Lewis T. Michener, and U. S. Treasurer George Nebeker. Throughout September and into October, Morgan kept up a rigorous round of high-level interviews, interspersed with telegrams to Utah, for the purpose of blocking Liberal efforts and securing an acceptable appointee as U.S. marshal for the territory. Morgan was satisfied when the president granted the appointment to I. A. Benton, a Salt Lake City postmaster. Then, after a brief effort to insure that the vacancy in the post office was also properly filled, the Utah emissaries returned home.[56]

A subsequent comment in Abraham Cannon's journal reveals not only how effective the lobbying had been but also that the First Presidency was fully apprised of its results. He recorded that George Q. Cannon had disclosed that the newly appointed marshal "had been instructed from Washington that he must do as he was directed by the heads of the Mormon church if he desired to retain the position." The concluding comment was that the marshal had sent word to the church presidency that he was willing to comply with those terms.[57]

Church leaders had also continued to be involved politically on the amnesty question. As the presidential campaign of 1892 approached, church insiders concluded, on the basis of information from Estee and others, that President Harrison was "so afraid of injuring his chances for renomination that he will not do anything that he thinks will offend any of this party." Thus expectation of an amnesty announcement waned. On the eve of the nominating conventions, the *Herald* rightly concluded that "the President's course in this business [amnesty] from the first has not been such as to suggest that his heart is in the matter." And during the ensuing campaign the Utah Democratic press persistently reminded voters of the unfulfilled Republican promises of amnesty.[58]

A complication in the progress toward amnesty, impossible to substantiate, was later recounted by Clarkson. He said that in the midst of the 1892 campaign the national committee sent him to appeal to Harrison for an immediate amnesty proclamation. The president replied that such action at that time would be "considered by the prejudiced people among the churches as an act influenced more by his needs and ambitions as a candidate than by his sense of justice and duty as a President." Expressing fear that the religious press would oppose and condemn such a proclamation, Harrison requested that Clarkson contact and gain assurance from each of a substantial number of editors of such papers. With the aid of Isaac Trumbo, the chairman recounted, they accomplished this large undertaking, securing a "favorable expression" from the various church papers for the president's immediate action on the matter.[59]

Along with the continued efforts in behalf of amnesty by church agents, Clarkson, and administration insiders, a key western senator had also become personally engaged in the cause. A letter from Francis E. Warren of Wyoming to Halford is informative of the broad implications of the struggle and the political tactics utilized in its behalf. The preliminaries of the letter, dated August 29, 1892, explained to the assumedly uninitiated Halford that the Mormon voters held the balance of power in the counties of western Wyoming. This situation was crucial to the make-up of the next state legislature, which would decide if Warren would be returned to the Senate for another term. He mentioned that the Gentiles in Utah and surrounding states were as anxious for amnesty as were the Mormons themselves, because it would "hasten the entire solution and settlement of troubles growing out of Mormonism in the past." The senator mentioned that he had seen Harrison several times on the matter during the spring and early summer of 1892 and reminded the secretary that the president's own reelection prospects would be enhanced throughout the West by granting amnesty prior to the November elections. Warren finally arrived at the real reason for writing. He stated that when

George Q. Cannon had left Washington earlier in the year, he had been convinced that the president was going to grant the amnesty sought. But, the senator continued, he had recently learned from a confidential source that Wilford Woodruff had come to believe that the pardon had been thwarted by Warren's having opposed it. The alarmed candidate assured the secretary that Woodruff was mistaken, but reported in desperation that, in consequence of the false assumptions, the Mormons in Wyoming were "in a mood to oppose a Republican legislature which might return me to the Senate." He pleaded for Halford to secure at least some acknowledgment from the president that Warren had in fact worked in behalf of the Mormons and requested the presidential confidant to prod Harrison into making the amnesty announcement.

Warren's existing correspondence indicates that during this period he was in contact with both Trumbo and Morris Estee. One of them probably was the source of the report concerning Woodruff's attitude. If the venerable church leader was of the opinion that Warren was to blame for Harrison's failure to act, he most likely received that idea from the source that informed Warren that Woodruff was angry with him. Such tactics had no noticeable effect on Harrison, who may have had his fill of Wyoming matters recently because of the intervention in the Johnson County War, which Warren had helped force upon him the previous month.[60]

At about this time, George Q. Cannon returned from another trip to the East, where he had discovered that the *Tribune* crowd had been making a secret attempt to revive the old strifes—probably in relation to the appointment of the U.S. marshal. These efforts had been partly averted by Cannon's visit. The personable Cannon was also apparently able to break down the final barriers in President Harrison's hesitancy toward the Latter-day Saints. This is best evidenced by the fact that soon after his return, Trumbo and Estee reported Harrison had requested the Mormon hierarchy to pray for his consumptive wife, with whom he had been sitting as his presidential campaign limped along without much attention from him. The telegram to Woodruff, which was read to other general authorities the same day as they offered prayers in behalf of Mrs. Harrison, assured that amnesty would be granted to the Mormons within a week.[61]

But in the ensuing days the president was preoccupied with grief over the death of his wife and with the imminent elections. It was not until the lame-duck period following his defeat that Harrison finally granted the petition. When it came, it was less than the Saints had been led to expect, and there was widespread disappointment in Mormondom. The problem, as those who continued to live with more than one wife understood, was that the proclamation promised more active prosecution of them, although their more submissive brethren, who had complied with the law, would be pardoned. However, by this time the last remnants of special restrictions on Utah and the Mormons were rapidly disappearing anyway, and one active polygamist reflected philosophically that the greatest effect of the presidential announcement was to improve public opinion toward the church.[62]

At about the time of Harrison's amnesty proclamation, Patrick Lannan, the long-time *Tribune* publisher, sought an interview with Mormon leaders. Conceding that there was no question about the approach of statehood, he expressed grave concern that the Latter-day Saints would yet seek to establish the kind of theocracy formerly preached as the "Kingdom of God." The former leader of the anti-Mormons sought a pledge that non-Mormons would not be disturbed or discriminated against if statehood were accomplished. In the absence of the First Presidency, Francis M. Lyman and John Henry Smith were authorized to deliver a resolution stating that church leaders would use whatever influence they had "that no non-Mormon whatever his past attitude towards the Mormon people may have been shall ever be disturbed in his person or business in any way whatever in the event of our territory being admitted into the Union." This was not enough for the apprehensive Lannan, and he decided to formulate a list of more specific questions to which the general authorities could respond.[63]

In subsequent days the questions were received. Besides a detailed question about establishment of a literal, temporal Kingdom of God, there were several about how unbelieving, nonconforming neighbors would be treated by—assumedly—Mormon state officials. The inevitable query regarding the finality of church authorities' pledges to have retired from politics specifically asked them to reaffirm their promise not to seek "to influence voters through the obedience of the rank and file to their priestly superiors." Finally, the dubious Gentile leader asked if all Utah citizens would be guaranteed complete equality before the law. This list of questions was carefully considered by at least a half-dozen church leaders, including historian B. H. Roberts and attorney F. S. Richards. All answers were completely reassuring, intending to convey the impression that conditions had changed in Utah and that the majority population of the territory could now be expected to conform to political standards prevalent throughout the nation.[64]

In spite of all assurances concerning withdrawal from politics and control over their members, there was an important internal exception to these statements. The First Presidency reserved the right to impose rather strict restraints on the political activities of other general authorities. This would be the basis for an open and heated controversy in the fall of 1895, but there was a significant private preliminary in the months surrounding the 1892 elections. Moses Thatcher and B. H. Roberts were involved in both situations.

Actually, the controversy stemming from Thatcher's speech at the Democratic convention and subsequent activities had never completely been resolved. In July Joseph F. Smith informed his sometime opponent "that the day would come when he would regret the stand he had taken upon the question of church and state which tends to prevent the Presidency from counseling the people in political matters." Within a week Thatcher was also taken to task for expressing ideas on bounties to sugar beet farmers, which would show in a negative light the Lehi sugar factory church leaders were striving diligently to establish. Subsequent discussion brought out the fact that the individualistic Thatcher was also not sustaining the political policy of the presidency, which required that all church general authorities "not to take up political or other work" without the knowledge and approval of the First Presidency.[65]

In the case of Thatcher and Roberts, it was October 11 before they called at the presidency's office to find out what they should do in politics. At that time they were advised to continue their efforts for the Democrats, "but very mildly."[66] This was prior to most of the bitter pamphlet campaign, which, though it did not implicate either directly, undoubtedly caused them to express themselves in less than mild terms. Even after the beginning of 1893, Thatcher, Roberts, and pamphleteer C. W. Penrose were considered "out of harmony" with their brethren. Apostles Lyman and Grant attempted to help Thatcher "see that he was in error in striking out in politics on his own hook," but there was no agreement on the matter then or in the following two months. Finally in the late March apostles' meeting the quorum declared that Thatcher must "be brought to see that he had been working against the policy of the presidency thus heading a faction against the presidency and bringing them to disgrace in the eyes of the Saints." Those present concluded that the defiant apostle would not be permitted to attend the approaching dedication of the Salt Lake Temple unless he changed his course and repented. Similar decisions applied to Roberts and Penrose, with brethren assigned to help persuade each of the error of his ways. Finally, all three recanted their views favoring political independence—at least for a time.[67]

During the short second session of the fifty-second Congress beginning early in December, 1892, several bills were introduced to enable Utah to become a state. The one sponsored by the lame-duck John T. Caine was favorably reported by the House Committee on Territories on January 24, 1893. But its progress had already been so severely delayed by the absence of Joseph Washington, the committee chairman, that Caine rightly feared there was hardly time to get it passed. Though he had been informed by the sympathetic Joseph Carey that the Senate was not disposed to do anything at that time toward the admission of new states, Caine induced C. W. Faulkner to introduce a Utah Enabling Act in the upper house anyway. The delegate agreed that such action was close to futile, feeling that the disposition in the upper house to link the admission of his territory to those of New Mexico, Arizona, and Oklahoma was the most serious obstacle to passage of the bill.[68]

Caine mentioned late in the session that President George Q. Cannon, his son Frank, H. B. Clawson, Estee, and Trumbo were all at the capital doing what they could for Utah "from their way of thinking." These efforts were also unsuccessful, but for an entirely different reason than Caine had mentioned. According to Clarkson, he and some of his associates had fervently wished to have the Republican-dominated Senate grant Utah statehood before the recently elected Democratic majority took their seats at the next term. He claimed that through their manner of persuasion they had gained practically the unanimous vote of the Senate in the territory's favor—only to be thwarted by the persistent individual efforts of Territorial Committee Chairman Orville H. Platt. Clarkson recalled that upon finding himself virtually alone on his committee in opposition to Utah, Platt threatened to resign as chairman if the majority of the committee would overrule him and report the bill favorably. He was reported to have carried the matter so far as to invoke senatorial courtesy to defeat what was said to have become a strong pro-Utah sentiment in the upper house.[69]

Other parliamentary maneuvers intended to bring the bill to the Senate floor when Platt was absent had been attempted through one of Clarkson's oldest and closest political friends, William B. Allison, the chairman of the Senate Committee on Appropriations. The powerful Iowa senator was certain he could provide the opening for Carey to bring the Utah measure up. But this had also failed.[70]

One of the methods still utilized by Clarkson in securing Senate support for Utah is indicated in an undated note from him found in Allison's papers for these months. The party chairman told how members of his national executive committee had just met and concluded that "the next President may lie in the action of the Mormon vote." An accompanying paper, not now available, was said to show "the number of votes of their people *outside* of Utah and the remarkable manner in which they [were] so diffused as to have the probable balance of power in 8 or 10 states." Clarkson explained that at a time when the Populist party and its free silver sentiments were gaining popularity in the western states, the Mormons were a great balance of conservatism against that drift. He continued that the information he had prepared was meant to influence senators who "may not understand the power of the Mormon vote," adding that all his committee agreed that the Utah bill should then pass the Senate and concluding that "it is a *vital* matter to the future of the party."[71]

In attempting to account for why Senator Platt had been so fervent in his opposition to Utah, Clarkson expressed near certainty that it had been a result of the influence of *Tribune* associates Lannan, Thomas, and Goodwin and their close ally from Idaho, Fred T. Dubois. Clarkson never questioned the integrity of Senator Platt, but he warned that the others had remained consistently, if secretly, opposed to Utah statehood. Dubois did have special ties to Platt because he and the senator's son had been roommates at Yale College some years before. Whatever their reasons for opposition, Clarkson was of the opinion that it had singly prevented the granting of Utah's admission in February, 1893.[72]

When Joseph L. Rawlins took his seat in the U.S. House of Representatives in September, 1893, one of his first acts was to introduce a joint resolution providing that the personal property of the church in the hands of the receiver be returned to its rightful owner. Part of the resolution defending such action stated that the church "no longer encourages or gives countenance in any manner to practices in violation of law." This bill breezed through the judiciary committees and passed both houses with impressive speed. Grover Cleveland signed the church property resititution resolution on October 25. A week later Franklin S. Richards, representing the church, petitioned the U.S. Supreme Court to remand the property in question to the Utah Territorial Supreme Court for final disposition to the church. On November 6, 1893, Chief Justice Melville Fuller handed down such a decree, which was subsequently carried out. All but the last of these steps took place in time to generate some political capital for the Democrats just as important off-year elections were held in Utah.[73]

Yet despite the restoration of church property by the Democratic administration, Utah Republicans were optimistic about the approaching election. The panic of 1893, especially devastating in the West, had gripped Utah for most of the year—with the party in power bearing the brunt of the blame. As the recently inaugurated second Cleveland administration sought remedies for the economic distress, the president called Congress into special session for the purpose of repealing the Sherman Silver Purchase Act of 1890. Although western senators opposed the measure to the end, it was accomplished in the weeks prior to Utah's election day. Also by that time it had become abundantly clear that Cleveland believed his party's mandate was tariff reform, including elimination or drastic reduction of protection for several vital Utah products, including wool, sugar, and lead. Republican spokesmen constantly reminded Utah voters of these facts.[74]

Under these circumstances the territory's Democrats were justifiably apprehensive. The *Herald* reminded voters that Utah was understood to be Democratic, then boldly warned they had better return a legislative majority for that party or those in Congress who could grant statehood may well lose interest in that goal. The newspaper also stressed that Utah should maintain harmony with the party in power not only nationally but in the territorial executive office, where Caleb W. West had been reappointed governor. However, to such arguments the *Tribune* pointedly replied that to remain Democratic Utah voters must desert silver and condone free importation of lead and wool.[75]

The election results indicated success for Utah's Republicans, the first for that party in the territory. The election began a string of four straight similar outcomes in the last political contests before statehood. Disregarding the short-lived Liberal allegiance retained by eight of the thirty-six legislators, the Republican party garnered majorities of seven to five in the upper house and fourteen to ten in the lower house of the territorial legislature. Frank J. Cannon's editorial comments labeled the Utah election as a "great rebuke" to the Cleveland administration and specifically referred to the attacks on silver, lead, and wool. He stated that an even stronger reason for Utah's repudiation of the Democrats was that the party had "given notice that they propose to prevent the establishment of home manufacturing institutions by refusing to grant bounties." Cannon referred to the struggling Lehi sugar works, observing that no such enterprise could hope to flourish without some initial aid from the government.[76]

When Delegate Rawlins returned home a week later, he admitted that the policies of the Democratic administration had not been such as would or ought to commend them to the people of Utah. And late in the month in a private University Club speech, he bitterly attacked President Cleveland for his policy on silver, citing fellow Democrat "Silver Dick" Bland as authority for the allegation that the fight on the white metal had been initiated by eastern party members at the behest of the Wall Street money power. Rawlins paid tribute to western Democrats for valiantly opposing repeal of the Silver Purchase Act despite impossible odds.[77]

This election was especially important to some doubtful Utah observers as proof of the actuality and good faith of the division along national party lines. Not long before, the *Tribune* had alleged that the Democratic party and the Mormon church had agreed to a deal through which statehood would be granted in exchange for continued election majorities for that party. After the election the *Herald* consoled Democrats by arguing that at least the outcome proved the allegations of such a conspiracy to be false. Soon after the *Tribune* pointed out that the preelection *Herald* warnings that a vote for the Republicans would jeopardize statehood had not dissuaded voters from their honest preferences. This, the paper concluded, was "the clearest evidence of their capacity for self-government that has ever been displayed in Utah and dispersed the fears of thousands of persons that with the trust imposed upon them they would use it unworthily." Significantly, this long-time opponent of statehood never again published articles against admission, and that week the *Tribune* began making comments sympathetic to the disbandment of the anti-Mormon party it had supported for so long.[78]

The Liberal party had essentially faded from existence in all except a few mining districts and the two largest Utah cities. Since the defeat in 1891 the party had not fared well in Ogden, but still held sway in Salt Lake City. However, November, 1893, also saw a crucial municipal election there, and many city residents were inclined to believe *Herald* allegations that the "malodorous" city council was the "exact antipodes" of honesty and capability in its conduct of public affairs. Although more restrained in its comments, a group of several dozen prominent Mormon and Gentile businessmen issued an invitation for others concerned to gather and discuss the future course of Salt Lake City government. The call commented that with the present financial distress gripping the region, it was "impossible for the community to stand the strain they are now put to by present municipal extravagance." When those interested in the matter assembled, many Gentiles criticized the incumbent Liberal administration, and it was concluded that since there was more prudence and economy needed than could be expected from a "political administration," a nonpartisan "Citizen's party" would be formed to oppose the Liberals for Salt Lake City's offices. Although the *Tribune* called this a revival of the People's party, only nine of the twenty Citizen's candidates were Saints and six of the Gentiles had recently been Liberals.[79]

Besides the threat from the Citizen's coalition movement, Liberals faced an even more formidable problem within their ranks. During the summer of 1893 a branch of the nativist American Protective Association, by then widespread in the nation, was established in Salt Lake City. Reportedly some 600 strong, this organization, most often referred to locally as the "Western Star" or "Amorines," was fundamentally anti-Catholic in its orientation.[80] Over twenty elected and appointed city officials were listed by the press among the members, some of whom had allegedly pledged to remove all Catholics from the municipal employment rolls. The *Salt Lake Tribune*, published by Catholic Patrick Lannan, was particularly outspoken in its criticism of the Amorines and their bigoted aims.[81]

Since the founder of the Liberal party and some of its long-standing sup-
ports were at least nominally Catholic, there was nothing but harm to
party fortunes anticipated as A.P.A. influence grew.

The *Deseret News* noted the considerable speculation on the relative
strength between the Amorines and the "Lannan Liberals" and predicted
that neither faction was likely to make sufficient concessions to the other
to enable the Liberals to be successful at the polls. At least three candidates on the Liberal slate were known to be Amorines, and some of their
fellows sought to expand the number. The mayoral candidate, J. C.
Conklin, refused to take a stand either for or against the A.P.A. and may
therefore have alienated both factions. At any rate, during the last days of
the campaign the matter caused the *Herald* to express confidence that
Citizen's party candidate Robert N. Baskin was assured of victory in the
mayor's race. The *Tribune* conceded that "if the Liberal ticket generally is
not elected this fall, it will be because of the unrest and indignation which
[the Amorines], as an organization, have caused in this community." It is
ironic that the anti-Mormon Liberal party in Utah, a coalition of diverse
groups generally united for more than twenty years, would be totally destroyed by one of the periodic waves of Protestant antipathy toward Ca-
tholicism, but that was the case. The Liberals lost all but a minority of
city council seats and the treasurer's office.[82]

Immediately after the election in which the Liberals polled only half
the votes they had gathered the year before, the *Tribune* conceded that the
party should soon disband. Interviews with a number of former anti-
Mormon activists indicated a near consensus in that regard. O. W. Powers expressed belief that statehood was now inevitable and that with
hindsight it would have been better to accept the Mormon professions of
good faith earlier. Although he was clearly in favor of dissolving the Liberal party, he stressed that such could not be accomplished by an individual or a newspaper, but must be done by the assembled members themselves. This was finally carried out a month later. At that time their long-
time organ, the *Tribune*, paid tribute to the heroic effort to Americanize
Utah: "They worked with the idea from the first that their final triumph
would at the same time be the death of the party." The feeling at the mass
meeting accomplishing the demise of the Liberal party seemed unanimous
that it had fulfilled its purpose.[83]

Prior to these important developments surrounding the 1893 elections,
Caine sent to Rawlins a draft of an enabling act for Utah, which prominent Utah Democrats had requested that he write. It was based on the
one reported favorably by the House Committee on Territories at the previous session, and that one, Caine confessed, had been copied to a large
extent from New Mexico and Arizona bills that had earlier cleared the

committee. The veteran lawmaker assured Rawlins that he was certain Charles Faulkner would be glad to present a similar bill in the Senate and that the process should be launched again.[84]

Rawlins introduced his bill in the new Congress on September 6, 1893. But this was complicated by the fact that new territorial committee chairman Joseph Wheeler also proposed one, less generous in school land allocations, and including Arizona, New Mexico, and Oklahoma. In addition, a recurring measure, this time introduced by William C. Oates, proposed that sparsely populated Nevada's respectability be bolstered by annexation of all Utah territory to it. As these bills were considered in the territorial committee, the *Tribune*—which at the time was still opposing statehood—published a special dispatch from the nation's capital alleging that the Cleveland administration, then repealing the silver purchase act, did not favor admission of additional silver states. The *Herald* countered that if such were the case, members of the House Committee on Territories, the majority of whom were in harmony with the administration, would not then be subjecting the Utah measures to such close scrutiny. The paper assured readers that there was no reason to believe that Cleveland and his associates were opposed to admission of further territories, particularly Utah.[85]

On November 2, just before the elections in Utah, the Democratic spokesmen were proven to be correct because the House committee reported the Rawlins Bill favorably. Rawlins had apparently secured authorization from each committee member, including Wheeler, to have his measure attached to virtually the same report the committee had made on the Caine bill in the previous January. Even the *Tribune* correspondent praised the "continuous and earnest" work in behalf of statehood done by Rawlins in his first weeks in Congress. This was accomplished at the short special session of Congress, which adjourned after the first week of November. But the Utah measure was placed high on the House calendar, with all concerned confident it would pass early in the approaching regular session.[86]

However, in the intervening weeks Utah's voters elected the Republican legislative majority, which threatened to bring progress toward statehood at the hands of the Democrat-dominated branches of the federal government to a halt. The *Tribune* taunted that it would be curious to see if Rawlins pursued his quest with his former zeal. When the delegate returned for a brief visit to the territory, he expressed disapointment at the outcome, but made it clear that he did not assume the election would interfere with Utah's progress toward statehood. He said Democratic leaders did not believe Utah was naturally Republican and the election could hardly offset that feeling. Besides, Rawlins continued, it would be poor party policy to antagonize the citizens of any territory by delaying state-hood when it was as deserving as Utah was.[87]

Proponents of Utah statehood may have received a scare when the sub-ject reappeared as Congress convened in the first week of December, 1893. Through a series of misunderstandings, the second ranking Democrat on the Committee on Territories, C. B. Kilgore, called up the Rawlins bill while Wheeler was absent. This brought considerable protest from House Republicans. As the *Tribune*'s perceptive Washington correspondent W. E. Annin explained, this was because the matter had been brought up at an early morning hour, before some members arrived and some of them who had previously opposed Utah statehood wished to express them-selves so that their constituents would understand why they had changed their position.[88]

The *Salt Lake Herald*'s version of the affair was quite different. The paper's capital dispatch appeared under headlines reporting that the Democrats were solidly anxious to admit Utah, but the Republicans con-tinued to be the stumbling block. The *Herald* reporter stated that "Mr. Trumbo and other Republicans are greatly chagrined at the conduct of the party in the House," singling out Maine party leaders Nelson Dingley and former Speaker Thomas B. Reed as the major opponents to further House action.[89]

There is probably an element of truth in this version of the delay be-cause long afterward, Trumbo's close associate, James S. Clarkson, re-counted a work they undertook at that time with Reed. Clarkson recalled that he had entered the capitol chamber in time to encounter some un-friendly words regarding Utah from Reed and other members of the Re-publican party, who he described as having already decided to defeat the bill. He immediately obtained an interview with the powerful represen-tative, who knew of Clarkson's past involvement with the Mormons on behalf of the Republican National Committee. He pointed out that the Mormons were in agreement with the Republican party on nearly all of the contemporary national issues. Still not convinced, Reed accepted Clarkson's offer for further arguments that evening at the former's hotel room, where, accompanied by Bishop H. B. Clawson, they held forth for three hours. After close questioning of the Mormon representative, Clarkson stated, Reed accepted their arguments as factual and withdrew his opposition. Although after the weekend he and his associates again protested the bill's coming up at the morning hour, they agreed it should be made the special order of business on the following day.[90]

Debate on the admission of Utah was finally staged on the floor of the House of Representatives on December 12, 1893. Compared to the ani-mosity engendered by the subject in the past, the mood that day was cordial. Delegate Rawlins impressively presented Utah's case and ably answered a good many friendly questions as to details of the bill and conditions in Utah. One of the two who occupied the time in opposition to statehood, Elijah A. Morse, a Republican from Massachusetts, showed himself so ignorant of Utah affairs as to bring ridicule and laughter upon himself and probably aided Rawlins's efforts. The other opponent was Michael D. Harter, a long time anti-silver Democrat from Ohio, who argued weakly that Utah was not entitled to statehood because proportionate to the most established states she did not have sufficient population and developed resources. Actually the quality of the opposition, with the laughter and derisive remarks aimed at it, showed the extent to which the great majority in the House agreed that Utah was now entitled to enter the union as a state. There were no more than a half-dozen nays in the final voice vote on the statehood matter taken that day.[91]

Thus the year 1893 ended on a high note with almost unopposed passage of the Utah Enabling Act in the House of Representatives. Developments of that year had been truly decisive in clearing the way for final enactment of the law midway through 1894. Amnesty for many Mormon polygamists and the return of the personal property of the church resolved undesirable situations that extended back into the 1880s. And the political developments involving the demise of the Liberal party and the Republican party's initial Utah victory were pivotal in eliminating long-standing opposition to Utah statehood.

NOTES

1. A. H. Cannon Journal, Oct. 2, 22, 1890. Smith was referring to an Edmunds bill concerning church personal property.

2. George Q. Cannon to "My Dear Judge" [Estee], Dec. 9, 1890, Woodruff, Cannon, and Smith to Judge M. M. Estee, Dec. 2, 1890, copies First Presidency Papers [Letterbooks].

3. A. H. Cannon Journal, Jan. 30, 1891.

4. W. H. H. Miller to James S. Clarkson, Nov. 7, 1890, W. H. H. Miller Papers [Letterbooks], Indiana State Library, Indianapolis, copy also in First Presidency Papers [Letterbook]. This letter enclosed one from Isaac Trumbo, suggesting "the manner in which the Edmunds law should be administered among the Mormons."

5. Woodruff, Cannon, and Smith to Estee, Dec. 2, 5, 1890, Woodruff, Cannon, and Smith to A. M. Musser, Nov. 28, 1890, Woodruff, Cannon, and Smith to W. W. Cluff, Nov. 28, 1890, First Presidency Papers [Letterbooks].

6. Woodruff, Cannon, and Smith to Estee, Dec. 2, 1890; First Presidency Papers [Letterbooks]. These statistics were only approximate and did not always reflect the more accurate figures that were then available at church headquarters in the semiannual stake statistical reports. The Wyoming figure, for example, did

not include a larger number of Latter-day Saints residing in Star Valley—then a part of Bear Lake, Idaho Stake. A. H. Cannon Journal, Jan. 30, 1891.

7. Benjamin Harrison to Clarkson, July 27, 1891, Clarkson to Harrison, July 22, Aug. 7, 1891, Benjamin Harrison Papers, Library of Congress, Washington, D.C.; Vincent P. DeSantis, *Republicans Face the Southern Question: The New Departure Years, 1877–1897* (New York, 1959), 208–26; Stanley P. Hirshson, *Farewell to the Bloody Shirt: Northern Republicans and the Southern Negro, 1877–1893* (Bloomington, Ind., 1962; rpt. Chicago, 1968), 233–56.

8. See, among others, Robert D. Marcus, *Grand Old Party: Political Structure in the Gilded Age, 1880–1896* (New York, 1971), 160; Richard J. Jensen, *The Winning of the Midwest: Social and Political Conflict, 1888–96* (Chicago, 1971), 122–77; Paul Kleppner, *The Cross of Culture: A Social Analysis of Midwestern Politics, 1850–1900* (New York, 1970), 92–178; Kleppner, *The Third Electoral System, 1853–1893: Parties, Voters, and Political Changes* (Chapel Hill, 1979), 198–237.

9. Jensen, *Winning of the Midwest*, 102–21, 200; Kleppner, *Third Electoral System*, 306–28.

10. Clarkson to E. W. Halford, Dec. 5, 1891, Harrison Papers. Professor R. Hal Williams of Southern Methodist University called my attention to this letter.

11. Clarkson was allied mainly with state party professionals who, while still favorable to some vestiges of the spoils system, were much more inclined to guide the Republican party toward a more pluralistic outlook. Many of President Harrison's leading supporters were amateur politicians who tended to oversimplify complex political and cultural forces into narrow standards of what was morally correct and fully American. See Jensen, *Winning of the Midwest*, 130–33; Kleppner, *Cross of Culture*, 162–64.

12. Clarkson to Woodruff, July 11, 1894, copy Volwiler Papers.

13. A. H. Cannon Journal, July 9, Oct. 15, 1891.

14. J. H. Smith Journal, Dec. 18–22, 1891.

15. A. H. Cannon Journal, Jan. 13, 1892.

16. Morgan Journal, Jan. 5, 1892; J. H. Smith Journal, Jan. 11, 20, 1892; *Salt Lake Tribune*, Jan. 7, 20, 1892.

17. *Salt Lake Tribune*, Feb. 14, 15, 16, 18, Mar. 1, 7, 1892.

18. Ibid., Mar. 23, 1892; *Salt Lake Herald*, Mar. 23, 1892; A. H. Cannon Journal, Apr. 1, 2, 28, 1892.

19. *Salt Lake Herald*, Mar. 23, May 10, 25, 1892.

20. F. S. Richards to John T. Caine, Dec. 21, 1891, Caine to S. A. Merritt, Jan. 23, 1892, H. P. Henderson to Caine, Feb. 7, 16, 1892, Caine to James Wallis, Jan. 26, 1892, John T. Caine Papers, H.D.C.; *Salt Lake Herald*, Jan. 6, 1892; *Congressional Record*, 52d Cong., 2d sess., 997, 1043, 1044.

21. *Salt Lake Tribune*, Jan. 7, 1892; Morgan Journal, Jan. 17, 18, 1892. C. W. Bennett said that the new Republican Executive Committee of Utah framed the Teller bill and sent it to Washington, D.C., for introduction. See *Salt Lake Tribune*, Jan. 20, 1892.

22. Caine to William H. King, Feb. 13, 1892, Caine to S. A. Merritt, Jan. 23, 1892, Caine to James Wallis, Jan. 26, 1892, Caine Papers.

23. *Salt Lake Tribune*, Feb. 24, 1892; *Salt Lake Herald*, Feb. 16, 18, 19, 20, 23, 24, 26, 1892.

24. *Salt Lake Herald*, Mar. 19, 31, Apr. 1, 17, 23, May 19, July 9, 1892; *Salt Lake Tribune*, Mar. 23, Apr. 1, 29, May 5, 1892.

25. *Salt Lake Tribune*, May 20, 1892.

26. R. Hal Williams, *Years of Decision: American Politics in the 1890's* (New York, 1978), 59–66; Marcus, *Grand Old Party*, 163–73; David S. Muzzey, *James G. Blaine: A Political Idol of Other Days* (New York, 1934), 467–80.

27. Gail Hamilton [Abigail Dodge], *Biography of James G. Blaine* (Norwich, Conn., 1895), 696–700. The author was a Blaine relative who had access to papers and materials not otherwise preserved.

28. *Salt Lake Herald*, Apr. 2, 1892; *Salt Lake Tribune*, Apr. 2, 1892.

29. George H. Roberts to J. H. Smith and [John] Morgan, May 19, 1892, J. H. Smith Papers. [Governor] Norman B. Willey to [Congressman] Willis Sweet, May 11, 1892, Norman B. Willey Papers, Idaho State Library, Boise. See also p. 220n71 herein.

30. *Salt Lake Tribune*, June 4, 1892.

31. *Salt Lake Herald*, June 7, 1892; Morgan Journal, June 5, 6, 1892.

32. *Salt Lake Tribune*, June 2, 1892.

33. Ibid., June 8, 11, 1892; *Salt Lake Herald*, June 10, 1892.

34. *Salt Lake Herald*, June 11, 14, 16, 1892; *Salt Lake Tribune*, June 11, 12, 14, 18, 22, 1892.

35. *Salt Lake Tribune*, June 19, 1892; *Salt Lake Herald*, June 17, 19, 22, 1892.

36. *Salt Lake Herald*, June 21, 22, 1892. See *The Facts in the Utah Case* (Salt Lake City, 1892), 5–23. See also copy, letter Jan. 12, 1892, signed by S. A. Merritt, chairman of the Democratic Territorial Central Committee, and Elias A. Smith, secretary, in Caine papers, Utah Historical Society, Salt Lake City.

37. *Salt Lake Herald*, June 24, 1892; *Salt Lake Tribune*, June 25, 28, 1892.

38. *Salt Lake Tribune*, June 25, 1892.

39. *Salt Lake Herald*, July 9, 10, 21, Aug. 10, 16, 18, 1892; *Salt Lake Tribune*, July 21, 22, 1892. Frequently, as on Aug. 18, the *Herald* noted defections from Liberal ranks, such as Salt Lake County Selectman John Butter, who had "decided to join the Republican party."

40. Charles Crane to George Veile, Feb. 6, 1892, Charles Crane Scrapbook, which a niece, Mrs. Naomi Melville Cottam, says she recently donated to Brigham Young University, Provo, Utah. Copy in possession of author.

41. *Salt Lake Herald*, June 17, 1892; Lyman Journal, Aug. 5, 1892; Lyman to Wilford Woodruff, Aug. 6, 1892, Francis Marion Lyman Papers, H.D.C.

42. *Salt Lake Herald*, Sept. 16, 17, 1892.

43. Ibid., *Salt Lake Tribune*, Sept. 17, 1892.

44. J. H. Smith to Frank J. Cannon, Sept. 30, 1892, J. H. Smith Papers; A. H. Cannon Journal, Aug. 30, 1892.

45. *Salt Lake Tribune*, Sept. 20, 21, Oct. 6, 1892; *Salt Lake Herald*, Oct. 6, 1892.

46. *Salt Lake Tribune*, Oct. 13, 1892; *Salt Lake Herald*, Oct. 13, 1892.

47. *Salt Lake Herald*, Oct. 17, 25, 27, 30, 1892; Cannon and O'Higgins, *Under the Prophet in Utah*, 124; *Nuggets of Truth* (Salt Lake City, 1892), 1–14, copy Utah Historical Society, Salt Lake City.

48. *Salt Lake Herald*, Oct. 11, 1892; Joseph F. Smith, *Another Plain Talk: Reasons Why the People of Utah Should Be Republicans* (Salt Lake City, 1892), 2–16, copy, Utah Historical Society; "Johnathon," *Joseph F. Smith Answered: His Plain Talk Shown to be Full of Errors and Misstatements* (N.p., n.d.), 1–4, copy Utah Historical Society; C. W. Penrose, *C. W. Penrose Replies to Joseph F. Smith* (N.p., n.d.), 1–4, copy, Lee Library, B.Y.U.; *Nuggets of Truth: Hear Ye the Whole Truths, As to Joseph Smith's Political Views* [an answer to the more famous tract by same name] (N.p., n.d.), 1–3, copy, B. H. Roberts Papers, H.D.C.

49. Thomas J. Stevens to J. F. Smith, Oct. 26, 1892, copy *Salt Lake Herald*, Oct. 30, 1892; *Voters of Utah, Beware!* (N.p., n.d.), 1–3, copy, Roberts Papers.

50. *Salt Lake Herald*, Nov. 2, 1892; *Salt Lake Tribune*, Oct. 31, 1892.

51. *Salt Lake Tribune*, Oct. 9, Nov. 6, 1892; *Salt Lake Herald*, Nov. 8, 1892.

52. A. H. Cannon Journal, Oct. 10, 23, 31, 1892.

53. Ibid., Nov. 3, 1892; *Salt Lake Herald*, Nov. 3, 6, 1892.

54. *Salt Lake Herald*, Nov. 10, 1892; *Ogden Standard*, Nov. 13, 1892.

55. *Salt Lake Herald*, Aug. 31, Sept. 1, 2, 1892; A. H. Cannon Journal, Aug. 30, 1892.

56. Morgan Journal, Sept. 1, 11, 12, 15–17, 22–30, Oct. 3–6, 1892. See also C. W. Bennett to Benjamin Harrison, Sept. 2, 1892, for letter of introduction for Willey L. Brown and George Nebeker to L. T. Michener, Oct. 6, 1892, enclosing a telegram from George F. Gibbs to John Morgan, Oct. 5, 1892, all in Harrison Papers. See also the Harrison Papers for correspondence aimed at blocking unfavorable Utah appointees.

57. A. H. Cannon Journal, Oct. 27, 1892.

58. Ibid., Apr. 28, 1892; *Salt Lake Herald*, Nov. 8, 1892.

59. Clarkson to Woodruff, July 11, 1894, copy Volwiler Papers.

60. Francis E. Warren to E. W. Halford, Aug. 29, 1892, Francis E. Warren Papers [Letterbooks], University of Wyoming Library, Laramie, copy also in Harrison Papers; Helena H. Smith, *The War on Powder River* (Lincoln, 1966, rpt. 1967), 183, 260–62.

61. A. H. Cannon Journal, Oct. 9, 13, 1892; W. Woodruff Journal, Oct. 11, 1892.

62. Harry J. Sievers, *Benjamin Harrison: Hoosier President* (Indianapolis, 1968), 242–43; Roberts, *Comprehensive History*, 6:289; A. H. Cannon Journal, Jan. 4, 1893.

63. Lyman Journal, Jan. 13, 1893.

64. Ibid., Jan. 26, 27, 1893; copy questions, unlabeled (index states they are from Lannan), undated (with other papers of Jan. 1893), Woodruff Papers, copy also inserted in Wilford Woodruff Political Letterbooks, 1893–1902, H.D.C.

65. A. H. Cannon Journal, July 12, 13, Aug. 4, 1892; Lyman Journal, July 12, 17, 28, 30, Aug. 4, 1892; Grant Journal, July 12, Aug. 4, 1892. In the latter entry Apostle Grant specified that "the policy of the presidency as I understood it is that

it is wise for our people not to consider it their bounden duty and that seeing the idea has gone on that we should all become Democrats that it is wisdom for the leading Democrats not to be too active in trying to made converts to their political faith." Lyman's July 28 entry stated, "The necessity of a good strong Republican element seemed to impress the presidency."

66. Lyman Journal, Oct. 11, 1892.

67. A. H. Cannon Journal, Mar. 22, 23, 1893; Lyman Journal, Mar. 22, 23, 27, 31, Ar. 3, 4, 6, 13, 16, 17, 1893.

68. Caine to J. E. Washington, Dec. 7, 1892, Caine to Charles C. Richards, Dec. 5, 1892, Jan. 31, 1893, Caine Papers, H.D.C.

69. Caine to C. C. Richards, Jan. 31, 1893, Caine Papers, H.D.C.; Clarkson to Woodruff, July 11, 1894, Volwiler Papers.

70. Clarkson to Woodruff, July 11, 1894, Volwiler Papers.

71. J. S. C. [Clarkson] to Dear Senator [William B. Allison], (undated with papers of Aug., 1893), William B. Allison Papers, Iowa State Library, Des Moines; Edward Leo Lyman, "Politicians' Perceptions of the Western Political Situation and Their Implications for Statemaking, 1887–1894," paper presented at the Twentieth Annual Conference of the Western History Association, October 17, 1980, Kansas City, Mo. A portion excerpted in Appendix 3 of Lyman, "Mormon Quest for Utah Statehood," 591–95, attempts to show that the Republican estimates of L.D.S. voter strength outside of Utah was grossly over-stated.

72. Clarkson to Woodruff, July 11, 1894, Volwiler Papers.

73. Joan Ray Harrow, "Joseph L. Rawlins: Father of Utah Statehood" (M.A. thesis, University of Utah, 1973), 82–83; Salt Lake Herald, Sept. 19, Oct. 6, 22, 26, 31, Nov. 7, 1893; Salt Lake Tribune, Oct. 28, 1893; Congressional Record, 53rd Cong., 1st sess., 1362.

74. Nevins, Grover Cleveland, 523–48; Ogden Standard, Aug. 22, 31, Oct. 14, 1893.

75. Salt Lake Herald, Sept. 28, Nov. 3, 5, 1893; Salt Lake Tribune, Oct. 1, 1893.

76. Ogden Standard, Nov. 8, 9, 11, 12, 1893; Salt Lake Tribune, Nov. 10, 1893.

77. Salt Lake Tribune, Nov. 15, 26, 1893; Salt Lake Herald, Nov. 15, 26, 1893.

78. Salt Lake Tribune, Nov. 5, 17, 1893; Salt Lake Herald, Nov. 14, 1893.

79. Salt Lake Herald, Aug. 29, Sept. 23, Oct. 22, 1893; Salt Lake Tribune, Sept. 7, 10, Oct. 26, Nov. 8, 1893.

80. Donald L. Kinzer, An Episode in Anti-Catholicism: The American Protective Associaion (Seattle, 1964), 93–139; Salt Lake Herald, Aug. 20, 29, 30, 31, 1893; Salt Lake Tribune, Aug. 27, 1893; "Journal History of the Church of Jesus Christ of Latter-day Saints," Aug. 25, 28, 30, 31, Oct. 5, 13, 27, 1893.

81. Salt Lake Herald, Aug. 30, 1893; Salt Lake Tribune, Aug. 27, Sept. 28, 1893.

82. Salt Lake Herald, Nov. 5, 1893; Salt Lake Tribune, Oct. 25, 1893; Deseret Evening News, Oct. 13, 27, Nov. 4, 1893.

83. Salt Lake Tribune, Nov. 10, 11, 12, Dec. 19, 1893; Salt Lake Herald, Nov. 11, 1893.

84. Caine to Rawlins, Aug. 18, 1893, Caine Papers, H.D.C.

85. *Ogden Standard*, Sept. 1, 1893; *Salt Lake Herald*, Sept. 16, 19, Oct. 28, 31, Nov. 1, 5, 1893; *Salt Lake Tribune*, Oct. 31, 1893; *Congressional Record*, 53rd Cong., 1st sess., 1273, 1276, 1469, 3100, 3116; *House Reports*, 53rd Cong., 1st sess., I, no. 162, Part 1, 1–24, part 2, 1–15.

86. *Salt Lake Herald*, Nov. 3, 8, 1893; *Salt Lake Tribune*, Nov. 4, 1893.

87. *Salt Lake Tribune*, Nov. 22, 1893; *Salt Lake Herald*, Nov. 15, 1893.

88. *Salt Lake Herald*, Dec. 9, 1893; *Salt Lake Tribune*, Dec. 9, 10, 1893; *Congressional Record*, 53rd Cong., 2d sess., 118, 136.

89. *Salt Lake Herald*, Dec. 9, 1893.

90. Clarkson to Theodore Roosevelt, Sept. 23, 1904, Theodore Roosevelt Papers, Library of Congress, Washington, D.C.; *Salt Lake Herald*, Dec. 12, 13, 14, 1893; *Salt lake Tribune*, Dec. 12, 13, 14, 1893.

91. *Congressional Record*, 53rd Cong., 2d sess., 174–87, 208, 319.

8

The Goal Accomplished—
But with Complications

After the Utah Enabling Act cleared its few hurdles in the House, Republican support for statehood seemed to increase rapidly. But ironically, the long-time Democratic champions of the territory's admission were simultaneously growing markedly more hesitant to grant what they had previously strived to attain. Recent election returns[1] did much to determine party position on the question, and the Democratic party included political realists not unlike those who had so long resisted Utah's cause when admission appeared to be detrimental to the Republican party. Yet through a series of unique circumstances, the remaining obstacles were rather quickly cleared and Utah's entrance into the union was assured within half a year. However, amid the jubilation at having statehood within sight, the highest Mormon authorities would come to regret the means through which the long-sought goal had been accomplished. Their attempts to extricate themselves and their people from unauthorized commitments made in exchange for admission of Utah became a complex and costly endeavor, the details of which further enhance our understanding of how Utah statehood was achieved.

At the beginning of 1894, *Salt Lake Tribune* dispatches were confident that there would be little difficulty in getting the Utah Enabling Act past the Senate Committee on Territories. Republicans on the committee indicated considerable support of the measure. In mid-January, 1894, the executive board of the Republican National Committee passed a resolution favoring the admission of Utah. Later in the month the powerful Senate Republican steering committee, after conferring primarily on statehood questions for several hours, agreed to recommend to the Republican caucus that party members should support the immediate admission of

Utah. Accounts of these proceedings mentioned Orville Platt's continued reservations but stated that he would withhold further opposition at least until the bill came to the Senate floor. These were decisive hurdles that Utah admission efforts had never before cleared. The *Tribune* observed that all Senate Republicans stood ready to vote for the measure as soon as it came up on the calendar and that "every day that Utah is kept out of statehood now can be charged fairly to the Democratic majority who have the matter in charge."[2]

The Republican press was by that time consistently chiding Utah Democrats, for their fellow party members in Washington, D.C., were becoming less inclined to bring the Utah matter forward. It was alleged that such former friends of the territory as A. P. Gorman and C. W. Faulkner were no longer certain Utah would support their party and were thus less in favor of admission of the new state. The *Tribune* republished a statement apparently originating in the *Washington Star* to the effect that "Mr. Cleveland is opposed to the admission of any more states at present and has passed the word to that effect." Another dispatch charged that Senator Gorman, head of the Democratic steering committee, had dictated the delay. Interviews with Republican members of the Senate Committee on Territories led the *Tribune* to suggest a plot to stall the Utah bill until the Senate became preoccupied with the House version of the Wilson Tariff bill, which would halt consideration of all other matters for an extended time.[3]

Delegate Joseph L. Rawlins was increasingly alarmed with his party's actions, and in late January, 1894, John T. Caine traveled east to assist his successor. "Greatly perturbed" at the failure of their party to bring the Utah admission bill before the full Senate, Caine and Rawlins summoned every pressure they could bring to bear on Senator Faulkner. The Utah Democrats warned party leaders, particularly those from the West, that "Democratic delay would mean the loss of church votes in all the adjoining states," adding that the obstruction had already done the party damage there and prompt action on the statehood matter was necessary to prevent permanent injury to their prospects.[4]

The territorial committee chairman had not even permitted the special subcommittee charged with initial consideration of the bill to convene. Although more regular meeting days of the committee passed without any such gatherings, the *Herald* finally reported its correspondent had been assured by Faulkner that the people of Utah had no need to fear because "in due course of time" the Utah bill would be reported favorably and passed. The assurance was couched in explanations about the Senate being a slow-moving body and that matters could not always be rushed.[5]

In subsequent days Rawlins informed Utah Democratic leader O. W.

Powers that he was no longer fearful of the outcome of the statehood bill in the upper house. He was certain that it would pass at the present session, though he confessed that "there is some reluctance to take up and pass the bill at once as Democratic senators are in some doubt as to whether Utah might conclude to do the foolish thing of sending two Republicans to the Senate." To prevent this eventuality from interfering with the party's pending legislative program, Rawlins divulged the Democratic intention to delay Utah's actual admission date until after the current congressional term had expired.[6]

The *Herald* loyally adopted that line of argument, saying the Democrats had been elected to effect certain national reforms and it would be suicidal to endanger their accomplishment by admitting two potentially Republican senators too soon. Probably but few Utahans were persuaded when the apologetic paper raised the question of whether the general party policies were not "of much wider concern to the nation than the immediate admission of one new state." Thereafter, rival capital correspondents to the Salt Lake dailies wired consistently contradictory reports on the status of the Utah bill. Yet points of agreement came through, nevertheless: that Faulkner's inaction continued, that there were no subcommittee meetings, and that almost all other members of the Senate Committee on Territories not only supported Utah's admission but also pointed to the chairman as the cause of continued delays.[7]

James S. Clarkson and his Republican associates had remained active throughout these weeks of frustrating delays. There was seemingly no way the Republican party, with its minority status in both houses, could hope to garner any credit for accomplishing Utah statehood during the present term of Congress. In fact, Clarkson later conceded that the territory's cause at the time looked hopeless. As he described the situation, it was plain that in spite of the seeming friendship of some long-time Democratic advocates of Utah's admission, "it was both the party intention and interest not to admit to statehood a territory whose two senators would be Republican and change the balance of power in the Senate." However, an unusual opportunity, arising out of factionalism among the Democrats, enabled the Republicans to play a greater role in securing Utah statehood than could otherwise have been expected.[8]

Much of the Democrats' divisiveness stemmed from party rivalries in New York state, where Grover Cleveland and his supporters were often at odds with the factions with which Senator David B. Hill was aligned. This was amplified on the national level by growing differences between the president's version of the pending tariff law and what some Democratic senators, particularly Hill and Gorman, thought it should be. This antagonism toward Cleveland and his policies eventually prompted Hill and Gorman to overcome their personal reservations concerning the wisdom of allowing Utah to be admitted as a state.[9]

Cleveland had previously nominated a respected New York attorney, William B. Hornblower, to fill a vacancy in the U.S. Supreme Court. It was a commendable appointment, except that because of the appointee's previous actions against Hill's Tammany Hall allies, it aroused the pent-up animosities in the senator. Because presidential action regarding the appointment had been unilateral and arbitrary—as conceded by both Hornblower and administration floor leader W. F. Vilas—it seemed a rather clear-cut case of infringement upon the sacred canons of senatorial courtesy.[10] Hill issued a bipartisan appeal to his fellow senators, accompanied by dire warnings of a complete overthrow of senatorial prerogatives unless the executive was checked. The failure of the administration attempt to get Hornblower confirmed was hailed in the New York press as a victory for Hill. But, as the *New York Times* observed, had it not been for the assistance of Senate Republicans, who were willing to participate in embarrassing the president, Hill would have been badly beaten in the contest because few Democrats wished to incur presidential wrath by opposing Cleveland, even on such traditional matters as senatorial courtesy.[11]

Clarkson's account of this situation stated that through the genial instrumentality of Isaac Trumbo, Hill was offered sufficient Republican aid to defeat Hornblower in exchange for pledges from Hill and Gorman that they would support the admission of Utah. This was reinforced in late January, 1894, when the stubborn Cleveland designated another New Yorker—even more offensive to Hill—Wheeler H. Peckham, as his next choice for the vacant court position. This time the *Times* predicted Hill would be hard-pressed to line up the necessary opponents, though it was reported that Fred T. Dubois, acting as Republican whip, appeared confident that he had gathered all the backing needed. This proved to be the case, and the *Times* again conceded that it was the Republican senators who supplied Hill with the forces necessary to defeat Peckham.[12]

A fervent Cleveland supporter, George W. Curtiss, observed in a *Harper's Weekly* editorial that New York senators Hill and Edward Murphy were "accused of making a trade with Republican politicians by which they agreed to vote against any tariff bill in return for Republican votes against Mr. Peckham and Hornblower." This may well be true because, as Curtiss pointed out, they joined Gorman, Stephen M. White, and several other Democratic senators in opposition to the administration's version of the tariff. But they also took an early stand in favor of Utah statehood. In fact Hill and White, both majority members of the Committee on Territories, subsequently played a crucial role in pressing Faulkner toward eventual action on the Utah bill.[13]

During the spring months there were almost weekly efforts on the part of Hill, White, and their Republican colleagues on the committee to get sufficient action for a favorable report on the Rawlins bill. On many Fridays the *Tribune* correspondent reported, that on the previous day—the regularly scheduled meeting time for the territories committee—Chairman Faulkner resisted efforts to take the matter up. The reporter had good access to Republican committeemen from Utah's neighboring states, George L. Shoup and Joseph Carey, who, with fellow westerner Henry L. Hansbrough, were particularly interested in placing Faulkner's opposition on record so that Republican support for Utah statehood could be clearly discerned by voters. On April 18 the reporter wired a detailed account of their presumed success in finally getting some results stating Senator White had called on Faulkner for an explanation of why the bill had been pigeonholed. He was informed that the bill's generous land provisions were objectionable and that it was not drawn entirely in accordance with precedents. Faulkner and fellow Democratic obstructionist William B. Bate expressed the opinion that further investigation and delay would be useful. But White, Hill, and the Republican members present insisted it was time for action. Further discussion substantiated Republican allegations that Democratic delays were primarily political. When the Republican committeemen finally acceded to an amendment preventing the possibility of new Republican senators from Utah entering their seats during the present term of Congress, some obstacles were removed.[14]

Yet despite these developments, several days later *Tribune* correspondent W. E. Annin reported that Rawlins had conceded it was doubtful if real progress had been made toward overcoming the policy of delay. This may have been because Faulkner and Bate stipulated that the committee report should not be brought up in any manner that might "antagonize" the tariff deliberations, which had been the order of Senate business for over three months. These were so increasingly disruptive to unity within Democratic ranks that the *New York Tribune* was merely stating the obvious when in early May it mentioned the "disorganized state of the party."[15] With no end in sight for consideration of the Wilson bill, there were few reasons for optimism for Utah's cause. Rawlins and territorial committee members continued their efforts, but were notably discouraged.

In a mid-May interview with Dubois, the *Salt Lake Tribune* correspondent discovered that Rawlins had admitted to the Idaho senator that he found it impossible to secure any satisfaction from Faulkner and despaired of anything being done for Utah. Despite Rawlins's subsequent denials of this action, he left for Utah with his family at that time. Although he had been persistent in his efforts throughout the winter and spring, his absence from his post on the day that the Utah statehood bill was successfully dislodged from the committee seriously detracts from the claims made then and more recently that he was the "father of Utah statehood."[16]

Meanwhile, Republican statehood advocates still had to cope with some opposition from Senator Orville H. Platt. Several sources, difficult to reconcile completely, tell of influences brought to bear on the stubborn, but conscientious Yankee. Platt's biographer describes an incident in which a Utah man, speaking for the Mormons, had previously gained the senator's confidence, apparently through his truthful responses to sensitive questions about polygamy. This man was undoubtedly Frank J. Cannon, who had been involved in lobby activities on several occasions in the nation's capital. Young Cannon's political autobiography related essentially the same details of Platt's test. According to this account, Platt summoned him to a private meeting, also attended by one of the Republican lobbyists for Utah. Describing arguments such as Trumbo and Clarkson had been utilizing about the disappearance of all semblance of Mormon polygamy, Platt pointedly asked Cannon of their truthfulness. His answer was that conditions in Utah were not exactly as described, since there was still some degree of disregard of the anti-polygamy decrees. But, he continued, the outlook was positive, and the problem was dissipating as rapidly as could be expected. Though he was later chastised by the lobbyist for being so candid, young Cannon credited himself with having won the senator to the favor of the Mormon cause that day. Platt's biographer agrees.[17]

This development may have occurred just prior to the time in mid-May when the Utah bill was finally retrieved from the Committee on Territories. Bishop Hiram B. Clawson wrote to Wilford Woodruff just after the statehood bill was reported out of committee on May 16 and revealed some details of how this crucial step was accomplished. Clawson, who had been working closely with Clarkson and Trumbo in the East, recalled that on May 15 it had been assumed that the Senate Democrats were so demoralized over the tariff bill that there was no hope for the Utah bill. Faulkner had promised to attend the committee meeting, but it had been discovered that the senator intended to be absent from the capital for two weeks. As the discouraged proponents of statehood discussed the situation, Senator White thought that it was not safe to press the matter in Faulkner's absence. But Clawson suggested that possibly this time of Democratic discouragement over the tariff was an opportune one for Utah. This idea prevailed, and with it in mind Trumbo conferred with the recently installed chairman of the Republican National Committee, Joseph H. Manley, and together they called on Platt.[18]

According to Clawson's report, during the ensuing conversation Platt stated that he was no longer opposed to the Utah bill. He promised to prove it by "taking hold of the matter in earnest." Resenting the fact that Democratic obstructionists had attempted to lay the blame for delays on him, he proposed to write to Faulkner, stating that he wanted the Utah statehood bill brought up and favorably acted on at once. In the resultant letter Platt informed the committee chairman that since the public had the impression that it was he who was responsible for committee inaction, the Connecticut senator was having the correspondence published to correct that view. Apparently this struck Faulkner at a vulnerable point because he immediately authorized the subcommittee to proceed. The result was that on the next day the hastily returned chairman announced to the press that his committee was prepared to report a bill for the admission of Utah as a state.[19]

A *Tribune* dispatch claimed Faulkner took this action in response to the repeated and urgent requests from the Republican members of his committee, along with Rawlins and Trumbo. The newspaper, which would consistently attempt to belittle Trumbo in the future, mentioned that the lobbyist was "representing something or somebody" in Washington and was the first to announce that Faulkner had ceased to resist the Utah measure. The *Herald* more charitably said, "Isaac Trumbo, of California, a native of Utah, has worked hard for the bill and no happier man was in town today than he when the committee decided to report the bill."[20]

Senator Faulkner continued to emphasize that the tariff had his party's top priority, but with the Utah bill out of the committee pigeonhole, its proponents expressed confidence that it would soon pass. As Clarkson stated, in his partisan way, that after the measure was so quickly placed on the Senate calendar, it was impossible for Democratic opponents to resist except through an open fight. No sensible politician wished to antagonize the yet-uncertain Utah electorate in such a manner.[21]

The element of disagreement yet remaining between the rival parties was as to the date at which Utah would have her own duly elected voting representatives in Congress. Republicans wanted this done promptly, but frankly conceded that they would never have been able to get the statehood bill out of committee if they had not given in to Democratic demands that the date of Utah's admission be postponed until 1896. As the time arrived, in early July, 1894, when both parties agreed the Utah bill should come to the floor of the Senate for final consideration, Carey disclosed that his Republican colleagues had caucused and discussed the possibility of fighting the delay in admission. They decided to honor their previous agreement and allow the amendment permitting the present term of Congress to expire before Utah's senators would be seated.[22]

However, as Shoup later revealed, Platt had not been a party to this promise. In fact, Shoup recalled, Platt had consistently reserved the right to propose alterations to the bill from the Senate floor. This was the reason, according to Carey, that he was not certain Platt would accede to Democratic demands that Utah not be admitted for another year and a half. When the Utah bill finally was brought up for Senate consideration on July 10, Platt did request a verbal amendment, but his proposal was a technicality.[23] The amended bill passed the Senate with almost no discussion and with no division of the House. On the final disposition of the bill, there were only two Democratic votes to the contrary.[24]

According to Rawlins's recollections, when the Utah bill was brought to the floor and Faulkner asked for unanimous consent for its immediate consideration, Platt arose, apparently to object. At that point, Rawlins remembered, Hansbrough whispered something to the Connecticut senator, after which Platt resumed his seat and the bill passed. Several years thereafter, Rawlins claimed that he discovered the subject of the conversation: Platt was told, according to these reminiscences, that "if Utah were admitted into the union she would line up as a Republican state," and it was that assurance which had supposedly quieted the senator.[25]

This entire account appears improbable in light of the fact that Platt had long been informed as to what his party could expect to gain from favorable treatment of the Utah question. That had not curbed his resistance until he was personally convinced that the people of Utah were prepared for the independence from federal control that statehood would allow them. In light of his recent actions in behalf of Utah, it is clear that Platt had concluded to favor Utah's admission before the bill came before the Senate. Besides this, on the day the upper house passed the Utah Enabling Act, Platt told the *Tribune* reporter that he was much pleased with the result and with the work of his Republican associates on the territorial committee.[26]

At that same time, the *Tribune* described the jubilant Trumbo shaking hands with half the senators at the capitol, while Bishop Clawson stood smilingly by. In subsequent days the colonel received numerous congratulatory telegrams from some of these legislators and others who knew of the importance and success of his quiet work. Senator Henry M. Teller said, "You have made the best fight ever before the American Congress and all sing your praises." Congressman Jonathan P. Dolliver stated, "No one ever came to this city who made so many friends and had so poor a cause." Senator J. C. Burrows noted, "You have been the peacemaker between a misunderstood people and this government, and I am sure the American people all join in praise to you." Platt himself remarked, "You have built yourself as well as the Mormons in good faith before the country." And another former opponent, Thomas B. Reed, expressed the sentiments of many colleagues when he said, "I feel assured that faithful work you have done will be recognized by a generous people."[27]

The congratulatory praise was not limited to the East. In response to a telegram from Clarkson, Trumbo, and Clawson (which said "statehood bill signed, your people are free and this ends our hard labor"), the First Presidency sent a reply to Trumbo: "We rejoice with, and congratulate you on the successful termination of your labor, which has resulted in Utah's enfranchisement, and political deliverance to her people." Reflecting their full awareness of the complexity of the lobbying effort, the church leaders acknowledged that "while your hand has not been seen, and others claim all the honor, those who know the facts fully appreciate your efforts, and fully accord to you their heartfelt gratitude for the deep interest you have taken in the matter."[28]

Possibly the long-time anti-Mormon lecturer and Washington commentator, Kate Field, best summed up the contribution of this dedicated lobbyist when she commented, "In all probability statehood would have been delayed but for the untiring vigilance of one man. Early and late, in season and out of season, Isaac Trumbo labored in behalf of immediate admission." Describing him as "kindly, courteous, popular with all, a born diplomatist," she observed that the colonel "converted enemies into friends, and accomplished with a smile what could not be obtained with an argument." Conceding others certainly had aided in the struggle for Utah statehood, Field admitted that she had "never seen so well-managed a campaign as the still hunt of Isaac Trumbo and Bishop Clawson during the last six months."[29] (A "still hunt" was a political strategy demanding a minimum of publicity, with efforts concentrated on small meetings and much canvassing "to reach wavering legislators without arousing partisan feelings or inviting vigorous counter-moves by the opposition." This approach was particularly effective when the opponents were not putting forth their full effort and when members "ordinarily fixed in their predilections are reachable because of hard times or specific local irritations." This being so, Trumbo and his associates enjoyed near-perfect circumstances for such a campaign, and their success entitled them to the praise given by contemporaries and far more credit for Utah statehood than has since been accorded.[30])

Clarkson, as he explained why his fellow Republicans had not more diligently sought to amend the enabling act to expedite quick admission of Utah, indicated awareness of another reason for a still hunt-type strategy: "It was not advisable to give any partisan color to it [the Utah bill] nor afford any partisan reason for Mr. Cleveland to disapprove it." He further explained to church leaders that they had intentionally conducted their efforts in such a way as "to tranquilize all the elements, and to bring Utah into the union a welcome member of the family and welcomed by all elements." This appears to have been impressively accomplished.[31]

To those aware of the numerous instances of bitter opposition formerly engendered by propositions of Utah statehood, the virtual absence of any semblance of such reactions on the eve of accomplishing that goal is truly remarkable. But a careful search for evidence to the contrary offers no reason to doubt that Utah's admission as a state was achieved in the manner detailed by the Mormon lobby agents and the *Salt Lake Tribune* Washington correspondent.

The key factor in the transformation among members of Congress and their constituents since the last attempt was the seemingly altered course of the Latter-day Saints regarding plural marriage. With the nation generally convinced that polygamy was at least in the process of eradication, the Senate, long the major obstacle to Utah's admission, was willing to accept the judgment of their colleagues on the territorial committee that there was no longer any reason to oppose the entry of the territory into the Union.

Certainly a still hunt may be impossible to document more fully than has been attempted herein, but all indications are that the quiet work that such a strategy entailed was effectively carried out amid circumstances in Congress almost uniquely advantageous to Utah's cause. The Democratic party had been the traditional champions of Utah's interests, although ardor for the cause had cooled somewhat with recent Republican election victories there. But even if the party had been totally united, as it was not amid the Wilson-Gorman tariff controversies, it could not abruptly abandon Utah without risking the long-range alienation of an electorate not yet entirely lost to them. There were undoubtedly innumerable contacts with individuals of both parties by the lobby agents, to overcome lingering apprehensions and bolster wavering resolves. And according to evidence subsequently brought forward, there were numerous offers of personal financial advantage linked to support for statehood. It is impossible to assess the full impact of such influences, but the implications from the agents responsible for such pledges indicate that they played a considerable role. Whatever their methodology, it is entirely probable that the role of Utah's untiring and resourceful lobbyists was greater than had ever been the case in accomplishing statehood for a territory in the United States.

Following passage of the bill in the Senate, it only remained for the House to ratify the amended version and send it to the president for his signature. Rawlins had difficulty locating signatories authorized to attest that the enabling act had been duly passed, finally securing the signatures of Vice-President Adlai Stevenson, the president of the Senate, and of acting House Speaker J. D. Richardson, to get the bill in proper order for submission to the president. Cleveland signed the Utah Enabling Act before bedtime on the evening of July 15, 1894.[32]

Utah received the long-awaited news with striking calmness and practically none of the spontaneous and noisy celebration characteristic of most new states. Possibly this was because of the disappointment that territorial status would continue. If the *Tribune* reaction on the subject was typical, this was the case. The *Salt Lake Herald* did announce that a statehood celebration day would be held at the Great Salt Lake resorts on August 1. Although the *Tribune* and some Republican leaders warned that this was intended to be a Democratic affair, the program outline was conspicuously nonpartisan and nondenominational. The well-attended proceedings were carried off in just such a manner. Rawlins was rightfully hailed for his role in securing the enabling act, but several prominent Republicans were also warmly received as speakers of the day. George Q. Cannon did not deliver his address personally, but its recounting of the previous half-dozen attempts at Utah statehood made the occasion for celebration all the more appreciated.[33]

However, even before this largest of the statehood celebrations had taken place, some who had most fervently desired Utah's admission into the union began to have reservations, due to ominous hints of huge political and financial obligations that were in some way related to the achievement of statehood. In each communication with church leaders, Trumbo, Clarkson, and Clawson alluded to numerous debts incurred in quest of the admission bill. Besides promises that Utah would vote Republican for years to come, the First Presidency started to recognize that their lobbyists had offered unnumbered political friends an interest in some of the enterprises, particularly railroads, which church leaders were in the process of developing in the territory.

In the summer of 1893, as the financial depression was reaching its nadir, members of the L.D.S. hierarchy had sought to promote a series of bold economic enterprises. They had two major purposes in mind. One was to provide work for unemployed church members, and the other was to develop some of the major resources and opportunities of the region, maintaining control while yet offering stock in the ventures to some outside capitalists in the hope of creating a body of influential friends in case of future need. When church leaders first embarked on these undertakings, Clarkson and Trumbo were visiting in Utah. Besides being honored at several Republican-sponsored affairs for their efforts in behalf of the party and the territory, they also traveled to the Lehi sugar factory and the Bullion Beck silver mine at Eureka. This was probably the time when

Clarkson informed Mormon authorities that since Utahans were becoming more inclined to conform to outside standards, he could now obtain capital from the nation's financial centers to help in building a railroad. This offer was deferred until the return of George Q. Cannon from an unsuccessful quest for loans, which took him all the way to the banking house of Rothschild in London. But on October 3, 1893, Trumbo and Clarkson signed a contract with Mormon leaders to be their agents in securing the necessary outside financial backing.[34]

This arrangement was aimed primarily at building a railroad from Utah to the Pacific Coast, expressly in competition with the line of Collis P. Huntington, the surviving partner controlling Southern Pacific Railway Company. The agreement stipulated that church leaders were to retain the majority of the corporate stock and were to carry out the construction. Clarkson and his associates were to sell the bonds and secure the rails for the road. Although some of the apostles were clearly apprehensive about the commitments being made, Woodruff favored boldly pursuing the enterprise.[35]

But when Cannon journeyed east again, he found out that the Bethlehem Steel officials to whom Clarkson had introduced him were only willing to agree to provide rails if the church offered a million-dollar guarantee and granted the eastern associates full approval over contracts affecting California and Nevada. There were also hints that the final propositions could not be fulfilled until Utah received statehood. Soon thereafter Cannon conveyed final word that the people with whom he, Trumbo, and Clarkson had been negotiating were not inclined to provide the necessary iron and steel without some portion thereof being paid for in cash. Since this was impossible, Cannon reported that all arrangements were terminated.[36]

However, while still in the East, Cannon met a more venturesome financier, George A. Purbeck, who quickly became interested in the railroad project and, it was gratefully noted, could produce the necessary monetary backing without any mention of the church needing to endorse the bonds. Within a few weeks Purbeck indicated interest in considerably expanding the scope of the proposed Utah schemes. Because of the depressed economic situation, this was not met with the unanimous approval of all general authorities. But the depression had been precisely the reason that the First Presidency had considered the project. Finally, Cannon predicted, with notable "warmth and force," that if they would unite and pursue the projected enterprise, they would succeed and prosper in it. After Woodruff added his own assurances, those present ratified the decision.[37]

The contract between the G. A. Purbeck Company and George Q.

Cannon, representing the Salt Lake and Los Angeles Railroad Company, aimed at developing transportation, manufacturing, and mining operations in the Salt Lake City vicinity, along with hydroelectric power, land, and irrigation projects near Ogden. The corporation was carefully designed to enable local stockholders to maintain control, while offering outside capitalists ample opportunity to become more interested in Utah's economic affairs.[38]

Only a few high church officials, acting as individuals, were involved in these endeavors. Yet these personal matters were so inextricably intermeshed with church finances that Woodruff may have been speaking only of the church leaders or of the broader church membership when he mentioned in his diary that Purbeck's backing had been divinely provided "to assist us in our temporal deliverance."[39] Certainly incorporation of this firm, significantly entitled "The Utah Company," was at least partly to relieve the individuals involved in the formerly projected Salt Lake and Los Angeles Railroad "of the personal responsibility of carrying to completion the businesses proposed."

These complex engagements were being finalized at the same time as the Utah statehood movement was reaching its successful climax. As the enabling act passed, several difficult problems involving the quiet heroes who did most to achieve that long-sought goal arose. Two days after Utah received news of the statehood bill passing the Senate, the *Salt Lake Herald* reprinted an Associated Press dispatch which stated that "the day the President's signature is affixed to the Utah admission bill will see the launching of the greatest railroad enterprise for years." The article continued that surveys and blueprints for a railroad from Salt Lake to Los Angeles had only been delayed until Utah became a state and that behind the plan of development was "the wealth and influence of the Mormon church." It was then disclosed that Bishop Clawson, who had been the chief of the lobby that put the statehood bill through, was the "active representative of Zion in this project," associated with Trumbo and Clarkson.[40]

When a *Herald* reporter contacted Nephi W. Clayton, general manager of the Salt Lake and Los Angeles Railway that, the paper assumed, must be involved in the project, he was informed there was no such connection and that the Utah railroad had not been delayed at all while awaiting statehood. A *Tribune* representative approached Cannon at his residence and apprised him of the contents of the dispatch. Cannon replied that neither the church nor its authorities were identified with the venture. He mentioned that it was possible that Clawson and Trumbo, who he stated were relatives, might have begun an independent project such as described in the newspaper, but he claimed no knowledge of it.[41]

Immediately thereafter a letter written by Clarkson, dated July 11, arrived at church headquarters. Its thirty-two typewritten pages recounted in detail the steps taken to gain statehood for Utah. Besides political information, reference was made to the railroad project of the previous year. Clarkson confided, "We have carried in parallel with our contest for statehood the material interest of Utah," bringing to the attention of all persons contacted politically the "material wealth and resources and industrial possibilities" of Utah, as well as the church leaders' ambition to develop them. He continued that the railroad venture has been in some degree "a backbone in our endeavors," then advised that such a project could be made "the means not only of fulfilling many obligations that we have incurred to many prominent men whose help has been vital, but also of gaining to your state their personal interest and valuable friendship." [42]

This and later inferences revealed that numerous individuals helpful in securing statehood were promised easy access to shares in Utah's prosperity when the boom, expected to accompany admission, began. Judging from his subsequent comments, Cannon was gravely disappointed upon receiving this information. It was a similarly rude shock to other inside associates who had been enjoying the exhilaration of knowing their territory was about to be freed from territorial restraints. Cannon later concluded that the accomplishment of statehood might not be worth the price that apparently was expected.

Besides the Clarkson letter, there was an attached memorandum written by Clawson, which was probably even more ominous in its suggestions of obligations incurred. The copy of this nine-page memo that exists contains enough undeciphered code words to render all discussion based on it as tentative. Clawson had been an inside observer of most of the efforts of Clarkson and Trumbo and recognized that he had an obligation to inform his ecclesiastical leaders of more of these activities than he had done previously. Cipher codes had been widely used within and outside the church for many years, and each word of his letter was clear to its recipients. Though it is apparently impossible to reconstruct that clarity, a sense of the magnitude of the obligations can be gained from some portions of the document.

Clawson began by mentioning that the six western states admitted into the union in 1889 and 1890 were reported to have expended, on the average, $500,000 to get their enabling acts passed, adding that "in their cases there was not the prejudice socially and religiously that there existed against our territory." He then reported that greater amounts had been raised and expended in Utah's behalf by Clarkson and Trumbo—"all of it in methods purely honorable and yet necessary." These funds were raised from one source, "Ralph" (code word probably railroads), "and all on the pledges of Clara" (Clarkson). The expenses had been incurred through employment of a "vast amount of clerk hire made necessary in reaching into every state, into every element, and in effecting organizations in our help." Much of this was apparently in connection with public relations work through the nation's press. Carefully detailing the large amount of time and personal cash expended by him and his two companions, Clawson confided, "The only thing I regret is the obligations that I in common with Tobias [Trumbo] have incurred from those who have helped us, and whose ambitions and interests in the future will lead them constantly to call upon us for assistance politically and otherwise." Adding that "all men in public affairs keep books. They render no service without expecting return," he stated that he expected to be called upon to repay thousands of debts, which would take a large part of his lifetime to accomplish.[43]

Actually, one of the major purposes of the letter and the memorandum was to elaborate on the long and faithful crusade for statehood conducted by Trumbo. Clarkson stated that Trumbo had dedicated his life "to the end of making the Mormon name as honorable and as accepted in honor in the sight of every highminded American" as any other people. In addition to the gratitude that should forever be owed to the colonel, Clarkson said, "I think he should be sent on your motion as one of the men to represent you in the United States Senate." Acknowledging that there was much potential senatorial timber in Utah, the Republican leader urged that no other man could possibly represent the state as well as his candidate. He pointed out that "if Colonel Trumbo had been a member of the Senate ten years he could not have garnered more acquaintance and friendship to your advantage than he has gained now."[44] The dark suggestions of extensive debts recurred when Clarkson stated that "no one else will ever know and therefore no one else could ever redeem as he can, the thousands and thousands of obligations that we have incurred in this long contest in your behalf." Clawson added his hope that Mormon leaders would see to it that the men selected as Utah representatives in Washington knew and appreciated the value of the favors rendered and "the honorable necessity of returning them."[45]

Trumbo and his associates had certainly set their sights on a Senate seat for the colonel, and although actual selection of Utah's representatives to the upper house was a year and a half away, they embarked on a unique newspaper campaign to get his name linked to one of those positions. The correspondence of Lemuel E. Quigg, a New York congressman, is revealing in this regard. On July 17, 1894, he wrote a letter of introduction for Trumbo to Donald Nicholson of the *New York Tribune*. It mentioned that the colonel was instrumental in achieving Utah statehood and that he was interested in securing 1,000 copies of the *Tribune* edition that recounted the event. The next day the congressman sent another letter to Nicholson, enclosing an article that detailed passage of the Utah bill and featured Trumbo's role. Quigg said that he had known the lobbyist for many years and that "the little praise I give him in this article is, to my personal knowledge, well deserved." He commented significantly that the article itself "will be very useful in Utah," where the Republican party will control the legislature responsible for selecting Utah's first two U.S. senators.[46]

The article was published in the respected Republican newspaper on July 20. After detailing the difficulty in convincing Gentiles in Utah and the nation that the Mormons had accepted in good faith the laws of the land and had abandoned polygamy, it stated that "no single influence has been so constant or more effective than that of Colonel Isaac Trumbo." Mentioning the Republican disfranchisement attempts, Liberal party opposition, national convention struggles, amnesty, and church property suits, as well as passage of the Utah Enabling Act, the lengthy column concluded, "All opposition disappeared in the face of the evidence marshalled by Colonel Trumbo."[47]

Soon after the Utah articles appeared in the New York paper, the *Salt Lake Herald* commented on potential Republican senatorial candidates, mentioning the strong claims Trumbo could muster. The editor observed that his name had been "very much in evidence in the eastern papers as a man who has done most to silence Republican opposition to Utah's admission." The same editorial also mentioned that the *Herald* had received a copy of the *New York Tribune* article directly from Trumbo; the paper had promptly reprinted it in its entirety. A man who had labored as long as the colonel in subsidizing and influencing newspaper coverage certainly was capable of utilizing those techniques in his own behalf.[48]

However, Trumbo's treatment by the rival *Salt Lake Tribune* was anything but positive and could easily—in connection with the ill-timed notice of the projected railroad scheme—have helped motivate Mormon church leaders to disengage from their former partners. On the last day of July, the paper noted that Trumbo appeared to have "a literary bureau of rather robust dimensions in active operation" because so many laudatory articles were appearing in the eastern press in connection with Utah statehood. The still-sensitive *Tribune* observed that many of these referred to the colonel as an "accredited agent" of the Mormons, making pledges on their behalf that it would be the church members' duty to fulfill. This, the paper stated, was news to the people of Utah, who were particularly unaware that the struggle for statehood was "distinctively a church fight." Editor C. C. Goodwin, who had his own senatorial ambitions, belittled Trumbo's claims, as he would consistently throughout the next two years.[49]

Just over a month after the Utah Enabling Act was passed, Cannon and some of his associates met in Salt Lake City with Trumbo and Clawson. At that time they discussed all that had been done in relation to the railroad project, which had been so closely associated with statehood. Some of the obligations but briefly mentioned in previous correspondence were detailed at this time. In response, Cannon told Trumbo that he and other church leaders "had no idea of the manner in which they were using the railroad as a means to get statehood or to create interest in the minds of prominent men in Utah affairs." He later confided to Clawson that "it spoiled the pleasure of the admission to know that such had been the case." It was probably a major reason ardor toward Trumbo, Clarkson, and their future ambitions was so rapidly cooling among the Mormon hierarchy.

Cannon reminded the political agents that the contract Clarkson had made the previous year had not been fulfilled. He recalled that he had gone east to meet the businessmen but found their terms for rails had been unsatisfactory and their demands for "entire control of the road" unthinkable. The church leader stated that the failure on Clarkson's part to provide acceptable financial backing had automatically terminated the contract. Cannon confessed that at the time he had been relieved at being freed from the danger of the church obligation to guarantee any bonds sold under those arrangements.

Cannon attempted to reassure Trumbo that his interests and those of his partners would be respected. The church leader made clear that he wanted them to share in the economic opportunity with the Utah participants, although they did have another financial agent in Purbeck. Trumbo admitted that he and Clarkson had counted on their former contract being honored, and, according to Cannon's account, "they had enlisted men in this and held out hopes to them concerning what was to be done: in fact, had entered into agreements with different parties for various interests." They had even used the reputation of the church leaders for probity and fair dealing as one of the inducements to these parties to get involved.[50]

A few days after the meeting with Trumbo and Clawson, the First Presidency forwarded a $3,000 draft to Clarkson at New York, explaining it had been brought to their attention that he had expended his own money in pursuing the successful statehood quest. They added that there would be no attempt at that time to express their appreciation for his "wonderful devotion" to their interests.[51] In a letter the following week to

Clawson, Clarkson acknowledged receipt of the money. He confessed understanding that the gesture was "kindly meant," undoubtedly at Trumbo's behest, but regretted that it had been done. Although he needed funds to meet pressing obligations, he promised to reimburse the gift when able, saying in a self-serving manner that "while I have given time and money in the service, and many times the money represented in the draft, it was all willingly given, and must stand to the end as my free will offering in a cause too sacred to be measured in any sense or form of money."

Yet the main portion of Clarkson's letter berated parties at Salt Lake City for ignoring his inquiries since statehood as to where the old business matter stood. Pledging that he was prepared to devote all his time and energies to the railroad enterprise "as the pulse of life was coming back to the business world," he added that it was an opportune moment to push the entire project to fruition and observed that they only had to devote equal power and effort as had been expended in achieving statehood to achieve similar success in completing the railroad.

Clarkson was especially anxious for a commitment because he had already established close ties with the Colorado Coal and Iron Company. This syndicate, headed by J. C. Osgood, was said to be not only anxious to provide rails and other material at advantageous prices but also interested in a long-term alliance with neighboring businessmen to aid in developing Utah iron deposits. Clarkson claimed that the Colorado company was prepared to take $5 million of the bonds at par and at 5 percent interest. He did admit uncertainty as to whether to pursue the negotiations and rather impatiently mentioned other business opportunities he had passed up while continuing to work in connection with what he hoped was his still-intact agreement with the Mormon leaders. Clarkson confessed embarrassment at the lack of any direction or authorization from Salt Lake City.[52]

Meanwhile, in the days following the meeting with Trumbo and Clawson, Abraham Cannon noted that his father was "worrying himself sick" over the entire engagement with Clarkson and Trumbo. The son observed that "they have doubtless promised their friends who worked for Utah's admission many things that will not be in the power of father and others who are associated in the railway enterprise to fulfill." It was acknowledged that the lobbyists had worked hard and done much good, but, young Cannon concluded, "the price they ask is very high." That same diary entry mentioned a proposal by Frank J. Cannon that the First Presidency be relieved of continuing anxiety over these matters through the appointment of trustees for the railroad who would have full authority to negotiate with Clarkson and Trumbo and "do by them all that is proper." Several days later, such an arrangement was put into effect.[53] The members of the presidency had long awaited the time when relative political and economic independence could be attained. Having expended time and effort in pursuit of those ends, they were anxious to more fully and exclusively resume their ecclesiastical responsibilities. The oversight of the interests in the Utah Company was therefore entrusted to younger men, chiefly Frank Cannon. His lobbying journeys had given him important experience and contacts in the East, and he would be a key participant in business dealings there and in Utah for several years thereafter.[54]

In letters and a telegram of September 14, 1894, Frank Cannon and another key Utah Company associate, Nephi W. Clayton, were instructed that "harmonious relations should be established between the general [Clarkson] and G.A.P. [Purbeck] to insure future union." When the presidency discussed the relationship with Clarkson and Trumbo, including the lobbyists' undoubted disappointment with the Purbeck association, they stressed the need not only to "deal very liberally with them," but to retain their good will because of the need for influence in California and in financial and political circles and for securing terminals and other concessions that they could presumably attain more effectively than Purbeck. Although church leaders confessed their dilemma as to what kind of financial reward or consideration that Clarkson and Trumbo should be given, it was clear that there was no intention to sever ties with them.[55]

Cannon and Clayton were also given a letter from Woodruff to Clarkson when they met him in New York. In it the aged but alert church leader apologized that communication from Salt Lake City had been so slight, explaining that he assumed Trumbo and Clawson had reported conversations they had with the presidency since success in the statehood matter. He expressed thanks for the lengthy July letter, saying "its historical value is priceless" because of the recital of unknown steps and measures that Clarkson and his associates had taken. He closed with the hope that satisfactory agreement concerning business matters could be attained. It is not clear whether Cannon and Clayton succeeded in delivering the letter to Clarkson. When they learned that he was contemplating a trip west, they sent a telegram asking him to wait until they could meet with him.[56] If the meeting was held, it accomplished little, because later in the month Clarkson came to Salt Lake City to confront his church associates.

After arrival in Utah, but prior to meeting with church leaders, George Q. Cannon sent Clarkson a long letter in reply to one dated September 18 in which the Iowan expressed his growing apprehensions. After voicing disappointment at a request for payment of a debt fully acknowledged, Cannon reiterated Woodruff's belated thanks to Clarkson and all the "friends unnamed in his communications" who had "assisted in the political redemption of Utah." He repeated a theme often expressed among his brethren since the first contact with the Republican lobbyists—that appreciation for their work was even deeper because it seemed to be a "free-will offering, tendered by yourself and your friends to a people whom you saw in the midst of an agonizing trial such as few races have met and survived." The sanctity of that service was said to have been diminished by the formal demand for a measure of that gratitude. Cannon expressed strong regrets over the commitments promised, confessing that "except for the sustaining influence of the Holy Spirit, we must be overwhelmed by the hints of obligations incurred and pledges made in our behalf. These debts are the more appalling because their extent is indefinite." But, the church leader added, "veiled as is their scope, your letter justifies the inference that we and our descendants, with all that we have or may justly hope to have, are mortgaged for all time to come."

Continuing along similar lines, Cannon said that "promises have evidently been made immeasurably beyond any right which we could have assumed in the name of our people." He explained that the general authorities had earlier given up plans to work for statehood because they realized that such could only be successful if "accompanied by barter" at which their souls revolted. This was another reason they had been so grateful for the aid offered by Clarkson and the manner in which they had previously thought the statehood campaign had been conducted. Thus the disappointment was increased at finding unknown strings attached to the attainment of that goal. Fervently determined to resist being committed in such a manner, Cannon declared that "the enfranchisement which has been assured is sweet in prospect; but other men have found that a so-called liberty can be purchased at too high a price." He then stated pointedly, "Vassalage under territorial form would be far preferable to the slavery which would put gyves [shackles] upon the consciences of ourselves and our descendants, in the form of an accepted obligation beyond the power of all with whom our pledge can have influence in this generation and in the time to come." The church leader concluded by promising that "all that honor and possibility permit we will give, and on this ground we believe that you will be our supporting friend."[57]

At a meeting on September 25, Clarkson initially neither shook hands nor took a seat. In a stiff and cold manner, he read a demand, couched in legal terms, tendering a contract with the J. C. Osgood company of Colorado in fulfillment of his part of the old agreement and asking for formal acceptance or refusal by Cannon and his associates. As the interview continued, Clarkson questioned how Cannon could assume that their contract had ended when subsequent to the meeting with the Bethlehem Steel officials they had together seen others "with the view of carrying out the agreement." Directly questioning Cannon's integrity, Clarkson blamed him for all the subsequent confusion and miscarriage of their plans.

Cannon replied that Presidents Woodruff and Smith could attest to his continuing concern that Trumbo and Clarkson's interests be treated fairly, affirming that he never intended that they be excluded from participation in the undertaking as stockholders. He then read excerpts from his personal journal recounting the instances when they had met and what had transpired. He showed that on the trip to New York, when he was to enter the arrangement with Purbeck and Company, he endeavored for nearly eight days to meet with Clarkson and Trumbo, who were engaged in important lobbying business in Washington, D.C. He read copies of telegrams sent that showed how annoyed he was at their seeming indifference to his position of delaying his meeting with the Purbeck officers when they knew their would-be partner was already in the city. He then recounted the eventual meeting with Trumbo and Clarkson at which he outlined to them the details of the proposed contract with Purbeck. Cannon confided, "It was necessary that I should prove this, because of the statement by General Clarkson, oft repeated, that he had had no notice that his contract was not still in force, and that he ought to have been advised." He went through many journal entries with Clarkson in an attempt to clarify and prove to him "that there had not been the least intention to do him any wrong, nor Colonel Trumbo, in all we had done." He stated that although he was certain the Purbeck contract was "not agreeable" to Clarkson, the First Presidency had every right to act as they did because "General Clarkson had exhausted, so far as I knew, every source that he had mentioned as likely to furnish funds." He reiterated, "There was therefore a complete failure on his part to obtain the means that had been agreed upon, and when the other opening presented itself, it did not seem an infringement of any arrangement that we had made for us to employ this firm as our financial agents." [58]

Clarkson's conciliatory letter of September 26 to Cannon and his associates acknowledged that many honest misunderstandings had been cleared up at the meeting. He was sorry for the lack of communication and hoped that "with faith in each other and a common zeal and industry to carry out our plans," they would yet succeed. However, a great degree of cordiality seems to have been lost from the relationship, probably because of the accusations against Cannon, who had a tendency to be overly sensitive to personal criticism. Undoubtedly the continuing specter of the financial and political promises expended in securing Utah statehood was also a factor in disrupting the closeness of the relationship.[59]

Although the personal confrontation had restored a more amicable relationship, there was yet the lingering problem of the nature of the commitment that Cannon supposedly approved in the East. At the same September 25 meeting, the church leader also drew upon his journal to recount a conversation he had with Trumbo and Clawson at the Hotel Rennart in Baltimore, probably in early 1894. He called untrue the statements, repeated by Clarkson, that he knew "that they were incurring heavy financial obligations for the admission of Utah with the expectation of paying these obligations out of the projects that should arise under the contract they had made." Cannon denied positively "that he had heard anything to the effect that they were spending money directly for the admission of Utah."

Another earlier meeting with Trumbo, at the Hoffman House in New York, was also reconstructed. Trumbo, it was said, wished to see the church leader concerning "certain propositions" he had received. Cannon recalled that these were to the effect that "a large fund was being raised by different parties on account of the tariff, the object being to prevent injurious legislation to certain interests. This sum was represented by Colonel Trumbo to me as being very large, and it was proposed that Utah should be included in the arrangment." The unnamed group was willing to have this done, "if they could have the assurance that two Republican senators would come from Utah." Cannon recalled that Trumbo had been sent to ask "if any pledge could be obtained to that effect." The church leader had replied that he "could not give a pledge of that kind" and "did not know anyone else that could." He said he would "do anything in my power to have Utah admitted as a state and to have it Republican, but could make no pledge of that kind." He recalled that this had seemed to satisfy Trumbo. At the time this interview was reconstructed, Cannon emphasized that Trumbo acknowledged that his version of that conversation was correct.[60] Notwithstanding this, it is easy to see how the lobbyist, listening for what he had wanted to hear, could construe Cannon's offer to do all he could to make Utah Republican as more than a strictly personal pledge. Much to the church leader's later regret, that was undoubtedly the way Trumbo reported it to his associates.

Cannon's mention of the fund that had been raised to prevent tariff legislation injurious to "certain interests" is significant. Grover Cleveland had been elected on a platform that denounced "the Republican protection as a fraud, a robbery of the great majority of the American people for the benefit of the few." And although the letter accepting the Democratic party's nomination toned this statement down to some extent, it was clear Cleveland would press for tariff reform.[61]

It was just as obvious that the nation's industrial interests, which were represented in Congress largely, but not exclusively, by Republicans, would seek to counter or at least soften this onslaught on the import duty structure that had so much benefited them. As was the case with previous—and subsequent—tariff bills, drastic downward revision of the rates was easily attained in the House of Representatives, but difficult if not impossible to pass the Senate, where many special interests were effectively overseen. During the legislative battles on the Wilson-Gorman Tariff, the Democrats enjoyed a majority of forty-four members to thirty-eight for the Republicans in the upper house. Two of the three Populist members sided with the Democrats and one with the Republicans. But matters were far from so simply divided. The income tax provision attached to the bill gave Senator Hill more than sufficient pretext to oppose the entire measure adamantly and consistently. And other Democrats declared to their Senate colleagues that they would not vote for any bill that did not offer substantial protection to certain products important to their constituents.

A revealing but unpublished article written by Clifford Rose of the *Louisville Courier-Journal*, read and revised by Senator James K. Jones, the official floor leader for the Cleveland forces in the tariff fight, states that a bill incorporating such reforms as the president and the majority of his party desired was impossible to get passed in the Senate. This was because eight Democrats—Arthur P. Gorman, Edward D. White, Donelson Caffrey, Calvin S. Brice, Edward Murphy, Stephen M. White, James Smith, and J. L. M. Irby—had declared that the bill sent from the House and reported favorably by the Senate Committee on Finance could never meet their approval. In fact Jones reported, "These senators had entered into a combination confined to themselves to stand by one another in their different demands."[62] In the end, they and their allies attained essentially what they aimed to accomplish in the final version of the Wilson-Gorman Act, although in doing so they incurred the wrath and denunciation of President Cleveland and the Democratic press.[63]

It is not possible to link further the prolonged and bitter tariff struggle of 1894 directly to Utah statehood, but it is significant that at least half of the insurgent Demcrats so firmly opposed to President Cleveland's tariff reform program had in like manner been supporters—and cooperators with the Republican party—in getting the Utah Enabling Act passed in the upper house.

George Q. Cannon also mentioned that the large anti-tariff combine had been interested in two Republican senators from Utah. In light of the closeness of the balance between the rival parties on tariff and other crucial issues, it is easy to see how welcome such additions to the Republican ranks would be to the protectionists. This would have been even more the case if the lobbyists for the Mormons stressed, as they undoubtedly did, Utah's marked preference for home industry, which stemmed from the preachings of Brigham Young.[64]

Toward the end of 1894, the First Presidency received a letter from Morris M. Estee, which candidly stated they had been fortunate that the financial arrangements with Trumbo and Clarkson had not been carried out as planned. In reply, the church leaders expressed, with equal frankness, the same sentiments. They still felt strongly compelled to exert themselves to do something to stimulate the local economy not only to relieve the unemployed but also "to maintain the hold which rightfully belongs to us in this country." But in response to Estee's comment that future troubles could have been of an economic rather than a political or religious character, they confessed, "We have already felt the weight of the pressure of financial obligations such as had not been known by us before." They commented significantly that "in endeavoring to emancipate ourselves from the bondage of hard times and the poverty which want of employment brings, we feel that we cannot be too careful in avoiding the bondage of debt."

The church leaders voiced apprehension about exhorbitant political as well as financial obligations when they confided that "one of the causes which has produced misunderstanding has been that we have not been kept informed of what was expected of us." Elaborating further they said, "Promises have been made so lavishly to accomplish the end in view—statehood—that we cannot, as we view it at present fulfill them in the manner that is desired." The presidency admitted that "we have desired very earnestly to be politically free, to enjoy the full measure of American citizenship which a state government furnishes." At the same time they confessed feeling that because of the many obligations created by Trumbo and others to obtain statehood "liberty of this kind may cost too much." If in achieving a measure of political independence, they were "placed in bondage of another kind that may be as hard to bear," statehood would hardly be worth the cost.

Yet in spite of these expressions of displeasure at the presumed debts incurred, the church leaders clearly acknowledged what they owed to Trumbo and Clarkson. Affirming the intention to do everything possible to avoid the very appearance of "a want of appreciation" for the important services rendered, they promised that "everything that honorable men can do and honorable men can ask of others to do, we propose to do to satisfy those gentlemen."[65]

During the next several months the Mormon authorities continued to consider the proper means to compensate their former agents. In mid-March, this matter was brought to a head by a letter from Clarkson to Clawson. It described an opportunity that Clarkson had long desired, to purchase control of a large metropolitan newspaper, in this case, the *Chicago Inter-Ocean*. He sought to interest the church leaders in investing $100,000 by describing the great advantages to be derived for them and their friends in the West. Although there was apparently little interest in such benefits, Cannon noted that his associates in the presidency were not averse to assisting Clarkson with his venture, if the money could be raised.

That night Cannon gave much thought to Clarkson's request. Although he still felt he had been unjustly accused the previous autumn, he re-affirmed his pledge to give whatever was necessary to relieve the presidency and their people of the continuing "sense of obligation" to Clarkson. In a meeting next day with Clawson, Cannon's valuable acre and a quarter original homesite in the center of Salt Lake City was offered as collateral on a low-interest loan that the presidency promised to secure for Clarkson's benefit. When Clarkson heard of the proposition from Clawson several days later, it was reported that tears coursed down his cheeks.[66]

By the end of the month the agreement had been finalized. It consisted of twenty promissory bond notes, payable to the holder at the First National Bank of Chicago at dates of maturity ranging from three to seven years. All notes were not only secured by the Cannon real estate but also were backed by the signatures of each member of the First Presidency. The next year, as Clarkson sought to convert these notes into immediate cash, either through actual sale or as security on a loan, he explained to a New York banker his original compensation from the church. Telling of the delays in the Utah railroad project, he stated that he had other opportunities more immediately available and was not willing to wait for the proposition with the Mormon leaders to reach fruition. He said that he sold his interest in the project, getting part of the payment in immediate cash and part in bonds. With this compensation, the association of Clarkson with the L.D.S. church and its leaders virtually ended, but on an apparently satisfactory note.[67]

Trumbo did not then press for such a settlement and probably never had as firm a financial claim on the church leaders. His hopes and efforts throughout the ensuing year remained centered on attaining election as a

Utah senator. After that effort failed, he simply left the state in disgust, telling Clarkson that he would eventually either make the "fellows in Utah" pay their debt—probably meaning the Senate seat—or he would "pay them a debt they won't like." Several years later Trumbo revealed to his former partner his plans. He had checked with some of his prominent California friends, and they had assured him that he still had a legitimate claim to a commission on the money he and Clarkson had belatedly located and offered for the benefit of the Salt Lake and Los Angeles Railroad Company. But before he could pursue the matter, Bishop Clawson arrived at the colonel's home, at the behest of the First Presidency, to soothe his hostile feelings and disappointment. After receiving $10,000 said to have been owed for refurbishing the Gardo House, Trumbo signed a legal paper attesting that he had no further financial claims on the L.D.S. church or its leaders. However, the document specifically charged that the other obligations incurred through him were still intact: "This paper has no political significance whatsoever, nor does it release them [the general authorities] from political promises made to the Republican party."[68] In light of the previously cited statements of George Q. Cannon, indications are that Trumbo was either deluding himself concerning those commitments or playing to the gallery of politicians to whom he had conveyed notice of such promises. In the final analysis Trumbo's downfall stemmed in large part from the distrust engendered among the most powerful men in Utah through his unauthorized political and economic commitments made on their behalf.

These alleged promises had a way of coming back to haunt the church leaders all too frequently in the following years. The first such instance occurrred during the 1894 congressional contest in Utah, when campaign speaker O. W. Powers alluded to deals between the Mormon hierarchy and business interests, particularly the sugar trust. And the following February, a detailed and partly accurate series of articles, written anonymously in Utah and published in the *New York Times*, so disturbed Cannon that he wrote a lengthy reply in an attempt to clarify the false allegations of improper agreements and deals with the Republican party and special interests.

Cannon's reply in the Salt Lake newspapers, forwarded to the *New York Times* by his son Frank and subsequently published there, successfully refuted the petty charges against him regarding his personal financial interests and his using his influence to secure employment for his many children. But in subsequent days the widely publicized allegations of political deals with Republican senators aroused considerable interest and comment from prominent Democrats. Senator M. W. Ransom stated the charges against Cannon were very serious and called for a complete investigation. Congressman William Springer complimented the *Times* on the exposures, saying he was convinced from his own knowledge that the paper was on the right track. His colleague, William Bynum, recalled his former efforts in behalf of his party in Utah and said he had no reason to doubt the *Times* assertions "that unfair methods have been employed to wrest the state from the control of the Democrats."[69]

Even more damaging than the political impact of this barrage of adverse publicity was its possible effect on the Mormon leaders' financial plans and aspirations. The *Times* fully acknowledged that as it predicted "when the investors in the East who have been invited to invest in the bonds of the Utah Company are made acquainted with all the facts," there was reason to believe they would "look closely into the matter before proceeding further in the direction of supplying the money which Mr. Cannon is so anxious to secure."[70] In his reply to the articles Cannon alleged that a primary purpose of the attack had been to destroy his credit. In fact, he stated, he would have refused to attempt a public clarification of the *Times* items had it not been for an obligation to others associated in his business enterprises.[71]

The *Times*' final mention of the Utah situation was published late in February, 1895, after which the storm subsided. But it is likely that damage was done to the prospects of the Utah Company. Purbeck, his agents, and Frank Cannon had made extensive contacts with potential investors throughout the East, in England, and in France but failed to obtain the necessary capital to proceed with their plans. Undoubtedly, the continuing economic depression was the main cause of their lack of success, but the negative publicity certainly had not benefited their efforts.

On June 25, 1895, at a meeting of the board of directors of the Salt Lake and Los Angeles Railway Company, it was unanimously resolved that the business relationship existing the previous year between their company and G. A. Purbeck and Company be terminated. This option had been provided for in the original contract, and with notice duly served on the New York company the ties with the unsuccessful financial agents were severed.[72]

Church leaders would experience even greater financial difficulties during the ensuing several years, and their promotion schemes were, if anything, even more extensive than in the past.[73] Yet in spite of further disappointments and the economic burdens that continued to press upon the First Presidency and their associates, they fully understood and appreciated the fact that the ultimate goal of Utah statehood was now within sight. Despite the additional anxieties that had been incurred in attaining that end, no one in a responsible position within the L.D.S. church regretted the final results of the effort.

NOTES

1. See p. 211 of present text. *Salt Lake Tribune*, Nov. 22, 1893, Washington dispatch noted that "the *Philadelphia Press* this morning prints a special stating that the news that the Republicans of Utah, as a result of the recent election, have, in connection with the Liberals, who are in sympathy with the Republicans in their opposition to the Democrats, secured control of both branches of the Legislature of that territory, is creating consternation in Democratic ranks here." The report continued that the party strategists who had intended to push the Utah statehood bill may cease such advocacy if it might ultimately result in two Republicans being elected to occupy Utah's seats in the U.S. Senate.

2. *Washington Post*, Jan. 11, 1894; *Salt Lake Tribune*, Jan. 13, 22, 28, Feb. 1, 1894.

3. *Salt Lake Tribune*, Jan. 22, 23, 25, 26, 27, 28, 30, Feb. 1, 2, 3, 4, 1894.

4. Ibid., Jan. 28, 30, Feb. 1, 6, 1894; *Salt Lake Herald*, Feb. 1, 1894; Andrew Jensen, *Latter-day Saint Biographical Encyclopedia*, 4 vols. (Salt Lake City, 1901), 1:737; *Salt Lake Herald*, Feb. 4, 1894.

5. *Salt Lake Herald*, Feb. 1, 1894.

6. J. L. Rawlins to O. W. Powers, Feb. 6, 1894, copy, ibid., Feb. 15, 1894.

7. Ibid., Feb. 15, Mar. 2, 1894; *Salt Lake Tribune*, Feb. 4, 6, 8, 1894.

8. James S. Clarkson to Wilford Woodruff, July 11, 1894, copy, Volwiler Papers.

9. Nevins, *Grover Cleveland*, 563–72; Herbert J. Bass, *"I Am Democrat": The Political Career of David Bennett Hill* (Syracuse, 1961), 161–62, 189, 207, 244. Much of Hill's unsuccessful strategy for winning the Democratic presidential nomination in 1892 had been based on an attempt to secure the support of western delegates by appearing to be more friendly than Cleveland toward silver and other western interests. However, his biographer indicated that subsequent to that bitter defeat, Hill became an orthodox eastern opponent of free silver. The often-biased Republican leader, James Clarkson, besides confirming Hill's position, also reported that the powerful Senator Gorman was opposed to Utah's statehood on similar grounds, as well as being fearful that the new state would vote Republican. See Clarkson to Woodruff, July 11, 1894, Volwiler Papers.

10. Nevins, *Grover Cleveland*, 563–72; "Memorials of William B. Hornblower: Data Bearing on His Nomination for U. S. Supreme Court," in Cleveland Papers, stated that Hill made it clear that the Supreme Court contest was strictly against Cleveland and his arbitrariness and in favor of senatorial courtesy. Hornblower also observed accurately that "it was characteristic of Mr. Cleveland not only to disdain the arts of conciliation but altogether to ignore the personal elements of the political world." *New York Times*, Jan. 16, 1894, quoted Vilas conceding that the president "had undoubtedly made a mistake in nominating Hornblower without consulting the two N.Y. Senators . . . had failed to follow the established custom." See also David J. Rothman, *Politics and Power: The United States Senate, 1869–1901* (Cambridge, Mass., 1966), 180–81, who uses the Hill-Cleveland Supreme Court controversy as his example of the use of senatorial courtesy.

11. *New York Tribune*, Jan. 9, 16, 1894; *New York Times*, Jan. 16, 1894.

12. Clarkson to Woodruff, July 11, 1894, Volwiler Papers; *New York Tribune*, Feb. 17, 18, 1894; *New York Times*, Feb. 13, 15, 17, 1894.

13. *Harper's Weekly*, Feb. 10, Apr. 7, 1894; John E. Osborne to David B. Hill, Mar. 26, 1894, David B. Hill Papers, New York State Library, Albany.

14. *Salt Lake Tribune*, Feb. 26, Mar. 3, 9, 17, 22, Apr. 11, 18, 19, 1894; *Salt Lake Herald*, Mar. 1, 2, 8, 20, 24, 28, 1894; *Washington Post*, Apr. 15, 1894. The Republicans finally acceded to the Democratic demands, which were as follows: that the subcommittee (on territories) should report a substitute bill, made to conform to prior admission bills; that in order to prevent the possibility of two new Republican senators during the Fifty-third Congress, no elections for delegates to a constitutional convention should take place earlier than the following Nov., and that the state government under the consitution should not be organized before the spring or summer of 1895. See *Salt Lake Tribune*, Apr. 19, 1894.

15. *Salt Lake Tribune*, Apr. 19, 21, 1894; *New York Tribune*, May 4, 1894.

16. *Salt Lake Tribune*, Apr. 22, 24, 26, May 4, 8, 11, 15, 16, 1894; *Salt Lake Herald*, May 17, 20, 1894. Harrow, "Joseph L. Rawlins," 88–91; *Deseret Evening News*, May 19, 1894.

17. Louis A. Coolidge, *Orville H. Platt: An Old-Fashioned Senator*, 2 vols. (1910 rpt. Port Washington, N.Y., 1971), 1:135–36; Cannon and O'Higgins, *Under the Prophet in Utah*, 91–93, 130–34.

18. Hiram B. Clawson to Woodruff, May 16, 1894, Hiram B. Clawson Papers, H.D.C.

19. Ibid.; *Salt Lake Tribune*, May 17, 18, 1894; *Salt Lake Herald*, May 17, 1894. The May 18 *Tribune* dispatch from Washington, D.C., reported that "Senator Faulkner was not decided until the meeting of the committee yesterday that he would consent to a report. Senator Shoup then called on him with a letter from Senator Platt, which stated that as a member of the subcommittee, he refused to be held any longer responsible for the pigeon-holing of the bill; that he favored a prompt report, but would reserve the right to offer amendments on the floor of the Senate." See *Salt Lake Tribune*, May 25, 1894, for a later denunciation of Democrats for delay of Utah statehood.

20. *Salt Lake Tribune*, May 17, 1894; *Salt Lake Herald*, May 17, 1894; *Congressional Record*, 53rd Cong., 2d sess., 4878; *Senate Reports*, 53rd Cong., 2d sess., V, no. 414, 1–29.

21. *Salt Lake Herald*, May 18, 1894, reported that Senator Faulkner said that the Utah bill "will be pressed to a vote as soon as the tariff bill is out of the way." The paper, generally supportive of Democratic decrees, also admitted that "friends of Utah think it could easily be arranged to have the admission take place next year, instead of the year after," as the party leaders were planning. Clarkson to Woodruff, July 11, 1894, Volwiler Papers.

22. *Salt Lake Tribune*, July 11, 1894, quoted Carey as saying, "When it was decided by the committee to take the bill out of the pigeon hole and permit it to be reported, there was a tacit understanding that the bill should be passed as amended. To be frank, we could never have gotten the bill out of committee unless the Republicans had agreed to postponing the date of admission, and particu-

larly to the agreement by which no United States Senators should be sent until 1896."

23. George L. Shoup to A. L. Thomas, July 12, 1894, copied in *Salt Lake Tribune*, July 29, 1894; *Congressional Record*, 53rd Cong., 2d sess., 7251, 7384. The *Tribune* correspondent mentioned several other senators who had been inclined to oppose, but had been dissuaded in one manner or another. He stated that it had been feared that James H. Kyle, the Populist senator from South Dakota, would "talk against the bill; and he was therefore dexterously called out of the chamber by a friend, who engaged him in conversation until the measure had been put upon its passage."

24. *Salt Lake Tribune*, July 11, 1894, reported that "there were only two viva voce votes cast in the negative on Utah's admission, and both were Democratic, Senators Gibson of Maryland and Cockrell of Missouri voting against the bill." With the partisanship of both *Tribune* and *Herald* properly weighed, in my judgment the *Tribune* accounts of passage of the bill are clearly the more accurate. *Salt Lake Herald*, July 11, 1894.

25. Joseph L. Rawlins, "Autobiography," ms., 126, Joseph L. Rawlins Papers, Marriott Library, University of Utah, Salt Lake City; Jensen, *The Unfavored Few*, 184–88; *Washington Post*, July 13, 1894.

26. *Salt Lake Tribune*, July 12, 1894.

27. Ibid.; telegrams (with many others) copied in campaign pamphlet "To the People of Utah" (Salt Lake City, Oct. 10, 1895), 6–8, copy, H.D.C.

28. "To the People of Utah," 1. In the senatorial campaign of the following year, Rawlins inquired of the First Presidency whether they were referring to him as claiming undue honors. He mentioned that he had been informed that the publication of the telegram had been unauthorized, but there was no question as to the authenticity of the dispatch. See Rawlins to First Presidency, Dec. 9, 1895, Clara, Tobias, Clio [Clarkson, Trumbo, Clawson] to Woodruff, July 17, 1894, Woodruff Papers.

29. "To the People of Utah," 11; "The Forty-fifth Star," *Kate Field's Washington*, July 25, 1894, 49–50.

30. Marcus, *Grand Old Party*, 186–87; *Ogden Standard*, July 11, 1894, quoted the exultant Trumbo as saying, "This is the ending of eight years of hard work. To me the most gratifying feature was the practically unanimous passage of the bill without debate."

31. Clarkson to Woodruff, July 11, 1894, Volwiler Papers.

32. *Congressional Record*, 53rd Cong., 2d sess., 7399, 7446, 7514, 7830; *Salt Lake Tribune*, July 17, 1894. The previous week, the crisis of the Pullman strike had cost the president most of his sleep. And perhaps just as disturbing, although far more distant, was the simultaneous violence in Utah's neighboring states, at Cripple Creek, Colorado, and Cour d'Alene, Idaho. Possibly amid these circumstances, Cleveland and numerous other Americans were then particularly appreciative of the widely known stability and conservatism of the majority of Utah's population.

33. *Salt Lake Tribune*, July 13, 18, Aug. 1, 1894; *Salt Lake Herald*, Aug. 2,

1894. The first *Tribune* citation editorialized, alluding to the long delay before actual admission, "There are no guns being fired over prospective statehood, are there? The people understand."

34. Leonard J. Arrington, "Utah and the Depression of the 1890's," *Utah Historical Quarterly* 29 (Jan., 1961), 3–18; Charles Hoffman, "The Depression of the Nineties," *Journal of Economic History* 16 (June, 1956), 137–64; A. H. Cannon Journal, June 1, 1893, Jan. 30, 1891, June 14, 24, 1893; Woodruff Journal, June 24, 27, 1893; Clarkson to Theodore Roosevelt, Sept. 23, 1904, Roosevelt Papers; *Salt Lake Tribune*, Oct. 6, 1893; Cannon to Clarkson, Sept. 24, 1894, Woodruff Papers, H.D.C.

35. Leonard J. Arrington, *Great Basin Kingdom: An Economic History of the Latter-day Saints* (Cambridge, Mass., 1958; rpt. Lincoln, 1966), 394–96; *Ogden Standard*, Nov. 29, 1893, Jan. 24, 1894; A. H. Cannon Journal, Nov. 29, 1893. Huntington's partner Stanford, more friendly to the Mormons, had died the year before. Trumbo was one of the executors of his estate.

36. A. H. Cannon Journal, Dec. 28, 29, 1893, Jan. 10, 11, Feb. 15, Mar. 2, 1894; Grant Journal, Feb. 15, Mar. 2, 1894; Lyman Journal, Dec. 28, 29, 1893; F. D. Richards Journal, Dec. 28, 1893, Feb. 14, 1894; Clarkson to Roosevelt, Sept. 23, 1904, Roosevelt Papers.

37. A. H. Cannon Journal, Mar. 2, 7, 1894; Grant Journal, Mar. 7, 1894; F. D. Richards Journal, Mar. 10, 1894.

38. Contract between George Q. Cannon and his associates and G. A. Purbeck and Company, Apr. 23, 1894; G. A. Purbeck to G. Q. Cannon, July 12, 1894; Articles of Incorporation Utah Company (extant copy undated, 1894); contract between G. Q. Cannon and his associates and G. A. Purbeck and Company, Aug. 29, 1894, First Presidency Miscellaneous [Financial] Papers; A. H. Cannon Journal, Sept. 13, 1894; "Journal History of the Church of Jesus Christ of Latter-day Saints," Sept. 13, 1894.

39. Arrington, *Great Basin Kingdom*, 386–400; F. D. Richards Journal, Apr. 18, May 15, 16, 17, 1894; Woodruff Journal, May 17, 1894.

40. *Salt Lake Herald*, July 13, 1894.

41. Ibid., July 13, 1894; *Salt Lake Tribune*, July 13, 1894.

42. Clarkson to Woodruff, July 11, 1894, Volwiler Papers. After a long search for this letter (known to exist because of Woodruff's reply), including checking the Clarkson Papers collections in the Library of Congress and the Iowa State Library at Des Moines, I stumbled onto the trail leading to the copy at Bloomington through luck. Aside from the A. H. Cannon Journal, the letter has proved to be the most valuable source material for the present work.

43. "Memoranda made by Clio [H. B. Clawson] of things he has learned at various times from personal observation or from being told by others, the past four years," accompanying Clarkson to Woodruff, July 11, 1894, Volwiler Papers.

44. Ibid.

45. Ibid.

46. L. E. Quigg to D. Nicholson, July 17, 18, 1894, Lemuel E. Quigg Papers [Letterbooks], New York Public Library. Quigg, until his election to Congress

that year, had been a star correspondent and editorial writer for Whitelaw Ried's widely respected *New York Tribune*. During his brief congressional career Quigg was closely associated with New York Republican "easy boss" Thomas Platt, with whom Clarkson had long been allied.

47. *New York Tribune*, July 20, 22, 1894.

48. *Salt Lake Herald*, July 16, 30, 1894.

49. *Salt Lake Tribune*, July 31, 1894.

50. George Q. Cannon Journal (excerpts), Aug. 17, 1894, notes of interview with General Clarkson and Colonel Trumbo, Sept. 25, 1894, both in George Q. Cannon Papers, H.D.C.

51. Woodruff, Cannon, and Smith to Clarkson, Aug. 21, 1894, Woodruff Papers.

52. Clarkson to Clawson, Sept. 1, 1894, G. Q. Cannon Papers.

53. A. H. Cannon Journal, Aug. 24, 1894.

54. Ibid.; Woodruff, G. Q. Cannon, and Smith to F. J. Cannon and Clayton, Sept. 14, 1894, Woodruff Papers.

55. Woodruff, G. Q. Cannon, and Smith to F. J. Cannon and Clayton, Sept. 14, 1894, Weber [First Presidency] to F. J. Cannon and Clayton, Sept. 14, 1894, Woodruff Papers.

56. Woodruff to Clarkson, Sept. 11, 1894, F. J. Cannon to Clarkson, Sept. 14, 1894, copy in Woodruff Papers.

57. G. Q. Cannon and his associates to Clarkson, for himself and his associates, Sept. 24, 1894, ibid.

58. Paper labeled "Interview with General Clarkson and Colonel Trumbo, Sept. 25, 1894," G. Q. Cannon Papers.

59. Clarkson to G. Q. Cannon and Associates, Sept. 26, 1894, ibid.

60. "Interview with Clarkson and Trumbo, Sept. 25, 1894," ibid.

61. Nevins, *Grover Cleveland*, 491, 563–64.

62. Ibid., 565–88; Lambert, *Gorman*, 200–238; Memorandum, Washington, J[an.], 1896, Allan Nevins Papers, Butler Library, Columbia University, New York City. Notes accompanying the 6-page typed memo, dated Feb. 3, 4, 5, 1896, explain that Rose, a fellow Washington news correspondent, had recently compiled the material in collaboration with Senators Harris, Vest, and Jones of Arkansas. Nevins, *Grover Cleveland*, 573, noted that this document, which he labeled the "Jones memorandum," was in his private possession. Lambert could not locate the material (see bibliographic note on manuscript material), but after a long search by me it is now easily accessible.

63. Nevins, *Grover Cleveland*, 581–88; Lambert, *Gorman*, 229–31; *Congressional Record*, 53rd Cong., 2d sess., 7712–13, 7801–9. The president stated that "this bill in its present form . . . means party perfidy and party dishonor." The Jones-Rose memorandum carefully explains that the administration agent in the Senate, Isham G. Harris, "informed the President that in his judgement there was not the remotest possibility of reaching an agreement on the propositions of the administration and the House." The senator and his associates concluded that Cleveland had understood the need for compromising with the protectionists and

they were consequently hurt and angered by the subsequent denunciation. Harris said, "I have no hesitancy in frankly stating that if there were 'party perfidy and dishonor' . . . then the President was the leading party thereto."

64. Nathaniel W. Stephenson, *Nelson W. Aldrich: A Leader in American Politics* (New York, 1930), 109–16, explained that "the most immediate furor created by this tariff concerned sugar" and that the Louisiana senators were acting as sugar agents pure and simple. H[erbert] Terrill to D. S. Lamont, Feb. 20, Mar. 6, 1894, Cleveland Papers, indicates desperate efforts to work with Cleveland and avoid bitterness. George Q. Cannon and other Mormon leaders were acutely interested in protecting their own infant sugar industry at this crucial juncture. For Brigham Young's stress on self-sufficiency, see Arington, *Great Basin Kingdom*, 195–231.

65. Woodruff, Cannon, and Smith to Estee, Dec. 18, 1894, Woodruff Papers.

66. "Extracts from Journal [of George Q. Cannon]," Mar. 11, 12, 15, 1895, Cannon Papers.

67. Indenture made Mar. 29, 1895 between John M. Cannon and Zena B. Cannon [banker for church interests] and Francis B. Peabody, Chicago, Ill., First Presidency Miscellaneous [Financial] Papers; W. McMaster Mills to John M. Cannon, Oct. 5, 1896, Oct. 3, 1897; E. O. Leach to J. M. Cannon, Dec. 3, 1896, ibid.; Clarkson to W. McMaster Mills, Aug. 25, 1896, James S. Clarkson Papers, Library of Congress, Washington, D.C.; Woodruff and Smith to F. J. Cannon, Apr. 2, 1898, Woodruff Papers.

68. Trumbo to Clarkson, Dec. 10, 1897, Clarkson Papers; Edward Leo Lyman, "Isaac Trumbo and the Politics of Utah Statehood," *Utah Historical Quarterly* 41 (Spring, 1973), 146–47; G. Q. Cannon Journal, Feb. 1, Mar. 29, 1898, excerpt notes in B. H. Roberts Papers.

69. *Salt Lake Herald*, Oct. 31, 1894, Feb. 19, 1895; *Salt Lake Tribune*, Oct. 30, 1894; *New York Times*, Feb. 13, 14, 15, 26, 1895; A. T. Schroeder, ed., "The N. Y. Times vs. Geo. Q. Cannon," *Lucifer's Lantern* 5 & 6 (Salt Lake City, June, 1899), 2–121, copy Lee Library, Brigham Young University, Provo, Utah. Cannon's son Abraham was later told that R. W. Sloan had written the *Times* exposé, assisted by another avid Democrat named H. J. Dinniny, explaining that they did it at the insistance of a man named Cater who came here from New York to provide special correspondence for the paper mentioned. See A. H. Cannon Journal, Feb. 20, Mar. 15, Apr. 19, 1895.

70. *New York Times*, Feb. 15, 1895.

71. *Salt Lake Herald*, Feb. 19, 1895;. Arrington, *Great Basin Kingdom*, 394–95.

72. G. Q. Cannon to George A. Purbeck, June 25, 1895, copy, First Presidency Miscellaneous [Financial] Papers. A provision for such dissolution had been provided for in the original contract.

73. At the end of the next year, Woodruff noted with great anxiety that "we the Presidency of the Church are so overwhelmed in financial matters it seems as though we should never live to get through with it. Unless the Lord opens the way in a marvelous manner, it looks as though we should never pay our debts." See Woodruff Journal, Dec. 30, 1896.

9

A Tumultuous Interim
to Statehood

Although the Utah Enabling Act had been passed, there was still a uniquely lengthy interim period before actual statehood arrived. With another campaign for a territorial representative to Congress, the selection of the delegates to the constitutional convention, and the election of the first state officers, including U.S. senators, this period was hardly anticlimactic. There were also intermittent threats of a rejuvenation of the Liberal party amid loud outcrys of church interference in politics. Yet with the arrival of statehood and the launching of self-government, both Mormon and Gentiles were finally inclined to forget the conflicts of the past and enjoy their new status as full-fledged citizens of the United States.[1]

During the month following the dissolution of the Liberal party in Utah, political observers were able to determine which major party would benefit most from its demise. Clarence Hall, a recently elected representative to the territorial legislature from Salt Lake City, died suddenly, necessitating a special election. W. C. Hall, an uncle of the deceased and a long-time Liberal, was selected as the Democratic party candidate. The Republicans nominated C. S. Varian, also a former Liberal. In the campaign of late December, 1893, the *Herald* repeatedly noted that a vote for the Democrat would be an indirect endorsement of the Cleveland administration and would strengthen the hand of Utah party leaders working for statehood. The *Tribune* countered with the reminder that a vote for Varian was the best way to protest against the wrongs heaped upon Utah by the Democratic administration.

The election of January 4, 1894, brought the Republicans victory by a margin of almost 1,000 votes. The *Tribune* proclaimed that Salt Lake City had thus placed the "stamp of disapproval on Cleveland's ways." Less biased observers more accurately surmised that the difference between the outcome and that of the legislative election two months earlier was that in the former there had been a Liberal candidate in the field and in the latter a large percentage of those who had supported that candidate were by natural inclination Republicans and now voted for Varian.[2]

One portion of the Democratic strategy in the unsuccessful campaign was significant as a portent for the more important contests of the future. In an attempt to divide the formerly Liberal voters, the *Herald* published an old letter in which Varian had criticized Arthur L. Thomas. The *Tribune*, whose editor and publisher were known to be close friends of the former governor, strongly defended Varian's past courageous actions without taking issue with his earlier disagreements with fellow Republicans. Nevertheless, the Democrats had recognized a potentially weak link in the Republican armor—the existence of rival factions within the party.[3]

During the ensuing months such schisms became more pronounced. On the one side was the so-called *Tribune* ring, whose members had most recently entered the Republican ranks from the defunct Gentile party. Their prime opponents were led by the party's territorial chairman, Charles Crane, who was becoming closely allied with Isaac Trumbo. At stake in the contest, as statehood became a certainty, were the two most prestigious offices available—the Utah governorship and the state's Gentile seat in the U.S. Senate. It was clear that Trumbo and Crane had set their sights on these positions, and it soon became equally evident that *Tribune* editor C. C. Goodwin and Thomas were aspirants for the same honors.[4]

Another aspect of the internal rivalry was between Salt Lake City Republicans and those in other portions of the territory. In his position as party chairman and as resident of Millard, one of the south-central counties, Crane had garnered much sympathy and support in the outlying areas. He was also exceptionally strong in Salt Lake's rival urban county, Weber. The *Tribune* editorialized for an entire year against Crane, accusing him of using his party position to his and Trumbo's advantage and consistently calling for his resignation if he were going to run for office.

The faction allied with the newspaper also planned more effective means to remove the rival party officer. During the Republican party territorial convention at Provo, in early September, 1894, an attempt was made to replace Crane with a Salt Lake banker, Samuel Kenyon. Efforts to garner support included comments about how the citizens of Salt Lake City were being discriminated against by the incumbent party chairman. This movement was thwarted, largely by Varian. Annoyed at not being informed of a previous caucus of Salt Lake County delegates, which had organized to implement the plan, he took occasion at a subsequent gathering of county delegates to complain about the arbitrary action, alleging it was part of a "scheme of a few designing and self-asserting office-seekers." After several other prominent delegates spoke in the same vein, there was no further effort to depose Crane and the ensuing convention proceedings were notably harmonious.[5]

The much more important accomplishment of the convention was the unanimous renomination of Frank J. Cannon as Republican candidate for delegate to Congress. The Democrats again selected Joseph L. Rawlins, so the opponents from the last congressional contest faced each other again. This time, however, it would be without the interference of a Liberal party candidate. The *Tribune* predicted confidently that the outcome would be different, observing that Cannon merely needed to maintain his former strength in the outer counties to win. This was based on the assumption that three-fourths of the 4,000 men in Salt Lake County who had voted for C. E. Allen two years before would now vote Republican. The Hall-Varian contest earlier in the year had cut heavily into the Democratic majorities, even in the supposed party strongholds of the city. And such outlying communities as Bingham, which had given 244 of its 300 votes to Allen, a former resident, were said to be solid for Cannon.[6]

Rawlins had been nominated in a speech which claimed that during his previous term his name had been associated with "unexampled achievements" in behalf of Utah. In his acceptance remarks he boasted of having enacted almost twice as many bills as any other territorial delegate. Rawlins detailed his efforts on behalf of statehood, charging that "from start to finish the Republican representatives and senators obstructed the passage of the bill," and only relented when they realized how destructive it would be to party support in the West. The delegate specifically mentioned the rumors that had been current of a "powerful and corrupt corporation" only awaiting statehood to build a certain railroad in Utah, and he stated that Trumbo was reportedly agreeable to the corporation as a senator from Utah. This was the source of Democratic campaign manager Powers's allegations, subsequently utilized in an effort to discredit the Republican party, Trumbo, and George Q. Cannon.[7]

Late in the campaign, on October 10, at a meeting illustrative of the harmonious relationships growing between the first Mormon Republicans, represented by John Henry Smith and the last of the Liberals to affiliate with that party, exemplified by C. C. Goodwin, President Joseph F. Smith gave what he called his first political speech. Challenging Rawlins's claims to the credit for achievement of statehood, he contended Utah did not owe imminent admission to the Democrats and charged that some Democrats had attempted to prevent statehood. The partisan church leader discounted Rawlins's statehood efforts and concluded that he was "not worthy of the honor" of being returned to Congress.[8]

Yet despite the rather unrestrained language of Smith, Rawlins, and others, this campaign was not nearly as bitter as that two years earlier—or the subsequent one. The writings of several Mormon leaders indicate a definite effort to prevent political differences from leading to personal animosities among church members. On one occasion the former political rivals, John Henry Smith and Moses Thatcher, appeared arm in arm to appeal to the people to maintain personal harmony amid partisan differences, a significant contrast to other contests.[9]

The stump speeches of the respective candidates for Congress were largely centered on financial issues. Rawlins and Cannon each blamed the opponent's party for the economic stagnation that had gripped the nation for a year and Utah for considerably longer. Rawlins asserted that calamity had come not because of the Democratic tariff laws but as a result of Republican monetary policies and encouragement of trusts. These often convoluted arguments were hardly persuasive, largely because the party in power is more easily blamed for economic distress. It was therefore more effective for Cannon to ask in his overdramatic, rhetorical style, "Who will give back the work, the wages, the prosperity, the dignity, and the hope to the mightiest nation under the sun"—to which the applauding audiences reiterated the desired answer.[10] Also, since all politicians in silver-producing states were constrained to support some coinage stance, whatever their national party platforms decreed, the major issue in this and other such contests of the era was the tariff. And the Republican party's position and record on that issue was far more appealing in Utah than any version of the Democratic policies that party spokesmen could muster.[11]

On election eve the *Herald* was still optimistic of Democratic victory. Although the paper admitted that if 75 percent of the former Liberal voters cast their ballots for the G.O.P., Cannon would win, it denied that the proportion would be so high. Yet when the time arrived, the Republicans emerged clearly victorious and when the *Herald* finally acknowledged that fact it attributed the outcome to the ex-Liberal element, which had affiliated with the Republican party. The Democratic spokesmen were correct in pointing out that with the increased voter turnout, their party had not lost support since the last election and in fact in the outlying areas had more than held its strength. However, the paper's editors were forced to admit that there were sections of Salt Lake City that were gravely in need of greater "organization and discipline in the Democratic army." As Goodwin had predicted, this was where Frank Cannon acquired his margin of victory.[12]

Another important aspect of the November, 1894, campaign was the contest for seats in the constitutional convention, which the recently passed enabling act had decreed would convene the following March. Utah voters were directed to select 107 delegates to frame a state constitution, and each party sought to dominate those proceedings.

In mid-September a group of Mormon Democrats reflected on the year-long ban on church leaders' participation in politics as candidates. Recognizing that such would deprive the constitutional convention of some of Utah's most capable citizens, they urged Apostles Thatcher and Franklin D. Richards to discuss the matter with the First Presidency. Wilford Woodruff and Joseph F. Smith were hesitant to engage in extensive conversation on the subject but did express a willingness that L.D.S. political activists "should make all proper efforts on both sides to carry their parties—only not slander, throw dirt and demean each other."[13] The next day the two apostles were joined by a third, Heber J. Grant, and invited to sit prominently on the speakers' stand during the Democratic territorial convention. Grant was surprised to be called upon to address the body and responded with brief remarks, which to his dismay were later printed and circulated as a partisan campaign tract. The following day he called upon Apostle Richards for further clarification of what the First Presidency had approved. He was assured that the church leaders had "no objection to any of the brethren doing any political work that they might think best . . . that all were at perfect liberty to do what they pleased as to making speeches for either party." This not only relieved Grant of apprehension concerning his recent political speech, but apparently convinced other churchmen that the former restrictions on ecclesiastical leaders participating in political affairs no longer applied.[14] Soon thereafter Francis M. Lyman noted from a conversation with Smith and Cannon that such partisan activity related only to the constitutional convention, not "ordinary politics." Unfortunately, this position was not widely clarified at the time or in the subsequent months and the next year would lead to further internal conflict.[15]

In the contest for convention delegates the Republicans were again triumphant, electing fifty-nine to forty-eight for the Democrats. Although twenty-eight of the delegates were non-Mormons, Latter-day Saints were in a large majority. This included four general authorities, Republican John Henry Smith and Democrats William B. Preston, Moses Thatcher, and B. H. Roberts, along with ten members of stake presidencies and fifteen members of bishoprics.[16]

Just after the beginning of the new year, some Democrats made a concerted effort to overcome their deficiency of convention delegates by challenging the results in several election districts. The Republicans countered by alleging serious irregularities, particularly in Sanpete County. Throughout the month of January, 1895, as the matter was investigated, the *Tribune* editor charged that Democrats had utilized forgeries of registration books and poll lists, with possible tampering with the ballot boxes to defeat the will of the people. On several occasions, territorial party leaders and specifically the Democratic majority currently dominating the Utah Commission were accused of gross dishonesty.

The matter was, if anything, regarded even more seriously among certain members of the Mormon hierarchy. Abraham H. Cannon, a trusted confidant of his father, in early January referred to information from the U. S. marshal's office that included mention of "the present effort of the Democrats to steal the control of the constitutional convention" through cases then pending in the party-dominated courts. He added, "This fraud is being perpetrated, with the help of the [Utah] Commission." He also expressed belief in an even more ominous plot, in case this one failed, of special investigators being sent from the nation's capital, possibly by the Cleveland administration, to investigate the current situation as to unlawful cohabitation "with the view to start anew the raid against the Mormons" should the convention-packing effort fail. Cannon indicated that the prosecuting attorney, John W. Judd, and Rawlins were reportedly the instigators of the movement.[17]

As time for the constitutional convention approached, the Democrats attempted to prevent Republicans supposedly elected from the third precinct of Salt Lake City, including John Henry Smith, from taking their seats. When these men defended their claims in court, evidence was presented showing that the ballot box in the case had been left in the hands of unauthorized persons within a Democratic party refreshment tent prior to the vote count. The *Tribune* version of the proceedings indicated a distinct possibility that the box was not only switched, but also implicated J. R. Letcher, chairman of the Utah Commission in the affair. Soon after the commission decreed that with such grave questions as to authenticity of the election results, no delegates would be allowed to occupy the contested seats. The *Tribune* called this an "outrageous attempt of Democrats to disfranchise the third precinct."[18]

When the delegates from the Republican majority held their pre-convention caucus they welcomed Smith and his fellow contestant, George R. Emery, even though the two did not possess official certificates of election. Thus the decrees of the Utah Commission were completely ignored. In fact, either to bolster legitimacy or in recognition for his valiant party service, Smith quickly emerged as the Republican choice for president of the convention. When this became known, according to the best historian of the convention, the Democrats declined to nominate a candidate in opposition to him to avoid placing Mormon Democrats in a position of having to vote against an apostle. The *Herald*, on occasion, hinted at Smith's questionable right to participate in the convention and in time would question his competence to preside over such crucial and complicated proceedings.[19]

The framers of the Utah constitution were engaged in their task for almost two months. Delegates were divided over many issues, and the regular proceedings included an abundance of debate. Yet the sessions demonstrated sufficient Mormon-Gentile harmony that Varian, clearly one of the more effective members of the convention, complimented his fellows on the fraternal spirit and the mutual understanding that they had been able to achieve through the close association of representatives of divergent viewpoints.[20] But despite this outward harmony, behind the scenes the convention's most controversial subject, woman's suffrage, threatened to revive old antagonisms among former adversaries. Both parties had previously declared themselves in favor of woman's suffrage. A measure providing that the right to vote and hold office "shall not be denied or abridged on account of sex" was duly introduced by David Evans, a Democrat from Ogden. The committee on elections and suffrage eventually issued a majority report in its favor. But as the matter progressed toward consideration on the floor, opposition began to develop. Along with a considerable number of Gentile Republicans, Democrat B. H. Roberts marshalled his impressive oratorical talents in opposition to inclusion of the woman's suffrage provision in the constitution. To his personal reasons for rejecting the measure, he added the warning that judging from President Grover Cleveland's previous comments and the provisions of the Edmunds-Tucker Act, inclusion of woman's suffrage would endanger acceptance of the Utah constitution and thus delay admission into the union.[21]

This stance considerably nettled some of the other church general authorities. At one meeting of the First Presidency and others, Woodruff expressed fear that the constitution would be defeated if woman suffrage was not a part of it. Joseph F. Smith held similar views, adding that Roberts had done more to injure church interests through his opposition than "any ten Liberals had done in the last fifteen years." This was an exaggeration, but it was repeated later by Woodruff. Particularly in light of subsequent conflicts involving Roberts, the statement indicates significant ill feelings toward the "blacksmith orator's" actions. It was noted that Roberts had been instructed by Smith and Woodruff not to oppose suffrage strongly, and Apostle John W. Taylor, a nominal Democrat, proposed that since he had "betrayed the church," he should be called to an account.[22] After further discussion, George Q. Cannon arose and lamented that the situation existed. He advised that they had better wait until after statehood to codify women's rights. He conceded that this was more because of growing opposition among Utah Gentiles than out of fear of the Cleveland administration rejecting a Utah constitution containing woman suffrage. Cannon had recently visited the nation's capital where he had interviews with the president, the attorney general, and several other cabinet officers. They assured him that such a constitutional provision would be acceptable and denied they had sent any investigators or instructions to the territorial officials regarding an anti-polygamy raid.[23]

At the same April 4 meeting of the church leaders, John Henry Smith divulged that the element associated with the exclusive Gentile Alta Club had concluded to work against the suffrage provision, and should it pass, they proposed to use their influence to defeat the constitution. Smith conceded that though he favored equal suffrage, he believed it best to leave it out since with the provision included the entire document was endangered. A week later he voiced alarm that "efforts were being made to resuscitate the Liberal party in order to defeat statehood," and suffrage was the main pretext for doing so. Although the wiser political counsel of Cannon and John Henry Smith was to concede the issue temporarily, there was no unanimity. Woodruff and Joseph F. Smith wished to direct Mormon delegates to stand firmly by woman suffrage, and Cannon soon agreed with them on the point.[24]

Roberts proposed submission of a separate suffrage amendment to the people, but this was decisively rejected by the convention. Of the twenty-nine votes in favor of the proposal, twenty-five were by Republicans and seventeen of these were non-Mormon. The suffrage provision subsequently passed, with the assistance of nationally prominent proponents of the cause. However, even such suffrage advocates as Henry Blackwell were eventually forced to concede that Utah women would have to forego their right to vote until after the new constitution went into effect.[25]

Later in the year Roberts argued that in the previous months he had been deeply involved in politics "without check or reproof" from ecclesiastical superiors, as far as he knew. Either Roberts's memory was deficient or the highest church leaders made the costly mistake of not directly communicating their displeasure to him. Yet even if this were the case, Roberts was still remiss in not more conscientiously seeking to understand where he stood with the First Presidency on the matter. Adverse comments concerning Roberts's activities had often been made in the presence of men who would have gladly confided such information to him if he had been seeking it.[26]

This ill will engendered by Roberts's actions in the constitutional convention is particularly important when linked with that long harbored toward his Democratic associate, Moses Thatcher. The Logan apostle had been too ill to attend the beginning sessions of the convention, but the letter he sent in explanation was so laced with partisan comments as to embroil the delegates in the first party clash of the convention. In light of the fact that Woodruff had expressed specific desire that political contentions be avoided during the constitution-framing process, it is easy to see how Thatcher's actions displeased the First Presidency. After Thatcher had recovered sufficiently to participate in the convention, the often dissident general authority was given "a mild reproof" by Woodruff "for his failure to seek counsel of the presidency in regard to the Constitutional Convention and other matters." [27]

This took place at the same meeting at which Woodruff had repeated Joseph F. Smith's observation that Roberts had "done the Saints more harm in his speeches in the convention than all the Liberal element" in Salt Lake City. When it is recalled that Thatcher and Roberts were the leading offenders of the presidency during the political campaign of 1892, and that it took great effort in the early part of the following year to bring them back into good standing with the brethren of their respective quorums, the displeasure incurred during the 1895 constitutional convention takes on added significance. It becomes clear that the greater controversy centering on the two during the ensuing autumn campaign was not an isolated incident. [28]

In early April, 1895, George Q. Cannon finalized his agreement to mortgage his city property for the purpose of paying off James S. Clarkson. By that time he had reason to believe that Isaac Trumbo and Hiram B. Clawson had been dishonest in their financial dealings with the First Presidency. Trumbo continued to hope Cannon would follow through on the arrangement as he understood it, which was that the two would together seek the Republican nominations for Utah's seats in the U.S. Senate. However, Cannon confided to John Henry Smith that he was as yet undecided about seeking that office. Abraham H. Cannon privately denied any such aspirations on the part of his father. [29]

One of the recipients of this quiet denial was the Salt Lake City fire-chief and Republican politician James Devine, who was interested in helping Frank J. Cannon win the Mormon senate seat. Devine was instrumental in uniting young Cannon's political interests with those of the *Tribune* faction of the party. They became nominal supporters of Goodwin's senatorial ambitions in exchange for the newspaper's support of Cannon. The rival *Herald*, while expressing surprise at the alliance, observed that it was a marriage of convenience. Cannon was looking for wider political support in Salt Lake City, where the *Tribune* crowd supposedly held sway, and Goodwin supporters were seeking a greater following in the outlying communities, which their new associate was thought to be able to provide.[30]

A month later, through Devine, *Tribune* publisher Patrick Lannan supposedly informed Abraham Cannon that Trumbo backer Charles Crane was "playing false to Frank [Cannon] in a political sense." Although it was highly unlikely that Crane would ever confide anything to a member of the *Tribune* faction, as Lannan alleged, at least some members of the Cannon family believed the report. They were notably sensitive concerning Frank Cannon's considerable human frailties and recognized the effect that printed accounts of some prior escapades might have on his political fortunes. The younger Cannon's candidacy for the Senate was soon to become an important wedge between the Crane-Trumbo combine and George Q. Cannon, on whom their senatorial hopes were largely hinged.[31]

According to his wife's recollections, when Trumbo returned to Utah after the enabling act was passed, he entered Salt Lake City on a Sunday to avoid the brass band and crowd he assumed would otherwise be on hand to greet him.[32] He could have spared himself the precaution because the people of Utah had not been apprised of the colonel's efforts in their behalf. Thus it was easy for his opponents to label him an "interloper," supremely presumptuous to be contending for the highest office Utah voters could offer a fellow citizen. The *Salt Lake Tribune*'s initial tactic was to ignore Trumbo completely, assuming that without publicity from the leading Republican paper, party voters would remain unaware of the man who had allied with the rival faction. But in May, 1895, the Goodwin-Thomas forces were dismayed to discover that the Salt Lake Republican League Clubs, which they presumed to dominate, had elected Trumbo as one of Utah's delegates to the organization's national convention to be held in Cleveland, Ohio. According to the biased *Herald* this was especially harmful to Goodwin because his chief claim to a seat in the U. S. Senate was as a long-time champion of the cause of silver in the West.

Trumbo went to Cleveland determined to overshadow the *Tribune* candidate on the silver issue, and according to subsequent *Herald* statements he "scooped Goodwin pretty badly."[33] The convention had not been particularly important to eastern delegations, but participants from the West planned to make the League of Republican Clubs annual convention a forum through which they could defend their monetary doctrines, already becoming a divisive intraparty controversy. Trumbo emerged as one of the leaders of that contest, presiding over several caucuses of silver advocates who planned to present resolutions boldly favoring free and unlimited coinage at a ratio of sixteen to one. Many easterners were just as intent on passing an anti-silver resolution, and all the westerners could accomplish was to block the opposition. But this was hailed as a victory, since it left the way free from negative encumbrances when the silver struggle was expected to resume during the party's 1896 convention.[34]

A notable segment of the nation's press recognized Trumbo as "silver champion of the West" and a leader of the struggles to protect the white metal. The notices that followed on a triumphal visit to New York City often mentioned him as certain of selection as one of Utah's first senators. He was rapidly becoming the best-known Utah political figure in the nation beyond the Great Basin. However, his accomplishments were carefully minimized in the *Salt Lake Tribune*. And even the *Salt Lake Herald*, often quite friendly to him, accused Trumbo of having acquired his publicity through a generous arrangement with the Associated Press news agency, which was undoubtedly true.[35]

In fact, it is apparent that the newspaper subsidization at which Trumbo had proved himself so adept on the national level helped lead to his and Crane's downfall in the 1895 Utah contest. The first to publicize these methods was Josiah F. Gibbs of the weekly *Blade*, then published at Nephi. In mid-July he editorialized under the heading "For Sale. One of the Utah Senatorships" that "it is currently reported that Colonel 'Ikey' has bid a hundred thousand dollars for the purpose of suborning the country press of Utah. That is not enough, Ikey, roll in another bar'l." The respected editor continued, "The country press of Utah may be poor in even debased silver dollars, but they won't sell out to a 13 carat, gold plated, tinsel-covered peacock for a hundred thousand dollars." In the ensuing weeks allegations of "boodle" and open subsidization of the press were widespread. *Provo Enquirer* editor John C. Graham, another constant opponent, stated that "there are so many evidences of boodle that we wonder sometimes what the people think of the newspaper men." Even the *Salt Lake Herald* was eventually accused of being a beneficiary of the Trumbo money barrel. Finally, Gibbs editorialized, "There is not a self-respecting Republican in Utah that cares to have future history record that Isaac Trumbo purchased a seat in the U. S. Senate."[36]

In this era of high political interest and participation, the best means of disseminating party information was the partisan newspaper. It was not considered an outright breach of acceptable practice for financially strapped editors to accept monetary support from politicians favored in their columns during a campaign. In fact if Trumbo and Crane had any hope of counteracting the influence of the *Tribune* faction, they certainly had to solicit aid from rival Republican papers. In July the *Blade* editor observed that before the campaign went much further, nine additional newspapers would be established in the territory, and he surmised that two-thirds of them would receive substantial financial support from the Crane-Trumbo organization. Among those papers that actually materialized was a Salt Lake weekly, the *Star*, which was soon launching direct attacks on the *Tribune* editor.[37] In addition, it soon became apparent that the Trumbo-Crane combine would use the prominent West Coast Republican organ, the *San Francisco Call*, in their behalf. It was reported that a *Call* correspondent was being stationed in Salt Lake City and that the paper would be distributed to doubtful voters throughout Utah.[38]

The *Salt Lake Tribune* would have been well advised to continue ignoring Trumbo and his efforts, but the paper apparently felt that inroads made into securing support within the Salt Lake delegation to the approaching territorial nominating convention made this impossible. Goodwin embarked on a personal onslaught of Trumbo as a Californian without requisite personal qualifications, merits of past service, or future potential who was simply seeking to buy high office. The *Tribune* editor said, "He came not only with the intention of debauching the people, but, so oblivious are his moral sensibilities that he actually sees no especial wrong and no particular impudence in attempting such a game." Other editors merely treated such items as final proof that Goodwin was attempting to belittle his chief rival for the Senate, and on occasion they commented that the attack had enhanced Trumbo's position in Utah.[39]

The *Tribune* had long been outspoken against Trumbo's running mate, Crane, for using his position as chairman of the Republican territorial committee for his own personal benefit. The paper conceded Crane's well-earned right to seek the gubernatorial nomination, but argued it was an unfair advantage for him to utilize his connections with the party machinery for such personal ends. Goodwin repeatedly called for his resignation and, whether accurately or not, took credit for Crane's doing so just weeks before the convention.[40]

There is evidence that Crane jeopardized his own popularity through his ties to Trumbo. Gibbs, who preferred Crane's candidacy to that of the *Tribune* man, Thomas, said Trumbo would "prove a veritable 'Jonas' to Crane's chances." Graham, speaking for a county delegation that had been most friendly to Crane the year before and without which he had little hope to win, observed that "if Charles Crane had rested on his laurels won last fall and not commenced his questionable wire pulling for office he could have anything in sight. His chances of success through his misdirected zeal are now slim. We fear he will never get the nomination."[41]

The questionable tactics referred to more than seeking newspaper support. There were reported attempts to secure delegate votes through similar "subsidization," and this was clearly beyond the bounds of propriety.

Such rumors of "corrupt agencies" had spread particularly through the crucial Provo area and caused considerable negative reaction. One delegate was proudly quoted as saying, "You cannot buy my vote with all the money in Utah County." His delegation headed for the last territorial convention unpledged, amid considerable talk of a compromise candidate for governor who would not widen the threatened breach within the Republican party.[42]

As Crane's forces added a sizable bloc of Salt Lake delegates to their solid ranks from Weber, Davis, Tooele, and Millard counties, some rivals adopted a strategy of placing in nomination the names of favorite sons from key uncommitted areas such as Beaver and Summit counties. This tactic would defeat Crane because it was assumed, that some delegates who felt an obligation to cast a complimentary vote for the man who had done so much to strengthen the party as its chairman would then abandon him and vote for someone else. The Crane group ridiculed the idea that any other man was as deserving of the nomination.

The plan for blocking Crane's selection was also advocated by Republicans who regarded the factional infighting as unforgivable. They were desirous of nominating a compromise candidate around whom both Crane and *Tribune* men could unite. Heber M. Wells had been mentioned as a possibility throughout the summer. Although he did not actively seek the nomination, he made it clear he would accept a party mandate if it were thrust upon him.[43]

When the convention opened on August 28, the race for the gubernatorial nomination remained the center of interest. When the formal proceedings began, the first speech referred to the warring factions and argued that it would be unwise to concede to either one and thus Wells's name was placed before the convention in the interest of party unity. Crane and Thomas were then nominated, along with two prominent Utah businessmen, Philo T. Farnsworth and George A. Lowe, from Beaver and Summit counties, respectively. On the first ballot Crane showed 200 votes to Wells's 172, with Thomas a surprisingly weak third. But since 269 votes were necessary for nomination, a second ballot was in order. In the hectic interim Crane's supporters "used every art to keep their forces from breaking and to add to their strength." But the next ballot proved decisive. Relieved from their first-ballot pledges, more delegates preferred to avoid party division, and Wells was nominated.[44] The following day Crane attributed his defeat more to the general feeling that a Mormon should head the ticket than to any influence of the *Tribune*. The *Tribune* issued another explanation: "The expression of the Wells men during the balloting for the governorship showed that a special reason for their fight on Crane was due to his alliance with Trumbo."[45]

Crane's defeat was a blow to Trumbo's hopes as well. If Crane had been victorious, a campaign tour with the gubernatorial candidate would have enhanced Trumbo's own prestige. Despite this setback Crane persistently remained involved. He and Trumbo assembled and financed their own program to supplement the main party campaign contingent of Wells, congressional candidate Clarence E. Allen, and territorial delegate and would-be senator Frank J. Cannon. In company with *Standard* editor William Glassman, a popular quartet of black singers, and a professional humorist, they stumped the territory with vigor. Asked why he continued to campaign, Crane explained that he did it for the good of the party, to rally his disappointed supporters behind the Republican nominees. Far from receiving any official party expressions of appreciation for these efforts, the former chairman rather bitterly complained that reports had reached him that the present chairman, George M. Cannon, was trying to discredit them.[46]

A second objective of Crane's continued campaigning was "the vindication of Colonel Trumbo" who, he felt, had been grossly misjudged and misrepresented in the party and beyond.[47] Crane authored a campaign pamphlet addressed to the Utah legislature and the general public to answer negative reports that had been spread about Trumbo. Denying the prevalent allegations of any connection with the sugar trust or the Southern Pacific Railroad, Crane stated that Trumbo was actually as much a long-time and permanent Utah resident as any of the aspiring senatorial candidates. As to Trumbo's being a boodler, "the only time he was ever a boodler was when he was giving of his money lavishly to elect Hon. Frank J. Cannon to Congress." Trumbo, Crane asserted, had legitimately contributed more to the party than any other man in Utah.[48]

In the days following the Republican convention the *Herald* exulted that because of the continued evidences of Republican factionalism, the outlook for the Democrats had never been brighter. The Democratic party convention was notable for its harmony. Although several men had been prominently mentioned as possible gubernatorial candidates, ex-delegate John T. Caine emerged with that nomination without engendering any perceptible bitterness. B. H. Roberts had declined the honor in favor of selection as a strong candidate for the Utah congressional seat. And the territorial gathering followed the lead of several county conventions in resolving to support Rawlins and Moses Thatcher for the U.S. Senate seats should the Democrats secure a majority in the first state legislature.[49]

The candidacies of Mormon general authorities Thatcher and Roberts eventually engulfed Utah in bitter strife over church interference in politics prior to the November election. Though the *Tribune*, immediately after their nomination, criticized this mingling of church and state on the part of the Democrats, there was little noticeable comment by members of the church leadership in the first week following the convention, except by Heber J. Grant, who in September noted at an apostles' meeting, where Thatcher's poor attendance was discussed, that he thought "Bro. Moses should not have accepted the nomination to be one of the United States Senators without first having a full and free chat with his brethren of the apostles and also with the Presidency."[50] Grant may have been particularly sensitive on this matter because he himself had been prominently mentioned as a favorite for the Democratic party gubernatorial nomination. After hearing a significant number of unsolicited expressions of preference for him by delegates enroute to the Democratic convention, Apostle Grant called at the office of the First Presidency and informed them of his opportunity. He assured the presidency that he had no intention of accepting the overtures without their permission but intimated that should they desire it, he would gladly become an active candidate. When no such encouragement was forthcoming, Grant wired his cousin, A. W. Ivins, a prominent Democratic convention delegate, to use his influence to see that his name was not presented, and it was not.[51]

On October 1, 1895, Apostle Brigham Young, Jr., engaged Thatcher in conversation on the streets of Salt Lake City. Young advised his fellow apostle to go to Woodruff and converse freely with him in relation to "some political complications." At first Thatcher refused, then reconsidered and promised to weigh the suggestion. In the course of further exchange, Young and most of his church associates were denounced as "too pliable" and not only failing to maintain their "individuality" but also, according to the notably "stiff" Thatcher, their "manhood." When Young subsequently repeated this conversation to some of his brethren, one of them recorded Thatcher's description of them as lacking "backbone."

The next day Thatcher did make an attempt to have an interview with Woodruff. Although the president of the church was apparently hesitant to talk with Thatcher in the absence of his counselors, the dissident apostle succeeded in stating his position. He did not see how Woodruff could "dictate to him or anyone else on political matters." The thrust of Thatcher's defense to Woodruff was that the First Presidency was trying to deprive him of his free agency, a right particularly valued in L.D.S. theology.[52]

If Joseph F. Smith understood Thatcher's remarks in the same light, this may have been what prompted him to make the statements he did just a few days later at general conference. On Monday, October 7, a conference priesthood session was held at the Assembly Hall on Temple Square. This was where final instruction to local church leaders was traditionally given. Among at least seven talks delivered that morning was one by Smith that included the remarks that precipitated perhaps the most heated political controversy in Utah's history. In the process of explaining that the church possessed living oracles whose counsel should be sought in all matters, he warned that a priesthood holder who undertook to do as he pleased without thought of the directions of his superiors was on dangerous ground. This statement led to mention, perhaps as an unplanned illustration by a man never known for being diplomatic or restrained in speech, of one of the apostles and one of the Seven Presidents of Seventies, who had recently "done wrong in accepting obligations without first consulting and obtaining the consent of those who presided over them." This was an obvious reference to Thatcher and Roberts, and the remarks that followed were a direct answer to Thatcher's recent comment about his brethren's lack of backbone. Smith stated that "no man surrenders his manhood by seeking the advice of his superiors." At the same meeting, Presidents Woodruff and Cannon endorsed Smith's sentiments, with the first counselor candidly admitting that although he would not have made such statements, he was glad they had been made.[53]

As news of these comments quickly spread throughout Utah, Democrats began to interpret them as a partisan threat to their campaign hopes. Four days later, at a meeting of the First Presidency and apostles, Smith forcefully denied that he had any intention of his statements being used for political purposes. During the ensuing week Woodruff published a statement, confirmed by a similar one by Smith, that no church influence was used or sought in political matters at the time. In a subsequent talk at an Ogden stake conference, Smith again denied his wish for a union of church and state, but also added that he did not wish to have the state interfere with church discipline. Several days later the presidency and half of the apostles discussed the political situation and resolved to "stand absolutely firm in maintaining church discipline, no matter how much political capital was attempted to be made out of the position."[54]

For almost a week after Smith's ill-advised conference remarks, the Salt Lake daily newspapers were remarkably restrained in reference to rumors that had emanated from the Assembly Hall. On October 11 the *Salt Lake Herald* advised calmness and affirmed that nothing had occurred which should damage the cause of the Democratic party in Utah, but next day it began to revise these views, possibly upon notice of the disclosures about to be made in the pages of the more sensationalist weekly *Salt Lake Argus*. Under a headline "Is The Old Fight On," the front-page *Argus* article mentioned rumors that notwithstanding the disclaimers repeatedly made, the Mormon church was still in politics and that at the proper time its leaders would "begin to wield the rod of discipline on the political anatomies of some of their subordinates." After repeating the persistent story of George Q. Cannon's bargain with Washington politicians in regard to Utah statehood, the article concluded that the highest church leaders had proven false to their declarations of aloofness from politics.[55]

The *Argus* detailed the proceedings of the priesthood meeting, charging that Joseph F. Smith had "administered the rod of discipline effectively." The paper then disclosed that the Utah Democratic executive committee had held emergency meetings to discuss the situation. They were said to be particularly alarmed that Thatcher and Roberts had been placed "under the ban," an allusion to a word-of-mouth technique that the Mormon hierarchy was known to have utilized previously to prevent "undesirable" political aspirants from gaining office. The efficacy of such tactics being duly recognized, Judge O. W. Powers stated that as party chairman he had "no right to procrastinate or delay taking some step that will save the party from defeat that they fear will come if the impression remains that we are under the ban of the First Presidency."

In an extensive interview published first in the *Argus*, Powers conceded the church leaders' right to discipline their members. But he questioned the uniformity in the application of the rules prohibiting political involvement, recalling that Apostle John Henry Smith had often been active politically and had never been criticized as had Thatcher and Roberts. In response to a direct question about the church leaders' right to require members to "take counsel before they enter politics or accept any nomination for political office," Powers replied, "Why should a Democrat be called upon to counsel with Joseph F. Smith, a Republican." The Democratic chairman concluded the interview by referring to the *Times* interview and other assurances that no man would be held accountable before ecclesiastical authority for his political actions and stated that his party had accepted such declarations in good faith. He demanded that those promises be kept more conscientiously than had recently been the case.[56]

In subsequent days the *Herald* contained numerous similar comments from leading Democrats, including Roberts. While the outspoken Mormon general authority claimed to hold himself respectfully answerable to the higher church leaders for any violation of their discipline or regulations, he did not consider his recent actions as a breach of such rules. Roberts's perception of the central problem, from the Democratic party point of view, was not that he had been denounced or his candidacy complained of, but that this had been done at such an inopportune time as far as injury to party prospects in the coming election was concerned.[57]

The *Salt Lake Tribune* was predictably incredulous in its comments. It charged Democratic managers with seizing the opportunity presented by

Smith's remarks to revive their declining hopes for success at the polls. Powers, whom the *Tribune* soon described as a master at stirring up a conflagration, was alleged to be undertaking the desperate game to create an issue that would generate new enthusiasm in his party ranks. It labeled the scheme as "rule or ruin," citing outright threats by Powers not only to wage war on the First Presidency but actually to appeal to President Cleveland to refuse Utah's admission as a state if such were deemed necessary to force the church leaders to cease using their influence in favor of the Republican party.

Indeed, if national Democratic leaders were inclined to look at Utah statehood solely as a matter of immediate partisan advantage, they had sufficient pretext for slowing the progress toward admission on the grounds of interference by Latter-day Saint leaders in political affairs. To the undoubted disappointment of some Utah Democrats, Cleveland showed no tolerance for delaying the territory's admission into the union. Thus even the most flagrant episode of church interference in politics was not sufficient to deny the political independence most Utah Mormons so fervently desired.

Actually, Joseph F. Smith's supposedly partisan comments were merely the latest of a number of Democratic grievances reaching back to 1891, when national party lines had first been drawn in Utah. When territorial party leaders subsequently reconvened their convention and drafted strongly worded articles declaring absolute separation of church and state, they were clearly aiming at other violations of such policy as well as the recent offenses. A *New York Times* correspondent reported accurately that "the convention was not summoned a second time simply because of the actions at the priesthood meeting. This was only the culmination of a long series of hostile and unfair influences exerted by the Mormon hierarchy."[58]

Besides the pointed criticism of ecclesiastical interference in the 1895 campaign, the reconvened Democratic convention enumerated what its leaders considered the most outrageous past violations of the principle of separation of church and state. After fully discussing the *Times* interview and similar pledges of 1891, George F. Gibbs's letter advising broader Cache Valley membership in the Republican party was detailed. Then the convention proceedings elaborated on Joseph F. Smith's role in the 1892 campaign, including his partisan speeches, the *Nuggets of Truth* pamphlet, and the bishop's recommend in behalf of Frank Cannon. They also accused the First Presidency of similarly aiding Cannon in the more successful 1894 contest, although Apostle Francis M. Lyman was more strongly denounced for his allegedly partisan role in that campaign. Another supposedly grave offense of that year was the telegram the presidency had sent to Trumbo, congratulating him for his role in securing Utah statehood. Trumbo supporters had recently circulated a political broadside replicating the rather laudatory telegram, and Democrats deeply resented the implication that their delegate, Rawlins, had been less instrumental in bringing about admission into the union. Finally, some party dignitaries were smarting over persistent comments by members of the First Presidency on the subject of home industry. These were construed, by those already sensitive on the subject, as a further attack on Democratic interests and doctrines.[59]

The *Salt Lake Tribune* promptly labeled the entire second Democratic convention as a huge "grandstand play." Some among the church leadership agreed, and the general authorities were particularly concerned over the undue bitterness generated by the renewed campaign. President Lorenzo Snow observed pessimistically that he had not seen such a "terrible spirit" among Mormon participants since the early days of great dissension and apostasy from the church in Kirkland, Ohio.[60] Although it is impossible to assess the effect of the newly revived church interference issue on the campaign, it clearly was not sufficient to overcome other Republican advantages.

In the more regular aspects of the contest personalities were first emphasized by the Democrats, particularly concerning the gubernatorial candidates. Caine certainly had the superior experience through his decade in Congress and other local offices before that. Wells, only thirty-six, was pictured as far too immature and inexperienced to be a serious alternative to the Democrat. But the Republican party rejoined that their man was of the future, not the past, and despite his relative youth, Wells had a good and extensive record of public service. The Democrats certainly had the advantage in the congressional race, since Roberts was the most popular Mormon orator of the day, and his opponent, Allen, was best remembered as a former bitter foe of the Saints. In candidacies for the other offices, both parties had a heavy preponderance of Mormons, but there, too, the Democrats seemed to have the better-known men. Yet in retrospect it was a contest in which issues certainly carried more weight in the outcome than did men.[61]

Again, the most widely discussed issue was the tariff. The national Republican party had long espoused the principle that the production of any article of general consumption that could be carried on in the United Stated should be encouraged. It advocated the theory that new and growing industries should be protected from foreign competition by tariffs until they were well enough established to stand on their own. Similarly, the Mormon church throughout its Utah history had encouraged its people to be self-sustaining and not dependent upon trade with outsiders.

Although Utah Democrats attempted to show a distinction between the Republican and Mormon doctrines, the Republicans were generally quite successful in uniting them during the 1895 campaign.

Utah Democrats had to stand by their national party position, which stated that it was wrong to protect industries from outside competition. They argued that if such industries could not thrive on their own, they should not be established in the locality. Utah campaigners for the party made it clear that they were not opposed to home industry, but only to offering it tariff and subsidy advantages at the cost of higher prices and taxes to the public, which the *Herald* termed "a form of robbery." They reasoned that it was better to import such products, leaving Utahans free to pursue endeavors more profitable to their vicinity. This party position, among a people imbued with a two-generation tradition of self-sufficiency, was certainly a liability for the Democrats.[62]

Early in the campaign the *Tribune* chided the Utah Democrats for being anxious to transfer attention away from the tariff to the silver question. Indeed the monetary issue was the stronger of the two for them in the West. Both parties in their state platforms had advocated the remonetization of silver at a ratio sixteen to one. Though there was some doubt as to whether either national party would commit itself in a similar way, there were more nationally prominent Democrats speaking out in its favor. The one about to become the most famous, William Jennings Bryan, lent his brilliant oratory to the Utah campaign at the height of the fight.

A segment of Utah voters, including some former members of the Republican party, had "come to the conclusion that there is absolutely no hope for silver in the Republican party" and had espoused the Populist party movement. This group nominated a partial list of candidates for state office, including the widely respected Henry W. Lawrence for governor. It was predicted that though the Populists were not, on the whole, a threat to either major party, the popular Lawrence and the silver issue would likely take votes away from Wells, a banker suspected of having been a "goldbug" until recently. The *Herald* predicted that "Heber M. Wells will wake up on election day and find that he has simply been cut to pieces by the third party man."[63]

The ballots themselves proved the inadequacy of this prediction. Wells ran somewhat behind his runningmates in Salt Lake City, but when all territorial returns were in, he had 20,833 votes to 18,519 for Caine and 2,051 for Lawrence. One eminent Utah historian explained these supposedly surprising results by noting that "Utah's first governor, Republican, was elected in 1895 only because silverite sentiment was divided between Democratic and Populist candidates." This might be partially true, but a look at the final election returns indicates a need for further explanation, since even the combined total of votes for Caine and Lawrence came 264 short of defeat for Wells.[64] Some voters clearly overlooked the Republican shortcomings on silver in favor of the party's tariff position.

A most perceptive explanation of the election outcome was offered by John Codman, a long-time observer of the Mormons, who published a letter in the *New York Times* after the Utah election results were announced. "The fact is that the Republican victory dates way back to the days of Brigham Young, whose policy was absolute protection, not only against foreign nations, but against the whole United States outside of Utah." Young had always maintained "that there was not a single article of necessity, and scarcely one of luxury, that could not be produced or manufactured in his domain." Codman concluded, "The whole Mormon people were imbued with this idea."

Although this assessment was correct, it was disputed even as it was published. In an accompanying note the *Times* editor alluded to the paper's allegations earlier in the year, saying George Q. Cannon was the man who possessed the true account of the election outcome—specifically mentioning the purported bargain between Republican party managers and members of the Mormon hierarchy. This argument was bolstered in subsequent days by an anonymous letter from the territory, which reiterated the contention that "the defeat of Democracy in Utah was compassed by the use of church influence." In prompt response Codman conceded Cannon's powerful influence in Utah affairs, but stuck to his contention that the deep-seated protectionist heritage was nevertheless the decisive key to the Utah Republican victory.[65]

No less an authority on Utah politics than Democratic Governor Caleb W. West also discounted church influence. He expressed personal disbelief of intentional church influence in the recent campaign, and stated that such a charge had been disastrous to his party. He asserted that if the church interference issue had not been injected, Utah would have gone Democratic. It was Powers's conduct of the campaign that came in for most of West's criticism and blame, but this viewpoint differed markedly from that of most Utah Democrats, who were appreciative of Powers's leadership. Although they were naturally disappointed by the defeat, their analysis of the election returns showed a narrowing of the Republican margin of victory over the figures of the previous year.[66] The *Deseret News* editor seized upon this as proof that church interference had not determined the outcome of the election after all. Referring to the widespread party defeats, he concluded that the "Democratic party has given as good if not better account of itself in Utah than in any other state of the union. Truly this appears to be 'a Democratic year'—for defeat."[67]

The entire slate of Republican state officers was elected. This included Heber M. Wells, Clarence E. Allen, and John R. Park of Salt Lake City; James T. Hammond of Logan; Morgan Richards of Parowan; A. C. Bishop of Ogden; and James Chipman of American Fork. All but Allen and Bishop were members of the Church of Jesus Christ of Latter-day Saints. The first state legislature was also clearly in the hands of a Republican majority, which at least temporarily frustrated the senatorial aspirations of Rawlins and Thatcher.[68]

Many in Utah expressed relief that with the election past there was hope that political strife would subside. To a great extent it did, but in the following two months there was still concerted infighting among Republican contestants for the Utah seats in the U.S. Senate. The earlier developments had largely favored Frank Cannon. A combination of farsightedness by his campaign managers, who committed Republican state legislative candidates to their man even before the state elections, help from a sympathetic cousin, George M. Cannon, in charge of territorial Republican machinery, and the tradition that the last territorial delegate to Congress was entitled to return to the capital in an elevated capacity all worked to his advantage over the other candidates.[69]

The only obstacle in Frank Cannon's path was the still-possible candidacy of his father—the only other Mormon seriously mentioned for the place of honor. At a meeting of general authorities just after the election, politics was the subject of lengthy deliberation. Lyman, Grant, and Woodruff expressed a desire that George Q. Cannon be sent to the Senate. Abraham Cannon dissented, saying that his father's services were more needed at home than in the nation's capital. In a conversation the next day President Cannon confided to his son Abraham that he did not actually desire to go to Congress but expressed hope that should he be selected, Frank would not be disappointed. After this exchange Abraham Cannon privately suspected that despite his father's denials, he would derive great satisfaction in being returned in triumph to the upper house.[70]

The *Tribune* forces had no difficulty in perceiving the danger that President Cannon's ambitions presented to C. C. Goodwin's candidacy. It would significantly enhance the position of their rival, Isaac Trumbo, who had long linked his race to that of the elder Cannon. In the ensuing weeks *Tribune* men labored through the editorial pages and behind the scenes to disuade the widely admired Cannon from his course. Upon private inquiry, in early December, Goodwin supporter Senator Fred T. Dubois was assured by Abraham Cannon that his father "had declared himself unequivocally out of the Senate race under all circumstances." He confided that President Cannon had conceded that Frank had earned the right to the honor. No public announcement of this shift of position would be made at the time, Dubois was informed, because such would give Trumbo sufficient time to retaliate by in some way undermining Frank Cannon's candidacy.[71] This change of stance indicated the continued decline of Trumbo in the estimation of George Q. Cannon. Undoubtedly Cannon had not only been hurt but had grown weary of the constant mention of their presumed senatorial partnership in the columns of the subsidized press. These artificially stimulated news items had been the root of much of the unfavorable publicity that Cannon and his church had received throughout the past year. Such items continued to persist not only in Utah papers but also throughout the country.

At a council meeting held November 21, some Mormon general authorities again discussed the senatorial question. President Woodruff reiterated his wish that George Q. Cannon go to the U.S. Senate and directed his fellow church leaders to adopt that policy. The several accounts of the gathering contain no indication that Cannon opposed this plan, but he did express hope that Trumbo would not be similarly supported. Cannon specified two principal reasons for this opinion: "He is not a person whose manner and characteristics we desire to represent us, for he is very ignorant, and then he would be, no doubt, a boodler, accepting bribes for services which he would have the power to render." One account of these deliberations included further reference to Trumbo as being primarily engaged in the interests of the Spreckles faction of the sugar trust and of the Southern Pacific Railroad. It was also assumed from these discussions among Mormon leaders that in his campaign work with the members-elect to the Utah legislature, Trumbo's notorious "money barrel" was open. Simon Bamberger, a business associate of the Cannon's, reported that not only was Trumbo leaving no stone unturned to get elected to the Senate, but also that he was intimating on occasion that he had "some kind of pull" on or through George Q. Cannon that would insure he got what he desired when the time came.[72]

Several years later President Cannon reflected in his diary on Trumbo's senatorial aspirations, admitting that there had been a time when he had been in sympathy with them. But, he continued, when the contest opened Trumbo had conducted himself in such a way as to alter this opinion, and he recalled he had so expressed himself at the time. The main offense specified in these reflections was that the aspirant had become the object of too much unfavorable comment and had thus alienated Cannon's affections. Another important reason for the church leader's growing coolness, though he denied active opposition, was that the presidency had never understood that Trumbo was to be repaid for his services to them by being made a senator.[73]

There is evidence that Trumbo had discerned Cannon's altered opinion toward himself and his senatorial ambitions. Soon after the colonel's departure for the nation's capital to work with Republicans interested in holding a Republican national convention in the West, his long-time associate, James S. Clarkson, wrote to Woodruff. This lengthy letter reflected a clear understanding of the Utah situation, undoubtedly as it had been described by Trumbo. It was obviously written for the purpose of rejuvenating the joint senatorial effort of Cannon and Trumbo.

Stating that Republicans across the nation were anxious to know who was to represent Utah in the Senate, Clarkson reminded church leaders that at an earlier interview it had been agreed that if amnesty, restitution of church property, and Utah statehood were attained with the aid of the Republicans, party spokesmen were to have some input into who should comprise the new state's congressional delegation. He had been designated to be the Republican representative in such deliberations, and after citing a consensus that the strongest men possible should occupy the positions, he named George Q. Cannon as the unanimous choice for the Mormon seat. Stressing his vast personal experience and the esteem in which he was widely held, he claimed that he could stand in any group and be the "equal of the greatest men." Clarkson admitted awareness of Cannon's disinclination to accept the office but expressed confidence that if convinced of the universality of the wish in Utah and beyond, he would hardly decline the honor.[74]

Clarkson then focused on the accompanying Senate seat. He claimed that there was almost "the same unanimity" in outside party circles in favor of Trumbo. He cited the colonel's lengthy service as the "evangel, the missionary, the herald" who had contacted so many influential men throughout the nation and who through the sheer force of his personality had paved the way for Utah's admission into the union. "He represents a power and a capacity to make friends and to make headway peculiar to him over any other man I have ever known." Using himself as an example, Clarkson cited Trumbo's remarkable faculty for transforming personal friendship into support for the Mormon cause. Trumbo was "a natural growth," and that while he did not possess "transcendent ability, he can accomplish more than any man of such ability" that the veteran politician had known in public affairs. While admitting an impetuous and sometimes overanxious aspect of the colonel's personality, which could easily have caused offense in the recent Utah campaign, Clarkson affirmed that Trumbo had never placed his personal interest above seeing the Mormon people vindicated and statehood properly attained. The party leader pointedly appealed in behalf of Trumbo's senatorial aspirations: "He has already established such relations with every prominent man in public life, in the Senate, in the House, in the national committee, in the leading newspapers, that it puts him where no other new man from Utah could possibly be if he should serve twenty years in the Senate." [75]

Clarkson then undertook the delicate task of discounting the candidacies of Frank Cannon and Goodwin. He expressed affection for young Cannon but admitted that Republican leaders did not believe him to be as yet anywhere near as influential at home or abroad as was his father. As for Goodwin, the lobby agent cited personal experience of frequently being confronted by arguments against Utah's claims that originated in the *Tribune*. He argued that to reward the hostile editor would seem to lend credence to what Goodwin had so long contended. [76]

Then returning again to the plea for the designated senators, Clarkson mentioned the troubling subject of the letter of the previous year, written just after the Utah Enabling Act had been passed. He alluded to the aid granted by friends who expected some kind of "alliance and mutual support in the future" and warned that to send to the Senate men who knew nothing of these tacit understandings and yet unpaid debts would do inestimable harm to Utah's future interests. Clarkson admitted special concern for the personal damage that would be inflicted upon those who had labored in behalf of statehood through such methods. This was particularly the case with Trumbo, who would be ruined. "It will bankrupt him and mortgage his whole life to repay what he owes in honor to these people who came to his help for your sake." Clarkson concluded with the frank warning that "you cannot keep the friends who were gained by President Cannon and Colonel Trumbo by elevating to the Senate men who all the time that Cannon and Trumbo were fighting for you, were fighting against you." [77]

Clarkson's letter was in line with Woodruff's prevailing inclinations, at least so far as George Q. Cannon's candidacy was concerned. On December 26 Abraham Cannon, more sympathetic to his brother's senatorial aspirations than his father's, recorded the latest decision of the church leader, noting that Woodruff had deemed it the will of the Lord that President Cannon be sent to the U.S. Senate. Some of his recent indecisiveness was explained when the president of the church said that he had consistently been in favor of the elder Cannon's candidacy, "but he had allowed fear of misrepresentation and abuse to change his mind for the time being," before having this resolve bolstered, perhaps by the Clarkson letter. [78]

While quiet efforts began to bring about the election of George Q. Cannon, Woodruff answered Clarkson's letter. Without mentioning his decision on his counselor's candidacy, he agreed that President Cannon would be a most suitable senator. But referring to the recent adverse publicity on church interference, which he assumed the Republican dignitary had noticed, he stated that since that storm broke church leaders had been most hesitant to express their political views in public. He also mentioned that these developments had made Mormon legislators decidedly more apprehensive about openly supporting Cannon, although he conceded that were the senatorial contest to be decided by popular vote, the church leader would have no trouble being elected.

Woodruff probably conveyed this pessimistic picture to help explain why he could not do more to help Trumbo. He was even more discouraging in his assessment of that situation. Acknowledging Trumbo's services and his own kind feeling for the colonel, Woodruff admitted that he sensed there were great obstacles in the way of Trumbo's election, especially since he was the Gentile candidate most closely allied with the L.D.S. church. "The non-Mormons of the community, as I understand, have thought that one Mormon should be sent as senator. I am told they have conceded this." But the Gentiles "look upon Colonal Trumbo as having come to the Territory merely for the sake of office, and that he secretly represents the Southern Pacific corporation." "Others believe that he represents us, and therefore are adverse to his selection, as it would mean too much Mormon influence." Finally, Woodruff confessed that the church leaders did not then have the power accredited to them of being able to decree their wishes and have them obeyed by the legislature. This current lack of political influence turned out to be even more prevalent than Woodruff had assumed.[79]

Meanwhile, the progress toward statehood was continuing. Despite threats that Utah Democrats might yet thwart it through appeals to the president of the United States, in early December, 1895, Frank J. Cannon received positive assurance to the contrary from Cleveland. Firmly discounting the negative rumors, the president indicated a strong desire to issue the proclamation admitting Utah into the union as soon as possible.[80]

A few days later an official delegation headed by Governor West presented Cleveland with a handsomely bound and engraved copy of the Utah constitution. Utah Commission Chairman J. R. Letcher attested to its having been properly approved by the Utah electorate the previous month and to its having complied with the stipulations of the enabling act. The president congratulated them on the imminence of statehood and promised to have the document examined by the proper authorities as promptly as possible. Although the anxious Utahans were subsequently informed by Attorney General Judson Harmon that this process could not be completed before the first of the year, he nevertheless announced his approval of the constitution on December 21. By that time the date for the president's statehood proclamation was set for Saturday, January 4, 1896, with the new state officers to be inaugurated the following Monday. Plans for this event were quickly laid, with prominent Utah Gentiles and Mormons cooperating at every point.[81]

At about mid-day on January 4, 1896, Salt Lake City erupted into an enthusiastic celebration. A shotgun fired in front of the Western Union Telegraph office signaled that word had arrived from Washington, D.C., that President Cleveland had signed the proclamation admitting Utah into the Union as the forty-fifth state. This set off a deafening clamor of shouts, fireworks, bells, and cannon salutes. A gigantic steam whistle especially provided for the occasion sounded incessantly for two hours from the tower of the Salt Lake City and County Building. The streets were thronged with people heartily congratulating each other on finally becoming full-fledged American citizens.[82]

Two days later the inauguration ceremonies were held in the Salt Lake Tabernacle. The ceiling of the historic auditorium was appropriately draped with a gigantic flag, and above the famous organ the forty-fifth star was illuminated electrically. More than 10,000 Utahans crowded inside the building, with thousands thronged outside on the Temple grounds. Prominently seated on the stand were the state officers-elect, along with a few of the outgoing territorial appointees.

Since Governor West had not yet returned from the East, Territorial Secretary Charles C. Richards presided and opened the proceedings with brief remarks. Interspersed betweeen a military band rendition and a children's chorus singing the national anthem, an invocation written by Woodruff was offered by George Q. Cannon. The former delegate to Congress, Joseph L. Rawlins, read Cleveland's admission proclamation and turning to Governor-elect Wells presented him with the pen that the president was supposed to have used over a year before in signing the Utah Enabling Act. Amid cheering and further band numbers, Richards declared, "The hour has arrived when the federal government is to withdraw from the control of the affairs of the territory, and surrender it up to the people; and to the native son of Utah, who has been chosen to be the governor of the state of Utah."

As the cannon at Fort Douglas boomed in the distance, Chief Justice Charles S. Zane administered the oath to Governor Wells. After the Tabernacle Choir sang "Utah, We Love Thee," written especially for the occasion, Governor Wells delivered his inaugural address. Much of the speech was a tasteful review of the uniquely long struggle to reach the point Utahans were then celebrating, which was, as the *Deseret News* characterized it later in the day, the moment when "the reigns [*sic*] of self government were placed in the hands of the people."[83]

At the conclusion of the inaugural ceremonies, the center of interest shifted to the city and county building several blocks away. This almost-new "joint building" had been offered for the use of the first state leg-islature, which Governor Wells had summoned by personal letters for that afternoon. When the expected confusion subsided, Wells, in a well-prepared address, focused attention on a large array of matters needing legislative attention as the new ship of state was launched. In the ensuing several months executive and legislative branches cooperated impressively in making the transition to statehood relatively smooth.[84]

The one matter remaining to bring Utah fully into the sisterhood of states was selection of the first U.S. senators to represent her in the halls of Congress. The struggles among aspirants for these positions con-tinued. On Utah's inauguration day the *Herald* reported authoritatively that George Q. Cannon was indeed a candidate for one of the seats. The account was vague as to the effect that this was expected to have on Gen-tile candidates, mentioning Trumbo, O. J. Saulisbury, C. W. Bennett, and Arthur Brown—but conspiciously ignoring Goodwin.[85]

When Frank J. Cannon returned from the nation's capital several days later, he declined to comment on his father's candidacy. But his *Tribune* ally, Goodwin, had no such reservations. While persistently booming the younger Cannon, the newspaper editor launched a strenuous effort, as the *Herald* described it, "by the use of every sort of innuendo, covert and open threats, to create a sentiment against Hon. George Q. Cannon." The *Tribune* editorials appeared to some to bear ominous portent for re-vival of the old issue of church interference in state affairs should Presi-dent Cannon enter the race. Despite this, the rival papers reported a con-siderable number of Democrats and Republicans ready to cast their vote for the church leader.[86]

A special committee of interested church authorities comprised of Apostles Abraham H. Cannon and John Henry Smith and the candidate's brother, Salt Lake Stake President Angus M. Cannon, made quiet inquir-ies among the legislators. They discovered considerable apprehension among Mormon lawmakers that supporting George Q. Cannon would precipitate the threatened controversy. The committee therefore con-cluded that Cannon could not safely carry a possible Republican caucus vote, which had been called for January 14. Thus on the eve of that party gathering, George Q. Cannon published a notice in the *Deseret News* de-claring that he would not allow his name to be considered for the U.S. Senate. He clearly alluded to the outburst his open declaration would in-cite: "I can't contribute to division by allowing my name to appear as a candidate."[87]

This was indeed a tragedy. Utah and the nation were thus deprived of the services of one of the potentially great statesmen of his era. Ironically, although some Democrats admitted Thatcher's senatorial candidacy had been at least partly an attempt to head off the elder Cannon's election to the Senate, it was actually his fellow counselor, the impetuous Joseph F. Smith, who had most surely denied Cannon the opportunity. Had there not been the preceding storm over church interference in politics, Cannon could easily have weathered whatever opposition might have arisen to his senatorial aspirations.[88]

As the Republican majority in the first state legislature sought to get organized, they held a caucus on the night of January 14. It was not intended that much would be said as yet about the selection of senators, but when the meeting got under way, the managers of several candidates, each confident of winning, concluded to press for an immediate vote on the senatorial nominees. Although many of the legislators were caught off guard, after considerable discussion they concluded to proceed with balloting.[89]

As the only remaining Mormon aspirant, Frank Cannon was chosen by acclamation. Then attention focused on the much less certain matter of the Gentile counterpart. The strategy of Goodwin's supporters, knowing they did not possess sufficient first ballot strength, was to support Brown against Bennett on the initial vote, then lead a breakaway from him to their man on a later ballot. They never dreamed that Brown's more capable floor agents had lined up sufficient support to win on the first ballot, but that was the case. Bennett came in second with a respectable vote. Although this was not the formal procedure through which the senators were selected, most promised to honor the choices when the matter was brought officially before the legislature.[90]

Two versions of Trumbo's status at the point of the caucus later emerged. The less favorable story—allegedly originating with a *Tribune* reporter— said that the colonel's "name was not presented because no one could be found to nominate him." The more friendly *Standard* explained that "it was a well-known fact that Col. Trumbo fought against a caucus and refused to have his name presented."[91]

Some other pieces of information can be assembled to indicate what probably happened to Trumbo. On the day the Utah legislature first convened he wrote a letter to the First Presidency. Attempting to rejuvenate the commitment he still hoped would place him in the Senate, he reminded the church leaders of his past efforts: "Statehood as an accomplished fact has been the dream of eight years of my life . . . and at last the consummation so devoutly sought for has become a reality." He hoped that "the closing scenes of this most realistic drama are about to be enacted, and my sequel is still to be told, but possessed of an equal confidence to that with which you viewed the progress and final achievement of *MY* portion of the understanding, I now look to you, believing and knowing that you will perform your part as faithfully and as perfectly as I have performed mine." Reminding the church leaders of what he at least believed was an old commitment, Trumbo concluded "that the finale to the agreement will terminate in a complete and perfect fulfillment of all promises, will be determined in a few days; and then I wish to rest with the satisfaction of being one of Utah's first senators." Apparently the First Presidency did not answer Trumbo's letter, thus leaving him in a rather helpless position of only being able to hope for what he thought was due him.[92]

On the day of the caucus—possibly after hearing rumors of the impending gathering—Isaac Trumbo called on the First Presidency and received their verbal answer to his letter of the previous week. Their response must have crushed his senatorial hopes, linked as they were to George Q. Cannon's candidacy for the other Senate seat. For on this very day President Cannon publicly announced that he was not a candidate.[93] Trumbo was caught, as intended, without the opportunity to cultivate sufficient support independent from Cannon. Without enough potential votes to be in contention, Trumbo abstained from participation in the caucus.

News of the selection of Utah's senators provoked considerable discussion among the members of Congress. Frank Cannon's choice was well accepted, but, as in Utah, Brown's choice met with little enthusiasm. A special news dispatch to the *Herald* reported, "The impression prevailed here that Colonel Trumbo would be selected as one of the senators. Some of his friends declare Trumbo's defeat to be a piece of rank ingratitude." His efforts for statehood were well remembered, and it was "expected that he would be rewarded for his loyalty to the Mormons." Some could not understand what had gone wrong.[94]

Trumbo was undoubtedly disappointed. He remained in Utah at least part of the year, having further conferences with Woodruff. Although he continued to hold some senatorial ambitions for several years longer, Trumbo moved back to San Francisco and was thereafter but infrequently heard from in Utah. Trumbo's friends had not exaggerated his valor in the eight-year personal crusade in behalf of the Mormon citizens. Nor were they far from the mark in praising the persuasiveness of his personality. But his critics were also correct, for his campaign tactics were certainly questionable. When he unintentionally alienated George Q. Cannon from his senatorial cause, he probably doomed himself to political oblivion.[95]

Thus the men who had worked longest and most directly in the successful struggle for Utah statehood, George Q. Cannon and Isaac Trumbo, failed to receive the senatorial rewards that many, including leaders of the national Republican party, desired them to attain. And Utahans would soon admit that Frank J. Cannon and Arthur Brown did little to merit their election to the U. S. Senate.[96]

Utah's entrance into the United States was thus fully accomplished. Certainly no other group of U.S. citizens of similar size ever struggled so long for statehood. Nor did any other territory have as much opposition to overcome to achieve its goals. The state had not yet arrived at full political and social maturity, but the progress in those areas had been sufficiently noticed by the nation that Utah was finally welcomed warmly into the union.

NOTES

1. This does not mean all conflicts were permanently eradicated. The most notable subsequent development was the recurring polygamy-political controversy surrounding the Reed Smoot hearings of 1903–6.

2. *Salt Lake Herald*, Dec. 27, 30, 1893; *Salt Lake Tribune*, Jan. 4, 5, 1894.

3. *Salt Lake Herald*, Dec. 27, 1893; *Salt Lake Tribune*, Jan. 3, 1894.

4. *Ogden Standard*, Jan. 5, 1894; *Salt Lake Herald*, Apr. 12, 1895.

5. *Ogden Standard*, Sept. 5, 1894; *Salt Lake Tribune*, July 1, 21, 25, 30, 1895; A. H. Cannon Journal, Aug. 28, 1894; *Salt Lake [Weekly] Argus*, Sept. 15, 1894.

6. *Salt Lake Tribune*, Sept. 12, 13, 1894; *Ogden Standard*, Sept. 12, 1894.

7. *Salt Lake Herald*, Sept. 15, 16, Oct. 17, 1894; *Salt Lake Tribune*, Sept. 16, 1894.

8. *Salt Lake Tribune*, Oct. 11, 21, 1894.

9. F. M. Lyman Journal, July 26, Aug. 25, Sept. 19, 1894. Democratic campaign strategist Orlando W. Powers, in a speech and political broadside, gave an exaggerated version of the details of the Utah Company and challenged Frank Cannon to comment on the same. It was obvious he was trying to make campaign capital out of the matter. In doing so he incurred animosity from George Q. Cannon and his associates that would continue for at least a year. On several subsequent occasions this hostility was shared by church members who were considered tarnished by too close contact with Powers, whom the First Presidency and some other general authorities considered worse than corrupt. See *Salt Lake Tribune*, Oct. 30, 1894; *Salt Lake Herald*, Oct. 31, 1894.

10. *Salt Lake Tribune*, Oct. 20, 1894; *Salt Lake Herald*, Oct. 3, 1894.

11. *Salt Lake Herald*, Oct. 30, 1894. President Cleveland's repeal of the Sherman Silver Purchase Act and the reduced duties on lead, wool, and sugar embodied in the Wilson-Gorman Tariff did little to endear the national Democratic party to most Utahans.

12. Ibid., Nov. 6, 8, 10, 1894.

13. F. D. Richards Journal, Sept. 14, 1894.

14. Grant Journal, Sept. 15, 16, 17, 27, 1894; "Speech of Hon. H. J. Grant: A Ringing Appeal to the Voters of Utah Territory," 2-page campaign broadside, no

publication information, copy, Lee Library, Brigham Young University, Provo, Utah.

15. Lyman Journal, Sept. 27, 1894.

16. Stanley S. Ivins, "A Constitution for Utah," *Utah Historical Quarterly* 25 (Apr., 1957), 100.

17. *Salt Lake Tribune*, Jan. 9, Feb. 27, 1895; A. H. Cannon Journal, Jan. 8, 1895.

18. *Salt Lake Tribune*, Jan. 9, 10, Feb. 27, Mar. 1, 2, 3, 1895.

19. Ivins, "Constitution for Utah," 101. Ivins's father was a prominent Democratic delegate. *Salt Lake Herald*, Mar. 16, 1895.

20. Ivins, "Constitution for Utah," 115.

21. *Official Report of the Proceedings and Debates of the Convention Assembled at Salt Lake City on the Fourth Day of Mar., 1895, to Adopt a Constitution for the State of Utah*, 2 vols. (Salt Lake City, 1898), 1:459–63; Brigham H. Roberts, "The Life Story of B. H. Roberts," ms., copy, Marriott Library, University of Utah, Salt Lake City; Jean Bickmore White, "Women's Place Is in the Constitution: The Struggle for Equal Rights in Utah in 1895," *Utah Historical Quarterly* 42 (Fall, 1974), 344–69; Truman G. Madsen, *B. H. Roberts: Defender of the Faith* (Salt Lake City, 1980), 217–20.

22. A. H. Cannon Journal, Apr. 4, 1895; Grant Journal, Apr. 4, 1895.

23. A. H. Cannon Journal, Apr. 4, 11, 12, 1895; Grant Journal, Apr. 4, 11, 1895.

24. A. H. Cannon Journal, Apr. 4, 11, 12, 1895; Grant Journal, Apr. 4, 11, 1895; Ivins, "Constitution for Utah," 112–13; *Salt Lake Tribune*, Jan. 7, Feb. 23, 27, Apr. 25, 1895.

25. Beverly Beeton, "Woman Suffrage in the American West, 1869–1896" (Ph.D. diss., University of Utah, 1976), 137–48, recounts events beyond the constitutional convention, including visits to Utah by Susan B. Anthony and Anna Howard Shaw in mid-May; *Salt Lake Herald*, Apr. 30, 1895; F. D. Richards Journal, Aug. 8, 1895.

26. B. H. Roberts to Woodruff, Cannon, and Smith, Oct. 8, 1895, copy Roberts Papers.

27. Lyman Journal, July 26, 1894: "Pres. Woodruff felt our Constitutional Convention should [be] as near as possible non-partisan." A. H. Cannon Journal, Apr. 25, 1895.

28. A. H. Cannon Journal, Apr. 25, 1895. See also pp. 201, 208 herein.

29. Grant Journal, Apr. 13, 1895; A. H. Cannon Journal, Apr. 4, 1895. Both diarists expressed to George Q. Cannon their distrust of Clawson when they were informed of the arrangement with Clarkson. Trumbo's recollection of the senatorial arrangement, as he recalled it several years later, was as follows: "When General Clarkson spoke to me in Washington in regard to the Senatorial position that I never had a thought pass my mind in respect to asking for anything, and when the agreement was made in New York that General Clarkson would have the naming of the senators, prior to that time I had no idea that the General in his generosity and good wishes would give me one of the places. Bishop Clawson

was present at the conversation in Washington when General Clarkson said what he was going to do. He spoke to Platt Quay, and Aldrich upon the subject, and they all selected me. I said then that they would make a mistake, and I wished that they would withdraw my name and give the senatorship to President George Q. Cannon, as he was the one it belongs to, and I did not wish it. Bishop Clawson at the same conversation joined me and said that President Cannon should be one of the senators and that Colonel Trumbo ought to be the other. General Clarkson, in answer to this said: we will take care of Mr. Cannon ourselves." Trumbo to First Presidency, Jan. 28, 1898, recorded in G. Q. Cannon Journal, Feb. 1, 1898, and copied from there by Roberts, Roberts Papers; J. H. Smith Journal, May 15, 1895.

30. A. H. Cannon Journal, Apr. 1, May 3, 14, 16, 1895.

31. Ibid., May 14, 16, 1895.

32. *Salt Lake Tribune*, Sept. 17, 1899.

33. *Salt Lake Herald*, May 15, 24, June 10, 17, 20, 1895.

34. Ibid.; Lyman, "Trumbo and Statehood," 136–37.

35. *Cleveland Plain Dealer*, June 16, 1895; *Cincinnati Enquirer*, June 21, 1895; *Cleveland Leader*, June 19, 1895; *Boston Herald*, June 28, 1895; *Buffalo Evening News*, June 19, 1895, and many other clippings, Isaac Trumbo Scrapbook, film copy, Utah Historical Society, Salt Lake City; *Salt Lake Herald*, June 29, 1895; *Salt Lake Tribune*, July 21, 1895.

36. *Nephi* [formerly *Deseret, Millard County] Blade*, July 13, Aug. 3, 1895; *Provo Enquirer*, Aug. 21, 1895; *Springville Independent*, June 21, 1895. See also Lyman, "Trumbo and Statehood," 138 n. 35 on Gibbs.

37. *Nephi Blade*, July 27, 1895; *Salt Lake Herald*, June 14, July 2, Aug. 13, 16, 1895.

38. *Salt Lake Tribune*, June 14, 1895; *Salt Lake Herald*, July 6, 1895; *San Francisco Call*, Aug. 25, 26, Sept. 1, 12, 1895.

39. *Salt Lake Tribune*, July 21, Aug. 3, 10, 1895; *Salt Lake Herald*, July 22, 1895.

40. *Salt Lake Tribune*, June 30, July 1, 21, 25, 30, 1895.

41. *Nephi Blade*, Aug. 10, 24, 1895; *Provo Enquirer*, Aug. 21, 1895.

42. *Provo Enquirer*, Aug. 22, 1895; A. H. Cannon Journal, July 25, 1895, recounted an interview with Charles Crane, who expressed hope that Apostle Cannon had not been referring to Trumbo in recent Sunday remarks at Provo. Cannon replied, "If Trumbo was guilty of bribery, they did apply to him."

43. *Salt Lake Herald*, July 29, Aug. 25, 26, 27, 1895.

44. Ibid., Aug. 29, 30, 1895; *Salt Lake Tribune*, Aug. 29, 30, 1895.

45. *Salt Lake Tribune*, Aug. 29, 30, 1895.

46. *Ogden Standard*, Nov. 14, 1895.

47. Charles Crane, "To the Members of the Utah Legislature and the General Public" (publication information not given), copy, Utah Historical Society, Salt Lake City.

48. Ibid.

49. *Salt Lake Herald*, Sept. 1–7, 1895.

50. *Salt Lake Tribune*, Sept. 7, 1895; Grant Journal, Sept. 26, 1895.

51. Grant Journal, Sept. 5, 1895. Besides, Grant's plural wife, Emily Wells, would not have been happy to have her husband running for office against her brother. Heber M. Wells and Heber J. Grant had also been lifelong friends.

52. Brigham Young, Jr., Journal, Oct. 1, 2, 1895, H.D.C.; A. H. Cannon Journal, Oct. 3, 1895; Grant Journal, Oct. 7, 1895.

53. Grant Journal, Oct. 7, 1895; A. H. Cannon Journal, Oct. 7, 1895.

54. Grant Journal, Oct. 10, 1895; *Salt Lake Tribune*, Oct. 14, 1895; *Deseret Evening News*, Oct. 14, 1895; A. H. Cannon Journal, Oct. 14, 21, 1895.

55. *Salt Lake Herald*, Oct. 11, 12, 1895; *Salt Lake [Weekly] Argus*, Oct. 12, 1895.

56. *Salt Lake [Weekly] Argus*, Oct. 12, 1895.

57. *Salt Lake Herald*, Oct. 13, 14, 1895.

58. *Salt Lake Tribune*, Oct. 13, 14, 18, 1895. On Oct. 18 Goodwin editorialized that the Democrats had little business crying church interference since they had nominated Roberts and Thatcher to capitalize on their ecclesiastical positions. *New York Times*, Nov. 3, 1895.

59. *Salt Lake Herald*, Oct. 23, 24, 1895.

60. *Salt Lake Tribune*, Oct. 24, 1895; Lyman Journal, Oct. 14, 23, 24, 25, Nov. 6, 1895, termed the proceedings "Powers' ghost-dance." Lyman was personally "roasted" by the Democratic convention for his alleged partisanship. He was generally successful in refuting specific charges. Young Jr. Journal, Nov. 14, 1895; A. H. Cannon Journal, Oct. 21, 1895.

61. *Salt Lake Herald*, Sept. 7, 1895; *Salt Lake Tribune*, Nov. 5, 1895.

62. Candidate Wells said, "Democrats will bring you a watch, but Republicans will bring you a watchmaker." The *Herald* retorted, "Does the watchmaker find it profitable to make his own shoes? . . . Does the Woods Cross fruit raiser waste his time in a futile effort to grow oranges? No. Why? It won't pay. . . . It don't pay to make things when you can buy them cheaper." See *Salt Lake Tribune*, Sept. 3, 1895; *Salt Lake Herald*, Aug. 24, 1895. The Democrats may have had the superior logic, but the Republicans had a long-standing Mormon tradition for home industry, which Brigham Young had fervently stressed. See note 65 below.

63. *Salt Lake Tribune*, Sept. 16, 1895; *Salt Lake Herald*, Sept. 4, Oct. 29, 1895.

64. Richard D. Poll, "Political Reconstruction of Utah Territory," *Pacific Historical Review* 27 (May, 1958), 125–26.

65. *New York Times*, Nov. 9, 25, 27, 1895. John Codman, *The Mormon Country: A Summer with the "Latter-day Saints"* (New York, 1874), 7–8, noted that "Brigham [Young] is an ultra-protectionist, and, as a worldly idol, would be worshipped in Pennsylvania. His great idea, before the advent of railroads, was to make Utah entirely independent of the outer world. He was on the high road to success. . . . Utah can, if need be, provide every article of food and clothing that its people require, and in addition to these almost every luxury."

66. *Salt Lake Herald*, Nov. 8, 18, 19, 1895.

67. *Deseret Evening News*, Nov. 6, 1895.

68. *Salt Lake Herald*, Dec. 5, 1895, contains a copy of the official election canvass figures.

69. There had long been an understanding that the Mormons would occupy

one Senate seat and the Gentiles the other. There was no other serious Mormon aspirant for the Senate except George Q. Cannon, whose recent political efforts were not nearly as well known as were his son's.

70. A. H. Cannon Journal, Aug. 6, 1895; *Salt Lake Herald*, Nov. 8, 10, 11, 1895.

71. Fred T. Dubois to A. H. Cannon, Dec. 6, 1895, Dubois to P. H. Lannan, Dec. 31, 1895, A. H. Cannon to Dubois (copy, undated, received Dec. 11, 1895), Fred T. Dubois Papers [Letterbooks], Idaho State University Library, Pocatello; A. H. Cannon Journal, Dec. 10, 1895.

72. F. D. Richards Journal, Nov. 21, 1895; A. H. Cannon Journal, Nov. 21, 27, 1895.

73. G. Q. Cannon Journal, Feb. 1, 1898, excerpts in Roberts Papers.

74. James S. Clarkson to Woodruff, Dec. 14, 1895, Cannon Papers.

75. Ibid.

76. Ibid.

77. Ibid.

78. A. H. Cannon Journal, Dec. 26, 1895; Jean Bickmore White, "Utah State Elections: 1895–1899" (Ph.D. diss., University of Utah, 1968), 95–109.

79. Woodruff to Clarkson, Dec. 30, 1895, Woodruff Papers [Letterbooks].

80. *Salt Lake Tribune*, Dec. 6, 1895.

81. Ibid., Dec. 17, 22, 1895; *Salt Lake Herald*, Dec. 14, 16, 17, 18, 22, 24, 1895.

82. *Salt Lake Tribune*, Jan. 5, 6, 1896.

83. *Deseret Evening News*, Jan. 6, 1896.

84. Edward Leo Lyman, "Heber M. Wells and the Beginnings of Utah's Statehood" (M.S. thesis, University of Utah, 1967), 30–90.

85. *Salt Lake Herald*, Jan. 6, 1896. The hostility among the leading Salt Lake dailies toward Trumbo had continued to build. When the *Washington Post* mentioned that the colonel was a possible selection as the Gentile senator, both the *Herald* and the *Tribune* strongly denounced the proposition the next day. *Washington Post*, Dec. 11, 1895; *Salt Lake Herald*, Dec. 12, 1895; *Salt Lake Tribune*, Dec. 12, 1895.

86. *Salt Lake Herald*, Jan. 9, 12, 13, 1896; *Salt Lake Tribune*, Jan. 10, 11, 1896; *Salt Lake [Weekly] Argus*, Jan. 11, 1896.

87. Cannon and O'Higgins, *Under the Prophet in Utah*, 165–67; *Deseret Evening News*, Jan. 14, 1896.

88. Several leading Republicans would continue to seek the leader George Q. Cannon's candidacy for some time to come. He would be something of an aspirant for the Senate at least three other times prior to his death.

89. *Salt Lake Herald*, Jan. 16, 1896.

90. *Ogden Standard*, Jan. 16, 1896.

91. Ibid., Jan. 18, 1896.

92. Letter copied in *Journal History of the Church of Jesus Christ of Latter-day Saints*, Jan. 6, 1896, H.D.C.

93. Ibid., Jan. 14, 1896.

94. *Salt Lake Herald*, Jan. 16, 1896.

95. Lyman, "Trumbo and Statehood," 146–49.

96. Frank J. Cannon left the Republican party within a year and soon severed his ties with the L.D.S. church. As a bitter apostate journalist, he sought to discredit the church leaders (after his father's death) through lectures and by co-authoring several series of muckraker-type exposé magazine articles. Arthur Brown served out the short term as U.S. senator and was not returned. He stayed in the East and some years later was shot to death in a Washington, D.C., hotel by a discarded mistress.

Conclusion

Utah's quest for statehood was accomplished after almost a half century of rather constant struggle. The Latter-day Saints had never been successful in living harmoniously among nonbelieving neighbors, particularly when, as was often the case, the reins of government were out of their hands. It was primarily for reasons of political autonomy and self-government that the Saints, guided by their ecclesiastical leaders, were so constantly in earnest to achieve statehood.

Although varying degrees of pressure were applied by a wide array of federal government officials at the nation's capital and within the territory, their various measures often served more to bolster resistance and unity among the Mormons rather than bring them to submission. If anything succeeded in stimulating a semblance of concession from the church hierarchy, it was the negotiations and high-level agreements finally made by general church authorities with similarly highly placed political party and government officials. But even then, much of what appeared outwardly to be substantive alterations of behavior regarding plural marriage and direct political involvement by the church hierarchy were intended to be but a temporary stance until after statehood was accomplished.

Much of the work of bringing about the accommodation between the highest church leaders and proper government authorities was carried out by lobbyists. First with the Democrats in the late 1880s, then with the Republicans in the early 1890s, cordial relations were established that did much to promote the understandings that resulted in the admission of Utah as a state.

An important adjunct to this work was altering public opinion toward the Mormons. At least a portion of this antipathy had been artificially aroused by individuals associated with Utah territorial officials and the *Salt Lake Tribune*, parties that had much to lose should Utah be admitted to statehood. But the extensive work of church agents with a large segment of the nation's press rather effectively diffused the emotional issue of Mormonism.

There may have been some alienation of high-ranking national Republicans from the Utah Mormons over the failure to select the "proper" U.S. senators. And undoubtedly some of the unredeemed obligations incurred in behalf of statehood by James S. Clarkson and Isaac Trumbo diminished the trust of others in the Saints' cause. But other events were probably more decisive in determining future developments. Control of the Republican party was passing to William McKinley and Mark Hanna, a move that largely removed Clarkson from the inner circle of party influence. Hanna would seek to establish a base of power in Utah during 1896, but the position his party was assuming on the silver issue did much to thwart such efforts.[1]

The actions of a number of western senators, including Frank J. Cannon, in walking out of the 1896 Republican National Convention in protest against the party's abandonment of silverite proposals completely disrupted the Utah Republican party, which had gained impressive preponderance during the preceding three years. The Republican factionalism over the silver controversy continued throughout the new state's first presidential election campaign and assured the Democrats a large majority for William Jennings Bryan. Many of these voters, like Frank J. Cannon, had been full-fledged Republicans not long before.

Despite these developments, some members of the Republican national hierarchy, particularly those charged with overseeing the party fortunes in the West, considered the L.D.S. vote more stable in resisting the supposed radicalism of the rival party's campaign than were most other voters in the region. An exchange between Clarkson and Redfield Proctor after the 1896 election noted that the Mormons had held more firmly to the Republican party than had been expected and were said to be "the best hold and hope of Republicanism in several states." They understood that despite the actions of his son, George Q. Cannon was not an avid advocate of free silver, and John Henry Smith was rapidly becoming a loyal McKinley representative in the area. Certainly some party leaders were confident that they could regain the influence in Utah so impressively won through the foresight and persistence of their fellows in recent years.[2]

Besides the excellent groundwork laid by Republicans in the early 1890s and a continued preference for the Republican position on the tariff, there was another important factor in the party's staying power among the Mormons. Despite receiving the electoral support of Utah in the previous election, Democrats assumed a stance of marked coolness toward the Latter-day Saints. In the 1904 national party platform the Democrats denounced polygamy in a manner reminiscent of the Republicans of an earlier era. Bryan and his followers assumed enough of the role of the nation's moral crusaders in politics to be a classic case of what Paul Kleppner has termed a "cross of culture." In so doing they did much to assure renewed Utah election majorities for the Republicans.[3]

While some Republicans participated in the often-heated Reed Smoot hearings, which attempted to unseat the Utah senator for being an apostle in a church that still appeared to condone plural marriage, their party platform in 1904 was silent in reference to polygamy and the Mormons. This would be appreciated by the still-influential and politically aware church leaders, some of whom had helped cause the furor by condoning the resumption of plural marriage. Clarkson, who had by this time regained some party prominence within the Theodore Roosevelt administration, had sought to acquaint the president with the Mormon question from his perspective. He also probably played a role in keeping the Republican platform silent on any statement offensive to the Latter-day Saints. After the final anti-Mormon storm (of the Smoot hearings) subsided, through the efforts of Senator Smoot and his political allies, the Mormons enjoyed cordial relations within the party for most of the next three decades.[4]

In the long run, the development of close relationships with highly placed members of both national parties may well have been more important for Mormon security than was Utah statehood. Members of the Latter-day Saint hierarchy finally realized, perhaps through hindsight, that cultivating such friendships was the best insurance available against the recurrence of harsh policies emanating from either the executive or legislative branches of the federal government.

Admission of Utah as a state resulted in most of the benefits of self-government that L.D.S. leaders had long anticipated. But some would undoubtedly be disappointed that the newly elected state officers and the electorate itself asserted so much independence. This was particularly true of Governor Heber M. Wells who, though a son, brother, and brother-in-law of polygamous L.D.S. general authoities, clearly demonstrated no tolerance for the continuance or resumption of plural marriage.[5] Some of the earlier statehood plans had specifically anticipated that the anti-polygamy laws could be enforced more leniently by friendly Mormon state officers, enabling the still-sacred principle of plural marriage to be quietly but safely practiced. But with Wells's and others' assertions to the contrary, all had not worked out as hoped.

The concessions of previous years relating to polygamy had been intended mainly to pacify the public and their elected representatives. The efforts at conciliation were done without actually altering any aspect of the practice, other than perhaps making it less visible and more of an individual responsibility. But each time a statement was made, Latter-day Saints who heeded the words of their ecclesiastical superiors were encouraged in their resolves not to practice polygamy. Though men with close ties to the general authorities knew that there had been no actual changes in the church's stance on polygamy, it would have been impossible to disseminate such tacit disclaimers widely throughout the church.

Thus John A. McClernand, a veteran of the Utah Commission, was correct when he reported to Cleveland in 1887 that progress was indeed being made, however slowly, against the Saints' peculiar institution. He predicted that "the more often the Mormons commit themselves, whether regularly or irregularly, against polygamy, the more they will have increased the obstacles to a retreat from the path of reform." Indeed, a significant number, especially of the younger generation, within the church hoped for a decline of plural marriage and were anxious to see the respectability of monogamous marital relationships enhanced within the Mormon community. After statehood there was some revival of polygamist activity, but it was becoming abundantly clear that a growing number who were in good standing as Latter-day Saints no longer condoned this flagrant defiance of civil authority. This attitude was at least partially the result of the public announcements that the church leaders had made in order to gain Utah's admittance into the union.[6]

In a strikingly similar manner political independence among the Mormons also arose primarily out of the public proclamations by the general church authorities that they were abandoning their long-held claims to dictate to other church members in politics. Again, these decrees had been at least partially necessitated by the efforts to gain statehood. Here, too, the assurances of noninvolvement in politics were most readily accepted and internalized among Mormon believers who had never before valued political independence. Some may have understood the statements were for outside consumption only, but many were encouraged to develop clear-cut political preferences too deeply ingrained to be altered by subsequent advice from church leaders.

On one occasion not long after statehood was granted, George Q. Cannon lamented the situation that he had helped to create. In describing circumstances where he felt advice should come from those most in tune with divine guidance—himself and other members of the First Presidency—the reaction was too often, "I don't care how much you know, you may have all the experience in the world; but I don't want to talk to you, you are an officer in the church and I don't want any ecclesiastical interference with me." In the following generation the most careful observer of Utah politics concluded in 1940 that "the church membership has not obeyed its leaders on any important political issue or candidacy during the last ten years."[7]

These matters were undoubtedly disappointments to those who had so long dominated all aspects of life among the Latter-day Saints in Utah, but they were an essential part of the process of shedding those facets of Mormonism that had proven unassimilable into the mainstream of American life. The adjustments accomplished during the years surrounding Utah statehood, largely sponsored by the First Presidency, did much to assure the vitality of the Church of Jesus Christ of Latter-day Saints in the twentieth century.

NOTES

1. John Henry Smith to Mark Hanna, Nov. 16, 1896, Hanna to Smith, Dec. 29, 1896, J. H. Smith Papers; Hanna to Heber M. Wells, Apr. 2, 1896, Heber M. Wells Papers, Utah State Archives, Salt Lake City; Lyman, "Beginnings of Utah's Statehood," 78–89. Clarkson had been working for several years to help William B. Allison secure the presidential nomination.

2. Redfield Proctor to James S. Clarkson, Nov. 21, 1896, Clarkson Papers, Library of Congress; Proctor to Henry Payne, Nov. 20, 1896 [Letterbooks], Redfield Proctor Papers, Proctor Free Library, Proctor, Vt.

3. Kleppner, *Cross of Culture*, 316–75. Porter and Johnson, comps., *National Party Platforms*, 133.

4. Clarkson to Theodore Roosevelt, Sept. 23, 1904, Roosevelt Papers; Isaac Trumbo to Clarkson, July 18, 1904, Clarkson Papers, responded to a convention report by saying that "I can assure you the way the platform was handled in Chicago—not making any comments at the people in Utah—it was a wonderful stroke in politics." I am well aware that during the Democratic interim of President Woodrow Wilson from 1912 to 1920 Utah also swung into the Democratic column. This had a great deal to do with the issue of prohibition, which had divided the Republicans; the Democrats' choice, Simon Bamberger, had a strong appeal on the subject.

5. The clearest instance of this was Wells's vocal opposition to polygamist B. H. Roberts's candidacy for Congress on the grounds of his marital relations. See also Lyman, "Beginnings of Utah's Statehood," 69–77.

6. For further McClernand comments, see p. 66n31 herein.

7. White, "Utah State Elections," 241. Frank Herman Jonas, "Utah: Sagebrush Democracy," in *Rocky Mountain Politics*, ed. Thomas C. Donnelly (Albuquerque, 1940), 34.

Appendix 1

Wilford Woodruff
Manifesto

OFFICIAL DECLARATION—1

To Whom It May Concern:

Press dispatches have been sent for political purposes, from Salt Lake City, which have been widely published, to the effect that the Utah Commission, in their recent report to the Secretary of the Interior, allege that plural marriages are still being solemnized and that forty or more such marriages have been contracted in Utah since last June or during the past year, also that in public discourses the leaders of the Church have taught, encouraged and urged the continuance of the practice of polygamy—

I, therefore, as President of the Church of Jesus Christ of Latter-day Saints, do hereby, in the most solemn manner, declare that these charges are false. We are not teaching polygamy or plural marriage, nor permitting any person to enter into its practice, and I deny that either forty or any other number of plural marriages have during that period been solemnized in our Temples or in any other place in the Territory.

One case has been reported, in which the parties allege that the marriage was performed in the Endowment House, in Salt Lake City, in the Spring of 1889, but I have not been able to learn who performed the ceremony; whatever was done in this matter was without my knowledge. In consequence of this alleged occurrence the Endowment House was, by my instructions, taken down without delay.

Inasmuch as laws have been enacted by Congress forbidding plural marriages, which laws have been pronounced constitutional by the court of last resort, I hereby declare my intention to submit to those laws, and to use my influence with the members of the Church over which I preside to have them do likewise.

There is nothing in my teachings to the Church or in those of my associates, during the time specified, which can be reasonably construed to inculcate or encourage polygamy; and when any Elder of the Church has used language which appeared to convey any such teaching, he has been promptly reproved. And I now publicly declare that my advice to the Latter-day Saints is to refrain from contracting any marriage forbidden by the law of the land.

WILFORD WOODRUFF
PRESIDENT OF THE CHURCH OF JESUS CHRIST
OF LATTER-DAY SAINTS.

President Lorenzo Snow offered the following:

"I move that, recognizing Wilford Woodruff as the President of the Church of Jesus Christ of Latter-day Saints, and the only man on the earth at the present time who holds the keys of the sealing ordinances, we consider him fully authorized by virtue of his position to issue the Manifesto which has been read in our hearing, and which is dated September 24th, 1890, and that as a Church in General Conference assembled, we accept his declaration concerning plural marriages as authoritative and binding."

The vote to sustain the foregoing motion was unanimous.

Salt Lake City, Utah, October 6, 1890.

From The Doctrine and Covenants of the Church of Jesus Christ of Latter-day Saints (Salt Lake City, 1981), 291–92.

Appendix 2

Excerpts from Three Addresses by President Wilford Woodruff Regarding the Manifesto

"The Lord will never permit me or any other man who stands as President of this Church to lead you astray. It is not in the programme. It is not in the mind of God. If I were to attempt that, the Lord would remove me out of my place, and so He will any other man who attempts to lead the children of men astray from the oracles of God and from their duty." (Sixty-first Semiannual General Conference of the Church, Monday, October 6, 1890, Salt Lake City, Utah. Reported in *Deseret Evening News*, Oct. 11, 1890.)

"It matters not who lives or who dies, or who is called to lead this Church, they have got to lead it by the inspiration of Almighty God. If they do not do it that way, they cannot do it at all. . . .

"I have had some revelations of late, and very important ones to me, and I will tell you what the Lord has said to me. Let me bring your minds to what is termed the manifesto. . . .

"The Lord has told me to ask the Latter-day Saints a question, and He also told me that if they would listen to what I said to them and answer the question put to them, by the Spirit and power of God, they would all answer alike, and they would all believe alike with regard to this matter.

"The question is this: Which is the wisest course for the Latter-day Saints to pursue—to continue to attempt to practice plural marriage, with the laws of the nation against it and the opposition of sixty millions of people, and at the cost of the confiscation and loss of all the Temples, and the stopping of all the ordinances therein, both for the living and the dead, and the imprisonment of the First Presidency and Twelve and the heads of families in the Church, and the confiscation of personal property of the people (all of which of themselves would stop the practice); or, after doing and suffering what we have through our adherence to this principle to cease the practice and submit to the law, and through doing so leave the Prophets, Apostles and fathers at home, so that they can instruct the people and attend to the duties of the Church, and also leave the Temples in the hands of the Saints, so that they can attend to the ordinances of the Gospel, both for the living and the dead?

"The Lord showed me by vision and revelation exactly what would take place if we did not stop this practice. If we had not stopped it, you would have had no use for . . . any of the men in this temple at Logan; for all ordinances would be stopped throughout the land of Zion. Confusion would reign throughout Israel, and many men would be made prisoners. This trouble would have come upon the whole Church, and we should have been compelled to stop the practice. Now, the question is, whether it should be stopped in this manner, or in the way the Lord has manifested to us, and leave our Prophets and Apostles and fathers free men, and the temples in the hands of the people, so that the dead may be redeemed. A large number has already been delivered from the prison house in the spirit world by this people, and shall the work go on or stop? This is the question I lay before the Latter-day Saints. You have to judge for yourselves. I want you to answer it for yourselves. I shall not answer it; but I say to you that that is exactly the condition we as a people would have been in had we not taken the course we have.

". . . I saw exactly what would come to pass if there was not something done. I have had this spirit upon me for a long time. But I want to say this: I should have let all the temples go out of our hands; I should have gone to prison myself, and let every other man go there, had not the God of heaven commanded me to do what I did do; and when the hour came that I was commanded to do that, it was all clear to me. I went before the Lord and wrote what the Lord told me to write. . . .

"I leave this with you, for you to contemplate and consider. The Lord is at work with us." (Cache Stake Conference, Logan, Utah, Sunday, November 1, 1891. Reported in *Deseret Weekly*, Nov. 14, 1891.)

"Now I will tell you what was manifested to me and what the Son of God performed in this thing. . . . All these things would have come to pass, as God Almighty lives, had not that Manifesto been given. Therefore, the Son of God felt disposed to have that thing presented to the Church and to the world for purposes in his own mind. The Lord had decreed the establishment of Zion. He had decreed the finishing of this temple. He had decreed that the salvation of the living and the dead should be given in those valleys of the mountains. And Almighty God decreed that the Devil should not thwart it. If you can understand that, that is a key to it." (From a discourse at the sixth session of the dedication of the Salt Lake Temple, April, 1893. Typescript of Dedicatory Services, Archives, Church Historical Department, Salt Lake City, Utah.)

Bibliographical Essay

My interest in the subject of Mormon politics began with the question of why the Latter-day Saints, who had been allied with the Democrats for over forty years, so abruptly became associated with their former enemies, the Republican party, in the 1890s and have retained that relationship to the present time. After completing a master's thesis in 1967 on Utah political history during the era—without locating much significant documentation on the subject—I consciously deferred further pursuit of his study until more of the source material, assumed to be held in the L.D.S. church historian's office, became available.

Even in the early stage of research I was struck by the wide array of excellent scholarly treatment of the earlier period of Utah Mormon history. Impressive contributions were made by Hubert H. Bancroft, Orson F. Whitney, Andrew L. Neff, Leland H. Creer, Dale L. Morgan, Nels Anderson, Juanita Brooks, Norman F. Furniss, Gustive O. Larson, Leonard J. Arrington, Robert J. Dwyer, Richard D. Poll, and Mark Cannon, among others. On the other hand, it was even more striking how little had been written on the years immediately after 1890. The last volume of Brigham H. Roberts's *Comprehensive History of the Church of Jesus Christ of Latter-day Saints* stood alone in providing significant detail on the period after Wilford Woodruff's Manifesto of 1890. Although several of the other authors listed above offered a few pages of treatment of the last decade of the nineteenth century, they mainly followed a course not unlike that set by Whitney, who merely listed the subjects that some future historian would have the opportunity to elaborate on.

Roberts, who like Whitney was sufficiently close to the Mormon hierarchy to have access to whatever church source material existed, began to write shortly after the turn of the century. A draft of his work appeared in serialized form in *Americana,* the bimonthly journal published by the American Historical Society, between June, 1909 and July, 1915. The author, who was often a participant in the political events of the 1890s, presented his material in a nonpartisan manner, although certainly from a pro-church viewpoint. While Roberts conceded some political involvement on the part of the highest church leaders, this crucial aspect of the era was far too carefully minimized in his work. And although the author, himself a polygamist, undoubtedly knew of the related background developments, he treated the Woodruff Manifesto as an abrupt announcement. He tied the declaration somewhat to the threat of the Cullom-Struble bill, but failed to discuss any of the preceding concessions or restrictions, something that cannot now be done as well by scholars attempting to reconstruct such developments from presently available source material. Admittedly Roberts was constrained by the breadth of his scope in the *Comprehensive History* to eliminate some important material from his treatment of the 1890s (for the sake of uniformity, several hundred pages of additional material had to be deleted from vol. 6 but exist in the original galley proofs in his papers at the church archives). But for whatever reasons, his coverage of the decade was tantalizingly brief. Thereafter, the church sources to which he had rather free access became far more restricted. Thus modern scholars had to draw rather exclusively from Roberts's *Comprehensive History of the Church* for internal insights on the Manifesto, political divisions, and the last statehood attempts.

The public documents necessary to study the government approaches to the Mormon question were certainly accessible, and Richard D. Poll and others had carefully analyzed and synthesized such material by the mid-1950s. In 1958 Leonard J. Arrington's *Great Basin Kingdom* appeared and, while tracing the economic development of nineteenth-century Mormondom, offered additional insights into the legislative and judicial treatment by the federal government. But even these excellent works remained relatively thin on behind-the-scene details of Utah history in the last decade of the century, since the source material necessary for greater depth remained unavailable.

Perhaps the treatment of the half-century Utah territorial period that is best known to the scholarly world is that portion of Howard R. Lamar's *The Far Southwest: 1846–1912, A Territorial History* dealing with the subject. His discussion of the years up to the Manifesto persuasively demonstrates that the existence of Mormon institutions and practices besides polygamy and political domination, such as land policies, educational practices, and civil court jurisdiction, were virtually certain to antagonize the non-Mormon officials who observed them firsthand. Lamar clearly demonstrated the need for additional federal intervention in Utah and showed that many who became involved in this effort acted with sincerity and commitment in attempting to bring the Mormons into the mainstream of American life. Lamar, who published the book in 1966, utilized an impressive variety of sources, but his admitted lack of access to church documents related to the latter portion of the territorial era certainly limited the work. Unable to penetrate into the private deliberations among the church hierarchy, he portrayed Delegate John T. Caine as a prime mover in the statehood attempts, instead of seeing his actual role as the loyal instrument of the First Presidency's will in such efforts. Lamar also followed the standard account of the Manifesto being suddenly announced, with no preliminaries other than extensive federal legislation and prosecution. However, this work was among the first to draw from the reminiscences of Frank J. Cannon and Robert N. Baskin to mention the presence of church lobbyists on the scene at the time that the Cullom-Struble bill was defeated and thereby implies their relationship to its suppression.

Certainly the most widely known study of Mormon politics is Klaus Hansen's *Quest for Empire*, first published in 1967. The book developed the thesis that "the idea of a political kingdom of God, promulgated by a secret 'Council of Fifty,' is by far the most important key to an understanding of the Mormon past." To Hansen, this was of vastly greater importance than the polygamy issue. The author was a leading proponent of the idea best expressed in the reminiscences of a longtime Mormon adversary, Fred T. Dubois, that polygamy was simply a convenient means of arousing public indignation in opposition to the Mormons, while the real source of contention to those who were most knowledgeable was the political domination that church leaders continued to exercise over their people. *Quest for Empire* contributed significantly to understanding the place of Mormonism in American political and cultural history in the years near the mid-point of the nineteenth century. The documentary evidence was sketchy, but adequate on this period. But when Hansen attempted to argue that the Council of Fifty continued dominant after the 1860s, he was basing his case on little more than extrapolation from the earlier evidence. Carrying this to the extreme, the author suggests that the Council of Fifty probably directed the defenses of the kingdom during the anti-Mormon onslaught of the 1880s, also assuming that Woodruff's Manifesto was motivated at least in part to preserve the political kingdom of God.

In the extensive research for this work, I have had the opportunity to examine papers or diaries of at least a dozen men whom Hansen lists as members of the Council of Fifty in 1880, along with similar confidential writings of more than a dozen Mormon general authorities closely associated with those on the membership lists. In all of these, there was but one reference to the Council of Fifty from 1886 to 1896. Just after the 1887 constitution was ratified by Mormon voters in Utah, at the October quarterly meetings of the church hierarchy, Apostle John W. Taylor "expressed it as his opinion that it would be much better if all of [their] business in relation to [admission as] a state was transacted through the Council of Fifty." President Woodruff responded, according to Apostle Heber J. Grant, that "it would be all right for the Council of Fifty to meet and attend to this matter, but under existing circumstances [the raid] it would not be safe to have them do so." The First Presidency had recently received the apostles' approval to act as a "confidential committee of three on statehood," and these men would continue to direct such affairs, with no further reference to the Council of Fifty, well beyond Utah's admission into the Union.

The appearance in 1967 of the personal journals of Abraham H. Cannon at Brigham Young University Library was a significant breakthrough for access to more detailed information into the workings of the church hierarchy during the era of the Manifesto, new political alignments, and the quest for Utah statehood. This young Mormon general authority, impressively candid and thorough in his daily journal entries, offered initial research leads to many developments occurring in this crucial period. In a real sense Cannon first suggested the course for further investigation of many of the subjects treated in the present work. Certainly the Cannon journal has been the most valuable single source utilized in this study.

In 1970 Gustive O. Larson's *The "Americanization" of Utah for Statehood* was published. In what was the most extensive treatment yet of the Mormon struggle for statehood, the author relied heavily on the A. H. Cannon journal. He also drew from other previously unused contemporary Mormon diaries and papers (mostly of non-general authorities) to present an impressive human interest story of the Mormon-Gentile conflict, with detailed treatment of the so-called raid, the pursuers and the persued, church leadership from hiding "on the underground," and life in the penitentiary for those who were apprehended. Larson argued that the conflict between the church and the government could have been avoided had the government been willing to allow "the corrective force of advancing civilization" to do its work as isolation in Utah continued to break down. He suggested that the monogamist element among the Utah Mormons would have acted to help bring the region into conformity with national standards by outlawing the practice of polygamy on their own. Larson was also a proponent of the viewpoint that polygamy was simply an emotion-laden tool used to help eradicate the more serious offense of political power and its use among the Mormon hierarchy.

In his study Larson utilized some of James S. Clarkson's papers to begin to document the mediation of nationally prominent Republicans in behalf of the Mormons, partially for the benefit of the party. He treated the Manifesto and the achievement of statehood in some detail, relying heavily on Frank J. Cannon's *Under the Prophet in Utah*. This source was previously considered suspect as an overly sensationalist exposé from the muckraker era. But now that many details can be corroborated by the more scrupulously honest personal journal of his half-brother, Abraham, the Frank Cannon book is considered, at least by many, to be more acceptable. Certainly Larson too readily accepted Frank Cannon's overlaudatory account of his own personal role in the coming of the Manifesto and preliminary negotiations regarding statehood, but more illuminating sources of such information were still unavailable.

This would finally change less than two years later, when former church historian Joseph Fielding Smith became president of the Church and in a far-reaching reorganization movement Leonard J. Arrington was appointed as church historian. With the accumulation of a much larger staff of trained professional historians came a far greater access to the vast store of documents long unavailable for research. Doing research at the church archives can be truly a dream for a historian because of the quantity of letters and diaries that have been preserved by a people who made a fetish of such preservation and journal writing. On occasion correspondence could be examined in the papers of both the writer (through letterpress copybooks) and the recipient, as well as comments in the diaries of one or both on the subject. Similarly, the Utah newspapers offered sufficient diversity of viewpoints that the stance on issues by each major political faction can be reconstructed.

Among the first to gain access to the materials relevant to the last portion of the nineteenth century was Henry J. Wolfinger, who soon demonstrated that the Woodruff Manifesto was preceded by earlier negotiations with federal governmental officials and by some partial concessions by church leaders. The hierarchy at least agreed to condone certain legislation that might be interpreted as allowing non-polygamist church members to accept legal restrictions against the practice. This has been regarded by some historians as the beginning of a revisionist trend in treatment of the Manifesto and related subjects.

This work has added to the background events leading to the Manifesto and presented suggestions as to its motivation. It thus has been regarded by R. Hal Williams and others as within the revisionist framework. Similarly, the primacy of the polygamy issue over political involvement, with the latter shown to be inoffensive to many nationally prominent party leaders, clearly challenges the previous treatments of the subject. This is also true of emphasis in *Political Deliverance* on the role of the First Presidency in directing the complex statehood efforts. In a broader sense, this work is revisionist in offering a depth and breadth of detail, garnered from the but recently accessible sources, which allow a clearer view of the entire Mormon struggle for statehood than was previously possible. Each chapter discusses developments never before recounted, and thus the book makes a significant contribution to the history of Utah and its entrance into the mainstream of American affairs.

Bibliography

MANUSCRIPTS: DIARIES, JOURNALS, LETTERS, AND PAPERS

Allison, William B. Papers. Iowa State Library. Des Moines, Iowa.
Budge, William. Papers. Historical Department Church of Jesus Christ of Latter-day Saints. Salt Lake City, Utah.
Caine, John T. Papers. H. D. C. Salt Lake City, Utah.
Caine, John T. Papers. Utah State Historical Society. Salt Lake City, Utah.
Cannon, Abraham H. Cannon. Journal. Lee Library. Brigham Young University. Provo, Utah.
Cannon, George Q. Papers. H. D. C. Salt Lake City, Utah.
Clarkson, James S. Papers. Library of Congress. Washington, D.C.
Clarkson, James S. Papers. Iowa State Library. Des Moines, Iowa.
Clawson, Hiram B. Papers. H. D. C. Salt Lake City, Utah.
Cleveland, Grover. Papers. Library of Congress. Washington, D.C.
Crane, Charles. Scrapbook, Lee Library. Brigham Young University. Provo, Utah.
Curtis, George T. Papers. H. D. C. Salt Lake City, Utah.
Dickinson, Don. Papers. Library of Congress. Washington, D.C.
Dubois, Fred T. Papers. Idaho State University Library. Pocatello, Idaho.
Eldredge, Alma. Diaries. H. D. C. Salt Lake City, Utah.
First Presidency. Miscellaneous Papers. H. D. C. Salt Lake City, Utah.
First Presidency. Papers. H. D. C. Salt Lake City, Utah.
Grant, Heber J. Journal. H. D. C. Salt Lake City, Utah.
Hammond, Francis A. Journal. H. D. C. Salt Lake City, Utah.
Harrison, Benjamin. Papers. Library of Congress. Washington, D.C.
Hill, David B. New York State Library. Albany, New York.
Jack, James. Papers. H. D. C. Salt Lake City, Utah.
Lund, Anton H. Diary. H. D. C. Salt Lake City, Utah.
Lyman, Francis M. Journal. H. D. C. Salt Lake City, Utah.

Lyman, Francis M. Papers. H. D. C. Salt Lake City, Utah.
McClernand, John A. Papers. Illinois Historical Society. Springfield, Illinois.
Merrill, Marriner W. Diary. H. D. C. Salt Lake City, Utah.
Miller, W. H. H. Papers. Indiana State Library. Indianapolis, Indiana.
Morgan, John. Journal. H. D. C. Salt Lake City, Utah.
Nevins, Allan. Papers. Butler Library. Columbia University. New York City, New York.
Nuttall, L. John. Journal. Lee Library. Brigham Young University. Provo, Utah.
Nuttall, L. John. Papers. Lee Library. Brigham Young University. Provo, Utah.
Penrose, Charles W. Papers. H. D. C. Salt Lake City, Utah.
Proctor, Redfield. Papers. Proctor Free Library. Proctor, Vermont.
Quigg, Lemuel E. Papers. New York Public Library. New York City, New York.
Rawlins, Joseph L. "Autobiography." ms. Marriott Library. University of Utah. Salt Lake City, Utah.
Richards, Franklin D. Journal. H. D. C. Salt Lake City, Utah.
Richards, Franklin D. Richards Family Papers. H. D. C. Salt Lake City, Utah.
Richards, Franklin S. Papers. H. D. C. Salt Lake City, Utah.
Richards, Franklin S. Papers. Utah State Historical Society. Salt Lake City, Utah.
Richards, Franklin S. "Reminiscences, 1887–1901." ms. Bancroft Library. University of California. Berkeley, California.
Roberts, Brigham H. Papers. H. D. C. Salt Lake City, Utah.
Roberts, Brigham H. "The Life Story of B. H. Roberts." ms. Marriott Library. University of Utah. Salt Lake City, Utah.
Rosborough, Joseph B. "Biographical Sketch." ms. Bancroft Library. University of California. Berkeley, California.
Roosevelt, Theodore. Papers. Library of Congress. Washington, D.C.
Smith, John Henry. Journal. Marriott Library. University of Utah. Salt Lake City, Utah.
Smith, John Henry. Papers. Marriott Library. University of Utah. Salt Lake City, Utah.
Smith, Joseph F. Papers. H. D. C. Salt Lake City, Utah.
Snow, Lorenzo. Papers. H. D. C. Salt Lake City, Utah.
Stewart, William M. Papers. Nevada Historical Society. Reno, Nevada.
Taylor, John. Papers. H. D. C. Salt Lake City, Utah.
Tolton, John F. "Memories of the Life of John Franklin Tolton." ms. H. D. C. Salt Lake City, Utah.
Trumbo, Isaac. Scrapbook. Utah State Historical Society. Salt Lake City, Utah.
Volwiler, A. T. Papers. Lilly Library. Indiana University. Bloomington, Indiana.
Warren, Francis E. Papers. University of Wyoming Library. Laramie, Wyoming.
Wells, Heber M. Papers. Utah State Archives. Salt Lake City, Utah.
Whitaker, John M. Journal. Marriott Library. University of Utah. Salt Lake City, Utah.
Willey, Norman B. Papers. Idaho State Library. Boise, Idaho.
Woodruff, Wilford. Journal. H. D. C. Salt Lake City, Utah.
Woodruff, Wilford. Papers. H. D. C. Salt Lake City, Utah.
Woodruff, Wilford. Political Letterbooks. H. D. C. Salt Lake City, Utah.

Young, Brigham Jr. Journal. H. D. C. Salt Lake City, Utah.
Young, John W. Papers. Beineke Library. Yale University. New Haven, Connecticut.
Young, John W. Papers. H. D. C. Salt Lake City, Utah.
Zane, Charles S. Journal. Illinois Historical Society. Springfield, Illinois.

NEWSPAPERS

Boston Herald. 1895.
Buffalo Evening News. 1895.
Chicago Times. 1887–89.
Chicago Tribune. 1895.
Cincinnati Enquirer. 1895.
Cleveland Plain Dealer. 1895.
Deseret Evening News. 1856–99.
Deseret Weekly News. 1886–96.
Journal History of the Church of Jesus Christ of Latter-day Saints. 1850–1900.
Louisville Courier-Journal. 1887–89.
Nephi Blade. 1895–6.
New York Evening Post. 1887–89.
New York Herald. 1887–89.
New York Star. 1887.
New York Sun. 1887–89.
New York Times. 1882–98.
New York Tribune. 1887–96.
New York World. 1887–89.
Ogden Daily Commercial. 1891–92.
Ogden Standard. 1887–96.
Provo Enquirer. 1891–92.
Salt Lake Argus. 1895–96.
Salt Lake Herald. 1886–98.
Salt Lake Times. 1891.
Salt Lake Tribune. 1880–1900.
San Francisco Alta California. 1887–89.
San Francisco Call. 1886–96.
San Francisco Chronicle. 1887–89.
San Francisco Examiner. 1887–89.
Springville Independent. 1891–95.
St. Louis Globe-Democrat. 1887–89.
Washington, D. C., National Republican. 1887–88.
Washington, D. C., Evening Star. 1890.
Washington, D. C., Post. 1886–96.

PUBLIC DOCUMENTS

U.S. *Congressional Globe.* [Thirty-forth through Forty-second Congress].

U.S. *Congressional Record.* [Forty-seventh through Fifty-third Congress].

U.S. House. *Executive Documents.* [Forty-ninth through Fifty-second Congress].

U.S. House. *Miscellaneous Documents.* [Forty-second and Fiftieth Congress].

U.S. House. *Reports.* [Fiftieth through Fifty-third Congress].

U.S. Senate. *Miscellaneous Documents.* [Fifty-first Congress].

U.S. Senate. *Reports.* [Fifty-third Congress].

U.S. Senate. *Hearings before the Committee on Territories in Relation to the Exercise of the Elective Franchise in the Territory of Utah.* [Fifty-first Congress]. (privately printed?)

U.S. Senate. *Proceedings before the Committee on Privileges and Elections of the United States Senate in the Matter of the Protests against the Right of Hon. Reed Smoot, A Senator from the State of Utah, to Hold His Seat.*

U.S. Utah Commission. *Minutebooks.* Utah State Archives. Salt Lake City.

Utah (Territory). Legislative Assembly of the Territory of Utah. *House Journals* [Twenty-eighth and twenty-ninth sessions].

Utah (Territory). *Governor's Message and Accompanying Documents.* 1888.

Utah (Territory). *Official Report of the Convention Assembled at Salt Lake City, Utah, March 4, 1895 to Adopt a Constitution for the State of Utah.* 1898.

Utah (State). Legislature of the State of Utah. *House Journal.* 1896.

MAGAZINES, JOURNAL ARTICLES, AND ESSAYS

Albright, Robert E. "Politics and Public Opinion in the Western Statehood Movement of the 1880's." *Pacific Historical Review* 3 (1934).

Alexander, Thomas G. "Charles S. Zane, Apostle of the New Era." *Utah Historical Quarterly* 34 (Fall, 1966).

Allen, James B. "'Good Guys' vs. 'Good Guys': Rudger Clawson, John Sharp and Civil Disobedience in Nineteenth-century Utah." *Utah Historical Quarterly* 48 (Spring, 1980).

Arrington, Leonard J. "Utah and the Depression of the 1890's." *Utah Historical Quarterly* 29 (Jan., 1961).

Campbell, Eugene. "Governmental Beginnings," in *Utah's History*, ed. Richard D. Poll (Provo, 1978).

Christensen, Joseph. "Life and Ancestry of Joseph Christensen." *The Utah Genealogical and Historical Magazine* 28 (Oct., 1937).

Cockerill, John A. "Brigham Young and Modern Utah." *Cosmopolitan* 21 (Sept., 1895).

DeVoto, Bernard. "Ogden: The Underwriters of Salvation," in *The Taming of the Frontier*, ed. Duncan Ackerman (New York, 1925).

Dix, Fae Decker. "Unwilling Martyr: The Death of Young Ed Dalton." *Utah Historical Quarterly* 41 (Spring, 1973).

Durham, G. Homer. "Administrative Organization of the Mormon Church."

Political Science Quarterly 57 (1942).

Edmunds, George F. "Political Aspects of Mormonism." *Harper's Magazine* 64 (Jan., 1882).

Farnham, Wallace D. "The Weakened Spring of Government: A Study in Nineteenth-Century American History." *American Historical Review* 68 (Apr., 1963).

Field, Kate. "The Forty-fifth Star." *Kate Field's Washington* July 25, 1894.

Goodwin, C.C. "The Political Attitude of the Mormons." *North American Review* 132 (Jan.-June, 1882).

Hoffman, Charles. "The Depression of the Nineties." *Journal of Economic History* 16 (June, 1956).

Ivins, Stanley S. "A Constitution for Utah." *Western Humanities Review* 10 (1956).

Jonas, Frank H. "Utah: Sagebrush Democracy," in *Rocky Mountain Politics*, ed. Thomas L. Donnelly (Albuquerque, 1940).

Jorgensen, Victor W., and B. Carmon Hardy. "The Taylor-Cowley Affair and the Watershed of Mormon History." *Utah Historical Quarterly* 48 (Winter, 1980.)

Lyman, Edward Leo. "The Alienation of an Apostle From His Quorum: The Moses Thatcher Case." *Dialogue: A Journal of Mormon Thought* 18 (Summer, 1985).

————. "The Elimination of the Mormon Issue from Arizona Politics, 1889–1894." *Arizona and the West* (Autumn, 1982).

————. "Isaac Trumbo and the Politics of Utah Statehood." *Utah Historical Quarterly* 41 (Spring, 1973).

————. "A Mormon Transition in Idaho Politics." *Idaho Yesterdays* 20 (Winter, 1977).

Morgan, Dale L. "The State of Deseret." *Utah Historical Quarterly* 8 (Apr.-Oct., 1940).

Parkin, Max H. "Mormon Political Involvement in Ohio." *Brigham Young University Studies* (Summer, 1969).

Paxson, Frederic L. "The Admission of the 'Omnibus' States." *Wisconsin State Historical Society Proceedings* 49 (1911).

Poll, Richard D. "Political Reconstruction of Utah Territory." *Pacific Historical Review* 27 (May, 1958).

Quinn, D. Michael. "L.D.S. Church Authority and New Plural Marriages, 1890–1904." *Dialogue: A Journal of Mormon Thought* 18 (Spring, 1985).

Thomason, Gordon C. "The Manifesto Was a Victory!" *Dialogue: A Journal of Mormon Thought* 6 (Spring, 1971).

Wells, Merle W. "The Idaho Admission Movement, 1888–1890." *Oregon Historical Quarterly* 56 (Mar., 1955).

White, Jean Bickmore. "Woman's Place Is in the Constitution: The Struggle for Equal Rights in Utah in 1895." *Utah Historical Quarterly* 42 (Fall, 1977).

Williams, J. D. "The Separation of Church and State in Mormon Theory and Practice." *Dialogue: A Journal of Mormon Thought* 1 (Summer, 1966).

Wills, John A. "The Twin Relic of Barbarism." *Publications of the Historical Society of Southern California* 1 (1890).

Wolfinger, Henry J. "A reexamination of the Woodruff Manifesto in Light of Utah Constitutional History." *Utah Historical Quarterly* 39 (Fall, 1971).

BOOKS

Alter, J. Cecil. *Early Utah Journalism.* Salt Lake City, 1938.

Arrington, Leonard J., and Davis Bitton. *The Mormon Experience: A History of the Latter-day Saints.* New York, 1979.

Arrington, Leonard J. *Great Basin Kingdom: An Economic History of the Latter-day Saints.* Cambridge, 1958; Lincoln, 1966.

Bancroft, Hubert H. *History of Utah.* San Francisco, 1889; Salt Lake City, 1964.

Baskin, Robert N. *Reminiscences of Early Utah.* Salt Lake City, 1914.

Bass, Herbert J. *"I Am a Democrat": The Political Career of David Bennett Hill.* Syracuse, 1961.

Blaine, James G. *Twenty Years of Congress: From Lincoln to Garfield.* Norwich, Conn., 1886.

Cannon, Frank J., and Harvey O'Higgins. *Under the Prophet in Utah.* Boston, 1911.

Cleland, Robert G., and Juanita Brooks. *A Mormon Chronicle: The Diaries of John D. Lee, 1848–1876.* 2 vols. San Marino, 1955.

Clements, Louis J., ed. *Fred T. Dubois' The Making of a State.* Rexburg, Idaho, 1971.

Codman, John. *The Mormon Country: A Summer with the "Latter-day Saints."* New York, 1874.

Coolidge, Louis A. *Orville H. Platt: An Old-Fashioned Senator.* 2 vols. Reprint. Port Washington, N.Y., 1971.

Creer Leland H. *The Founding of an Empire: The Exploration and Colonization of Utah, 1776–1856.* Salt Lake City, 1947.

Cullom, Shelby M. *Fifty Years of Public Service: Personal Recollections of Shelby M. Cullom.* Chicago, 1911.

DeSantis, Vincent P. *Republicans Face the Southern Question: The New Departure Years, 1877–1897.* New York, 1959.

Donnelly, Thomas G., ed. *Rocky Mountain Politics.* Albuquerque, 1940.

Durham, G. Homer, ed. *The Discourses of Wilford Woodruff.* Salt Lake City, 1946.

Dwyer, Robert J. *The Gentile Comes to Utah: A Study in Religious and Social Conflict, 1862–1890.* Washington, D.C., 1941; Salt Lake City, 1971.

Flanders, Robert B. *Nauvoo: Kingdom on the Mississippi.* Urbana, 1965.

Furniss, Norman F. *The Mormon Conflict, 1850–1859.* New Haven, 1960.

Hamilton, Gail. *Biography of James G. Blaine.* Norwich, Conn., 1895.

Hansen, Klaus J. *Quest for Empire: The Political Kingdom of God and the Council of Fifty in Mormon History.* East Lansing, 1967; Lincoln, 1974.

Hirshson, Stanley P. *Farewell to the Bloody Shirt: Northern Republicans and the Southern Negro, 1877–1893.* Bloomington, 1962; Chicago, 1968.

Jensen, Alta R. *The Unfavored Few: The Autobiography of Joseph L. Rawlins.* Monterey, Calif., 1965.

Jensen, Andrew. *Latter-day Saint Biographical Encyclopedia.* 4 vols. Salt Lake City, 1901.

Jensen, Richard J. *The Winning of the Midwest: Social and Political Conflict, 1888–96.* Chicago, 1971.

Josephson, Matthew. *The Politicos.* New York, 1938.

Kenner, Scipio A. *The Practical Politician.* Salt Lake City, 1892.

———. *Utah as It Is.* Salt Lake City, 1902.

Kinzer, Donald L. *An Episode in Anti-Catholicism: The American Protective Association.* Seattle, 1964.

Kleppner, Paul. *The Cross of Culture: A Social Analysis of Midwestern Politics, 1850–1900.* New York, 1970.

———. *The Third Electoral System, 1853–1892: Parties, Voters, and Political Changes.* Chapel Hill, 1979.

Lamar, Howard R. *Dakota Territory, 1861–1889: A Study of Frontier Politics.* New Haven, 1956.

———. *The Far Southwest, 1846–1912: A Territorial History.* New Haven, 1966; New York, 1970.

Lambert, John R. *Arthur Pue Gorman.* Baton Rouge, 1953.

Larson, Gustive O. *The "Americanization" of Utah for Statehood.* San Marino, Calif., 1971.

———. *Outline History of Utah and the Mormons.* Salt Lake City, 1958, 1961.

Larson, Robert W. *New Mexico's Quest for Statehood: 1846–1912.* Albuquerque, 1968.

Long, E. B. *The Saints and the Union: Utah Territory during the Civil War.* Urbana, 1981.

Madsen, Truman G. *B. H. Roberts: Defender of the Faith.* Salt Lake City, 1980.

Malmquist, O. N. *The First 100 Years: A History of the Salt Lake Tribune, 1871–1971.* Salt Lake City, 1971.

Marcus, Robert D. *Grand Old Party: Political Structure in the Gilded Age, 1880–1896.* New York, 1971.

McKiernan, F. Mark, ed. *Restoration Movement: Essays in Mormon History.* Lawrence, Kansas, 1973.

Moyle, James H. *Mormon Democrat: The Religious and Political Memories of James Henry Moyle.* Edited by Gene A. Sessions. Salt Lake City, 1975.

Muzzey, David S. *James G. Blaine: A Political Idol of Other Days.* New York, 1934.

Neff, Andrew L. *History of Utah.* Salt Lake City, 1940.

Nevins, Allan. *Grover Cleveland: A Study in Courage.* New York, 1932.

Oberholtzer, Ellis Paxson. *A History of the United States since the Civil War.* 5 vols. New York, 1917–37, 1969.

Poll, Richard D., ed. *Utah's History.* Provo, 1978.

Porter, Kirk H., and Donald B. Johnson, comps. *National Party Platforms, 1840–1964.* Urbana, 1966.

Richardson, James J D., comp. *A Compilation of the Messages and Papers of the Presidents, 1789–1897.* 20 vols. Washington, D.C., 1898.

Rhodes, James Ford. *History of the United States from the Compromise of 1850.* 8 vols. New York, 1910.

Roberts, Brigham H. *A Comprehensive History of the Church of Jesus Christ of Latter-day Saints*. 6 vols. Salt Lake City, 1930.

Rothman, David J. *Politics and Power: The United States Senate, 1869–1901*. Cambridge, Mass., 1966.

Sievers, Harry J. *Benjamin Harrison: Hoosier President*. Indianapolis, 1968.

Smith, Helena H. *The War on Powder River*. Lincoln, 1967.

Stanwood, Edward. *James Gillespie Blaine*. Boston, 1905.

Stephenson, Nathaniel W. *Nelson W. Aldrich: A Leader in American Politics*. New York, 1930.

Tullidge, Edward W. *Tullidge's Histories: Containing the History of All the Northern, Eastern and Western Counties of Utah; Also the Counties of Southern Idaho*. 2 vols. Salt Lake City, 1889.

Wells, Merle W. *Anti-Mormonism in Idaho, 1872–92*. Provo, 1978.

Whitney, Orson F. *History of Utah*. 4 vols. Salt Lake City, 1892–1904.

Williams, R. Hal. *Years of Decision: American Politics in the 1890's*. New York, 1978.

THESES AND DISSERTATIONS

Anderson, Robert D. "History of the Provo *Times* and *Enquirer*, 1873–1897." Master's thesis, Brigham Young University, 1951.

Beeton, Beverly. "Woman Suffrage in the American West, 1869–1896." Ph.D. dissertation, University of Utah, 1976.

Bernstein, Jerome. "A History of the Constitutional Conventions of the Territory of Utah from 1849–1895." Master's thesis, Utah State University, 1961.

Brown, Vernal A. "The United States Marshals in Utah Territory to 1896." Master's thesis, Utah State University, 1970.

Caldwell, Gaylon L. "Mormon Conceptions of Individual Rights and Political Obligation." Ph.D. dissertation, Stanford University, 1952.

Cannon, Mark W. "The Mormon Issue in Congress, 1872–1882: Drawing on the Experience of Territorial Delegate George Q. Cannon." Ph.D. dissertation, Harvard University, 1960.

Cook, Lyndon W. "George Q. Cannon's Views on Church and State." Master's thesis, Brigham Young niversity, 1977.

Grow, Stewart L. "A Study of the Utah Commission, 1882–96." Ph.D. dissertation, University of Utah. 1954.

Harrow, Joan Ray. "Joseph L. Rawlins, Father of Utah Statehood." Master's thesis, University of Utah, 1973.

Haynes, Alan E. "The Federal Government and Its Policies Regarding the Frontier Era of Utah Territory, 1850–1877." Ph.D. dissertation, Catholic University of America, 1968.

Jack, Ronald C. "Utah Territorial Politics: 1874–1896." Ph.D. dissertation, University of Utah, 1970.

Jensen, Therald N. "Mormon Theory of Church and State." Ph.D. dissertation, University of Chicago, 1938.

Kotter, Richard E. "An Examination of Mormon and Non-Mormon Influences in Ogden City Politics, 1847–1896." Master's thesis, Utah State University, 1967.

Linford, Orma. "The Mormons and the Law: The Polygamy Cases." Ph.D. dissertation, University of Wisconsin, 1964.

Lyman, Edward Leo. "Heber M. Wells and the Beginnings of Utah Statehood." Master's thesis, University of Utah, 1967.

———. "Mormon Quest for Utah Statehood, 1886–1896." Ph.D. dissertation, University of California, Riverside, 1981.

Lythgoe, Dennis L. "The Changing Image of Mormonism in Periodical Literature." Ph.D. dissertation, University of Utah, 1969.

Middleton, Henry J. "The Life of Charles Franklin Middleton: A Man and His Times." Master's thesis, Utah State University, 1965.

Poll, Richard D. "The Mormon Question, 1850–1865: A Study in Politics and Public Opinion." Ph.D. dissertation, University of California, Berkeley, 1948.

———. "The Twin Relic: A Study of Mormon Polygamy and the Campaign by the Government of the United States for Its Abolition, 1852–1890." Master's thesis, Texas Christian University, 1939.

Quinn, D. Michael. "The Mormon Hierarchy, 1832–1932: An American Elite." Ph.D. dissertation, Yale University, 1976.

Roderick, Judith Ann. "A Historical Study of the Congressional Career of John T. Caine." Master's thesis, Brigham Young University, 1959.

Shipps, JoAnn Barnett. "The Mormons in Politics: The First Hundred Years." Ph.D. dissertation, University of Colorado, 1965.

Thompson, Margaret S. "The Spider Web: Congressional Lobbying in the Age of Grant." Ph.D. dissertation, University of Wisconsin, 1979.

White, Jean Bickmore. "Utah State Elections: 1895–1899." Ph.D. dissertation, University of Utah, 1968.

POLITICAL PAMPHLETS AND BROADSIDES

Cannon, George Q. *A Review of the Decision of the Supreme Court of the United States in the case of George Reynolds vs. The United States.* 1879.

Crane, Charles. "To the Members of the Utah Legislature and the General Public." [1895].

"Don't Be A 'Bastard'." [1891].

Grant, Jedediah M. *Three Letters to the New York Herald from J. M. Grant of Utah.* 1852.

"Jonathon." *Joseph F. Smith Answered: His Plain Talk Shown to be Full of Errors and Misstatements.* [1892].

Nuggets of Truth. 1892.

Nuggets of Truth: Hear Ye the Whole Truths, As to Joseph Smith's Political Views. [1892].

Penrose, C. W. *Penrose Replies to Joseph F. Smith.* [1892].

"Rawlins in Congress: The Work of a Strong, Modest, Untiring Man." [1894].

Schroeder, A. T., ed. "The N. Y. Times vs. Geo Q. Cannon." *Lucifer's Lantern.* 1899.

Smith, Joseph F. *Another Plain Talk: Reasons Why the People of Utah Should Be Republicans.* 1892.

"Speech of Hon. H. J. Grant: A Ringing Appeal to the Voters of Utah Territory." [1894].

The Facts of the Utah Case. 1892.

"To the People of Utah." 1895.

"Utah Statehood, Reasons Why It Should Not be Granted." 1887.

Voters of Utah, Beware! [1892].

Index

Index

Index

Nelson, William, 33, 70, 80–81
Nephi Blade, 265
Nevada, 10, 126, 186–87, 214, 233
Newman, Angie F., 88
New Mexico, 7, 35, 125–26, 130, 186–87, 209
New York City Press Association, 71
New York Evening Post, 50, 74, 80, 85
New York Herald, 8, 72, 84–85
New York Star, 71
New York Sun, 72, 80, 84–85
New York Times, 50, 71–72, 74, 80, 84–85, 90, 225, 247–48, 272, 275
New York Tribune, 84–85, 226, 236–37
New York Tribune Index, 85
New York World, 84
Nibley, Charles W., 134
Nicholson, Donald, 236–37
Nuttall, L. John, 130

Oates, William C., 214
O'Brien, T. B., 127–28, 130
Ogden Daily Commercial, 151–52, 154
Ogden Daily Union, 152
Ogden Standard, 151–54, 180, 203
Ogden, Utah, 111–12, 127
Oklahoma, 209, 214
Omaha Herald, 26
Omnibus statehood bill, 41, 104–5, 107
Outhwaite, J. H., 105

Park, John R., 276
Paddock, Algernon, 57, 191
Pamphlet campaign, 201
Panquitch Stake Presidency, 167
Panic of 1893, 232–33
Parowan Stake Presidency, 167
Parsons, Eli H., 204
Peckham, Wheeler H., 225
Penrose, Charles W., 43, 47–48, 51, 56–59, 62, 76–77, 79, 84, 103–4, 156, 160, 166, 202, 209
People's party (Mormon), 3, 48, 97, 101, 111–12, 117, 151, 161, 164
Philadelphia Times, 74, 80
Pierce, Franklin, 8
Platt, Orville H., 60, 145*n*29, 192–93, 209–10, 223, 227–29
Plural marriage, 2–5, 8–9, 11, 13, 15, 21, 23–34, 28, 31, 35, 44, 47, 49–50, 58, 60,
88, 90, 125, 133, 140–41, 175, 185; abandonment urged, 12, 16, 18, 43, 45–46, 53–54, 59, 106, 294; barrier to statehood, 1–2, 18, 58, 60, 109, 114; concessions on, 12, 45, 294; definition distinctions, 44–45, 60; determination to continue, 53–54, 63, 89, 106, 109, 114
Poland Act, 19
Poland, Luke P., 16
Polygamy. *See* Plural marriage
Populist party, 209, 274
Powers, Orlando W., 116, 193, 197–98, 200, 213, 223–24, 247, 271
Pratt, Arthur, 112
Presiding bishopric: defined, 6*n*1
Preston, William B., 259
Probate courts in Utah, 15
Proctor, Redfield, 292
Provo Enquirer, 162–63, 265
Public Opinion, 85–86, 94*n*45
Pulitzer, Joseph, 84–85
Purbeck, George A., 233–34, 248

Quigg, Lemuel E., 236–37
Quinn, D. Michael, 146*n*34, 170
Quorum of Twelve Apostles. *See* Apostles quorum

Radical Republicans, 152
R-Co. *See* Southern Pacific Railroad
Raid. *See* Anti-polygamy raid
Railroads, 14, 16, 38*n*27; lobby, 42; promotion, 233–34
Ransom, Mathew W., 247
Rawlins, Joseph L., 193, 201–3, 210–11, 213–14, 216, 223–24, 226–27, 229, 251*n*28, 268, 273
Reasoner, Calvin, 154
Reed, Thomas B., 215, 229
Reid, Whitelaw, 85
Republican appointees in Utah, 29, 33
Republican clubs. *See* National League of Republican Clubs
Republican national committee, 174, 187, 189, 222
Republican newspapers, 9, 223
Republican party
—National, 3–4, 9, 11, 187–96; additional Senate seats, 35, 104, 125–26, 187–88; demanded concessions, 2, 21, 142–43;

J. Wilson Shaffer, 14; Arthur L. Thomas, 23–24, 109; Caleb W. West, 33, 42, 81, 128; George L. Woods, 17; Brigham Young, 8, 41
Utah territorial legislature, 10, 13, 24, 97–99
Utah territorial supreme court, 73

Varian, Charles S., 135, 141, 199, 255–56, 261
Vilas, W. F., 225
Voter registration in Utah, 114–15

Wade, Benjamin, 14
Waite, Morrison, 21
Warner, Ernst F., 116
Warren, Charles, 196
Warren, Francis E., 205–6
Washington County, Utah, 175
Washington Evening Star, 136–37, 223
Washington state, 35, 107
Watson, Robert, 86–87
Watterson, Henry, 82
Weber County, Utah, 150, 153, 159, 200
Weber Stake Presidency, 151
Wells, Heber M., 114, 267–68, 273–74, 276, 281–82
West, Caleb W., 33–34, 42, 81, 97–99, 106, 109, 128, 193, 202, 211, 275, 281
Wheeler, Joseph, 214–15
Wheeler, William A., 21
Whitbeck, John, 116
White, Edward D., 244

White, Stephen M., 225–26, 244
Whitney, Orson F., 10, 139
Williams, C. *See* Penrole, C. W.
Williams, George B., 190
Williams, Parley, 30
Wilmot, David, 9
Wilson, Jeremiah M., 61, 126
Wilson, William L., 198
Winder, John R., 158, 161, 203
Woman's suffrage, 34, 88, 261
Wood, Ruth, 88
Woodruff, Wilford, 52–53, 87, 89–92, 106, 114, 120, 130, 132–37, 139–41, 147n42, 174, 178, 190, 240, 261–62, 269–70, 276–81; epistle of, 89; manifesto of, 135–40, 146n38, 175
Wyoming, 108, 125–26, 133, 186–87, 205–6

Young, Brigham, 10–11, 13–14, 275
Young, Brigham, Jr., 269
Young, John W., 41–42, 44, 46–47, 54–56, 58, 61, 63, 70, 72–73, 76–77, 96–97, 106, 113–14, 161
Young, LeGrand, 53, 176
Young, Richard W., 114–15, 133, 145n32
Young, Seymour B., 90

Zane, John M., 158–59, 162, 192
Zane, Charles S., 24–25, 70, 109, 117, 148n55, 157, 190, 281
Z.C.M.I., 28, 86
Zundell, I. E. D., 142

Note on the Author

Edward Leo Lyman's interest in Utah-Mormon history has been lifelong. After completing bachelor's and master's degrees in history at Brigham Young University and University of Utah, he took a high school teaching and coaching position in Riverside, California. While working full-time, helping his wife, Pam, in rearing five children, and devoting considerable time to church and community activities, he began working part-time on a doctorate in history at University of California at Riverside, which was completed in 1981. After receiving one of the first research fellowships to study in the Archives of the Church of Jesus Christ of Latter-day Saints in the summer of 1972, Lyman's appearance there virtually every vacation period during the next decade became a standing prediction among some department employees. As his work on Mormon politics continued, he began to publish articles and deliver papers at professional conferences rather consistently, and his work has been well received. He now teaches full-time at Victor Valley College in Victorville, California.